Praise for PassPorter®

It's the first and only book that covers Disney cruises in detail. And what splendid detail! Jennifer and Dave tell you everything you need and want to know, from embarkation to debarkation. Even if you don't currently have a Disney cruise planned, this is great armchair reading. It certainly took me back to happy thoughts of my last Disney cruise and made me want to plan the next one!

— Mary Waring
MouseSavers.com

With PassPorter, we knew what to expect on our first cruise rather than feeling like novices. It was a wonderful resource and saved us from many "first timer" mistakes!

— Laurie Smith
in Arizona

I love how much information is packed into PassPorter! This is a fantastic tool for people who need to know everything before they cruise.

— Deborah DeCaire
in Ontario

PassPorter takes away all the guesswork. It has complete information and all the insider tips. Passporter was our "bible" when planning our Disney cruise.

— Judith Bauer
in Indiana

PassPorter has saved us time and money. Thank you, thank you, Dave and Jennifer. PassPorters are the perfect guides and easy to read!

— Lee Townsend
in Massachusetts

I love the excellent and helpful information in PassPorter! I couldn't imagine cruising without it!

— Sue Ann Daniels
in Florida

PassPorter is one of the few comprehensive resources for the Disney Cruise Line. Everything is covered. Thanks for putting together a fantastic resource for Disney fans!

— Brian Hubbard
in Indiana

What's New in This Edition

Major Enhancements:

✓ **More than 20 brand new pages** filled with valuable information, advice, details, reviews, ratings, and photos.

✓ **More photos** than our previous edition—many of which include your authors in the picture, too!

✓ **Coverage of all new Mexican Riviera and Panama Canal repositioning ports**, including extra information for the Los Angeles port, including travel and lodging.

✓ **Sneak peek at new itineraries and new ships**—our thoughts and speculations on the future of the Disney cruises.

✓ **Coverage of all the recent changes** aboard, including the onboard airline check-in program, increased pricing for parking and Palo, the new stage show on the Wonder, and more!

✓ **Updated details** on shore excursions for all ports.

✓ **Comparison grid** of car rental companies offering one-way rentals between Orlando Intl. Airport and Cocoa Beach.

✓ **More information** on the new passport regulations, including how and when to get yours.

✓ **More details** on Internet access, including in-stateroom wireless (wi-fi), and using your cell phone at sea.

✓ **Enhanced details** on cruising with kids, including more tips and photos for Flounder's Reef Nursery.

✓ **Cruise Journal** for you to keep notes on your adventure.

Fun Features and Information:

✓ Thousands of small tweaks to further improve our guide.

✓ Current rates, prices, menus, and shore excursions.

✓ Expanded index to make it easier to find things.

✓ More new reader tips, magical memories, and stories.

✓ New peer reviewers to ensure accuracy and thoroughness.

...and much, much more! Visit us at http://www.passporter.com/dcl for a complete list of what's new and changed in this edition!

Disney Magic/Wonder Deck Plans

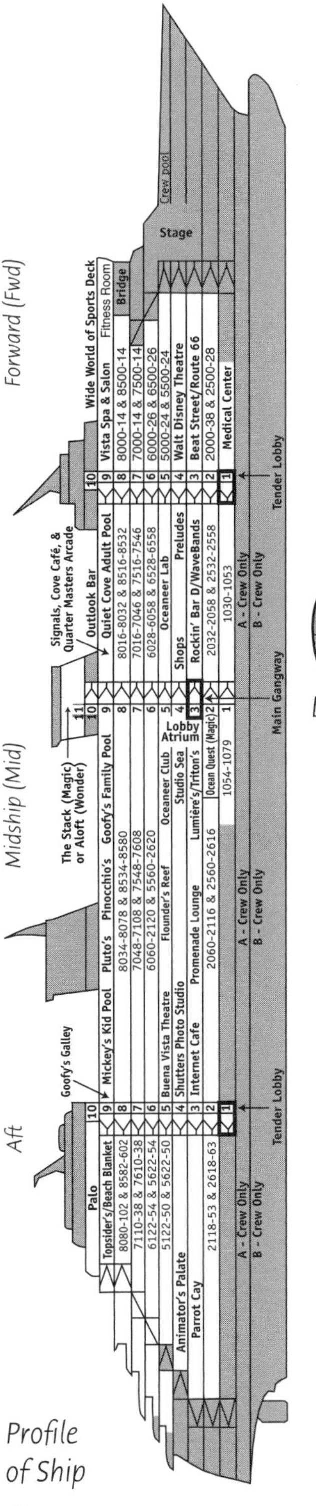

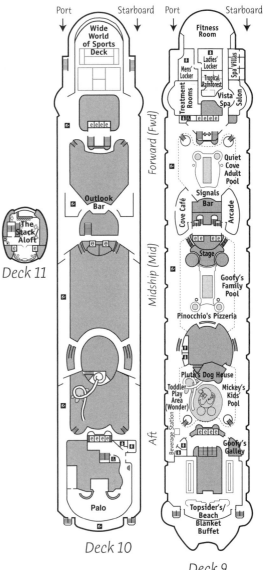

Tip: Once you know your stateroom number, note it on this page and highlight the section of the ship where it is located in the profile map to the left.

Our stateroom number: _____

Port   Starboard   Port   Starboard

Forward (Fwd)

Wide World of Sports Deck

Midship (Mid)

Aft

Profile of Ship

Profile map labels

Forward (Fwd)

Wide World of Sports Deck — Fitness Room — Bridge

10	9	Vista Spa & Salon	8000-14 & 8516-8532
	8		7000-14 & 7500-14
	7		7046 & 7516-7546
	6		6000-26 & 6500-26
	5		6028-6058 & 6528-6558
	5		5000-24 & 5500-24
	4		5000-24 & 5500-24
	3	Beat Street/Route 66	2000-38 & 2500-28
	1	Medical Center	

Tender Lobby

Outlook Bar
Quiet Cove Adult Pool
8016-8032 & 8516-8532

Signals, Cove Café, & Quarter Masters Arcade

Preludes
Rockin' Bar D/WaveBands — 2032-2058 & 2532-2558
Shops — 2060-2116 & 2560-2616
Oceaneer Lab — 1030-1053

A - Crew Only
B - Crew Only

Main Gangway

The Stack (Magic) or Aloft (Wonder)

10	Goofy's Family Pool	8034-8078 & 8534-8580
8	Pinocchio's Pluto's	7048-7108 & 7548-7608
7		6060-2120 & 5560-2620
6	Oceaneer Club	
5	Studio Sea	
4	Lumiere's/Triton's	1054-1079

Lobby Atrium
Flounder's Reef
Promenade Lounge

Goofy's Galley

Mickey's Kid Pool
Topsider's/Beach Blanket
8080-102 & 8582-602
7110-38 & 7610-38
6122-54 & 5622-54
5122-50 & 5622-50
2118-53 & 2618-63

Buena Vista Theatre
Shutters Photo Studio
Internet Cafe
Animator's Palate
Parrot Cay

A - Crew Only
B - Crew Only

Tender Lobby

Deck 11

The Stack / Aloft

Deck 11

Deck 10

Wide World of Sports Deck

Outlook Bar

Palo

Deck 10

Deck 9

Fitness Room
Mens Locker — Ladies' Locker — Spa Villas
Treatment Rooms — Tropical Rainforest — Vista Spa — Salon

Quiet Cove Adult Pool

Cove Café — Signals Bar — Arcade

Stage

Goofy's Family Pool

Pinocchio's Pizzeria

Pluto's Dog House

Toddler Play Area (Wonder) — Mickey's Kids' Pool

Beverage Station

Goofy's Galley

Topsider's/Beach Blanket Buffet

Deck 9

Key to Deck Plans

- ☐ guest area
- ▨ crew only/inaccessible
- e elevator
- ▥ stairs
- ♿ wheelchair accessible
- 🚺 women's restroom
- 🚹 men's restroom
- ✂ smoking allowed
- ⑪ stateroom category

Decks 8, 7, 6, and 5

Stateroom Categories

- ❶ Cat. 1 (deck 8)
- ❷ Cat. 2 (deck 8)
- ❸ Cat. 3 (deck 8)
- ❹ Cat. 4 (deck 8)
- ❺ Cat. 5 (deck 7)
- ❻ Cat. 6 (decks 5–6)
- ❼ Cat. 7 (decks 5–7)
- ❽ Cat. 8 (decks 5–7)
- ❾ Cat. 9 (decks 1–2)
- ❿ Cat. 10 (decks 1–2, 5, 7)
- ⓫ Cat. 11 (decks 5–7)
- ⓬ Cat. 12 (deck 2)

Port ↓ **Starboard** ↓ (Deck 8)

Bridge

Forward (Fwd)

Midship (Mid)

Aft

8030 Walter E. Disney Suite ❶
8530 Roy O. Disney Suite ❶

8100, 8102, 8600, 8602 — Public Deck

Deck 8

Port ↓ **Starboard** ↓ (Deck 7)

Forward (Fwd)

Midship (Mid)

Laundry

Aft

7134, 7136, 7138 — Public Deck

Deck 7

Port ↓ **Starboard** ↓ (Deck 6)

Forward (Fwd)

Midship (Mid)

Laundry

Aft

Deck 6

Port ↓ **Starboard** ↓ (Deck 5)

Crew Pool

Forward (Fwd)

Oceaneer Lab — Ocean Quest (Wonder)

Top of Atrium

Oceaneer Club

Flounder's Reef

Buena Vista Movie Theatre

Midship (Mid)

Aft

Deck 5

Decks 4, 3, 2, and 1

Get These Deck Plans Online!
Owners of this guide have free access to more detailed, color versions of all our deck plans—you can even zoom in closer! Access requires an Internet connection for downloading the files. Visit http://www.passporter.com/dcl/deckplans.htm

Deck 4

Port · Starboard

Stage

Walt Disney Theatre

Forward (Fwd)

Mickey's Mates · Drinks · Snacks

Preludes · Treasure Ketch

Middle of Atrium

Midship (Mid)

Walking/Jogging Track

Studio Sea

Shutters · Bottom of Movie Theater

Aft

Galley

Animator's Palate

Deck 3

Port · Starboard

Forward (Fwd)

Sessions/Cadillac Lounge · UpBeat/Radar Trap

Diversions

Rockin' Bar D/WaveBands

Guest Services · Shore Excursion Desk

Lobby Atrium · Main Gangway

Midship (Mid)

Lumière's/Triton's

Galley

Promenade Lounge · Internet Cafe

Aft

Galley

Parrot Cay

Deck 2

Port · Starboard

Forward (Fwd)

Port		Starboard	
2000		2500	
2002		2502	
2004		2504	
2006		2506	
2008	2009 2509	2508	
2010	2011 2511	2510	
2012	2013 2513	2512	
2014	2015 2515	2514	
2016	2017 2517	2516	
2018	2019 2519	2518	
2020	2021	2520	
2022		2522	
2024		2524	
2026		2526	
2028		2528	
2030		2530	
2032		2532	
2034	2035 2535	2534	
2036	2037 2537	2536	
2038	2039 2539	2538	
2040	2041 2541	2540	
2042	2043 2543	2542	
2044	2045 2545	2544	
2046	2047 2547	2546	
2048		2548	
2050		2550	
2052		2552	
2054		2554	
2056		2556	
2058		2558	
2060		2560	

Ocean Quest *(Magic)*

2062		2562	
2064		2564	
2066		2566	
2068		2568	
2070	2071 2571	2570	
2072	2073 2573	2572	
2074	2075 2575	2574	
2076	2077 2577	2576	
2078	2079 2579	2578	
2080	2081 2581	2580	
2082	2083 2583	2582	
2084	2085 2585	2584	
2086		2586	
2088		2588	
2090		2590	
2092		2592	
2094		2594	
2096	Laundry	2596	
2098		2598	
2100	2101 2601	2600	
2102	2103 2603	2602	
2104	2105 2605	2604	
2106	2107 2607	2606	
2108	2109 2609	2608	
2110	2111 2611	2610	
2112		2612	
2114		2614	
2116		2616	
2118		2618	
2120		2620	
2122		2622	
2124		2624	
2126		2626	
2128	2129 2629	2628	
2130	2131 2631	2630	
2132	2133 2633	2632	
2134	2135 2635		
2136	2137 2637		
2138	2139 2639	2638	
2140	2141 2641	2640	
2142	2143 2643	2642	
2144	2145 2645	2644	
2146	2147 2647	2646	
2148		2648	
2150		2650	
2152	2153	2653	2652

Midship (Mid)

Aft

Deck 1

Port · Starboard

Forward (Fwd)

Medical Health Center

Forward Tender Lobby

Port	Starboard
1030	
1032	
1034	
1036	1037 1039
	1041
1040	1043
1042	1045
1046	1047
1048	1049
1050	1051
1052	1053
1054	
1056	
1058	
1060	
1062	
1064	1065
1066	1067
1068	1069
1070	1071
1072	1073
1074	1075
1076	1077
1078	1079

Midship (Mid)

Aft Tender Lobby

Aft

What's Your Heading?

(M) = Disney Magic; (W) = Disney Wonder

Location	Deck	Page	Location	Deck	Page
Adult pool	9 Fwd	3	Nightclubs	3 Fwd	5
Adult cafe	9 Mid	3	Nursery	5 Mid	4
Adult district	3 Fwd	5	Ocean Quest (M)	2 Mid	5
Adult restaurant	10 Aft	3	Ocean Quest (W)	5 Mid	4
Aerobics studio	9 Fwd	3	Oceaneer Club & Lab	5 Mid	4
Aloft (W)	11 Mid	3	Outdoor movies	9 Mid	3
Animator's Palate	4 Aft	5	Outlook Bar	10 Mid	3
Assembly stations	4	5	Palo	10 Aft	3
Atrium (Lobby)	3-5 Mid	5,4	Parrot Cay	3 Aft	5
Arcade	9 Mid	3	Photo studio	4 Aft	5
Bars	3,4,9,10,11	5,4,3	Piano lounge	3 Fwd	5
Beach Blanket Buffet (W)	9 Aft	3	Ping-Pong tables	9	3
Beat Street (M)	3 Fwd	5	Pinocchio's Pizzeria	9 Mid	3
Beverage station	9 Aft	3	Pluto's Dog House	9 Aft	3
Buena Vista Theatre	5 Aft	4	Pools	9	3
Buffet restaurant	9 Aft	3	Preludes Bar	4 Fwd	5
Cadillac Lounge (W)	3 Fwd	5	Promenade Lounge	3 Aft	5
Casual dining	9	3	Pub (Diversions)	3 Fwd	5
Children's clubs	5 Mid	4	Quarter Masters arcade	9 Mid	3
Children's pool	9 Aft	3	Quiet Cove adult pool	9 Fwd	3
Conference rooms	2 Mid	5	Radar Trap duty free (W)	3 Mid	5
Cove Café	9 Mid	3	Restrooms	3,4,5,9,10	5,4,3
Dance club	3 Fwd	5	Rockin' Bar D (M)	3 Fwd	5
Deck parties	9 Mid	3	Route 66 (W)	3 Fwd	5
Diversions	3 Fwd	5	Salon	9 Fwd	3
Duty-free shops	3 Fwd	5	Sessions lounge (M)	3 Fwd	5
Family nightclub	4 Mid	5	Shore excursion desk	3 Mid	5
Family pool	9 Mid	3	Shuffleboard	4	5
Fast food	9	3	Shutters photo studio	4 Aft	5
Fitness center	9 Fwd	3	Shops	4 Mid	5
Flounder's Reef	5 Mid	4	Sickbay	1 Fwd	5
Fruit station	9 Aft	3	Signals	9 Mid	3
Goofy's Family Pool	9 Mid	3	Snack bars	9	3
Goofy's Galley	9 Aft	3	Spa (Vista Spa)	9 Fwd	3
Guest Services	3 Mid	5	Sports deck	10 Fwd	3
Hair salon	9 Fwd	3	The Stack (M)	11 Mid	3
Hot tubs	9	3	Teen club	11 Mid	3
Ice cream station	9 Aft	3	Tender lobbies	1 Fwd & Aft	5
Internet Cafe	3 Aft	5	Theater (movies)	5 Aft	4
Kids pool	9 Aft	3	Theater (stage shows)	4 Fwd	5
Kids clubs	5 Mid	4	Toddler water play area	9 Aft	3
Laundry rooms	2,6,7 Mid	5,4	Topsider's Buffet (M)	9 Aft	3
Liquor shop	3 Fwd	5	Treasure Ketch	4 Mid	5
Lobby (Atrium)	3 Mid	5	Triton's (W)	3 Mid	5
Lounges	3,4,9,10,11	5,3	UpBeat duty free (W)	3 Mid	5
Lumière's (M)	3 Mid	5	Vista Spa & Salon	9 Fwd	3
Medical Center	1 Fwd	5	Walt Disney Theatre	4 Fwd	5
Mickey's kids' pool	9 Aft	3	Waterslide	9 Aft	3
Mickey's Mates	4 Mid	5	Whirlpools	9	3
Movie theater	5 Aft	4	WaveBands (W)	3 Fwd	5

Fwd, Mid, or Aft? These common abbreviations are for the Forward (front), Midship (middle), and Aft (rear) of the ship. Refer to the labels on our deck plans.

PassPorter's®
Disney Cruise Line®
and Its Ports of Call
2008

Sixth Edition

The take-along travel guide and planner

Jennifer Marx
and
Dave Marx

with contributions by
Chad Larner and Nicole Larner

PassPorter Travel Press

An imprint of MediaMarx, Inc.
P.O. Box 3880, Ann Arbor, Michigan 48106
877-WAYFARER
http://www.passporter.com

PassPorter's® Disney Cruise Line® and Its Ports of Call—2008 (Sixth Edition)

by Jennifer Marx and Dave Marx

© 2008 by PassPorter Travel Press, an imprint of MediaMarx, Inc.

P.O. Box 3880, Ann Arbor, Michigan 48106
877-WAYFARER or 877-929-3273 (toll-free)
Visit us on the World Wide Web at http://www.passporter.com

Distributed by Publishers Group West

ISBN-10: 1-58771-055-2
ISBN-13: 978-1-58771-055-1

10 9 8 7 6 5 4 3 2 1

Printed in the United States of America

About the Authors

Name: Jennifer Marx
Date of birth: 10/09/68
Residence: Ann Arbor, MI
Signature: *Jennifer Marx*

Jennifer Marx grew up in Michigan, where you can stand anywhere within the state and be less than six miles from a lake, river, or stream. Her shipboard experiences include two weeks aboard a sailboat as a crew member and nine months working aboard the sternwheeler "Michigan" on Lake Biwa, Japan. Her first Disney Cruise Line adventure was for three nights in October 1999. A four-night cruise followed in May 2001. She had the good fortune to be aboard the Panama Canal crossing (eastbound) in August 2005. Her most recent cruise was aboard the Disney Wonder on the four-night MouseFest cruise in December 2007. Jennifer is the author of more than 30 books, including the guide that started it all: *PassPorter's Walt Disney World*. Jennifer makes her home in the university town of Ann Arbor, Michigan, where she lives with her husband Dave and their son, Alexander.

Dave Marx may be considered a Renaissance Man, a jack-of-all-trades, or a dilettante, depending on how you look at things. He took a 20-year hiatus between his early journalism training and the start of his full-time writing career. Beyond co-authoring more than 20 books with Jennifer, he's been a radio writer/producer; recording engineer; motion picture music editor; broadcast engineer supervisor; whitewater safety and rescue instructor; developer of online publishing courses; and newsletter editor and promotions chief for an online forum. He discovered the Walt Disney World Resort in March 1997 and first cruised in October 1999. He's since cruised 12 more times, including his award cruise for being a Million-Point Winner at the retired "Who Wants to Be a Millionaire—Play It!" attraction at Walt Disney World. Dave lives in Ann Arbor, Michigan.

Name: Dave Marx
Date of birth: 04/07/55
Residence: Ann Arbor, MI
Signature: *Dave Marx*

About the Contributors

Chad Larner and Nicole Larner are PassPorter's in-house research team. This phenomenal brother-and-sister duo unearthed tidbits of new and updated information, checked the accuracy of addresses and phone numbers, and assisted in the peer review process. Their contributions really shine in chapter 6— Chad researched and wrote all shore excursion reviews for the new ports, and Nikki did the primary page layout work. Their essential position on the team enables PassPorter to grow and thrive! Nikki and Chad are both fans of the Disney Cruise and have cruised several times each.

PassPorter Team

Our 18 Expert Peer Reviewers—We recruited a group of knowledgeable Disney experts. Each painstakingly checked our guide to ensure its accuracy, readability, and thoroughness. Thank you from the bottom of our hearts! A special thank you to Debbie Hendrickson!

Amy Bedore has visited Walt Disney World many times and took her first Disney cruise in 2006. Now Disney is the only way to sail! Amy is a PassPorter Message Board Guide and enjoys sharing her Disney experiences.

Dyan K. Chaplin enjoys traveling with her husband, Jeffrey, and teenage son, Kyle, who share her enthusiasm for all things Disney. Dyan serves as a PassPorter Message Board Guide, has a love for baseball and the Boston Red Sox.

Dianne Cook and husband Tom had a Disney honeymoon and now "do Disney" twice a year with their sons Andrew and Matthew. A Disney Vacation Club member since 1996, Dianne is also a PassPorter Guide.

Lesley Duncan is a PassPorter Message Board Guide who first visited Walt Disney World in 1972. She is looking forward to her first Disney cruise aboard the Magic on the Westbound Panama Canal cruise this May.

Marisa Garber-Brown is a Destination Specialist with MouseEarVacations.com. Her parents brought her to Disney in 1979 and she has visited and cruised multiple times every year since. She enjoys being a PassPorter Guide and spending time with her husband Tim.

LauraBelle Hime is a PassPorter message board guide and enjoys 4–5 Disney trips a year. Disney cruising is her newest passion and she finds each cruise to be a unique experience whether she travels solo, with family, or with friends.

Terri Jordan is a Disney Vacation Club member, PassPorter Guide, and avid Disney vacation fan. She recently completed her third Disney cruise in the Mediterranean and is planning her fourth on the Westbound Panama Canal Repositioning.

Barb Nefer Lesniak and her husband Tony have taken over 60 Disney cruises. Their web site, The Platinum Castaway Club (http://www.castawayclub.com), has been providing helpful Disney cruise planning information since 1999. Barb is also a travel agent (http://www.dclexpert.com) devoted exclusively to booking Disney cruises.

Sandy Livingston is a freelance proofreader. She's taken 20+ Disney trips, including a four-night Disney cruise several years ago and a seven-night cruise in December 2007. She and her husband Bob are Disney Vacation Club members.

Bruce Metcalf works at a major Central Florida resort, so cruising is his preferred form of vacation. He enjoys "messing about in boats" of all sizes from the Tomorrowland Phantom Boats to the Disney Wonder.

Lynn Mirante and family sailed the Disney Magic's inaugural year and fell in love with cruising. Four cruises later and the westbound Panama Cruise is their next adventure! Lynn is also a PassPorter Message Board Guide and co-owner of Ears To You Travel.

Sharon Moore is an avid Disney fan. She makes an annual pilgrimage for the International Food and Wine Festival at Walt Disney World, and recently enjoyed her first, but not last, Disney Cruise.

Sarah Mudd is a military wife, PassPorter Message Board Guide, and frequent visitor to Disney's U.S. parks. She, her husband Mike, and 7-year-ol daughter Emilie live in Virginia and is hoping to go on her first Disney cruise in the near future.

Rebecca Oberg has enjoyed three Disney cruises and six visits to Walt Disney World since her first trip in November 2004. She is a PassPorter Message Board Guide and is currently planning a third Disney cruise.

Cheryl Pendry is a PassPorter Guide and a Disney Vacation Club member. She and her husband Mark are regular Disney visitors, despite living in England. They recently enjoyed their second Disney cruise around the Mediterranean in summer 2007.

Jennifer Savickas, her husband Jim, and her son Jameson have made the trek from New Hampshire to Disney more than 18 times since 1996 (four times in one year alone)! Jenn is currently planning her first cruise for 2009.

Marnie Urmaza and her family took their first Disney cruise in 2006 and have booked their next one for 2009. What a magical way to vacation! Marnie also enjoys being a PassPorter Message Board Guide.

Don Willis is a retired government appraiser living in North California. His first visit to Disneyland was in 1962, and he just enjoyed his first Disney Cruise. He is a Guide on the PassPorter message boards.

Acknowledgments

Oceans of thanks to our readers, who've contributed loads of tips and stories since the debut of the first PassPorter in 1999. A special thanks to those who allowed us to include their contributions in this field guide:

Mary Waring, Laurie Smith, Deborah DeCaire, Judith Bauer, Lee Townsend, Sue Ann Daniels, Brian Hubbard (page 1); Jim Anders, Susan Kile (page 30); Lynn Mirante, Dave Huiner, Annette Konicek (page 84); Renee Latta, Michelle Spurrier, Christina Robin (page 110); Diana Barthelemy, Tom Herman (page 134); Grant Torre, Jeff D., Dawn Dobson (page 168); Diana Barthelemy (page 304); Gina Peterson, Susan Zanovitch, and Bruce Metcalf (page 324) . May you each receive a new memory for every reader your words touch.

PassPorter would not be where it is today without the support of the Internet community. Our thanks to the friendly folks below and to all those we didn't have room to include!

- AllEars®.net (http://www.allears.net). Thanks, Deb!
- CruiseCritic.com (http://cruisecritic.com). Thanks, Laura!
- MEI-Travel and Mouse Fan Travel (http://www.mei-travel.com). Thanks, Beci!
- MouseEarVacations.com (http://www.mouseearvacations.com). Thanks, Jami!
- MousePlanet (http://www.mouseplanet.com). Thanks, Mark, Alex, Lani, and Shoshana!
- MouseSavers.com (http://www.mousesavers.com). Thanks, Mary!
- The Platinum Castaway Club (http://www.castawayclub.com). Thanks, Barb & Tony!
- Unofficial Disney Information Station (http://www.wdwinfo.com). Thanks, Pete!

A special thank you to the Guides (moderators) of our own message boards: Maureen Austin, Amy Bedore, Tiffany Bendes, Dyan Chaplin, Michelle Clark, Dianne Cook, Lesley Duncan, Dawn Erickson, Joanne and Tim Ernest, Marisa Garber-Brown, Rob Gatto, Kristin Grey, Debbie Hendrickson, LauraBelle Hime, Linda Holland, Christina Holland-Radvon, Claudine Jamba, Terri Jordan, Deb Kendall, Robin Krening-Capra, Susan Kulick, Marcie LaCava, Denise Lang, Kris Lindsey, Keri Madeira, Lynn Mirante, Yvonne Mitchell, Sarah Mudd, Bill Myers, Michelle Nash, Rebecca Oberg, Allison Palmer-Gleicher, Cheryl Pendry, Sheana Perry, Tina Peterson, Susan Rannestad, Sabine Rautenberg, Carol Ray, Crystal Remaly, Jennifer Sanborn, Jennifer Savickas, Ann Smith, Donna Sonmor, Kelly Spratt, Marie St. Martin, Suzanne Torrey, Marnie Urmaza, Sara Varney, Susan Wagner, Suzi Waters, Don Willis, Debbie Wright, Tammy Wright, and the 24,000+ readers in our amazing community at http://www.passporterboards.com.

A heartfelt thank you to our family and friends for their patience while we were away on research trips or cloistered at our computers, and for their support of our dream: Allison Cerel Marx; Alexander Marx; Carolyn Tody; Tom Anderson; Fred and Adele Marx; Kim, Chad, Megan and Natalie Larner; Dan, Jeannie, Kayleigh, Melanie, and Nina Marx; Gale Cerel; Jeanne and David Beroza; Robert, Sharon, and Nicole Larner, Gordon Watson; and Marta Metcalf.

Printer: Malloy Incorporated in Ann Arbor, Michigan
Visibility Specialists: Kate and Doug Bandos, KSB Promotions
Newsletter Editor and Online Coordinator: Sara Varney
Office Managers and Research Assistants: Nicole Larner and Chad Larner
Proofreader: Sandy Livingston
Sorcerers' Apprentices: Kim Larner, Carolyn Tody, and Tom Anderson
Special thank yous to Ernie Sabella, Phil Adelman, Jeff Howell, Fred Marx, Paul McGill, Christy Erwin, Jason Lasecki, and the Disney crew members.

Last but not least, we thank Walter Elias Disney for his dream.

Contents

Jennifer poses by a porthole

List of
Maps, Worksheets, and Charts

Dave anticipates a fine meal at Palo

Goofin" around at the Mickey Pool

Contents
(continued)

Bonus Features...

Bookplate for personalization
.... inside front cover

2008/2009 Planning Calendars
.... inside back cover

Important Phone Numbers
.... inside back cover

Web Site Index
.... pages 333–337

Photos, including many original
shots by your authors
.... throughout the book

Planning Timeline Worksheet
.... page 351

Cruise at a Glance Worksheet
....page 352

A little extra magic
.... sprinkled throughout

Bon Voyage!

You're about to embark on a marvelous voyage aboard one of the most beautiful and celebrated cruise lines in the world. You couldn't have made a better choice—the Disney Cruise Line will surprise and delight you with its stunning architecture, legendary service, and fun-for-the-whole-family activities. Boy, we wish we could go with you!

Our original travel guide, *PassPorter's Walt Disney World*, contains the basic information for the Disney Cruise Line. Even so, our readers sent in many requests to add more details on the cruises. Our answer is this field guide, which is chock-a-block with information on virtually every aspect of cruising with Disney. We designed it to stand alone or work with our Disney World guidebook and/or the PassPorter travel planning system. Everything you need to know to plan and enjoy a magical cruise is within these pages!

You're holding the sixth edition of the first guidebook dedicated to the Disney Cruise Line! As always, we include in-depth coverage of scheduled "special itinerary" ports along with Disney's regular stops. Changes and updates aboard the Disney Cruise Line since our last edition are highlighted in gray, too! The Disney Cruise Line is constantly evolving, which makes this travel guide a perpetual work in progress. Please tell us what you like and where we've missed the boat so we can improve our next edition!

This field guide is the embodiment of not just our knowledge and experience, but that of our fellow cruisers and PassPorter readers as well. In essence, this is a cruise guide by cruisers, for cruisers. We share what we like and don't like, and you may find some differing opinions just within the pages of this guide. Reader opinion plays a big part of our shore excursion reviews in chapter 6. And our expert reviewers shared their own opinions and experiences to enrich our information.

Use this field guide for planning before you embark, and then keep it handy onboard during your voyage. We hope you find this field guide a useful companion on your adventure!

We'd love to hear from you! Visit us on the Internet (http://www.passporter.com) or drop us a postcard from Castaway Cay!

Jennifer and *Dave*

P.S. This edition was last revised in February 2008. To check for new revisions or view our latest online update list, visit us on the Internet at this address: http://www.passporter.com/dcl

Preparing to Cast Off

Cruising doesn't just refer to the time you're onboard—it's a state of mind. To help you get into the spirit of the adventure that awaits, try out our favorite ways to build excitement for a Disney cruise. You may discover they help you "cruise" through the planning process without a hitch!

Check Out the Literature

A trip to your local travel agent will reward you with the free Disney Cruise Line Vacations booklet—it's in full color and crammed with photos. You can also request one at 888-325-2500 or at http://www.disneycruise.com. The Disney web site is also a great source for photos, excursions, etc.

Watch the Video or DVD

Request your free Disney Cruise Line video or DVD by calling 888-325-2500 or on the web at http://www.disneycruise.com. It arrives in about 3-4 weeks. Both the video and DVD offer a fun peek at the ship and ports.

Network With Other Cruisers

Fans of Disney cruises are scattered far and wide—chances are you know someone who has been on a Disney cruise. If not, come join us on the Internet, where many Disney cruisers congregate to share tips. See page 28 for links to popular gathering places, including PassPorter.com.

Tune In to TV

Watch the Travel Channel and the Discovery Channel for specials about cruises and the Caribbean. Or have fun with reruns of "The Love Boat."

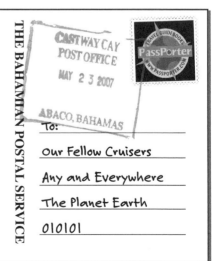

FROM CASTAWAY CAY

Being on Castaway Cay and hearing all this great music reminds us that there's nothing like steel drums to conjure up visions of cruising through the Caribbean. Find some Caribbean-style music and play it as you plan. We guarantee it'll get you in the mood. If you have access to iTunes, try the Reggae/Island radio stations. If you're on AOL, try the Surf or Reggae channel at AOL keyword: Radio.

Your field guide authors,
Jennifer and Dave

THE BAHAMIAN POSTAL SERVICE

CASTAWAY CAY
POST OFFICE
MAY 2 3 2007

ABACO, BAHAMAS

To:

Our Fellow Cruisers

Any and Everywhere

The Planet Earth

010101

Getting Your Feet Wet

So, you've decided to take a Disney cruise! The Disney cruise attracts many first-time cruisers. If you're among them, welcome to the world of cruising! If you're a cruise veteran, welcome back!

Now that you've decided to cruise, you're likely to have one of two reactions. You may feel overwhelmed by the complexity that looms ahead. Or you may be lulled into a sense of complacency, sure that all the details will be taken care of. We understand—before our early cruises, we wavered between these two reactions ourselves. It wasn't until we learned more about the Disney cruises that we received a welcome splash of cold water. Thanks to a boatload of knowledge and the experience of other cruisers, we were able to dispel that feeling of drifting into uncharted waters.

We figure you don't want a splash of cold water in your face, so instead we offer this chapter as a friendly introduction to the world of cruising with Disney. We filled the chapter with highlights and histories, as well as facts and figures. You can read the chapter straight through or jump to the sections that interest you. We've included articles on the Disney Cruise Line, cruising in general, hints for first-time cruisers, comparisons with other cruise lines and Walt Disney World, fleet facts, the differences between the two ships, budgeting, money-saving ideas, and the best places to find more information. We wrap up the chapter with tips and memories.

Before you delve deeper, we want to share a secret. Yes, it's true that you could plunk down your money and just show up. But you wouldn't be getting your money's worth—not by a long shot. Planning is the secret to any successful vacation. Not only do you learn the tips and tricks, but you get to start your cruise early through anticipation. By the end of this guide, you'll know more than the vast majority of your shipmates. You'll know the way to get those coveted reservations. You'll know the way to pack and what to bring. You'll even know your way around the ship before you board it. In short, you'll be cruising your way ... straight out of those uncharted waters and into the true "magic" and "wonder" of a cruise.

Introduction

Reservations

Staterooms

Dining

Activities

Ports of Call

Magic

Index

The Disney Cruise Line

The Disney Cruise Line is more than just another cruise. Disney designed its ships to be **innovative**, offering unique facilities and programs, each with Disney's hallmark, first-class service.

The **history** of the Disney Cruise Line began in November 1985, when Premier Cruise Lines become the official cruise line of Walt Disney World Resort. Premier's "Big Red Boat" offered Disney characters and packages that included stays at the Walt Disney World Resort. When the ten-year contract with Premier was up, Disney set off on its own with an ambitious goal: To become the best cruise line in the world. Disney commissioned the Fincantieri Shipyard (in Venice, Italy) to build a 350-million-dollar liner reminiscent of the grand, trans-Atlantic liners of the early 20th century. A private island was developed into the delightful Castaway Cay, a stop on each cruise itinerary. On July 30, 1998, the Disney Magic set sail on her maiden voyage. The magnificent new ship boasted a classic, streamlined silhouette, twin funnels, and well-appointed interiors. The Disney Magic sailed from her dedicated, art deco-inspired cruise terminal in Port Canaveral, Florida on three- and four-night cruises to the Bahamas. The Disney Wonder set sail on August 15, 1999. Seven-night itineraries to the Eastern Caribbean on the Disney Magic were added in 2000, leaving the shorter cruises to the Wonder. In 2002, seven-night Western Caribbean cruises were added. The Disney Magic sailed the Mediterranean in summer 2007 and returns to the West Coast in summer 2008. Both ships have received upgrades over the years, enhancing their comforts. What lies ahead? See page 29 for a discussion of the future, including scuttlebutt and our own personal theories.

The **Disney Magic** and the **Disney Wonder** are almost identical vessels, with only a few minor differences (see page 23). The ships' hulls are painted dark blue-black, white, yellow, and red (Mickey's colors) with elegant gold scrollwork that cleverly reveals the silhouettes of classic Disney characters. As you board, you are greeted by friendly crew members in the three-story lobby atrium, distinguished by a sweeping staircase and a bronze statue (Mickey on the Magic, Ariel on the Wonder). Warm woods, polished metal

railings, and nautical touches embrace passengers in elegance. Subtle Disney touches are abundant, from character silhouettes along the staircase to valuable Disney prints and artwork on the walls. Every area of the ship is decorated and themed. Both ships are a delight to the senses.

© Disney

The Disney Magic and the Disney Wonder

Why Cruise?

Cruising is something very special. Imagine yourself on a big—really big—beautiful ship. A low hum of excitement fills the air. The ship's whistle sounds smartly (Where have you heard that tune before?) and the ship begins to glide out of her berth. The ship is yours—deck upon deck of dining rooms, lounges, theaters, and staterooms.

People cruise with Disney for many reasons. Some love everything Disney, some want to be pampered, others enjoy the onboard activities, and still others want to visit foreign ports. Some families love the together-time they can have onboard, while other families appreciate the many activities for different ages. Adults love the peace of the adults-only pool, the gourmet tastes at Palo, and the evening fun at Beat Street/Route 66. Teens love having their own hangout and meeting fellow teens. Kids love the Oceaneer Club/Lab and the pools. What about us? Our first Disney cruise was to experience Disney's "next new thing." What brought us back again and again? Pure relaxation! A vacation to Disney World is wonderful, but very intense. On the cruise, we take a deep breath and slow down. We disembark refreshed and renewed, ready to tackle anything.

© MediaMarx, Inc.

Jennifer blows bubbles during the sailaway deck party

Cruising Myths

Here are some oft-quoted reasons why some people don't cruise—each is a common myth that we're happy to dispel. Myth #1: *It's too expensive.* Actually, cruising costs the same as a land-based vacation—a Disney Cruise is equivalent to a comparable stay at the Walt Disney World Resort. Myth #2: *I'll be bored.* If anything, there's too much to do! You'll find it hard to choose between activities, and you'll probably disembark with a list of things you wish you'd had time to do. Myth #3: *I'll get seasick.* Most people don't, but there's a chance you could be one of the unlucky few. But if you follow our tips on page 317, you should be just fine. Myth #4: *Cruises are too formal.* Hey, this is a Disney cruise! Yes, the cruise is luxurious, but you won't feel out of place. Casual clothing is the norm onboard (most of the time). Myth #5: *The Disney Cruise is for kids (or people with kids).* Kids love the Disney Cruise, but so do adults (we cruised many times sans kids). There are plenty of adult activities and areas. Myth #6: *I'll feel claustrophobic or unsteady on my feet.* Disney ships' staterooms are 25% larger than most other lines, and the ships have stabilizers to minimize rolling.

Introduction · Reservations · Staterooms · Dining · Activities · Ports of Call · Magic · Index

Introduction

Reservations

Staterooms

Dining

Activities

Ports of Call

Magic

Index

First-Time Cruisers

Are you going on your first cruise and wondering what to expect?

You're not alone—many of your fellow cruisers will also be on their first cruise. We remember our first cruise well—we had only "The Love Boat" reruns and stories from friends and family to rely upon. We fretted over getting seasick, which wasn't a problem at all. We worried there wouldn't be enough to do, but in fact there was too much—a cruise is quite overwhelming (especially for first-timers) and we wished we had more time. We were even concerned we'd feel like "poor relations" mingling with wealthier cruisers, but we fit right in.

Life aboard a Disney cruise ship is unlike most land-based vacations, unless perhaps you live the lifestyle of the rich and famous. Even if you're staying in budget lodgings, you'll receive the same level of luxurious, personal service as the deluxe guests. Your stateroom attendant will keep your room ship-shape (cleaning twice a day), see to your special needs, and turn down the bed every night (perhaps even with a cute animal made from towels). You'll form a personal relationship with your dining room team, who'll attend you at every shipboard dinner (apart from Palo).

And you'll eat! **Nearly all food and soft drinks onboard are included** in your Disney cruise—meals, snacks, room service, more snacks—so order anything you want, even if it's "seconds" or two different entrées.

The **ship hums with activity**, from sunup to the wee hours. Parties, live shows, children's programs, recreational activities, first-run movies, seminars, and guest lectures ... nearly everything is included in the price of your cruise, as is the right to do "none of the above."

Some say that modern cruise ships are "floating hotels," but "traveling resort" is a better description. Each day brings new vistas and often a new port. No matter how distracted you may be by onboard activities, the subtle vibration and motion of the ship whispers that your **luxurious little world** is going somewhere. Unlike long road trips or jet flights, your life doesn't go into an uncomfortable state of suspended animation while en route to your destination. Getting there can be far more than half the fun!

Our **advice to first-time cruisers** is two-fold: Learn as much as you can about cruising, and then leave your expectations at home. Keep an open mind and be willing to try new things. You can rest assured that Disney has taken the needs of first-time cruisers into mind and considered your needs even before you realize you have them.

What's Included in a Disney Cruise?

Shipboard Accommodations: Up to 25% larger rooms than other ships—from 184 sq. ft. to 304 sq. ft. for non-suite staterooms.

Shipboard Meals: Three full-service dining room meals daily (breakfast, lunch, and dinner). Alternatives for breakfast, lunch, and dinner, such as buffets, quick-service, and room service, are also included. Let's not forget the snacks (soft-serve ice cream, fruit, hot dogs, sandwiches, pizza), afternoon cookies, evening hors d'oeurves, and at least one late-night dessert buffet. The seven-night cruises serve up even more late-night munchies. Soft drinks (Coke, Diet Coke, Caffeine-Free Diet Coke, Sprite, Diet Sprite, Hi-C pink lemonade, and Hi-C fruit punch), milk, coffee, tea (Twinings hot and Nestea iced), hot cocoa, water, and ice are always free at meals and at the Beverage Station (deck 9), but are mostly not free through room service or at the bars. Lunch (with soda) at Castaway Cay is also included.

Shipboard Entertainment and Activities: Disney offers a wide variety of entertainment, including live stage shows, first-run movies, deck parties, live bands, dancing, nightclubs, karaoke, trivia games, Disney character meet and greets, seminars, tours, art auctions, and social gatherings.

Sports and Recreation: There are three pools, four whirlpool tubs, fitness center, aerobics studio (and some classes), walking/jogging track, Ping-Pong, shuffleboard, basketball, and the Wide World of Sports deck.

Kids' Activities: Participation in kids' programs is included for ages 3–17, with activities and areas for varying age groups. Kids' shore excursions (other than Castaway Cay programming) are not included, however.

Ports of Call: Stops at all ports on the itinerary are included, as is transportation to the shore by tender (small boat), if necessary. Port charges are included in the price quote, unlike some other cruises.

What Isn't Included?

Your airfare may or may not be included in your cruise package—check when making your reservation. This goes for insurance and ground transfers between the airport to the ship as well. Accommodations, meals, and park passes for any time you spend at Walt Disney World are not included, unless you book a land/sea package that specifically includes these. Other extras: alcoholic beverages, specialty beverages (i.e., smoothies), soft drinks (at a bar or from room service), Internet Cafe, bingo games, spa and beauty treatments, Palo meals ($15/adult), childcare for kids under 3, arcade games, onboard or off-ship shopping, photos, formalwear rental, shore excursions, meals off-ship (except Castaway Cay), medical treatment, laundry services (including the self-service washers and dryers, though you can use the iron and ironing board freely), parking at the cruise terminal, and gratuities.

Introduction

Reservations

Staterooms

Dining

Activities

Ports of Call

Magic

Index

Introduction

Reservations

Staterooms

Dining

Activities

Ports of Call

Magic

Index

How Do They Measure Up?

Compared to **other cruise ships**, the Disney Magic and the Disney Wonder are among the most spacious ships afloat. Staterooms are 25% larger on average than those found on other ships. Other unique aspects of the Disney Cruise Line include split bathrooms (in stateroom categories 10 and up), rotational dining (different dining rooms, same servers), half a deck designed just for kids (with programs for specific age groups), areas reserved just for adults (pool, restaurant, Cove Café, spa, beach on Castaway Cay, and an entertainment district that's reserved just for adults after 9:00 pm), a visit to Castaway Cay (Disney's private island), Disney's famous characters, and that Disney magic!

Experienced cruisers may miss having a casino or a library aboard. The sentiment seems to be that the Disney Cruise Line offers the best family cruise afloat, but that it lacks enough activities for adults without children. We disagree (especially after several "drydock" upgrades)—we've sailed without kids and never lack adult activities. The generous adults-only areas deliver welcome isolation and surpass other "family" cruise lines. Some cruisers have also reported that the Disney Cruise Line is too, well, "Disney." Let's face it: If you don't like Disney, you may not like this cruise either. But these aren't theme parks. The quality service and elegant surroundings could easily outweigh any negative associations you have with Mickey Mouse.

Safety and **cleanliness** is a big deal on cruise ships, and all international ships are inspected by the U.S. Centers for Disease Control (CDC) on a regular basis. The Disney Magic and Disney Wonder were most recently inspected in September 2007 and December 2007. Both passed their inspections, receiving 99 and 95 out of 100 points, respectively. To view the latest inspection results, visit: http://www.cdc.gov/nceh/vsp/default.htm.

If you've been to the Walt Disney World Resort and wonder how a Disney cruise compares to a **resort vacation**, it is really quite different. The cruise feels more laid-back yet formal at the same time. The excitement of dashing from attraction to attraction is gone, and you may feel like you're missing "something" that you can't identify. On the upside, everything is within walking distance, the food is "free," and rain isn't the same party-pooper it is at the theme parks. You'll take things a bit slower on the cruise (although there's still plenty to do), all the while feeling pampered by the gorgeous setting and excellent service. Walt Disney World and the Disney cruise do share many perks, however: single key-card access for rooms and purchases, Disney character greetings, and that "red carpet" guest service. Don't expect to find "Walt Disney World on water." You'll discover the Disney Cruise Line has its own unique charm.

Fleet Facts

Home Port: Port Canaveral, Florida, USA
Country of Registry: The Bahamas
Radio Call Signs: C6PT7-Magic and C6QM8-Wonder
Captains: Captain Tom Forberg, Captain Henry Andersson, Captain John Barwis, Captain Gus Verhulst, and Captain Thord Haugen
Crews: 950 crew members, multinational
Guests: 2,400 (1,750 at double occupancy)—maximum is near 3,000
Space ratio: 48.3 (the ratio of passengers to space, namely 4,830 cubic feet per passenger; a ratio this high means a roomy, uncrowded ship.)
Tonnage: 83,000 (measured by volume, not weight—for an explanation, see http://www.m-i-link.com/dictionary/default.asp?s=s&q=tonnage)
Length: 964 ft./294 m. (longer than the *Titanic* at 882 ft./268 m.)
Beam: 106 ft./32.25 m. (the width of the ships at their widest)
Draft: 25.3 ft./7.7 m. (the depth below the waterline when full)
Speed: 21.5 knots, or 25 mph/40 kph (max. is 24 knots/28 mph/44 kph)
Systems: Five 16-cylinder diesel engines, two 19-megawatt GE propulsion motors, three bow and two stern thrusters, and one pair of fin stabilizers
Passenger Decks: 11 (see front of book for our detailed deck plans)
Lifeboats: 20, with each seating 150 passengers (plus 50 life rafts)
Staterooms: 877 (252 inside, 625 outside)—see chap. 3
Theatres: 2 (975 seats and 268 seats)
Restaurants: 4 (138 seats in Palo, 442 seats in the others)—see chap. 4
Buffets and Snack Bars: 4 (294 seats inside, 332 seats outside)
Lounges: 5 (or 8 if you count the three nightclubs)
Shops: 5   **Pools**: 4 (one is for crew)   **Hot Tubs**: 4   **Spa**: 1

Differences Between the Magic and the Wonder

Feature	Disney Magic	Disney Wonder
Year built:	1998	1999
Itineraries:	7-night and up cruises	3- and 4-night cruises
Decor:	Art Deco	Art Nouveau
Bow decoration:	Sorcerer Mickey	Steamboat Willie (Mickey)
Stern adornment:	Boatswain Goofy	Donald and Huey
Atrium statue:	Helmsman Mickey	Ariel, The Little Mermaid
Grand dining room:	Lumière's	Triton's
Casual dining room:	Topsider's Buffet	Beach Blanket Buffet
Adults-only district:	Beat Street + Cove Café	Route 66 + Cove Café
Dance club:	Rockin' Bar D	WaveBands
Jazz piano bar:	Sessions	Cadillac Lounge
Deck 2 public space	Ocean Quest kids' area	Conference rooms
Teen club:	The Stack	Aloft
Navigator's Verandah:	Round porthole	Larger oblong porthole

Introduction
Reservations
Staterooms
Dining
Activities
Ports of Call
Magic
Index

Can I Afford It?

Cruises were once reserved for wealthy globetrotters. These days, cruises are **more affordable**, but not always "inexpensive." Disney Cruise Line's popularity and "demand-based" pricing keep pushing rates up. Still, a seven-night Disney cruise can be comparable in price to a seven-night land vacation at Walt Disney World. To determine what you can afford, make a budget (see below). Budgeting not only keeps you from spending too much, it encourages you to seek out ways to save money. With a little research, you can often get **more for less**. To get an idea of what an actual cruise costs, check out our recent 2007 cruise expenses at the bottom of the page.

A **cruise package** may include ground transportation, airfare, insurance, lodging at Walt Disney World, theme park admission, and other extras. This may seem convenient, but planning each aspect of your cruise yourself saves you more money. Learn about cruise packages on pages 43 and 46.

Your **cruise expenses** fall into six categories: planning, transportation, lodging, cruise passage, port activities, and extras. How you budget for each depends upon the total amount you have available to spend and your priorities. Planning, transportation, lodging, and cruise passage are the easiest to factor ahead of time as costs are fixed. The final two—port activities and extras—are harder to control, but we provide sample costs throughout this field guide to help you estimate.

Begin your budget with the **worksheet** on the next page (use pencil at the start). Enter the minimum you prefer to spend and the most you can afford in the topmost row. Set as many of these ranges as possible before you delve into the other chapters of this book. Your excitement may grow as you read more, but it is doubtful your bank account will.

As you uncover costs and ways to save money, return to your worksheet and **update it**. Your budget is a work in progress—try to be flexible within your minimums and maximums. As plans crystallize, write the amount you expect (and can afford) in the Goals column. If you are using PassPockets (see the Deluxe Edition on page 348), **transfer the amounts** from the Goals column to the back of each PassPocket when you are satisfied with your budget.

Our Dec. 2007 Expenses
(2 adults, 1 child)

Round-trip airfare: $491
Rental mini-van: $120
4-night cruise (cat. 7): $1,879
Port activities: $10
Souvenirs: $119
Beverages/Palo: $30
Phone/Internet: $150
Childcare: $18
Gratuities: $85

TOTAL: $2,902

Budget Worksheet

Electronic, interactive worksheet available— see page 350

As you work through this field guide, use this worksheet to identify your resources, record estimated costs, and create a budget. We provide prices and estimates throughout the book.

	Minimum	Maximum	Goals
Total Projected Expenses	$	$	$
Planning:			
Phone calls/faxes:			
Guides/magazines:			
Transportation: *(to/from)*			
Travel/airline tickets:			
Rental car:			
Fuel/maintenance:			
Ground transfer/shuttle:			
Town car/taxi:			
Wheelchair/ECV:			
Parking:			
Lodging: *(pre-/post-cruise)*			
Resort/hotel/motel:			
Meals/extras:			
Cruise Passage:			
Cruise:			
Protection plan/insurance:			

Port Activities:	Per Port	Total	Per Port	Total	Per Port	Total
Excursions:						
Meals:						
Attractions:						
Rentals:						
Transportation/taxis:						

	Minimum	Maximum	Goals
Extras:			
Souvenirs/photos:			
Beverages:			
Resortwear/accessories:			
Palo/formal wear:			
Spa treatments:			
Childcare (nursery):			
Phone/Internet/stamps:			
Gratuities/duties:			
Other:			
Total Budgeted Expenses	$	$	$

Introduction

Reservations

Staterooms

Dining

Activities

Ports of Call

Magic

Index

Money-Saving Ideas and Programs

The Disney Cruise Line enjoys great popularity, so discounts can be scarce. Here are the ways we've found to save money on your cruise:

Reserve Early to Get Early Booking Savings

Reserve early enough and you could save approximately $100–$890 per stateroom (7-night cruises) or $30–$650 per stateroom (3- and 4-night cruises). Staterooms at this discount are limited, however. To get the best early booking savings, reserve your cruise as soon as dates are announced (generally up to 18 months in advance).

Go à la Carte

Disney emphasizes the 7-night Land and Sea package combining 3 or 4 nights at the Walt Disney World Resort with a cruise. This is appealing to many vacationers, but it is pricier than making your own arrangements as you can usually find better deals on hotel rooms at Walt Disney World.

Find Promotions and Discounts

As with most cruise lines, Disney uses demand-based pricing. Unlike most cruise lines, this means prices almost always rise as a cruise date approaches. The last-minute specials common with other lines are rare at Disney. With Disney Cruise Line, the earlier you reserve, the better your rate. That said, deals and specials are available, if you're alert. Check about 75 days before you want to cruise (this is the final payment deadline for current reservations). Visit http://www.disneycruise.com to learn more. Also visit MouseSavers.com (http://www.mousesavers.com), which summarizes available discounts, and http://www.themouseforless.com.

Use a Travel Agent

Larger travel agencies are able to pre-book blocks of staterooms, locking in discounts for you to snag later on. Check with agents before booking on your own (see page 47 for a list). Travel agents are very good at finding the best prices, too! Mouse Fan Travel (http://www.mousefantravel.com) and MouseEarVacations.com (http://www.mouseearvacations.com) have saved us considerable money on our cruises (yes, we find travel agents quite helpful!), and other agencies can do the same.

Watch for Onboard Credits

Wouldn't it be nice to have an extra $25 or $100 sitting in your onboard account? Keep an eye out for onboard credit specials. At the time of writing, guests who book online get a $25 credit. Onboard credits may also be available when you book onboard (see next page) and through special deals offered by travel agents. Credits for repeat cruisers have generally been replaced by in-stateroom gifts.

Move to Florida

We're not serious about moving, but if you're already a Florida resident you may get discounts up to 50% off select cruises (limited staterooms). Call Disney at 888-325-2500 to inquire about Florida resident discounts, or check http://www.mousesavers.com. Proof of residency is required.

Book Your Next Cruise Onboard

On your next Disney cruise, check the *Personal Navigator* or the Cruise Sales Desk on Deck 4 for onboard specials. Not only can booking onboard offer great prices ($100 less than land-based prices recently), but sometimes onboard credits, too. Two catches: The best rates are often for cruises sailing the same time next year, and you must reserve before you disembark. If you see a deal, grab it—you can change or cancel your reservation later if necessary; just call Disney at 888-325-2500. Tip: You can transfer your booking to your travel agent when you return home.

Stay Off-Site Before Your Cruise

If you're like us and prefer to arrive at least a day ahead of your cruise, look for an inexpensive hotel or motel. In-airport hotels can be pricey—to save money, see page 62. See pages 61–62 and 68–70 for lodging. It can sometimes be less expensive to fly in a day early, so always investigate.

Compare Local Transportation Costs

Depending on your party size, it can be less expensive to rent a car to drive from the airport to the port and back again. On the other hand, transportation companies such as Quicksilver Tours & Transportation may offer price plus convenience. Explore your options on pages 63–65.

Special Tips for Special People

✔ **Infants and kids** 12 and under are less expensive than adults, but only if there are two adults along as well (the first two stateroom guests always pay full adult fare). The third and fourth adults in a stateroom also cruise at a lower price. See page 44.

✔ **AAA and Costco** members can get rates and make reservations through these companies and often get excellent deals. AAA members: Ask about your local AAA chapter's "Disney Month" for extra savings and goodies, and be sure to inquire about any extras (such as an onboard credit) with your AAA Disney package.

✔ **Disney Vacation Club** members may be eligible for exclusive cruises at good rates. Check with this program or the Disney Cruise Line for details.

✔ **Canadian residents** may get special rates on select cruises. Contact the Disney Cruise Line or a travel agent.

✔ **Military personnel** may be eligible for some last-minute rates, similar to those offered to Florida residents. Call the Disney Cruise Line or a travel agent for more details.

✔ **Repeat cruisers** are automatically members of the Castaway Club. You'll receive a gift (one per stateroom) when you cruise again, and enjoy special features at the Castaway Club web page. For details and rates, call Disney Cruise Line, or visit http://www.disneycruise.com and click Castaway Club.

Introduction
Reservations
Staterooms
Dining
Activities
Ports of Call
Magic
Index

Porthole to More Cruising Information

While this field guide could serve as your single source, we recommend you gather as much information as possible. Each of the sources described below offers its own unique porthole into the world of Disney cruising.

Official Disney Information—Definitely get the free booklet and video/DVD we mention on page 16, and visit the web site (http://www.disneycruise.com). Any other brochures you can get from your travel agent will be helpful, too. Disney also sends cruise documentation (more about this on page 50) that contains some basic information.

Books—Disney published an official guidebook, *Birnbaum's Disney Cruise Line*, starting in 2004, but we were disappointed to find little detail beyond what's available at the Disney Cruise Line's web site—the shore excursion reviews are insightful, however. And while virtually all Walt Disney World Resort guidebooks mention the Disney Cruise Line, most only give it a few pages. The two with the most information are *Walt Disney World with Kids* by Kim Wright Wiley (Fodor's) and *The Unofficial Guide to Walt Disney World* by Bob Sehlinger (Wiley). Both have about 10 pages on the topic. Two other PassPorter books contain information on Disney Cruise Line: *PassPorter's Open Mouse for Walt Disney World and the Disney Cruise Line* and *PassPorter's Treasure Hunts* have sections on Disney Cruise Line.

Magical Disney Cruise Guide—This excellent, free online guide offers a detailed overview of Disney cruising, including reviews. http://www.allears.net/cruise/cruise.htm.

Web Sites—Some of the best sources of information are the official and unofficial sites for the Disney Cruise Line. Here are our picks:

Disney Cruise Line Official Site—http://www.disneycruise.com
Disney Cruise Line Official News Site—http://www.dclnews.com
PassPorter.com (that's us!)—http://www.passporter.com/dcl
PassPorterBoards.com (advice from fellow cruisers)—http://www.passporterboards.com
Magical Disney Cruise Guide—http://www.allears.net/cruise/cruise.shtml
Platinum Castaway Club—http://www.castawayclub.com
DIS—http://www.wdwinfo.com (click "Disney Cruise Line") and http://www.disboards.com
Disney Echo—http://disneyecho.emuck.com
AllEars.net—http://www.allears.net/cruise/cruise.htm
Kolb Family—http://www.kolbfamily.com/2000cruise/disney_cruise.htm
Disney World Online Guide—http://www.wdisneyw.co.uk/cruise.html
Pettit's Page—http://www.richpettit.com/vacations/ourvacations.htm
epinions.com—http://www.epinions.com (search on the ship names)

These are excellent sites on general cruising:
CruiseCritic—http://www.cruisecritic.com
About.com—http://cruises.about.com
CruiseMates—http://cruisemates.com
AvidCruiser—http://avidcruiser.com
Cruise2.com—http://www.cruise2.com

The Future of the Disney Cruise Line

What's next for Disney Cruise Line? Here are some facts and theories.

There are **two new ships on the horizon** for Disney Cruise Line, the first new ships to be added to the Disney fleet since the launch of the Disney Magic and Disney Wonder! This exciting and long-awaited news was announced on February 22, 2007, by Walt Disney Company President Robert Iger. Disney is very quiet about details (and will be for a couple more years), so we'll try to fill in some of the blanks with our thoughts, too.

What do we know about Disney's new ships at this time? Two ships, scheduled for delivery in **2011 and 2012**, will be constructed by Germany's Meyer Werft shipyards. The ships' sizes are 122,00-124,000 Gross Register Tons (GRT)—the Magic and Wonder are each 83,000 GRT, and the largest cruise ship in service is Royal Caribbean's Freedom of the Seas, at 154,407 GRT. The new ships will have 1,250 staterooms each (up from 875 on the Magic and Wonder—that's 2,500 passengers at double occupancy, compared to Freedom of the Seas' 3,634), and 13 passenger decks, up from the current 11 (two more decks). The artist's renderings reveal ships with the familiar Disney Cruise Line "look," only bigger. When all four ships are in service, Disney will have nearly 2 1/2 times the passenger capacity it has today. In other words, the two new ships are equal to three Disney Magics. Meantime, the Panama Canal is undergoing a dramatic expansion, so by 2014 the canal won't be an obstacle to the huge, new ships.

Now the **guesswork** begins. How much will the new ships differ from the Magic and Wonder? We expect the new staterooms will be very similar in size and amenity to the current rooms, right down to the very popular split bathrooms. The percentage of verandah staterooms grows, thanks to two extra stateroom decks sporting verandahs. We think there may be a new category of stateroom for larger families, roughly 50% wider than a standard room. The biggest suites will probably be bigger, and there will, of course, be more suites available. It's hard to tell from the drawings whether the ships will have indoor/outdoor pools, a feature common to ships that visit Alaska, but we can certainly hope! Other cruise industry trends we think we'll see include a version of the grand, stem-to-stern lobby found on Royal Caribbean's larger ships, and additional optional restaurants to supplement Palo. What we don't think Disney will borrow from its competition are rock climbing walls and surfing machines—expect larger kids' spaces instead. It's a foregone conclusion that one ship will "live" in California—will it be a new one, or the Magic or Wonder? We think two ships will stay in Port Canaveral, which is great for Caribbean and Bahamian itineraries. Will a third ship alternate between Port Canaveral and special destinations elsewhere in the world? Maybe the third ship will sail 10- and 11-night itineraries? Larger ships may require an expansion of facilities on Disney's private island, Castaway Cay. We can't imagine the family beach being more crowded than it already is. We also suspect that if Disney adds major new features to the new ships, we'll see them on the Magic and Wonder, too (if they'll fit). Disney will probably give its older ships a serious makeover after the new ships arrive. Other lines have stretched their older ships to increase stateroom count and add facilities.

Construction begins in 2010. The shipyard's construction docks are indoors and the ultra-modern manufacturing facility is a wonder (http://www.meyerwerft.de). Walt Disney Imagineering already has a project team at Meyer Werft, so there's plenty of magic afoot.

What about **special itineraries** for 2010 and beyond? It's hard to guess. Disney surprised us by announcing relatively tame special itineraries for 2009. Swapping Tortola or St. Croix for St. Maarten on the Eastern itineraries can best be classified a fuel economy measure.

Introduction

Reservations

Staterooms

Dining

Activities

Ports of Call

Magic

Index

Introduction
Reservations
Staterooms
Dining
Activities
Ports of Call
Magic
Index

Cruise Reviews You Can Use

Cruiser reviews and reports are one of the absolute best ways to evaluate and get acquainted with the Disney Cruise Line before you embark. With that in mind, we've collected several tips and memories from our own experiences and those of our readers. Enjoy!

If you have access to the **Internet**, make it a point to get online and explore the web sites listed throughout this field guide. PassPorter's readers post many interesting, detailed trip reports on their cruises at http://www.passporterboards.com/forums/sharing-your-adventure-disney-cruise-reports. We also recommend you visit MousePlanet's Trip Reports web site, which offers a nice collection of cruise reports at http://www.mouseplanet.com/dtp/trip.rpt.

One of the first "guides" to Disney Cruise Line was a free online publication by Mickey Morgan, the "Magical Disney Cruise Guide." You can still find this **informative online guide** at AllEarsNet. Read it at http://www.allears.net/cruise/cruise.htm.

"Keep a **journal of your trip**, starting with your thoughts and notes on the planning process. Take the journal with you and make notes at the end of each day before you go to bed, as a sort of end-of-day recap. You'll be surprised how such a simple thing can really enrich your travels. When you get home, share your trip report with the friendly folks at the PassPorter Message Boards—it'll be like reliving your trip all over again!" – *contributed by Disney vacationer Jim Anders*

Magical Memory

"We had a Magical Gathering with my family over the July 4th holiday. It was an absolutely amazing experience, but building up to the event itself was at least half of the fun. My husband, two sons, and I always make a yearly Disney pilgrimage. This time, we took along my in-laws, both of whom had never been on an airplane. My brother-in-law and his fiancé were also included. The family usually gets together every Sunday afternoon, and we used this as a great opportunity to build anticipation for the big trip. Every week, we would divulge a Disney tip, factoid, or a story from a previous Mouse vacation. Boy, did this generate a lot of discussion. With each passing week, you could just see the excitement grow and grow. The week prior to departing, everyone was taken with Mouse fever. We all tie-dyed and decorated T-shirts for our upcoming adventure. This activity culminated our planning and signified that the time for our trip had finally arrived. Not only had we created unusual and different pieces of memorabilia for our vacation, but our T-shirts allowed us to easily identify each other in crowds. This was definitely an experience of a lifetime."

...as told by Disney vacationer Susan Kile

Plotting Your Course

DISCOVER the best times to cruise with Disney

CHART your journey and make cruise plans

FIND many ways to get to the port

PACK just what you need to bring on the cruise

By now, we're certain you're hooked on the idea of a Disney cruise vacation. The time has come, the Walrus said, to turn those Disney dreams into a voyage filled with "wonder" and "magic."

Every journey starts with the first step, and this vacation is no exception. That step, of course, is planning. Planning is the keel upon which the rest of your cruise is built. This chapter is filled with the principal planning steps you'll need to take, plus a cargo of savvy advice and a chartroom filled with maps, charts, and worksheets to help keep you on course.

Some of you may be embarking on a cruise and/or leaving the United States for the very first time. While you will be visiting cozy, nearby ports, you'll encounter some subtle and not-so-subtle differences between cruise preparations and land journeys. Start your planning as far ahead as possible. Not only can you save some money, but you may need that head start to obtain the proper identity documents.

So just how do you plot the course that takes you from your front door to the gangway of your Disney cruise ship? In this chapter, we'll chart the many steps in the journey, from selecting your cruise itinerary and sail dates to steering your way around tropical storms. You'll be able to pick your way through the turbulent waters of cruise rates and packages and safely reserve your snug stateroom.

Your ship's captain will ably plot your course on the high seas, but you'll need your own map and compass to get to port. We cover the many highways and byways that form your journey-before-the-journey, including fair lodgings at the port itself.

Finally, it's Embarkation Day! We make sure you aren't waylaid enroute to the cruise terminal, that your important identity papers are all in order, and that your trunks and sea bags are packed!

Introduction

Reservations

Staterooms

Dining

Activities

Ports of Call

Magic

Index

Choosing Your Itinerary

Disney Cruise Line offers **several different itineraries** in 2008–2009: one 3-night cruise, two 4-night cruises, a special 5-night cruise, two 7-night land/sea combinations, six different 7-night cruises, and two special 15-night repositioning cruises. Your choice of itineraries may be solely based on price or length, particularly if you combine your cruise with a stay at Walt Disney World (see page 43). If you can't decide which itinerary works best for you, read our descriptions and comments below for insight:

3-Night Cruise Itinerary: The shortest and least expensive cruise, with three nights at sea aboard the Disney Wonder and two ports of call: Nassau and Castaway Cay. Actual time spent afloat: about 68 hours (almost three days). This cruise whizzes by, and you may feel like it's over before it's barely begun. On the flip side, this is a great cruise on

> **3-Night Itinerary:**
> Thursday: Set sail
> Friday: Nassau
> Saturday: Castaway Cay
> Sunday: Return to port

which to get your feet wet if you're new to cruising. If you plan to stay at the Walt Disney World Resort before your cruise, the 3-night cruise works best for this as it falls at the end of the week. Also, this cruise departs on Thursdays, which also happens to be the day that most space shuttles depart from Cape Canaveral (see pages 176–177 for more details on shuttle launches).

4-Night Cruise Itinerary: More sailing time with four nights at sea on the Disney Wonder. Like the 3-night, the 4-night stops at Nassau and Castaway Cay. The extra day is spent at sea—there used to be a stop in Freeport instead of a day at sea, but this ceased in 2004. Actual time spent afloat: about 92 hours (almost four days). If cruising is your focus,

> **4-Night Itinerary:**
> Sunday: Set sail
> Monday: Nassau
> Tuesday: Castaway Cay
> Wednesday: At sea
> Thursday: Return
> to port

you'll be happier with a 4-night cruise than a 3-night—the extra night is more relaxing and it gives you a greater chance of dining at Palo without missing one of the other three restaurants. A benefit: If the Captain has to bypass Castaway Cay due to weather, he has the option to try again the next day. A special version of this itinerary visits Castaway Cay twice (see below)!

Special 4- and 5-Night Bahamian Cruises

In 2008, Disney Cruise Line is offering two special Bahamian cruises with itinerary variations. The first is a 4-night Bahamian cruise that stops at Castaway Cay twice—its port of call itinerary is Castaway Cay, Nassau, Castaway Cay. This special 4-night itinerary is available throughout May, June, July, and August 2008. A special 5-night Bahamian cruise available just once on September 1, 2008, follows the same itinerary with double Castaway Cay stops but adds a day at sea after the stop at Nassau.

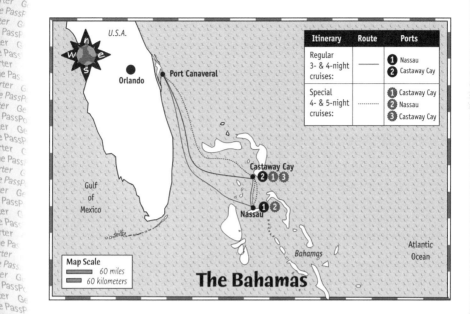

The Bahamas

Itinerary	Route	Ports
Regular 3- & 4-night cruises:	———	① Nassau ② Castaway Cay
Special 4- & 5-night cruises:	·········	① Castaway Cay ② Nassau ③ Castaway Cay

The 7-night land/sea combination itineraries are really just Walt Disney World resort vacations combined with the 3-night and 4-night cruises.

4 Nights on Land/3 Nights at Sea Itinerary: Of the two land/sea itineraries, this is the one we recommend. If you're a fan of Walt Disney World, you may find anything less than four days at Walt Disney World is just too short. With four major parks, you need at least a day to visit each. The cruise portion of this itinerary is identical to the 3-night cruise. The cruise is short, yes, but after four days at Walt Disney World, that may feel just right. Another advantage to this itinerary is how neatly it falls within the space of one week—you leave on Sunday and return on Sunday. If you're a fan of Walt Disney World but new to cruising, we think you'll like this itinerary best—it gives you a reasonable amount of time in the parks and a taste of the cruise. Of course, you can book a 3-night cruise-only and arrange your accommodations on your own. See page 43 for details.

3 Nights on Land/4 Nights at Sea Itinerary: We think three days at Walt Disney World is too short. And this itinerary does start and stop on Thursday, which makes for a lopsided week. There are some advantages, however. First, you get four nights on the cruise, which also means four days of meals. If you'd spent that extra day at Walt Disney World, you'd have to feed yourselves for that day, so you get more bang for your buck. And the 4-night cruise has some added perks that you don't get on the 3-night cruise, such as an at-sea day, a variety show, and the Pirates in the Caribbean menu (the theme night itself is the same). (See the chart on page 38 for a comparison.) If your focus is on cruising and you want to save some money on your vacation, then this may be the itinerary for you!

Choosing Your Itinerary (continued)

7-Night Caribbean Cruise Itineraries: Almost an entire week onboard the Disney Magic with several itineraries to the Eastern or Western Caribbean. Note: There are no 7-night Caribbean cruises from May to September in 2008.

Disney Cruise Line's original 7-night itinerary, the **Eastern Caribbean cruise**, has three ports of call (St. Maarten, St. Thomas, and Castaway Cay) and three days at sea. The **Western Caribbean cruise** offers four ports of call (typically Key West, Grand Cayman, Cozumel, and Castaway Cay) plus two days at sea. In 2008, a special Western Caribbean itinerary visits Costa Maya and Cozumel, plus two visits to Castaway Cay—this itinerary is available on September 27, October 25, November 22, and December 20, 2008. In summer 2009, variations on the Eastern itinerary are offered, with stops in St. Thomas and Tortola or St. Croix. Actual time spent afloat: 164 hours (almost seven days). The 7-night cruise is a great choice for experienced cruisers or those who really want to relax. Cruisers on 7-night itineraries also enjoy formal and semi-formal evenings, theme nights, and a wider variety of onboard activities. Night for night, the 7-nights are no more costly than shorter cruises. Land/sea packages for these cruises are typically only offered to international guests.

> **7-Nt. E. Caribbean:**
> Saturday: Set sail
> Sunday: At sea
> Monday: At sea
> Tuesday: St. Maarten
> Wednesday: St. Thomas
> Thursday: At sea
> Friday: Castaway Cay
> Saturday: Return to port

> **7-Nt. W. Caribbean:**
> Saturday: Set sail
> Sunday: Key West
> Monday: At sea
> Tuesday: Grand Cayman
> Wednesday: Cozumel
> Thursday: At sea
> Friday: Castaway Cay
> Saturday: Return to port

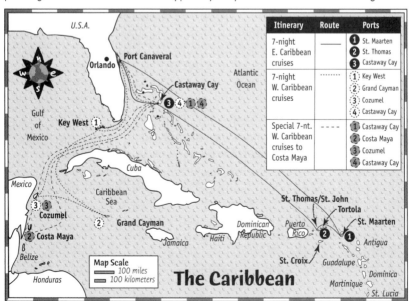

Itinerary	Route	Ports
7-night E. Caribbean cruises	———	❶ St. Maarten ❷ St. Thomas ❸ Castaway Cay
7-night W. Caribbean cruises	·········	① Key West ② Grand Cayman ③ Cozumel ④ Castaway Cay
Special 7-nt. W. Caribbean cruises to Costa Maya	- - - -	❶ Castaway Cay ❷ Costa Maya ❸ Cozumel ❹ Castaway Cay

The Caribbean

Introduction
Reservations
Staterooms
Dining
Activities
Ports of Call
Magic
Index

West Coast Itineraries: In summer 2008, the Disney Magic returns to the West Coast for several Mexican Riviera itineraries.

15-Nt. Westbound:

Saturday: Sail from Port Canaveral
Sunday: Castaway Cay
Monday: At sea
Tuesday: At sea
Wednesday: Aruba
Thursday: At sea
Friday: Pass through Panama Canal
Saturday: At sea
Sunday: At sea
Monday: Acapulco
Tuesday: At sea
Wednesday: Puerto Vallarta
Thursday: Cabo San Lucas
Friday: At sea
Saturday: At sea
Saturday: Los Angeles (San Pedro)

Two 15-night itineraries between Port Canaveral and Los Angeles via the Panama Canal are offered: intinerary #1 leaves on May 10, 2008 from Port Canaveral, stops at Castaway Cay and Aruba, sails through the Panama Canal, stops along the Mexican Riviera, and ends in Los Angeles, while itinerary #2 departs on August 17, 2008 and reverses the above route with an extra stop in Cartagena (see itinerary boxes for full schedules). These are the "repositioning" cruises that allow the Disney Magic to be on the West Coast during the summer of 2008 (see next page). Traditionally, the per diem (daily) price of repositioning cruises is less than for cruises that embark and disembark from the same port, and this is true of Disney Cruise Line's repositioning cruises as well.

Alas, if you haven't already booked one of these two cruises, you may be out of luck—at the time of writing, both itineraries were **fully booked**. It's likely there will be cancellations, however, so keep checking back. If you can swing it, we highly recommend a verandah stateroom—you'll find it invaluable during the Panama Canal crossing. We were lucky enough to sail one of the two repositioning cruises (the eastbound itinerary) offered in 2005, so we've got firsthand experience to share with you in our port chapter—ah, the sacrifices we make for our craft! Actual time spent afloat: 356 hours (almost fifteen days). Cruisers on 15-night itineraries can expect several formal and semi-formal evenings and a wider variety of onboard activities. Land/ sea packages are offered with these itineraries—you can add a 2- or 3-night pre- or post-stay at Disneyland! To read our Panama Canal Crossing trip report, visit http://www.passporter.com/dcl/panamacanalcruise.asp.

15-Nt. Eastbound:

Sunday: Sail from San Pedro (LA)
Monday: At sea
Tuesday: Cabo San Lucas
Wednesday: Puerto Vallarta
Thursday: At sea
Friday: Acapulco
Saturday: At sea
Sunday: At sea
Monday: Pass through Panama Canal
Tuesday: Cartagena
Wednesday: At sea
Thursday: Aruba
Friday: At sea
Saturday: At sea
Sunday: Castaway Cay
Monday: Port Canaveral

Introduction

Reservations

Staterooms

Dining

Activities

Ports of Call

Magic

Index

Choosing Your Itinerary *(continued)*

7-Night Mexican Riviera Itineraries: In light of the very successful West Coast cruises back in summer 2005, Disney is again offering 12 popular Mexican Riviera cruises departing from Los Angeles in summer 2008. The itinerary leaves from the port of San Pedro (22 miles from Disneyland), enjoys a day at sea, stops at Cabo San Lucas, Mazatlán, Puerto Vallarta, another two days at sea, and then back to San Pedro. These are all the same ports visited in 2005, though the port order and departure weekday is different (it's now Sunday rather than Saturday). Departure dates are May 25, June 1, June 8, June 15, June 22, June 29, July 6, July 13, July 20, July 27, August 3, and August 10, 2008. Actual time spent afloat: 164 hours (almost seven days). These special 7-night cruises have plenty of availability at the time of writing.

7-Nt. West Coast:
Sunday: Set sail
Monday: At sea
Tuesday: Cabo San Lucas
Wednesday: Mazatlán
Thursday: Puerto Vallarta
Friday: At sea
Saturday: At sea
Sunday: Return to port

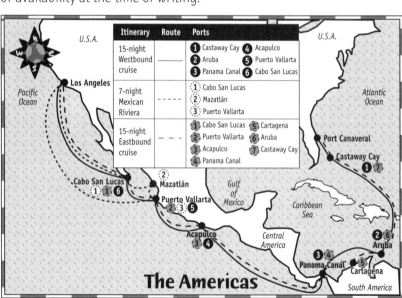

Itinerary	Route	Ports	
15-night Westbound cruise	———	① Castaway Cay ② Aruba ③ Panama Canal	④ Acapulco ⑤ Puerto Vallarta ⑥ Cabo San Lucas
7-night Mexican Riviera	– – – –	⑴ Cabo San Lucas ⑵ Mazatlán ⑶ Puerto Vallarta	
15-night Eastbound cruise	— — —	① Cabo San Lucas ② Puerto Vallarta ③ Acapulco ④ Panama Canal	⑤ Cartagena ⑥ Aruba ⑦ Castaway Cay

The Americas

Does This Book Cover the West Coast Ports of Call?

Yes! We include full reports on each of the ports for the West Coast itineraries, as well as interesting information on passing through the Panama Canal. We've also added details on getting to California, the San Pedro cruise terminal, and lodging near the port, and the majority of this information is based on firsthand experience from your authors, peer reviewers, and readers. Please keep in mind that California is a huge destination and it would really take an entire guidebook to cover—in fact, you may want to check out our award-winning guidebook, *PassPorter's Disneyland Resort and Southern California Attractions* (see page 348).

What about other destinations? Some rumors have floated about Alaskan cruises, but as of yet, nada. 2007's special Mediterranean itineraries were immensely successful, but are not likely to be repeated in the near term. How about Hawaii, South America, or back to Europe? Probably after Disney's fleet grows.

We should note that the **special 10-night holiday cruise** that has been offered between the Christmas and New Year holidays is not appearing on the December 2008 or 2009 schedule. But perhaps it will return in December 2010 or beyond when the new ships debut. Who knows?

If you're eager for other destinations with that "Disney touch," whether as an add-on to a cruise, theme park vacation, or just for its own sake, look into **Adventures by Disney**. While these aren't cruises, they are special, immersive guided tours—designed and led by Disney cast members—to popular destinations like Europe and the American Southwest. These tours are for adults and kids ages 4 and older. There are several itineraries for California and the Southwest which might be ideal as add-ons to a West Coast cruise. We have not yet had the pleasure of experiencing Adventures by Disney, but we are planning a group expedition to try one out in fall 2009 during PassPorter's "Decade of Dreams" Tour (our 10th anniversary coast-to-coast celebration—see page 347)! We are hearing great things from folks who have returned from these "adventures." For more details and rates, visit http://www.AdventuresByDisney.com.

How Many Days to Cruise?

Should you do three days at Walt Disney World and four days at sea, or vice versa? We don't think you can possibly see everything at Walt Disney World in three days, so take four nights at Walt Disney World and three nights on the cruise, giving you a taste of cruising for a future return trip. And if four days at Disney World still isn't enough, you can always book extra days at Disney after your cruise when you're rested.

Do Itineraries Ever Change?

Yes, as you can see by the mention of the special 2008 cruises, itineraries can and do change. For the most part, these itineraries are announced before reservations are accepted for those sailing dates. Occasionally, though, changes occur after you've made a booking. If so, Disney Cruise Line will contact you about your options. Occasionally itineraries are modified immediately before or during your cruise, but it is rare. Most last-minute itinerary changes are due to bad weather, and usually other ports are substituted. Castaway Cay is the port most often bypassed due to weather (as it is the most frequently visited), but even that is an uncommon occurrence (it seems to happen most in January and February). If you have plans at a port that cannot be modified (e.g., a wedding), you shouldn't count on a cruise to get you there—you're best off flying in and leaving the cruise for another time.

Itinerary Comparison Chart

Wondering about the specific differences between the various cruise itineraries? Below is a chart of the **differences only** between the regular itineraries (not the special itineraries). As you read through the book, you can assume that any feature mentioned applies to all cruise itineraries unless we specifically state otherwise.

Feature	3-Night	4-Night	7-Night E. Caribbean	7-Night W. Caribbean
Ports of call	2	2	3	4
Sea days	0	1	3	2
Embarkation day	Thursday	Sunday	Saturday	Saturday
Debarkation day	Sunday	Thursday	Saturday	Saturday
Hours afloat	68	92	164	164
Special dinner menus		1	4	4
Character breakfast			✔	✔
Champagne brunch		✔	✔	✔
High tea			✔	✔
Tea with Wendy			✔	✔
Dessert buffets	1	1	2	2
Formal nights			1	1
Semi-formal nights			1	1
Dress-up nights	1	1		
Stage shows	3	3	3	3
Variety shows		1	3	3
Adult seminars		✔	✔	✔

As you might imagine, the 7-night cruise offers more activities than the 3- or 4-night cruises—there are more days to fill, after all! Activities differ from cruise to cruise, but here's a list of some of the extra activities that have been offered on the 7-night cruises in the past:

- ✔ Intro to Internet session
- ✔ Dance lessons
- ✔ Family & Adult Talent Show
- ✔ Team Trivia
- ✔ Family Mini Olympics
- ✔ Mr. Toad's Wild Race
- ✔ Mickey 200 Race
- ✔ Ping-Pong tournament
- ✔ NHL Skills Challenge
- ✔ Mixology demonstrations
- ✔ Ice carving demonstrations
- ✔ Artist-led workshops

See chapter 5, "Playing and Relaxing Onboard," starting on page 135 for many more details on the various activities aboard.

Selecting Your Sail Dates

Once you've selected an itinerary, it's time to choose a sail date. The Disney Cruise Line operates year-round, so you have many choices. Deciding when to go is based on many factors: your schedules, your plans, price, itinerary availability, and weather. Let's go over each of these in detail:

Your Schedules—It's better to book as far ahead as possible, so check now with your employer/school for available vacation dates.

Your Plans—Do you want to go to Walt Disney World? If so, do you want to go before and/or after your cruise? If you do plan a visit to a Disney resort, you'll want to select a sail date that works in tandem with your resort plans—see the "To Go To Walt Disney World or Not?" topic on page 43 for tips. Are you hoping to visit relatives or spend some time at Kennedy Space Center in Cape Canaveral? If so, you will want to go when you can add extra time before and/or after your cruise.

Price—The Disney Cruise Line has rate trends that correspond to demand (check out our rate trends chart on page 45). In general, cruising is more affordable in January and September through early December (excluding Thanksgiving). Spring, summer, and major holidays are the most expensive times to cruise. See pages 44–45 for more pricing details.

Itinerary Availability—The various cruise itineraries depart and return on particular days of the week (see chart below), which may be important to your vacation schedule. Additionally, the 7-night cruise usually alternates between the Eastern Caribbean and Western Caribbean every other week. For specific dates of future cruises, visit http://www.disneycruise.com, or check your Disney Cruise Line booklet.

Cruise	Depart	Return
3-Night	Thurs.	Sun.
4-Night	Sun.	Thurs.
7-Night	Sat.	Sat.

When do we like to sail? We're fond of May—great weather, great rates!

Are Any Dates Unavailable?

Typically, yes. Ships do fill up near certain dates—such as Christmas and New Year's Eve. And some dates may be reserved for members of a certain group only, such as the Disney Vacation Club member-only cruises (there's one September 21-25, 2008). Also, the ships go into drydock for maintenance once every couple of years. For example, the Disney Magic will be in drydock September 6-27, 2008. A quick call to the Disney Cruise Line can tell you if your preferred dates are available.

Caribbean and Bahamian Weather

The Caribbean and the Bahamas generally enjoy **delightful weather** year-round. Even so, it can get cool in the winter and a little warm in the summer. The summer also brings more rain than usual. See our weather chart below for details. The most important weather condition to consider is hurricane season, which runs from late May through November (see tropical storm levels in the chart below). The worst months for hurricane activity are August and September. Cruising during hurricane season means you're more likely to have a port change or two and have a rocky ride on rough seas. Even so, cruising during hurricane conditions isn't very dangerous, as modern storm forecasting gives the cruise lines plenty of time to modify itineraries to dodge the storms.

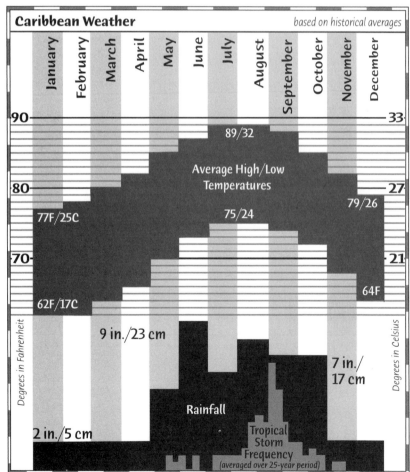

Caribbean Weather — based on historical averages

Average High/Low Temperatures

89/32 · 79/26 · 77F/25C · 75/24 · 64F · 62F/17C

90 / 33 · 80 / 27 · 70 / 21

Degrees in Fahrenheit · Degrees in Celsius

Rainfall — 9 in./23 cm · 7 in./17 cm · 2 in./5 cm

Tropical Storm Frequency (averaged over 25-year period)

Mexican Riviera Weather

Wondering what the weather will be like on your **West Coast cruise**? The Mexican Riviera, which includes the ports of Cabo San Lucas, Mazatlán, Puerto Vallarta, and Acapulco, is a pretty nice place to be in May, June, July, and August. Warm temperatures are the norm, with some rain in the latter half of summer. The hurricane season here begins in May and peaks in late August, so there is always a possibility of itinerary changes during storms. Here are the details on each port:

Cabo San Lucas	May	June	July	August
Average High	88°F/31°C	93°F/34°C	96°F/36°C	96°F/36°C
Average Low	68°F/20°C	68°F/20°C	74°F/23°C	75°F/23°C
Average Rainfall	0 in.	.3 in./0.8 cm.	.3 in./0.8 cm.	.3 in./0.8 cm.

Mazatlán	May	June	July	August
Average High	81°F/27°C	85°F/30°C	86°F/30°C	87°F/31°C
Average Low	71°F/21°C	77°F/25°C	78°F/26°C	78°F/26°C
Average Rainfall	0 in.	1.2 in./3 cm.	6.0 in./15 cm.	8.0 in./20 cm.

Puerto Vallarta	May	June	July	August
Average High	85°F/30°C	86°F/30°C	87°F/31°C	86°F/30°C
Average Low	71°F/21°C	77°F/25°C	78°F/26°C	76°F/25°C
Average Rainfall	1.1 in./3 cm.	3.7 in./9 cm.	4.1 in./10 cm.	11.0 in./28 cm.

Acapulco	May	June	July	August
Average High	90°F/32°C	91°F/32°C	91°F/32°C	90°F/32°C
Average Low	76°F/25°C	77°F/25°C	77°F/25°C	77°F/25°C
Average Rainfall	1.1 in./3 cm.	10.4 in./26 cm.	8.9 in./23 cm.	10.4 in./26 cm.

Panama Canal Weather

The 50-mile Panama Canal enjoys an average temperature of 84°F/ 29°C the entire year. The summer months are also the rainy months— you can expect occasional afternoon rains or thunderstorms that last for an hour or two. Rainfall averages for May to August are 8 in./ 19 cm. per month. Expect hazy skies during your passage.

Hurricanes

Following historic Atlantic hurricane seasons in recent years, we can't blame you for thinking long and hard on whether a major storm will affect your vacation. However, we were at sea for three and a half weeks during the 2005 season, and the **impact was far less than you might expect**. A storm near Baja, California forced the Disney Magic to bypass Cabo San Lucas and took us to the alternate port of Manzanillo, but the rest of our two-week Panama Canal journey was smooth sailing (although farther north, Hurricane Katrina was doing its worst). On a Western Caribbean cruise in June, our ship changed the order of its port visits and dashed to dodge a storm near Cuba. Other cruisers didn't do as well. Port Canaveral closed for several days, with embarkation/debarkation delayed and relocated to Fort Lauderdale (Disney bused cruisers there and back). Another time, the Disney Magic and Wonder huddled together in Galveston, Texas, dodging a storm. Most important is that the passengers and ships were kept safe. Modern mariners have plenty of warning about storms and are quite adept at keeping their passengers safe. We all hope for risk-free journeys, but it helps to prepare yourself mentally for the chance that all may not go as planned. When compared to the dangers of bygone eras, we're way far ahead of the game. One thing we wouldn't do is dissuade you from taking a hurricane-season cruise. After unexpectedly cold, icy, soggy, or scorching vacations on land, there's something to be said for a trip where you can lift anchor and head for fair weather. We'd rather be "stuck" on a cruise ship with all its facilities than be holed up in a motel room playing endless hands of cards, even if the deck heaves occasionally.

Unfortunately, we have **more stormy weather in our future**. Atlantic hurricanes follow roughly 25-year cycles of above- and below-average activity, and we're not quite halfway through an up cycle. The National Weather Service releases its annual storm outlook in May, with an update in August (see http://www.nhc.noaa.gov). Forecasters predict a "modestly more active" hurricane season in 2008. We hope everyone on land and sea enjoys a respite from the recent extremes, but a return to relatively fair weather seems unlikely.

There's not much you can do to **prepare for a stormy voyage**. Try out seasickness medication in advance if you're susceptible and bring it with you (see page 317). Vacation insurance may add peace of mind, but insurance is typically more useful for your journey to and from the cruise ship than for the voyage itself. Disney Cruise Line has to put passenger safety first, and the company is not obligated to "make good" weather-related changes, but they have an admirable record of delivering passenger satisfaction, even in such difficult cases.

To Go To Walt Disney World or Not?

Perhaps you're tempted by the Caribbean land/sea vacation package, or you just can't resist the urge to visit Walt Disney World. Whatever your reason for visiting the Walt Disney World Resort, you're not alone—the majority of your fellow cruisers will also visit the parks on their trip. If you're just not quite sure yet, let's weigh the pros and cons:

Reasons to Visit the Mouse House:
- ✔ You love Disney parks and can't be nearby without a visit.
- ✔ You've never been, and this is a great opportunity.
- ✔ You're not sure you'll feel the "Disney magic" if you skip the parks.

Reasons to Just Cruise:
- ✔ You want a laid-back, really relaxing vacation.
- ✔ You've been there, done that, and don't need to go back yet.
- ✔ You don't have the time or money.

If you do **decide to go** to Walt Disney World, you'll need to choose between a land/sea vacation package and arranging it yourself. We always make our own arrangements—we save money and enjoy greater flexibility. The land/sea package does not include meals on land (unless you add the optional Disney Dining Plan) and only offers a limited choice of Disney resort hotels, based on your choice of stateroom (though you can pay to upgrade to a different resort). Would you like to stretch your dollars at a value resort but book a comfortable verandah stateroom? Not on the land/sea! You also can't grab hotel-only discounts that are often available. We prefer a minimum of a four-night cruise and at least a four-night stay at Walt Disney World. That's not in the package, either, though you can add it. You finally, however, get the full value out of the Magic Your Way (Park Hopping) tickets that come with the packages—you no longer pay for the day you embark on your cruise. And you can't beat the land/sea for convenience—you'll be ushered everywhere with a minimum of fuss. No matter what, we refer you to our *PassPorter's Walt Disney World* guidebook for loads of details, tips, strategies, maps, and plans. *PassPorter's Open Mouse for Walt Disney World and the Disney Cruise Line* guidebook adds invaluable information for travelers with all sorts of special challenges. You can pick up our guidebooks at most bookstores, online at http://www.passporter.com, and at 877-929-3273.

Should you visit Disney parks **before or after** you cruise? The Disney land/sea vacation package places the Walt Disney World leg before the cruise leg by default, though you can request it be switched. If you're new to Walt Disney World, visit the parks first—Walt Disney World is an intense vacation experience, and the cruise will be a relaxing break. Walt Disney World fans may prefer visiting the parks after the cruise, as "dessert."

Cruise Rates

While we can't give you exact prices, we can give you rate ranges for various itineraries and stateroom categories. The rates below are based on our own research of 2008 rates—we feel these are realistic numbers, but we can virtually guarantee that you'll get different rates when you do your own research. Use these as **guidelines only**. Actual rates are based on demand and fluctuate during the year. To get actual rate quotes, call the Disney Cruise Line, visit http://www.disneycruise.com, or talk to your travel agent. The rates below are for **two adult fares** with taxes and early booking savings, but do not include air, insurance, or ground transfers.

Typical Cruise Rate Ranges (for two adults in one stateroom)

Category	3-Night Cruise Low to High	4-Night Cruise Low to High	7-Night Cruise Low to High	7-Night Land/Sea Low to High
1	$4,598–5,698	$5,398–6,498	$8,398–10,398	$7,398–10,398
2	$3,998–5,098	$4,598–5,698	$7,798–9,998	$6,798–9,998
3	$2,478–4,498	$3,098–4,898	$5,998–8,998	$5,398–8,998
4	$1,673–3,386	$1,866–3,586	$3,900–6,420	$3,466–5,672
5	$1,473–2,793	$1,666–3,226	$3,418–5,412	$3,006–4,706
6	$1,433–2,693	$1,606–3,006	$3,208–5,202	$2,786–4,496
7	$1,373–2,453	$1,526–2,706	$2,998–4,992	$2,586–4,286
8	$1,273–2,313	$1,486–2,366	$2,640–3,942	$2,366–3,762
9	$1,173–2,213	$1,386–2,186	$2,326–3,732	$2,166–3,552
10	$973–2,013	$1,106–2,066	$2,120–3,522	$1,986–3,342
11	$873–1,913	$1,046–2,006	$2,000–3,416	$1,872–3,236
12	$773–1,733	$966–2,026	$1,900–3,374	$1,766–3,194
3rd & 4th Guest: Kids Under 3	$171	$171	$200	$200
3rd & 4th Guest: Kids 3-12	$222–1,099	$333–1,199	$550–2,199	$550–2,199
3rd & 4th Guest: Ages 13 & up	$287–1,099	$383–1,199	$650–2,199	$650–2,199

✔ Each stateroom booked must include at least one adult, and no more than 3–5 total guests may occupy a stateroom, depending on occupancy limits. If your party size is greater than five, you'll need to book a suite (categories 1–2) or more than one stateroom.

✔ Staterooms with just one adult and one child are charged the price of two adults.

✔ Guests cruising alone (one adult in a room) are charged roughly 87% of the above rates.

✔ Guests booking a land/sea package can choose to stay at the Grand Floridian with categories 1–3; a deluxe resort (Beach Club, Polynesian, Animal Kingdom Lodge, Saratoga Springs, Swan, or Dolphin) with categories 4–7; or a moderate resort (Port Orleans French Quarter, Port Orleans Riverside, or Caribbean Beach) with categories 8–12. No other resorts are options.

✔ Note: Women who are past their 24th week of pregnancy and infants under 12 weeks cannot sail with the Disney Cruise Line.

Confused by all those rate ranges? We feel the same way. Before we went to press, **we researched every regular 2008 cruise** and its rates (at early booking discounts). We then graphed the minimum rates (for two adults in a category 12 stateroom) into the chart below. This chart gives you a very useful overview of the general trends for specific times in 2008 (and 2009 will likely be very similar). Rates for higher categories follow the same basic trends as category 12, so you can use this chart to pinpoint seasons for the best rates. Keep in mind, however, that these rates can change at any time. Don't take the numbers in this chart at face value—concentrate on the trends instead. Also note that this chart does not take into account seasonal discounts that may be offered, thereby reducing the rates for a specific period. You may want to compare this to the chart on page 40 to pick the best compromise between great cruise rates and great weather (we're partial to May ourselves).

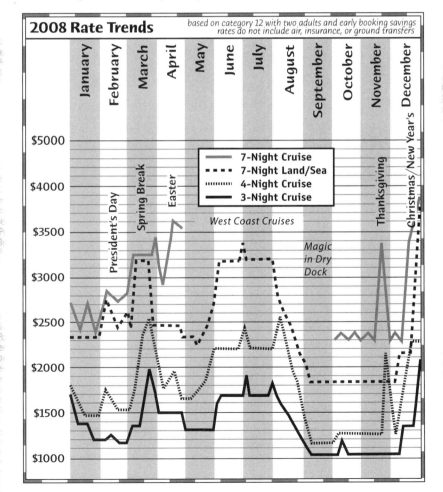

2008 Rate Trends — based on category 12 with two adults and early booking savings rates do not include air, insurance, or ground transfers

Legend:
- 7-Night Cruise
- 7-Night Land/Sea
- 4-Night Cruise
- 3-Night Cruise

West Coast Cruises

Magic in Dry Dock

President's Day · Spring Break · Easter · Thanksgiving · Christmas/New Year's

Cruise Add-Ons

If you're looking for a little more magic in your cruise and/or Walt Disney World vacation, there are a number of packages and add-ons designed to help you get the most out of it. Below are the basic packages offered at press time. Please call the Disney Cruise Line for specific packages and prices. Prices quoted below are for 2008, and we expect 2009 to be similiar.

Romantic Escape at Sea—Guests on a 3-, 4-, or 7-night cruise can add a collection of "romantic" services and items to their voyage. This package includes a romantic gift amenity (this may be a gift basket with photo album or frame, sparkling wine, and chocolates, but some cruisers report getting two spa robes instead of the sparkling wine), romance turndown service (one night), champagne breakfast in bed (one morning), priority seating at Palo (one evening), a bottle of wine from the premium wine list at Palo, and a Tropical Rainforest pass for two at the Vista Spa for the length of the cruise. Some cruisers also report receiving a free 8 x 10 photo with their package. Another unadvertised perk of this package is the ability to book your reservations (such as Palo and Vista Spa) up to 105 days in advance (assuming you've paid for your cruise in full). The massage previously included in this package is no longer included. The ability to make reservations early may be the best piece of this package considering the popularity of Palo. Cruisers report mixed feelings about this package—some love the extra goodies and feel they are "worth the price," while others enjoy the services but think the gifts are "less than stellar" and of "mediocre quality." Price is $359 per couple (ages 21 and older only). Confirm all amenities before booking. This package must be booked prior to 30 days before sailing. Note that this package is not available on cruises longer than 7 nights. (Booking Code: ESC)

Family Reunion—Guests on a 3-, 4-, or 7-night cruise or 7-night land/sea package can add a personalized Disney Cruise Line family reunion shirt (one per person), a leather photo portfolio with a complimentary photo (one per stateroom), and a commemorative family reunion certificate (one per person). Families booking 8 or more staterooms can also choose one of the following: an hour-long reception with open bar and snacks, a Bon Voyage Memory Box (one per stateroom), or a bottle of wine (one per stateroom). Costs $59 per person for the first and second guests in the room, $19 per person for extra guests in the same room. Package must be purchased for all guests (regardless of age) in the party. (Booking Code: FAMILY)

Two other "packages" are the **Wedding at Sea** starting at $3,698 per couple and the **Vow Renewal** starting at $1,798 per couple. Both are available on 3-, 4-, and 7-night cruises, as well as 7-night land & sea packages. See page 316 for more information.

Walt Disney World Packages

If you book your stay at Walt Disney World separately from your cruise, you can take advantage of a number of other packages. The Magic Your Way packages start with the basics (accommodations plus Magic Your Way base tickets) and add on dining plans, recreation plans, and premium Magic Your Way tickets. Magic Your Way packages start at about $330/person. To learn more about the available packages for Walt Disney World vacations, call the Walt Disney Travel Company at 800-828-0228, ask your travel agent, or visit http://www.disneyworld.com.

Reserving Your Cruise

Once you know when, how, and where you want to cruise, it's time to **make reservations**. You can call the Disney Cruise Line directly, book online at DisneyCruise.com, or use a travel agent (see sidebar at bottom). There are pros and cons to all. Dealing directly with Disney may give you more control over stateroom selection, while travel agents may get better deals. Disney Vacation Club (DVC) members who want to cruise on points (see sidebar on page 48) should contact DVC directly.

Before you make your reservations, **use the worksheet** on page 51 to jot down your preferred sailing dates along with alternates. Even a small change in your travel dates can open the door to a great deal. Be familiar with all stateroom categories (see chapter 3) in your price range, too.

To make reservations, call **888-325-2500**, 8:00 am to 10:00 pm Eastern Time (weekdays) and 9:00 am to 8:00 pm ET (weekends). From outside the U.S., call +1-800-511-9444 or +1-407-566-6921. Representatives offer help in English, Spanish, Japanese, French, Portuguese, and German. Castaway Club members have a special phone number (see page 323). You can also reserve at http://www.disneycruise.com and at cruise-related sites—see below.

Call Disney Cruise Reservations as far in advance as possible. Ask for any **special deals or packages** for your dates—Disney generally doesn't volunteer this information. If you have a Disney Visa or are a Disney Vacation Club member or Florida resident, ask about those discounts. If your dates aren't available, check alternates.

Shopping Around
You can also make reservations through various travel reservation sites or travel agents specializing in Disney Cruise reservations (in alphabetical order):

Travel Reservation Sites	Travel Agents
http://www.cruise.com	http://www.aaa.com
http://www.cruise411.com	http://www.costco.com
http://www.cruise-locator.com	http://www.dreamsunlimitedtravel.com
http://www.expedia.com	http://www.earstoyoutravel.com
http://www.orbitz.com	http://www.mei-travel.com
http://www.travelocity.com	http://www.mouseearvacations.com
http://www.vacationstogo.com	http://www.themagicforless.com

Get Your Passports Together Now
Your cruise takes you to foreign ports, so you must have proper ID. Passports are highly recommended and may be required, depending upon your sail date. It can take months to obtain passports if you haven't already, so get started now! See pages 52-53 for more details.

Introduction

Reservations

Staterooms

Dining

Activities

Ports of Call

Magic

Index

Reserving Your Cruise *(continued)*

Make any **special requests**, such as a handicap-accessible room or the need for special meals, at the time of reservation. If you have a particular stateroom or deck in mind (see chapter 3), make sure to tell the reservations agent at the time of booking.

You will be asked if you want the **Vacation Protection Plan**, and the cruise line agents automatically include it in their quote. This insurance plan covers trip cancellations, travel delays, emergency medical/dental, emergency medical transportation/assistance, and baggage delay, loss, theft, or damage. The plan price is based on the length of your cruise vacation—$59 (3 nights), $69 (4 nights), and $109 (7 nights) per person for the first and second individuals in your stateroom (additional guests are $39, $49, and $59 respectively). If your flight could be affected by weather, seriously consider insurance. Note that your airfare and your air travel-related delays will not be covered unless you're also using the Disney Air Program. So if you book your own air travel, use an insurance policy other than Disney's—air travel delays can cause you to miss your cruise departure, so be sure you're covered! Also note that the Protection Plan does not cover some preexisting medical conditions. If you don't want this insurance, ask to have it removed from your quote.

Save on **vacation insurance** by booking it yourself—visit http://www.insuremytrip.com or call your insurance agent. But don't delay—most companies will waive preexisting medical conditions only if you buy insurance within 7-14 days after making your trip deposit. Trip interruption/cancellation coverage is great for circumstances beyond your control, but it doesn't help if you simply change your mind. If the cruise is only part of your vacation, make sure your policy covers the entire trip. Policies vary, so shop carefully. You may already have life, medical, theft, and car rental protection in your regular policies (be sure you're covered overseas). Credit cards, AAA, and/or other memberships may also include useful coverage. Airlines already cover lost baggage—make sure your policy exceeds their limits. Seniors and travelers with preexisting conditions should seriously consider insurance—the costs of evacuation, overseas medical care, and travel/lodging for a companion while you're under treatment are very high.

Disney Vacation Club Members

Members of Disney's innovative time-share program, the Disney Vacation Club (DVC), can pay a fee to use their points for cruises. Contact Disney Vacation Club directly at 800-800-9100 or visit http://www.disneyvacationclub.com to get point charts and details on reserving cruises. Note that you can use a combination of points and cash (or credit) for a cruise. Reservations with points can be made up to 24 months in advance. We've heard mixed reports from guests who use DVC points to cruise—some feel it works out well for them, while others feel the cruise requires too many points. Disney Vacation Club members booking cruises without points may also be entitled to an onboard credit—inquire when making reservations.

Introduction
Reservations
Staterooms
Dining
Activities
Ports of Call
Magic
Index

You may also be asked if you want **airfare**. In general, we've found it is less expensive to book our own airfare, but you may prefer to leave the flight details up to Disney. The biggest drawback to using the Disney Air Program is that they decide which flight you'll take, and you may arrive later than you prefer or have tight flight transfers. If you do use Disney Air, ground transfers are automatically included in your package (see below). All Disney cruisers flying on participating airlines can take advantage of Disney's Onboard Airline Check-In program (see page 57).

Ground transfers are automatic for those using the Disney Air Program and an option for those arranging their own flights. Disney roundtrip ground transfers are available to/from the airport to the cruise terminal and/or between Walt Disney World/Disneyland and the cruise terminal. Price is $69/guest (Caribbean cruises) and $59/guest (Mexican Riviera cruises). The ground transfers include transportation and baggage handling. For cruisers arriving at Orlando Intl. Airport, your bags go directly from the plane to your ship (provided you affix the Disney-supplied labels prior to checking your bags with your airline and you're flying in on the day of your cruise). One-way transfers to or from the airport are $35/guest. See page 64. If you're traveling between the airport and Walt Disney World (and staying at a Disney resort hotel), those transfers are included free of charge as part of Disney's Magical Express program (see below).

A **deposit** of $200/guest (3-/4-night), $250/guest (7-night), or $500/guest (repositioning cruises) is required to confirm your reservation. Note that the per-person deposit for stateroom categories 1–3 is double the above rates. Reservations are held for 1–7 days without confirmation (24 hours for cruises within the final payment window, three days for popular holiday cruises, and seven days for all other cruises), and then they are deleted if no deposit is received. Pay your deposit by 10:00 pm ET on the necessary day (or by 8:00 pm if the necessary day is a Saturday or Sunday)—you can do it over the phone with Visa, MasterCard, Discover, JCB, Diner's Club, or

Disney's Magical Express

Disney offers its resort guests free bus transportation between Orlando International Airport (MCO) and Disney resort hotels. Modeled after Disney Cruise Line's ground transportation program, guests arriving at MCO can bypass baggage claim and head right to the bus loading area—as long as they've affixed special luggage tags back home, their luggage will be gathered right off the plane and delivered to their resort room. Provided their airline participates in the program (see list on page 57), guests headed back to the airport can do their airline check-in (including baggage) right at their hotel before boarding their bus. Reservations must be made at least one day in advance, but try to do it at least 10 days in advance to allow time to receive your luggage tags and instruction booklet in the mail. If you're staying at a Disney resort hotel before or after your cruise, inquire at 866-599-0951. If you're on a Disney Cruise Line land/sea package, Disney's Magical Express is already built in—ask your reservation agent for details.

Reserving Your Cruise *(continued)*

American Express. Record deposits on the worksheet on page 51.

Once your cruise is confirmed, Disney mails a **confirmation** of your reservation. Payment is due in full 90 days (stateroom categories 1–3) or 75 days (stateroom categories 4–12) prior to sailing. You must provide passport numbers 75 days prior to departure (see pages 52–53). If you need to cancel, reservations can be cancelled for full credit up to 75 days (categories 4–12) prior to your vacation. The deposit is nonrefundable for reservations in stateroom categories 1–3. If you cancel 45–74 days (categories 4–12) prior to your cruise/package, you lose your deposit. If you cancel 8–44 days prior, you lose 50% of the cruise fare. There is no refund if you cancel seven days or less prior to your cruise/package (applies to all categories). There is a $35/person fee for document reissue and name/air changes within 30 days of your vacation. There is a $50/person fee if you change your sail dates 0–59 days prior to your cruise, and you may need to pay that $35/person fee on top of it if your documents must be reissued. Insurance may help with these penalties.

Your **cruise documents** are mailed to you 10–14 days before sailing. Read everything in your cruise document package and fill out the mandatory guest information form, cruise contract, immigration form(s), and payment authorization before you leave home. Note: You can fill out this paperwork for your cruise at http://www.disneycruise.com, but **be sure to print it out and bring it with you**. Four additional forms may also need to be filled out: the flight information form (to tell Disney your flight details), flight modification form (to change flights when you're using Disney Air), Medical Information Form (to notify Disney of a pre-existing medical condition or special need), and the Minor Authorization Form (if you are traveling with a child of whom you are not the parent or legal guardian)—these forms are available online. Luggage tags are included with each cruise booklet and should be placed on your bags before you arrive (see page 80 for details). Included with your cruise document package is the recently redesigned "Ship and Shore Vacation Guides," a collection of mini-guides covering a checklist of action items, shore excursions, quick tips, onboard gifts, "Setting Sail" (a brief guide to the cruise), and Disney's Vacation Plan (insurance). Your cruise documents are required to board, and you should have them with you (or in your carry-on) on the day of departure. Don't make the mistake of putting them in a suitcase that gets checked through.

Once your cruise is reserved, you may be eager to **meet other families** sailing with you on the same cruise. You can do this in advance of your cruise by posting your own sail dates on Disney Cruise Line message boards such as our own PassPorter Message Boards (http://www. passporterboards.com) or at DIS (http://www.disboards.com). You can use these resources to plan get-togethers, find companions for your table in the dining rooms, or find playmates for your kids. You'd be surprised at

Cruise Reservation Worksheet

Electronic, interactive worksheet available— see page 350

Use this worksheet to jot down preferences, scribble information during phone calls, and keep all your discoveries together. Don't worry about being neat—just be thorough! ✎ Circle the cruise you finally select to avoid any confusion.

Cruise length: *3 nights   4 nights   7 nights   7 nights land/sea   15 nights*

Departure date: _____ Alternate: _____

Return date: _____ Alternate: _____

We prefer to stay in category: _____ Alternates: _____

Discounts: *Disney Visa   Disney Vacation Club   Castaway Club*

AAA   Seasonal   Florida Resident   Canadian Resident   Other: _____

Dates	Itinerary	Category	Rates	Insurance	Total

Reservation number: _____

Confirm reservation by this date: _____

Deposit due by: _____ Deposit paid on: _____

Balance due by: _____ Balance paid on: _____

Do we need to order passports/birth certificates? _____

Introduction

Reservations

Staterooms

Dining

Activities

Ports of Call

Magic

Index

Introduction

Reservations

Staterooms

Dining

Activities

Ports of Call

Magic

Index

Have Your Passports Ready

Do you need a passport? Short answer: It's a good idea to have a passport. Long answer: In 2007, the U.S. government **extended the deadline** for citizens to obtain passports for sea (and land) travel to/from the Caribbean (including the Bahamas), Canada, Mexico, and Bermuda. The newest deadline is "a later date to be determined." (How's that for specific?) The rules keep changing, so for the latest news, check at http://travel.state.gov and/or the Disney Cruise Line web site. Here are the facts:

FACT: All **air travelers returning to the United States** from the Caribbean, Bahamas, and Mexico must have a passport, a trusted traveler card such as NEXUS, FAST, or SENTRI, or U.S. Coast Guard Merchant Mariner Document. Passports are already required for air, land, and sea travel to/from nearly everywhere else in the world.

FACT: The highly touted **Passport Card** (a credit card-sized alternate passport) is only valid for land and sea travel between the United States, Canada, Mexico, the Caribbean, and Bermuda. It is not valid for air travel or for other destinations. The PASS Card is cheaper than a passport, but its limited use makes it a false economy. If you feel it meets your needs, you may apply for one as of February 1, 2008—get details at http://travel.state.gov.

FACT: The U.S. government, the Cruise Line Industry Association (CLIA), and the Disney Cruise Line all **recommend that you obtain passports** as soon as possible.

Our Keep It Simple Suggestion: Get passports for your entire traveling party, now! Even if a passport is not required for your cruise, it's a smart idea to have one if you have to abandon your cruise and fly back to the United States. (While passport regulations do allow for re-entry without a passport due to unforeseen emergencies, better safe than sorry.)

At the time of writing, U.S. citizens returning from the Caribbean, Canada, and Mexico by sea (or land) can use **government-issued photo IDs** (such as a current driver's license) plus a certified birth certificate (with a raised seal or multiple colors) to re-enter the country. Be sure to bring original or official documents; no copies will be accepted. (Birth certificates only are acceptable for minors traveling with their parents and/or legal guardians.) We also recommend you bring a backup photo ID for emergencies.

If your cruise returns to the United States on or after that to-be-determined-later deadline we mentioned earlier (perhaps sometime in mid-2009?), or if you're flying to/from destinations outside the United States as of now, you will need a valid passport for **each member of your party, even infants**. This requirement is especially challenging with newborns (who may cruise as early as 12 weeks), as there's barely time to get the birth certificate, then apply for and receive a passport in that 12 weeks.

Disney Cruise Line asks that all guests with passports supply their passport numbers at least **75 days prior to departure** (once passports become mandatory, expect this to become a requirement). If you have applied for passports but fear you may not receive them in time, discuss the situation with a Disney Cruise Line representative prior to the 75-day deadline.

Passport applications are accepted at **more than 9,000 locations in the United States**, including many post offices, county clerks' offices, and city halls. For a full listing, including hours of operation, visit http://travel.state.gov or call the National Passport Information Center (NPIC) phone number at 877-487-2778. The same site also provides application forms for download and full information on the application process.

It typically takes **6-8 weeks to receive a passport** after you file the application, so apply for your passport(s) no later than 135 days (four months) prior to sailing, or pay extra to expedite your application. See the below for details on getting a rush passport.

New applications for everyone including infants must be made in person, but passport renewals can be made by mail provided the current passport is undamaged, your name hasn't changed (or you can legally document the change), the passport is no more than 15 years old, and you were 16 years or older when it was issued.

Are you in a rush? **Expedited passport applications** can be processed for an extra fee. If you apply through a regular passport "acceptance facility," you can get your passport within two weeks—pay an extra $60 with each application, plus overnight shipping. If you are traveling within two weeks, urgent passport applications can be processed at 14 Passport Agencies in the U.S., by appointment only. If you cannot get to one of those Agencies, services such as U.S. Birth Certificate.net (http://www.usbirthcertificate.net) can do it for you, provided you first visit a local passport acceptance facility to handle the preliminaries.

Important: You will need a **birth certificate or other birth/naturalization record** before you can apply for your passport, so you may need even more time! While there are services (such as USBirthCertificate.net) that can obtain a domestic birth certificate in as little as 2-3 days, if you were born outside the U.S., the process may take weeks or even months.

Budget **$97 for a "standard" adult passport application**, $82 for each child under 16. Expedited (two-week) processing brings the cost up to $157/adult, $142/child, plus next-day shipping costs. Passport renewals are $67. Duplicate/replacement birth certificate fees vary by state, but cost about $5–$15. Naturally, the help of a passport/birth certificate service adds even more to the price—typically an extra $100/passport, $50/birth certificate.

Make sure you **don't get caught without your papers**. Use this timeline to calculate your due dates, and use the following worksheet to get all your ducks in a row.

Passport Timeline

My Cruise Date:	
Subtract 135 days from cruise date:	Passport application (regular) due:
Subtract 90 days from cruise date:	Passport application (expedited) due:
Subtract 75 days from cruise date:	Passport # to Disney Cruise Line due:
Need birth certificates, too? Subtract 15 days from the passport application due date (for those born in the U.S.), 120 days (for those born outside the U.S.):	

Passport Worksheet

Name	Passport Number	Completed Application	Proof of Citizenship	Proof of Identity	Passport Photos (2)	Fees

Going on a West Coast cruise? See transportation options on page 74.

Getting to Florida

By Car, Van, Truck, or Motorcycle

Most vacationers still arrive in Florida in their own vehicle. It's hard to beat the **slowly rising sense of excitement** as you draw closer or the freedom of having your own wheels once you arrive (helpful when you're combining your cruise with a land vacation). Driving may also eliminate any concerns you or family members may have with air travel. And driving can be less expensive than air travel, especially with large families. On the downside, you may spend long hours or even days on the road, which cuts deeply into your vacation time. And you'll need to park your car while you're cruising, which is pricey (see pages 67 and 71).

If you opt to drive, carefully **map your course** ahead of time. You can do this with a AAA TripTik—a strip map that guides you to your destination. You must be a AAA member (see page 27) to get a TripTik, but you can easily join for $60–$75/year. If you're driving I-75, we recommend *Along Interstate-75* (Mile Oak Publishing, http://www.i75online.com) by Dave Hunter. I-95 drivers will benefit from the *Drive I-95* guide by Stan and Sandra Posner (Travelsmart, http://www.drivei95.com) or a visit to http://www.usastar.com/i95/homepage.htm. For navigating the Sunshine State, look for Dave Hunter's *Along Florida's Freeways* guidebook. Or try a trip-routing service such as AutoPilot at http://www.freetrip.com.

If you live more than 500 miles away, **spread out your drive** over more than one day, allotting one day for every 500 miles. If your journey spans more than a day, decide in advance where to stop each night and make reservations. If possible, arrive a day ahead of your cruise departure day for a more relaxing start to the cruise (see pages 68–70 for lodging in Cape Canaveral). Compare the price of driving versus flying, too.

By Train

The train is a uniquely relaxing way to travel to Central Florida. **Amtrak** serves the Orlando area daily with both **passenger trains** and an Auto Train, which carries your family and your car. The **Auto Train** runs between suburban Washington, D.C. and suburban Orlando (Sanford, FL). Prices vary depending on the season, the direction, and how far in advance you make your reservation. The Auto Train is also available one-way, and in many seasons, one direction is less expensive than the other. Late arrivals are the norm, so allow extra time. Keep in mind that you may need to take a taxi or town car from the train station, or you can rent a car from the nearby Hertz office. For Amtrak's rates, schedules, reservations, and more information, call 800-USA-RAIL or visit them at http://www.amtrak.com.

By Bus

Greyhound serves Melbourne, Orlando, and Kissimmee. Buses take longer to reach a destination than cars driving the same route. Fares are lowest if you live within ten hours of Central Florida. For fares and tickets, call Greyhound at 800-231-2222 or visit them at http://www.greyhound.com.

By Airplane

Air travel is the fastest way for many vacationers, but we recommend you fly in at least a day before in the event there are any flight delays. You have two choices: use the Disney Air Program and let them include your airfare in your package—inquire about pricing when you book your cruise—or book your own flight. It'll be less expensive and more flexible if you book your own flight—Disney Air Program arrival and departure times aren't always optimal. To find an **affordable flight**, be flexible on the day and time of departure and return—fares can differ greatly depending on when you fly and how long you stay. Second, take advantage of the many "fare sales" available—to learn about sales, visit airlines' web sites or travel sites such as Travelocity (http://www.travelocity.com), Expedia (http://www.expedia.com), or Orbitz (http://www.orbitz.com). Third, try alternate airports and airlines (including low-fare airlines like Southwest and jetBlue). Fourth, be persistent. Ask for their lowest fare and work from there. When you find a good deal, put it on hold immediately (if possible), note your reservation on page 59, and cancel later if necessary. Consider researching fares on your **airline's web site**—you can experiment with different flights and may get a deal for booking online. Priceline.com (http://www.priceline.com) is an option—you can name your own price. But only use it if you are flying out a day or more ahead and/or returning a day or more later. To arrange **ground transportation**, see pages 63-67.

Our Top 10 Flying Tips, Reminders, and Warnings

1. Visit http://www.tsa.gov for travel security news and updates.
2. Check the status of your flight before departing for the airport. Use online check-in if it is offered by your airline (most now offer it).
3. Pick up a meal and drinks for the flight after you pass through security, as most domestic flights have discontinued meal service for security reasons.
4. Pack sharp or dangerous items in checked luggage (or just leave them at home). This includes pocket knives and sport sticks. Lithium batteries must be installed in electronic devices when packed in checked luggage, or in original packaging or in a protective travel case in carry-on luggage. Cigarette lighters, scissors with blades under 4" and nail clippers are allowed. For details, visit http://www.tsa.gov. Call the Disney Cruise Line to confirm any questionable objects.
5. Remember the **3-1-1 rule** for liquids/gels in carry-ons: They must be in **3 oz. or less** bottle(s), all in **1 quart-sized, clear, zip-top bag**, and **1 bag per person**, placed in screening bin. Limit your carry-ons to one bag and one personal item (e.g., purse).
6. Keep your luggage unlocked for inspections, or it may be damaged.
7. Plan to arrive at the airport at least two hours prior to departure.
8. Curbside check-in may be available (fee may apply), but you may need to obtain a boarding pass from your airline's customer service desk anyway.
9. E-ticket holders need a confirmation and/or boarding pass. Get it from your airline's web site or from Disney's Onboard Check-In Desk (see page 57).

Introduction · Reservations · Staterooms · Dining · Activities · Ports of Call · Magic · Index

Introduction
Reservations
Staterooms
Dining
Activities
Ports of Call
Magic
Index

Getting Around the Orlando International Airport

Most cruise-bound passengers will arrive in the Orlando International Airport, a large, sprawling hub and one of the better airports we've flown into. Your plane docks at one of the **satellite terminals** (see map on next page). Follow the signs to the automated **shuttle** to the main terminal— there you'll find **baggage claim** and ground transportation. Once you reach the main terminal, follow signs down to baggage claim (Level 2). If you're using Disney ground transportation (and have previously affixed Disney luggage tags), head directly to the Disney's Magical Express check-in desk on "B" side, Level 1. Shuttles, town cars, taxis, and rental cars are also found on Level 1 (take the elevators opposite the baggage carousels). Each transportation company has its own ticket booth, so keep your eyes open. If you get lost, look for signs that can get you back on track.

© MediaMarx, Inc.

Disney's Magical Express check-in desk on level 1, side B

As your authors used to live in entirely different parts of the country, we became quite good at **meeting up at the airport**. It's best to meet your party at their baggage claim area as you won't be allowed past security without a valid boarding pass. The trick here is knowing which airline and baggage claim area. Use the map and airline list on the next page, or call the airport directly at 407-825-2001. Be careful when differentiating between the side A and side B baggage claim. Also note that gates 1–29 and 100–129 use side A, while gates 30–99 use side B. Check the arrival/departure boards in the terminal for flight status, too! Other terminal meeting spots are the Disney Stores (see stars on map on next page), the Borders bookstore (noted on map—they carry PassPorter books!), or an eatery. Be sure to exchange cell phone numbers, too. Another meeting option is an **airport restaurant**, especially for long waits.

For **more details** on the Orlando International Airport, call 407-825-2001 or visit http://www.orlandoairports.net. Air travelers can be paged at 407-825-2000.

Upon your return to the Orlando International Airport for your flight back home, be sure to give yourself ample time to check in (if you didn't use Disney's Onboard Airline Check-In Program—see sidebar below) and get through security. The security checkpoint can be lengthy during peak travel times, so we suggest you go directly to security when you arrive at the airport. Small eateries and convenience stores are located in the satellite terminals, where you'll wait for your flight after passing security. There are also InMotion DVD rental kiosks at the terminals for gates 30-59 and gates 60-99 (as well as an InMotion store in the main terminal itself)—see http://www.inmotionpictures.com for details.

Air Canada, Alaska Airlines, American Airlines, CanJet, Continental, Midwest, and Sun Country use Gates 1-29; America West, ANA, KLM, Northwest, Spirit, Ted, United, and US Airways use Gates 30-59; Air France, AirTran, British Airways, Delta, Frontier Airlines, and Virgin Atlantic use Gates 60-99; and ATA, JetBlue, and Southwest use Gates 100-129.

Disney's Onboard Airline Check-In Program

All Disney cruisers can now take advantage of Disney's Onboard Airline Check-In Program to get your return boarding passes and luggage transferred from ship to plane, whether or not you purchased Disney ground transfers and/or Disney Air. What's the catch? Your flight must come through the Orlando International Airport, you must be flying on one of the participating airlines (currently AirTran Airways, Alaska Airlines, American Airlines, Continental Airlines, Delta Airlines, Northwest Airlines, or United Airlines/Ted), and you must be flying home directly after your cruise. If you qualify, you can register for onboard airline check-in at the cruise terminal or at a Disney Cruise Line hospitality desk at your Disney resort before your cruise. There may also be a form in your cruise documents, which you can then turn in at the cruise terminal or Disney resort. If you use this program, your boarding pass will be delivered to your stateroom on the day prior to disembarkation. And your luggage is trucked to the airport and loaded onto your plane for you!

Introduction

Reservations

Staterooms

Dining

Activities

Ports of Call

Magic

Index

Getting Around the Orlando Sanford Airport

Travelers flying to Orlando **from Europe or via group charter** may arrive at the smaller Orlando Sanford International Airport (FSB), located about 18 miles northeast of Orlando and 67 miles from Port Canaveral. Airlines with scheduled service into Sanford include Allegiant Air, Icelandair, and flyglobespan, as well as six international charter services with flights from the United Kingdom and Ireland (First Choice Air, Monarch, MyTravel, Thomas Cook, Thomsonfly, and XL Airways).

Alamo/National, Avis, Dollar, Enterprise, Hertz, and Thrifty all operate **in-terminal car rental desks**. Budget has an off-site rental office. Mears Transportation and several shuttle services provide bus/van service from Sanford to Orlando-area attractions and Port Canaveral.

International passengers arrive and depart from Terminal A, while domestic travelers use Terminal B. A Welcome Center is located across the street from Terminal A and is home to ground transportation services.

Dining options here include the Budweiser Tap Room (terminal A) and basic food courts (terminals A & B).

For more details on the Orlando Sanford International Airport, phone 407-322-7771 or visit http://www.orlandosanfordairport.com. If you plan to rent a car at the airport and drive to Port Canaveral, use a map routing service such as MapQuest.com before you leave home to get directions (the airport is located at 1 Red Cleveland Blvd., Sanford, FL 32773).

Orlando Sanford International Airport

Travel Worksheet

Electronic, interactive worksheet available—see page 350

Use this worksheet to jot down preferences, scribble information during phone calls, and keep all your discoveries together. Don't worry about being neat—just be thorough! 🖋 Circle the names and numbers once you decide to go with them to avoid confusion.

Arrival date: _____   Alternate: _____

Return date: _____   Alternate: _____

We plan to travel by: ❏ Car/Van   ❏ Airplane   ❏ Train   ❏ Bus   ❏ Tour
❏ Other: _____

For Drivers:

Miles to get to Port Canaveral: _____ ÷ 500 = ____ days on the road

We need to stay at a motel on: _____

Tune-up scheduled for: _____

Rental car info: _____

_____

For Riders:

Train/bus phone numbers: _____

Ride preferences: _____

Ride availabilities: _____

Reserved ride times and numbers: _____

Routes: _____

For Tour-Takers:

Tour company phone numbers: _____

Tour preferences: _____

Tour availabilities: _____

Reserved tour times and numbers: _____

Routes: _____

Introduction

Reservations

Staterooms

Dining

Activities

Ports of Call

Magic

Index

For Fliers:

Airline phone numbers: _____

Flight preferences: _____

Flight availabilities: _____

_____

_____

_____

Reserved flight times and numbers: _____

_____

For Ground Transportation:

Town car/shuttle/rental car phone numbers: _____

_____

Town car/shuttle/rental car reservations: _____

_____

Package ground transportation details: _____

_____

Additional Notes:

Reminder: Don't forget to confirm holds or cancel reservations (whenever possible) within the allotted time frame.

Lodging Near Orlando Intl. Airport

If you fly into Orlando a day ahead of time but arrive too late in the day to make the trek to Port Canaveral, consider bunking near the airport the night before. We describe several hotels near the airport below—even one hotel that's actually in the airport itself! Here are the details:

▮ Hyatt Regency Orlando $239+   0 mi./0 km. from airport

You can't beat the convenience of staying right in the airport at this Hyatt, but you will pay for the privilege. This six-story hotel is built right into the main terminal at the Orlando International Airport, offering 445 sound-proof, luxurious rooms at a whopping 400 sq. ft. each. While we haven't had the opportunity to stay here, a walk around the hotel spaces gives the impression of a very upscale business hotel. Standard room amenities include two double "Grand Beds," oversized work desk with dataport, armchairs, cable TV, balcony (not all rooms), iHome clock radio, refrigerator, coffeemaker, hair dryer, iron and ironing board, daily newspaper, voice mail, and wireless Internet (fee)—there are no in-room safes. Hotel amenities include room service, arcade, beauty salon, heated outdoor pool, sundeck with a view of the runway, 24-hour fitness room, and access to the shopping mall in the airport. The Hyatt has three restaurants: Hemispheres serves breakfast buffets and elegant dinners on the top two floors; McCoy's Bar and Grill is a casual eatery serving American food, and Hiro's Sushi Bar. The Lobby South lounge offers drinks and appetizers in front of its big screen TV. Check-in time: 4:00 pm; check-out time: 12:00 pm. The hotel was built in 1992 and renovated in 2000. Visit http://orlandoairport.hyatt.com or call 407-825-1234. Address: 9300 Airport Boulevard, Orlando, FL 32827. Note that when you purchase air travel through Disney Cruise Line and they fly you in the night before your cruise, this appears to be the hotel that Disney puts you up at most frequently (but no guarantees, of course!).

▮ Orlando Airport Marriott $189+   2.5 mi./4 km. from airport

© MediaMarx, Inc.

We enjoyed a night at this Marriott before a Disney cruise in May 2003 and found it both convenient and affordable (we got a great rate here via Priceline.com—see sidebar on next page). The Marriott is a mere 5 minutes from the Orlando Airport via a 24-hour complimentary shuttle (available by using a courtesy phone in the terminal). The 484 renovated rooms at this 10-story business hotel offer two double beds, work desk with dataport, 27-in. cable TV, two-line speakerphone, coffeemaker, hair dryer, iron and ironing board, daily newspaper, voice mail, and wireless high-speed Internet access (fee)—there are no in-room

A standard room

safes or balconies. Hotel amenities include room service, arcade, indoor/outdoor heated pool, hot tub, sauna, fitness center, tennis courts, and basketball court. Dining options include LUXE, serving casual American food for breakfast, lunch, and dinner. A full-service steakhouse, Porterhouse, is open daily for dinner. A pool bar, The Landings, serves drinks and sandwiches seasonally. The hotel was built in 1983 and renovated in 2007. Check-in time: 3:00 pm; check-out time: 12:00 pm. Visit http://marriott.com/property/propertypage/MCOAP or call 407-851-9000 or 800-380-6751. Address: 7499 Augusta National Drive, Orlando, FL 32833. See our detailed review of this hotel, complete with photos, at http://www.passporter. com/articles/orlandoairportmarriott.asp. We would stay here again without hesitation.

Introduction

Reservations

Staterooms

Dining

Activities

Ports of Call

Magic

Index

☐ Sheraton Suites $215+   2.5 mi./4 km. from airport

This all-suite, three-story hotel offers 150 suites at affordable rates. Suite amenities include a separate living room with sofa bed, work desk, two-line phones with dataports, TV, armchair, and kitchenette area with refrigerator, coffeemaker, and microwave, private bedroom with French doors, two pillowtop double beds (or one king bed), another TV, marble bathroom with hair dryer, iron and ironing board, voice mail, and wireless Internet access—there are no in-room safes, but there are balconies in some rooms. Hotel amenities include room service, a heated indoor/outdoor pool, sundeck, hot tub, and fitness room. The on-site restaurant, Mahogany Grille, offers a breakfast buffet plus lunch and dinner. Several restaurants—Chili's, Tony Roma's, and Bennigan's—are within walking distance. A 24-hour shuttle is available between the airport and hotel—use the courtesy phone in the terminal to request it. Check-in time: 3:00 pm; check-out time: 12:00 pm. Visit http://www.sheratonairport.com or call 407-240-5555 or 800-325-3535. Address: 7550 Augusta National Drive, Orlando, FL 32833.

☐ La Quinta Inn & Suites North $119+   3 mi./5 km. from airport

This five-story, 148-room motel offers clean rooms, free continental breakfasts, and free high-speed Internet access in all rooms. Room amenities include two double beds (or one king bed), 25-in. cable TV, dataport phone, coffeemaker, hair dryer, iron and ironing board, voice mail, free local calls, and newspaper delivery—there are no balconies or in-room safes. There are also five suites with a separate living room, sofa bed, microwave, and refrigerator. Motel amenities include an outdoor heated swimming pool, hot tub, sundeck, and fitness center. No on-site restaurant, but a TGIFriday's is adjacent and Tony Roma's, Cracker Barrel, Bennigan's, and Chili's are within walking distance. This motel was built in 1998. A free airport shuttle is available from 5:00 am to 11:00 pm daily. Check-in time: 3:00 pm; check-out time: 12:00 pm. Visit http://www.laquinta.com or call 407-240-5000. Address: 7160 N. Frontage Rd., Orlando, FL 32812

☐ AmeriSuites Airport NW $107+   3 mi./5 km. from airport

Enjoy a 480 sq. ft. suite in this six-story hotel. Each suite has a living room with a cable TV, two-line phone with dataport, desk, and sofa bed, kitchenette with wet bar, coffeemaker, refrigerator, and microwave, and a bedroom with two double beds (or one king bed), hair dryer, iron and ironing board, voice mail, and high-speed Internet. The living and sleeping areas are separated by half walls. Hotel amenities include an outdoor heated splash pool and fitness center. Complimentary continental breakfast. TGIFriday's, Tony Roma's, Cracker Barrel, Bennigan's, and Chili's are within walking distance. A free shuttle is available within a 5-mile radius of the hotel from 5:00 am to midnight. Check-in time: 3:00 pm; check-out time: 11:00 am. Visit http://www.amerisuites.com or call 407-816-7800. Address: 5435 Forbes Place, Orlando, FL 32812

Priceline.com

We've had great success with Priceline.com (http://www.priceline.com), where you can bid on hotel rates in particular areas. Before one of our cruise trips, we got the Marriott Orlando Airport (see previous page) through Priceline.com for about $35. If you do decide to try Priceline.com, read the directions thoroughly, and keep in mind that once your bid is accepted, you can't cancel. We recommend you visit BiddingForTravel.com (http://www.biddingfortravel.com) for Priceline.com advice and tips. Note that as of January 2008, each of the hotels we describe in the Lodging Near Orlando Intl. Airport section is a potential hotel available via Priceline.com. Not sure about Priceline.com? Another place to try for hotel deals is Hotwire.com at http://www.hotwire.com.

Want to stay near or at Walt Disney World before or after your cruise? For Disney resorts and hotels nearby, we recommend you pick up a copy of PassPorter's Walt Disney World guidebook (see page 348)—it goes into great detail on Walt Disney World lodging.

Getting to Port Canaveral

Port Canaveral, Florida, is Disney's home port. Situated in the city of Cape Canaveral, it's easily accessible from anywhere in Central Florida.

From the Orlando International Airport
Port Canaveral is about one hour (45 mi./72 km.) east of the airport. You have four options: transfer, town car/limo, taxi, or rental car.

Disney Cruise Line Ground Transfer—If you're sailing the day you arrive at the airport and you've booked ground transfers, a Disney Cruise Line representative meets you at the airport and directs you to a motorcoach. Check your cruise documents for transfer details. If you're not on a package, you can purchase these transfers for $69/person roundtrip—inquire at 800-395-9374, extension 1. If you're departing in the next day or so, just fill out the Transfer Purchase Option in your cruise documents and hand it over at the Disney's Magical Express counter on the first floor of the airport (a $69/person charge will appear on your shipboard account). For more details on motorcoaches, see page 66.

Note: Mears Transportation no longer provides shuttle transportation to Port Canaveral (no doubt because they operate the Disney Cruise motorcoaches).

Town Car/Limo—A luxurious alternative is a town car or limo, through a company like Quicksilver (888-468-6939) or Happy Limo (888-394-4277). The driver meets you in baggage claim, helps you with your luggage, and drives you to the port. Cost is around $190 for a town car ($210 for a van) round-trip to and from the port.

© MediaMarx, Inc.

Dave relaxes in a limo on the way to the port

Taxi—At approximately $100 one-way, it's not the best value. You can get taxis at the airport on level 1.

Rental Car—This option works well if you'll be spending time elsewhere before you cruise and need the wheels (thus, this is usually our preference). It can also be less expensive than the other options, but you must spend time for pickup/dropoff. For our tips on choosing the best rental car company for your needs, see the next page.

Introduction

Reservations

Staterooms

Dining

Activities

Ports of Call

Magic

Index

Getting to Port Canaveral

(continued)

Rental Cars *(continued)*

All the major car rental companies are located at the airport, but we prefer Budget (800-527-0700), Hertz (800-654-3131), or Avis (800-331-1212) because they are convenient, affordable, and offer a complimentary shuttle to the cruise terminal. Which car rental company you pick depends a great deal on the best rates for your rental period and car class. Check http://www.mousesavers.com/rentalcar.html for current discount codes—be sure to try all codes that apply! Note that while National/Alamo has an office in Port Canaveral, it does not offer a complimentary shuttle. All above-mentioned rental car companies have offices near the cruise terminal for drop off/pick up. For more rental car tips, see http://www.passporter.com/rentalcars.asp. Here are our rankings for the three best rental companies (chart inspired by the much-missed DCLTribute.com):

Rank	Company	Price	Dist.	Where to Check Rates
#1	Avis	$39.99[1] $33.00[2]	4 miles P3F[3]	Check rates at http://www.avis.com (rent at MCO, return to P3F), or call 800-331-1212. Local address: 6650 N. Atlantic Ave.; local phone: 321-783-3643.
	Avis is usually the rental car company we go with, thanks to its excellent combination of low rates, convenient office location, and great service.			
#2	Hertz	$54.99[1] $49.49[2]	2 miles COIC10[3] New location!	Check rates at http://www.hertz.com (rent at MCO, return to COIC10), or call 800-654-3131. Local address: 8963 Astronaut Blvd.; local phone: 321-783-7771.
#3	Budget	$67.99[1] $29.14[2]	3 miles CC5[3]	Check rates at http://www.budget.com (rent at MCO, return to CC5), or call 800-527-0700. Local address: 8401 Astronaut Blvd.; local phone: 321-951-4813.

[1] First sample price was based on a non-discounted, economy-class car picked up at Orlando Airport on Friday, May 9 at 10:00 am and returned to the local rental office on Saturday, May 10 at 10:00 am.

[2] Second sample price is based on the best public discount we could find for the same rental day and time as above, based on the discount codes posted at http://www.mousesavers.com.

[3] This code represents the exact location of the corresponding car rental company's office in Port Canaveral—use it when checking rates online or over the phone!

Will you need your rental car for a longer period? If you'll be picking up and dropping off your rental at Orlando International Airport, price out the companies above ... then try Hotwire.com. We've gotten daily rentals from Hotwire.com for as low as $18 and week-long rentals for as low as $14 per day. In December 2007, we booked through Hotwire.com and got an Avis mini-van for 12 days for just $17 per day! Hotwire.com does not currently offer one-way car rentals, however.

Getting to Port Canaveral

(continued)

Driving directions from the Orlando airport: Follow airport signs to the "North Exit" and take the Beachline Expressway (528) east 43 mi. (69 km.) to Cape Canaveral. You'll need $1.25 in small bills/coins for tolls.

From Orlando and Walt Disney World—You have four options: ground transfer, town car/limo, rental car, and your own car. Disney offers ground transfers, and Quicksilver and Happy Limo offer town cars/limos/vans to Port Canaveral (see previous page). If you're driving, take I-4 to exit 72 and then take the Beachline Expressway (528) east 53 mi. (85 km.) to Port Canaveral. Allow at least one hour and $2.75 for tolls. See directions below to the terminal.

From I-75—Take I-75 south to Florida's Turnpike. Take the turnpike south to exit 254 and take the Beachline Expressway (528) east 50 mi. (80 km.) to Port Canaveral. Expect $6.00 in tolls. See directions below to terminal.

From I-95—Take I-95 to exit 205 East and take the Beachline Expressway (528) east 12 mi. (19 km.) to Port Canaveral.

From Port Canaveral to the Disney Cruise Line Terminal—As you drive east on the Beachline Expressway (528), you'll cross two bridges (see if you can spot your ship when you're atop these bridges). After the second bridge, take the Route 401 exit to the "A" cruise terminals and follow the signs to the Disney Cruise Line Terminal (detailed on page 71).

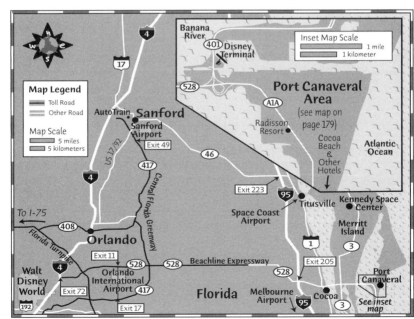

Sidebar tabs: Introduction · Reservations · Staterooms · Dining · Activities · Ports of Call · Magic · Index

Disney Cruise Line Motorcoach (Ground Transfers)

Passengers on a Disney land/sea vacation package and those who've booked ground transfers separately (see page 49) may get to ride in a Disney Cruise Line motorcoach. These handicap-accessible **deluxe buses** were re-painted in 2007 with the classic round portholes. On board, the cushy seats recline and there's even a restroom in the back. On the way to Port Canaveral, you're treated to a delightful video that heightens your anticipation. On the way back, you may watch a Disney movie on the overhead monitors.

Disney Cruise Line Motorcoach

There are some **downsides** to the ground transfers. There's no guarantee you'll get a Disney Cruise Line motorcoach just because you purchased the transfers. When we used the transfers, we rode in the motorcoach on the way to Port Canaveral, but on the way back to the Walt Disney World Resort, we were squeezed into a drab Mears shuttle van instead. This is more likely to happen if you're going to the Walt Disney World Resort after your cruise. Another downside is that you usually need to wait to board the bus. This could mean you may feel rushed when you arrive at the airport. And check-in goes slower, since you're in the midst of a large group of people who've arrived with you. You'll need to decide which is more important: convenience (take the bus) or speed (use another method). If you opt for the transfer, sit as near to the front as you can to be among the first off.

Boarding at the airport: Passengers with ground transfers who arrive between 9:00 am and 1:30 pm will be met in the terminal by a Disney representative and told where to board the motorcoach (usually near the Disney's Magical Express desk on level 1, side B). Your luggage (if properly tagged) is conveniently intercepted and transported to the ship.

Boarding at Walt Disney World: If you're staying at one of the Disney hotels affiliated with the Disney Cruise Line (Grand Floridian, Beach Club, Polynesian, Disney's Animal Kingdom Lodge, Saratoga Springs, Swan, Dolphin, Port Orleans, and Caribbean Beach), you'll be instructed to set your luggage by the door for pickup on the morning of your cruise. Around 10:00 am to 11:00 am, you meet in a central location in the resort and then proceed to the motorcoach, which generally leaves between 11:00 am and 11:45 am. You may have the option to depart from Disney's Animal Kingdom theme park the morning of your cruise, giving you an extra half-day in the park—inquire at the cruise hospitality desk at your resort (generally open from 8:00 am to noon daily).

Ground Transportation Worksheet

Use this worksheet to research, record, and plan your transportation to and from Port Canaveral.

Method	Price	Details	Reservation #
Disney Cruise Line Transfers: 800-395-9374			
Town Car/Limo/Van: *Quicksilver Tours*: *888-468-6939* *Tiffany Town Car*: *888-838-2161*			
Rental Car: *Avis*: 800-331-1212 *Budget*: 800-527-0700 *Hertz*: 800-654-3131		*(don't forget tolls)*	

Scheduling Pick-Up and Departure Times

Allow 90 minutes to get to Port Canaveral from either Orlando Airport or Walt Disney World. Thus, if you hope to board the ship as soon as possible, a pickup/departure time of 9:30 am or 10:00 am is good. If necessary, you could depart as late as 1:00 pm or 1:30 pm to reach Port Canaveral by 3:00 pm at the latest. For your return trip, the earliest you can expect to disembark the ship is 7:45 am to 8:30 am (and yes, you can still do the sit-down breakfast). It takes about 15 to 20 minutes to collect your bags and go through customs. Thus your pickup/departure time could be set between 8:00 am and 9:15 am. We do not recommend you book a flight with a departure time before 12:30 pm. A 2:00 pm or later flight would give you more breathing room.

Introduction
Reservations
Staterooms
Dining
Activities
Ports of Call
Magic
Index

Lodging Near Port Canaveral

You may want to take advantage of the visit to the "Space Coast" to squeeze in a trip to Kennedy Space Center or a day at the beach. Or perhaps you want to arrive in advance to avoid stress on the morning of your cruise. While there are many motels and hotels in the area, we've stayed at five (Radisson, Quality Suites, Ron Jon, Motel 6, and Residence Inn), all of which we recommend. We also detail one other hotel. To see the location of each, check the map on page 179.

☐ Radisson Resort at the Port $129+   2.7 mi./4.3 km. to port

This 284-room luxury resort was the closest lodging to the Disney Cruise Line terminal (until the Country Inn and Suites opened) and is quite popular with cruisers. While it is not an oceanfront hotel, it does feature a themed pool (see photo below), wading pool, hot tub, tennis court, fitness center, room service, and 1- and 2-bedroom suites in addition

to its standard, Caribbean-themed rooms (see photo at left). All rooms have ceiling fans, TVs, coffeemakers, hair dryers, voice mail, and high-speed Internet access. Suites add another TV and phone line, whirlpool tub, microwave, refrigerator, and walk-in showers. An on-site restaurant, Flamingos, is open from 6:30 am to 10:00 pm daily and serves American food, with Caribbean/Floridian cuisine on Saturday nights and a champagne brunch

Our standard, king bed room at the Radisson on Sundays. Check-in time: 3:00 pm; check-out time: 12:00 pm. One notable feature is the complimentary shuttle between the hotel and the port (you can make your shuttle reservation up to two weeks in advance—don't wait until you check in to reserve it or you may get a late pickup or none at all). Avis has moved; the closest car rental office is now Hertz. Special cruise prices allow you to park in their lot while you cruise. Great promotional rates are often available on the Internet for less than $100, but pay attention to the cancellation details, as you may have to pay a $25 fee to cancel. Visit http://www.radisson.com/capecanaveralfl or call 321-784-0000. Address: 8701 Astronaut Boulevard, Cape Canaveral, FL 32920

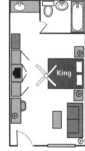

Typical floor plan

The beautiful, themed pool, complete with a waterfall and perching lioness and eagle

Quality Suites $98+   6.1 mi./9.8 km. to port

This small, all-suite hotel offers 48 spacious rooms and reasonable rates. The two-room suites offer a living room with a queen sofa bed, TV, phone, kitchenette with sink, microwave, refrigerator, and coffeepot, and in the bedroom, a king bed (no double beds available), another TV, phone, and a desk. All rooms have hair dryers, irons, and high-speed Internet access (free). A free continental breakfast is offered on the second floor.

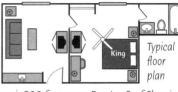

Typical floor plan

There's no on-site restaurant, but a Taco Bell and Waffle House are next door. This hotel has no swimming pool; it does have a large

Quality Suites

Suite living room

whirlpool, and the ocean is 300 feet away. Ron Jon Surf Shop is one block away. Free shuttle to the port with most rates—make a reservation at the desk the day before. Cruise parking packages are available, but you'll need to drive to and park at the Radisson. Check-in time: 3:00 pm; check-out time: 12:00 pm. For details, visit http://www.qualitysuitescocoabeach-portcanaveral.com or call 321-783-6868. 3655 N. Atlantic, Cocoa Beach, FL 32931

Motel 6 Cocoa Beach $59+   6.1 mi./9.8 km. to port

The Motel 6 in Cocoa Beach has the lowest published rates in the area. The clean motel features an outdoor swimming pool, cable TV, and a laundry room. While there is no restaurant on-site, a Waffle House is within walking distance. This motel is also close to tourist attractions such as Ron Jon Surf Shop, and it's only one block from the beach. No shuttle is available to the port; expect to pay about $11 to $15 for a taxi. Check-in time: 2:00 pm; check-out time: 12:00 pm. Visit http://www.motel6.com or call 321-783-3103. Address: 3701 N. Atlantic Avenue, Cocoa Beach, FL 32931

Motel 6 room

Resort on Cocoa Beach $140+   7.2 mi./11.6 km. to port

Resort on Cocoa Beach

A gorgeous, 8-story beach resort within reasonable distance of the port. The 147-suite resort features two-bedroom "condominiums" which sleep six with one king bed, two queen beds, and a sleeper sofa. Features include balconies, two bathrooms, full kitchens, two phone lines, two TVs, DVD, whirlpool tub, washer/dryer, and high-speed Internet access (no extra fee). Resort amenities include beach access, outdoor pool with kid's water play area, sauna, hot tub, fitness center, playground, tennis and basketball courts, a 50-seat movie theater, and a drop-in childcare center. This is a true resort! An on-site restaurant, Mug's, is an ocean grill and sushi bar (open 11:00 am to 10:00 pm daily). No shuttle is available to the port; expect to pay about $11 to $15 for a taxi. Check-in time: 4:00 pm; check-out time: 10:00 am. Visit http://www.theresortoncocoabeach.com or call 866-469-8222. Address: 1600 N. Atlantic Avenue, Cocoa Beach, FL 32931

Introduction

Reservations

Staterooms

Dining

Activities

Ports of Call

Magic

Index

Introduction
Reservations
Staterooms
Dining
Activities
Ports of Call
Magic
Index

Lodging Near Port Canaveral *(continued)*

■ Holiday Inn Express $128+   4.7 mi./7.5 km. to port

Holiday Inn Express

This hotel opened in late 2000, offering 60 guest rooms in a variety of family-friendly configurations. Beyond the standard queen bed and king bed rooms, Holiday Inn Express offers KidSuites with a separate room for the kids, Family Suites (for older kids or two couples traveling together), Romantic Suites with whirlpool tubs, and Executive Suites with workspace. All rooms have a microwave, refrigerator, coffeemaker, free wireless Internet access, hair dryer, iron and ironing board, and free newspaper delivery. A free continental breakfast is provided each morning. Amentities include an outdoor pool, whirlpool, and a fitness center ($3 fee), plus it is just two blocks from the beach. There is no on-site restaurant, but Durango Steakhouse, Florida Seafood, and The Omelette Station are nearby. You can take Art's Shuttle (http://www.artsshuttle.com, 800-567-5099) for $3/person to the cruise terminal. Check-in time: 3:00 pm; check-out: 11:00 am. For details, visit http://www.hiexpress.com/es-cocoabeach or call 321-868-2525 (local) or 800-465-4329 (toll-free). Address: 5575 N. Atlantic, Cocoa Beach, FL 32931

■ Residence Inn $149+   1.9 mi./3 km. to port

This all-suite hotel opened in 2006 and is already proving popular with cruisers—we've stayed here twice already and love it! Each of the 150 suites has separate living and dining areas, as well as fully-equipped kitchens. Rooms come with either two queen-size beds or one king bed, plus a sofa bed. Among its amenities are complimentary high-speed Internet access, free hot breakfasts, free happy hour (Mondays–Thursdays), free parking, and a $6 round-trip port shuttle (departs at 10:00 or 10:30 am—signup when you check-in). Check-in time: 2:00 pm; check-out: 12:00 pm. For details, visit http://www.residenceinn.com/mlbri or call 321-323-1100 (local) or 800-331-3131 (toll-free). Address: 8959 Astronaut Blvd., Cape Canaveral, FL 32920

Residence Inn dining area and living room

■ Ron Jon Cape Caribe Resort $156+   3.2 mi./5.2 km. to port

Anyone can rent the studios (up to 4 people), one-bedroom (6 people), two-bedroom (8–10 people), and three-bedroom villas (12 people) at this lovely resort. All villas have a sitting or living room, refrigerator, microwave, and coffeemaker. The one-, two-, and three-bedroom villas add a patio/balcony and full kitchen. Two- and three-bedroom villas also have a whirlpool tub (our one-bedroom villa had only a shower, no tub at all). Resort amenities include a "water park" with large heated pool, 248-ft. water slide, lazy river, and beach, plus an on-site restaurant, fitness center, children's play center, movie theater, miniature golf, and organized activities. This resort is 600 yards (about 3 blocks) from the beach, but it does provide a shuttle to the beach. Guests receive a discount at Ron Jon Surf Shop in Cocoa Beach. You can arrange for a shuttle to the cruise terminal through the concierge for an additional fee, or expect to pay about $9 to $12 for a taxi. We loved our one-bedroom villa here in December 2004—we found it bright, cheery, very spacious, clean, and full of amenities. Check-in time: 4:00 pm; check-out time: 10:00 am. Visit http://www.ronjonresort.com or call 888-933-3030 or 321-799-4900. Address: 1000 Shorewood Drive, Cape Canaveral, FL 32920

Ron Jon living room and kitchen

The Disney Cruise Line Terminal

Not content to use an existing, plain-Jane terminal for its cruise line, Disney had a **beautiful terminal** built in Port Canaveral to its exact specifications for $27 million. The Disney Cruise Line Terminal (terminal #8) is easily recognized by its 90-foot glass tower and art deco design. The terminal opens between 10:00 am and 10:30 am on cruise days for embarking passengers.

© MediaMarx, Inc.

The cruise terminal

If you're driving to the terminal, a gated, fenced lot with 965 parking spaces is available across from the terminal for $15 per 24-hour period (vehicles over 20 ft. long pay $26/day). (Note: Repositioning cruisers cannot park their cars while they cruise.) You'll need to **pay for parking up front** with cash, U.S. traveler's checks, Visa, or MasterCard. The Canaveral Port Authority operates the parking and we know of no discounts. If you do not drop off your luggage curbside (see below), you can take it to one of the white tents in the parking lot. You may find it less expensive to rent a car, drive, return the car to a rental office in Cape Canaveral, and catch a shuttle to the terminal than to park at the terminal. Warning: Ants are plentiful around here and may be attracted to food or crumbs in your car.

Security at the terminal is excellent. Have photo IDs for everyone in the car handy when you drive up. Guests and their luggage may be dropped off at the terminal curbside or the parking lot. A porter **collects all luggage** (tip $1 to $2/bag) except your carry-ons before you enter the terminal—luggage is scanned and delivered to your stateroom later, so be sure to attach those luggage tags. Security scans your carry-ons before you enter the terminal. Inside the terminal doors are escalators and an elevator that take you upstairs for check-in and embarkation.

In the terminal, look down at the gorgeous, 13,000 sq. ft. terrazzo tile Bahamas map.

Plan to arrive before 1:00 pm. Ships are scheduled to leave at 5:00 pm, but they may leave as early as 4:00 pm when weather dictates. Federal rules require all passengers be onboard one hour prior to sailing.

Address: 9150 Christopher Columbus Drive, Port Canaveral, FL 32920

Phone: 321-868-1400

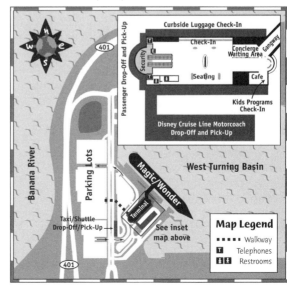

Curbside Luggage Check-In
Check-In
Concierge
Waiting Area
Gangway
Security
Passenger Drop-Off and Pick-Up
401
Seating
Cafe
Kids Programs
Check-In
Disney Cruise Line Motorcoach
Drop-Off and Pick-Up
West Turning Basin
Banana River
Parking Lots
Magic/Wonder
Terminal
Taxi/Shuttle
Drop-Off/Pick-Up
See inset
map above
401

Map Legend
■■■■ Walkway
T Telephones
🚻 Restrooms

Sidebar navigation: Introduction · Reservations · Staterooms · Dining · Activities · Ports of Call · Magic · Index

Check-In and Embarkation

If you're on a Disney land/sea vacation package, your check-in was completed when you checked in to your Walt Disney World resort hotel. Have your **Key to the World card and passporters/photo identification** out and proceed down the gangway (discussed on the next page).

If you've booked a cruise only or made your hotel arrangements on your own, don't worry—the check-in/embarkation procedure is remarkably smooth, especially if you **fill out the cruise forms before arrival**, which you can do online. Check your Travel Booklet (which comes in your cruise document package—see page 50) for the forms to be completed in advance.

When you arrive, a cast member may first check to ensure your cruise documents are together. You then proceed to the **check-in counters** (28 in total) which are lined up along the left-hand side. Check-in generally begins around 10:30 am or 11:00 am. If you are a member of the Castaway Club (see page 323) or staying in a suite, you may be directed to special counters.

Have your cruise travel booklets and passports/ID handy. If you've misplaced your immigration forms (included in your cruise documents), you can get extra copies in the terminal. You can do this paperwork online, but you'll need to print out and sign the waiver (and bring it with you). Be sure to bring **original or official documents**; no copies will be accepted.

Check-in takes about 10 minutes (you may spend more time in line). Once your forms are filed, you'll each get a **Key to the World card**, which is your ID/charging card and room key for the duration of the cruise (see below). Keep this card with you at all times.

A Key to the World card
(repeat cruiser version)

Your Key to the World Card and Money

It's your stateroom key, ship boarding pass, and shipboard charge card—no wonder Disney calls it your Key to the World. Everyone will have his or her own card—be sure to sign them as soon as you get them, and keep them safe. Disney ships are a cash-free society—everything you buy onboard and at Castaway Cay (except stamps) must be charged to that card. Stash your wallet in your room safe, grab your Key to the World Card, and travel ultra-light. At check-in, you'll need to make a deposit of at least $500 toward your on-board spending using a credit card (any of those listed on page 48 work), traveler's checks, cash, and/or Disney Dollars. You can even put a different credit card on each person's room key (great for friends traveling together). Disney charges your credit card whenever your shipboard account reaches its limit. If you deposited cash or cash-equivalent, you'll be called down to the Guest Services desk (Purser) to replenish the account. Cruising with kids? You can give them full charging privileges, deny them any charge privileges, or place a limited amount of cash on their account. Whatever you decide, you can make changes later at the Guest Services desk on deck 3 midship.

Non-U.S. citizens (including alien residents of the U.S.) have special check-in counters—look for the signs as you approach the counters. You will need to present your passport with any necessary visas at check-in to ensure that you can reenter the U.S. upon the ship's return. (Canadian citizens must also present a passport, according to Canada's Passport Office at http://www.ppt.gc.ca.) If you live in a country that participates in the U.S. Visa Waiver Program (see http://travel.state.gov) and plan to be in the U.S. for 90 days or less, you don't need a visa, but you do need to present proof of return transport and a signed visa waiver arrival/departure form (I-94W form) that you get from your airline. For more information on visas, check with the U.S. consulate or embassy in your country (see http://usembassy.state.gov). Note that non-U.S. citizens must surrender their passports at check-in; they will be returned upon disembarkation—see page 323. For this reason, you should bring extra forms of photo identification, which you will use when you leave and reenter the ship in your ports of call.

Embarkation usually begins between noon and 1:00 pm. Upon arriving at the terminal, you will receive a boarding number and may board when your number is called; there is no need to wait in line. While you're waiting to embark, you can relax on cushy sofas, watch Disney cartoons, and read the papers Disney gave you (usually a *Personal Navigator* or summary sheet). Around 11:00 am, Captain Mickey, Donald, or other characters may appear for photos and autographs. You may also be able to sign up your kids for Oceaneer Club/Lab—look for a sign-up desk inside the cafe at the far end of the terminal. Be sure to visit the museum-quality, 20-foot-long model of the Disney Magic in the middle of the terminal. You'll also find a small cafe with convenience items and stateroom gifts (but no seating). Look for more than 50 images of Mickey (both obvious and hidden) in and around the terminal! See the terminal map on page 71 to get your bearings before you arrive.

When it's **your turn to board**, you'll walk through the 16 ft. (5 m.) high Mickey-shaped embarkation portal (see photo) and present your Key to the World card, which is swiped through a card reader and handed back to you. Just before you reach the ship, photographers will arrange your party for the first of many ships' photo opportunities. Flash! That's it! You've made it! Proceed on up the gangway to the magic and wonder that await you.

© MediaMarx, Inc.

Inside the Disney Cruise Line Terminal

Going on the West Coast cruise? This part's just for you!

Getting to California

If you opt to **drive** to California, or from points within California, our best advice is to get a good map. Drivers unfamiliar with Southern California laws and freeways should visit **California Driving: A Survival Guide** at http://www.caldrive.com. This web site provides an excellent introduction to the "car culture" of California.

Air travel is the best way for many to get to Southern California—and it's a great way to strengthen the air travel industry and the U.S. economy. Use the tips on page 51 for booking the best airfare to California. There are three airports you could fly into—Los Angeles International (LAX), John Wayne/Orange County (SNA, http://www.ocair.com), and Long Beach (LGB, http://www.lgb.org). The vast majority of our readers are likely to use LAX, however, so we focus on that in this guidebook.

The granddaddy of California airports, **Los Angeles International Airport** is the third busiest airport in the entire world. It's located about 30 miles from Disneyland and 20 miles from the Port of Los Angeles. When you arrive, your plane docks at one of the nine terminals (see map below). From there, follow signs to baggage claim. Most ground transportation, including rental cars and shuttles, is located on the Lower/Arrival Level.

For **more details** on the Los Angeles International Airport, call 310-646-5252 or visit http://www.lawa.org and click the "LAX" tab. Airport address: 1 World Way, Los Angeles, CA 90045.

Los Angeles International (LAX) Airport

Introduction · Reservations · Staterooms · Dining · Activities · Ports of Call · Magic · Index

Getting to the Port of Los Angeles

The Disney Magic berths at the Port of Los Angeles in San Pedro while it is on the West Coast in the summer of 2008.

From the Los Angeles International Airport

The Port of Los Angeles is about 30–60 min. (20 mi./32 km.) south of the airport. You have five options: Disney ground transfer, shuttle, town car/limo, taxi, or rental car.

Taking a Disney Ground Transfer—Available to/from the airport, cruise terminal, and Disneyland. Just add it onto your cruise reservation. For more details, see page 49.

Using a Shared-Ride Van Service or Shuttle—SuperShuttle (714-517-6600 or 800-BLUE-VAN, http://www.supershuttle.com) and Prime Time Shuttle (310-342-7200 or 800-RED-VANS, http://www.primetimeshuttle.com) will take you nearly anywhere in the greater Los Angeles vicinity. From LAX, follow the signs to the Lower/Arrival Level island and request a pickup under the Shared-Ride Vans sign. From other locations, call or go online to make reservations at least 24 hours in advance—upon arrival, you may also need to use a courtesy phone to request pickup. At press time, a one-way fare from LAX to the port is $29 for the first person and $9 for each additional person (SuperShuttle) or $27/person (Prime Time Shuttle). Kids ride free under age 3 (on SuperShuttle) and under age 2 (on Prime Time Shuttle). Parents take note: If you're traveling with a child under 6 years of age or under 60 lbs. (27 kg.), you must bring an approved child safety seat to use on the shuttle. What about hotel shuttles? Generally speaking, hotels near the port are just too far away from airports to offer shuttles—the Holiday Inn near the port is the exception (see next page). If you're staying in a hotel within 5-10 miles of an airport, inquire with that hotel directly.

Using a Car Service, Town Car, or Limo—Both SuperShuttle and Prime Time Shuttle offer car services, though they're pricey—about $75 for a one-way trip from LAX to the port for up to three adults. We've found better rates through LAX Shuttle and Limo (877-529-7433, http://www.laxshuttlelimo.com) which offers a $58/one-way fare for up to four adults. Reservations are required.

Taking a Taxi—This is not our favored method of transportation, as it can be expensive—figure about $55+ tip for a one-way fare from LAX to the port. Large parties may be able to ride in a taxi mini-van economically, however. From LAX, follow the signs to the Lower/Arrival Level and look for a yellow taxi sign.

Rental Car—The only national rental car company in San Pedro is Enterprise, but they don't specialize in one-way rentals. There are rental offices about five miles away in Long Beach. You'll need a taxi to get to/from the ship (allow $15–$20). Drop off your companions at the ship before dropping off the rental, as the cabs can't carry much baggage.

Driving directions from LAX Airport: Follow signs to the San Diego Freeway (I-405) South, take it to the Harbor Freeway (I-110), then go south on the Harbor Freeway to the "CA 47–Terminal Island" exit. Merge right to the Harbor Blvd. Exit. Proceed straight through the Harbor Blvd. intersection and turn right into the World Cruise Center parking lot.

Driving directions from the Disneyland Resort: Take I-5 north to CA-91 west to the Harbor Freeway (I-110), then south on the Harbor Freeway to the "CA 47–Terminal Island" exit. Merge right to the Harbor Blvd. exit. Proceed straight through the Harbor Blvd. intersection and turn right into the World Cruise Center parking lot.

Lodging Near the Port of Los Angeles

You may find it most convenient to stay near the port the night before your cruise. These are the San Pedro hotels near the cruise terminals.

▪ Holiday Inn San Pedro $80+   .5 mi/1 km to port

This faux Victorian building houses 60 guest rooms, each with 10 foot ceilings. Rooms offer two queen beds (or one king bed), 25 in. cable TV, refrigerator, coffeemaker, hair dryer, iron and ironing board, newspaper delivery, voice mail, and free high-speed Internet access. The hotel has an outdoor heated pool, hot tub, and fitness center. There is an on-site restaurant—Club 111—which serves breakfast, lunch, dinner, and room service. The hotel was built in 1986 and renovated in 2001. A shuttle to the World Cruise Center is available for $5/person. Fly & Cruise packages are available with transfers from the airport to the pier—call or check their web site for details. Good advance rates are available at their web site. Check-in time: 3:00 pm; check-out time: 12:00 pm. Visit http://www.holidayinn.com or call 310-514-1414. Address: 111 S. Gaffey Street, San Pedro, CA 90731

▪ Sunrise Hotel San Pedro $96+   .5 mi/1 km to port

From all accounts this hotel won't win awards for amenities or style, but it is convenient and reasonably priced. The 110-room hotel has three stories and was renovated in 2001. Rooms have two queen beds (or one king bed), cable TV, refrigerator/minibar, coffeemaker, free high-speed Internet access, free local calls, hair dryer, iron and ironing board, and voice mail—there are no balconies, but the windows do open. Complimentary newspapers and continental breakfast are provided each morning in the lobby. There is an outdoor heated swimming pool and hot tub. The hotel has no restaurant, but the Grinders eatery is adjacent. The Ports o' Call Village across the street has restaurants and shops, too. A complimentary shuttle is available to the World Cruise Center, which is just four blocks away. Note: This hotel is no longer run by Best Western. Check-in time: 3:00 pm; check-out time: 12:00 pm. For details, call 310-548-1080 (no web site at press time). Address: 525 S. Harbor Blvd., San Pedro, CA 90731

▪ Doubletree Hotel San Pedro $134+   2.5 mi/4 km to port

Formerly known as the Marina Hotel, this Portofino-inspired, three-story hotel offers 226 rooms and suites. Rooms come equipped with two queen beds (or one king bed), high-speed Internet access, two-line phones, cable TV, minibar, coffeemaker, hair dryer, iron and ironing board, and newspaper delivery. Hotel amenities include an outdoor heated pool, hot tub, tennis court, and fitness center. Deals may be had via Priceline.com (see page 55). Park and cruise packages may be available—inquire with hotel. A free shuttle is available to the World Cruise Center, plus a complimentary van service within a five-mile radius. Check-in time: 3:00 pm; check-out time: 12:00 pm. Visit http://www.doubletreesanpedro.com or call 310-514-3344. Address: 2800 Via Cabrillo, San Pedro, CA 90731

▪ Crowne Plaza Los Angeles Harbor $140+   .6 mi/1 km to port

The 244 rooms at this well-reviewed hotel offer two queen beds (or one king bed), cable TV, desk, dataport, refrigerator, coffeemaker, hair dryer, iron and ironing board, voice mail, and wireless Internet access ($10/day). Hotel amenities include an outdoor heated pool, hot tub, arcade, and fitness center. Juliette's Restaurant is open all day until 10:00 pm. Cruise packages may be available—inquire with hotel. A free shuttle is available to the World Cruise Center and other nearby attractions. Good deals may be found on Priceline.com (see page 55). Formerly a Sheraton. Check-in time: 3:00 pm; check-out time: 12:00 pm. Visit http://www.crowneplaza.com or call 310-519-8200. Address: 601 S. Palos Verdes Street, San Pedro, CA 90731

■ The Queen Mary $149+   7.5 mi/12 km to port

Want to stay somewhere <u>really</u> interesting? On the night before our 2005 repositioning cruise, we stayed on the Queen Mary, just across the harbor from the World Cruise Center! The Queen Mary is the original "grandest ocean liner ever built," playing hostess to the rich and famous during the 1930s. The ship is now permanently moored and operates as a museum and hotel within very reasonable driving distance of the Magic's berth in San Pedro. There is even a Disney connection with the Queen Mary, as Disney owned her and

Strolling the deck on the Queen Mary

planned to build a major waterfront attraction around her. Disney's plans changed, but that fact simply added to the mystique. The "hotel" is comprised of the ship's original 365 staterooms, which span three decks. Each historic stateroom is unique, and many include original rich wood paneling, lovely Art Deco built-ins, and small portholes (outside cabins only). Seven classes of staterooms are available: deluxe staterooms (recently renovated), family staterooms (with an extra bed), first-class staterooms (the original cabins reserved for first-class passengers), tourist staterooms (no wood paneling, but they do have portholes), inside stateroom (two twin beds for the budget-minded), mini suites (separate living room and bedroom, all with original wood paneling), and the royalty suites (several rooms, original wood paneling, and originally occupied by nobility and heads of state). Stateroom amenities include air conditioning, room service, satellite TV, and high-speed Internet access. Accommodations include a self-guided tour of the ship, too. On the ship you'll find four restaurants: Sir Winston's is an elegant, reservations-required restaurant serving dinner only; Chelsea Restaurant is an award-winning seafood restaurant; The Promenade Cafe serves a diner-style menu at breakfast, lunch, and dinner; and Champagnes serves a festive Sunday brunch in the Grand Salon (the ship's original first-class dining room). Also available is Tibbies Cabaret and Dinner Theater, which serves dinner along with a Broadway-style cabaret show; Vamp Lounge, featuring a modern interpretation of classic 1930s burlesque (really!); and The Observation Bar in the original first class lounge with an impressive view. Hotel services include a business center, fitness rooms, and The Queen Mary Spa. Numerous boutiques are also available, as are several museum-like attractions. Of particular interest

Our first-class stateroom on the Queen Mary

to some is the reported paranormal activity onboard, which we think is part of the ship's charm. There's even a "Ghosts & Legends Tour" for $27/adults ($25/kids age 3-11, seniors, and military). We really enjoyed our night on the Queen Mary, but we wouldn't classify it as a five- or even four-star hotel. It's a bit rundown in places—our bathroom had peeling wallpaper, for example. In all honesty, we didn't mind this—we felt this obvious wear made the whole experience seem more authentic. Parking is $10/day. Check-in time: 4:00 pm; check-out time: 12:00 pm. Visit http://www.queenmary.com, e-mail reservations@queenmary.com, or call 562-435-3511. Address: 1126 Queen'sHighway, Long Beach, CA 90802

Introduction

Reservations

Staterooms

Dining

Activities

Ports of Call

Magic

Index

The World Cruise Center

While the Disney Magic is on the West Coast, it sails out of the World Cruise Center at the Port of Los Angeles in San Pedro. (Don't confuse this with the port at Long Beach—they are two entirely different ports.) The World Cruise Center is the **busiest cruise port on the West Coast**—you may remember it as the home port of "The Love Boat" TV series. It's located at berths 91–93 and encompasses two terminal buildings. More information is available at http://www.portoflosangeles.org and http://www.pcsterminals.com.

The Disney Magic docks at **berth 93** at the World Cruise Center. The recently remodeled terminal that serves this berth is spacious, providing plenty of seating and several large flat-screen TVs. This is the larger of the two cruise terminals at World Cruise Center.

If you're driving, a gated, fenced lot with 2,560 **parking spaces** is available for $12 per 24-hour period (or $1/hour for the first ten hours). You can pay with cash, U.S. traveler's checks, and major credit cards. Parking Concepts (http://www.lacruisecenter.com) operates the parking, and we know of no discounts. Lots 1 and 2 are closest to the terminal. Lots 6, 7, and 8 are further away, but courtesy shuttles (which are not wheelchair accessible) are available to and from the cruise terminals.

Security checks photo IDs for everyone in your car when you drive up. Porters are on hand to **collect all luggage** (tip $1 to $2/bag) except your carry-ons before you enter the terminal—luggage is scanned and delivered to your stateroom later, so be sure to attach those luggage tags you received with your cruise documents. Security scans your carry-ons before you enter the terminal.

Plan to arrive before 12:00 pm. Ships are scheduled to leave at 4:00 pm.

Address: 425 S. Palos Verdes St., Berth 93, San Pedro, CA 90731

Telephone: 310-514-4049

© MediaMarx, Inc.

The Disney Magic berthed at the World Cruise Center terminal in San Pedro, California

Our Mexican Riviera and Panama Canal Cruise Experiences

When Disney Cruise Line announced its first Mexican Riviera and Panama Canal itineraries for 2005, we and a legion of Disney cruise fans were seriously geeked! This would be the first time any Disney ship would sail through the **fabled Panama Canal**, and who knew when Disney might repeat that voyage? (Little did we know it would happen just three years later.) While West Coast-based Disney fans were excited about having the Magic call California "home" for the summer, what really pushed our buttons was a chance to spend two weeks onboard as the ship made its way from Florida to California. Plus, we'd have eight days at sea, which is one of our favorite parts of the cruising experience. Alas, our work commitments did not allow that, so we did the next best thing—we booked passage as soon as we could for the return trip through the canal, from California back to Florida.

Since we were flying to California from Michigan, the first edition of *PassPorter's Disneyland and Southern California* guidebook was still in development, and Disneyland was celebrating its 50th anniversary, how could we not include a **stay at Disneyland**? To "plus" things even more, we spent the night before our cruise departure in Long Beach, California, aboard that Grand Dame of the seas, the Queen Mary. We'd delve briefly into old-fashioned luxury ocean travel before embarking on our modern voyage. While it wasn't the only way to spend a night before a cruise, we thought it was the perfect choice for us.

Passage through the Panama Canal is more amazing than we ever imagined. Read a good book about it, preferably while lounging in a deck chair. (Dave recommends *The Path Between the Seas* by David McCullough.) Do not sleep in that day, and do some deck-hopping. While you have a great overview of the canal passage and the process of transiting the locks from deck 10, experience at least one lock from down on deck 3, where you'll see it all up close and personal. Don't spend the whole day on your verandah, either, since there's much you can't see from that vantage point. And wherever you are that day, the Panama Canal Authority narrates the day's events over the ship's PA system.

Despite it being the Magic's second trans-canal trip, it was a **very special two weeks**. A tropical storm cost us our visit to Cabo San Lucas (Manzanillo was the surprise substitute port). The ship was abuzz with the news that Roy and Patty Disney, the ship's godparents, Disney Cruise Line President Tom McAlpin, and several Hollywood celebrities were aboard for all or part of the voyage—all first-timers through the canal, like us. There were more than 1,400 Castaway Club members on board, so the club reception took over deck 9! Our son Alexander took his first, toddling steps as we were passing through the canal. The risqué "Sea Skit," which has since become a late-night tradition in Route 66/Beat Street on the last night of a cruise, was performed on the stage of the Walt Disney Theatre during a special late-night crew talent show. We also spied the cruise line's head of hotel operations dressed in full chef's regalia, manning a buffet carving station so that rank-and-file crew members could witness part of the canal passage. That's what we call a team effort! Somehow, we managed to survive two weeks in an inside stateroom (when we tell folks, "Don't count on an upgrade," we speak from experience). And when the Magic finally returned home to Port Canaveral, we were sorry to see the cruise end.

Read our **in-depth report** at http://www.passporter.com/dcl/panamacanalcruise.asp.

Packing for Your Cruise

Some folks hear "cruise" and start packing enough clothes for an around-the-world tour. If you tend to overpack, a cruise is the best place to do it. Guests on land/sea vacations or with ground transfers may only need to handle their bags at the very start and end of their trip. But if you're combining your cruise with a stay in Florida without Disney's help, you'll appreciate having **less luggage**. The Disney Cruise Line limits each guest to two suitcases and one carry-on. Need help packing light? Visit http://www.travelite.org.

When you arrive at the terminal, luggage is collected and you won't see it again until later that day, when it's delivered to your stateroom (usually between 2:00 pm and 6:00 pm). Pack a **separate carry-on** (no larger than 22" x 14"/56 x 36 cm) with your ID, cruise documents, prescriptions, and a swimsuit. Keep this bag light as you may be carrying it around for a few hours. You'll also need this carry-on for your last night, when you place the rest of your luggage outside your stateroom by 11:00 pm for collection.

A word about your **personal documentation**: We strongly recommend that U.S. citizens obtain and use passports, although they may or may not be required depending upon your sail date. For more information and tips on passports, see pages 52–53. If a passport is not required for your cruise and you'll be presenting your birth certificate and photo ID instead, do not pack your birth certificate in your luggage—keep it with you.

When your cruise documentation arrives, you'll find two **luggage tags** for each individual, with your ship, name, stateroom, and departure date. Read your cruise documentation to find out if you should tag your luggage before or after you arrive at the terminal. In general, if you're not on a land/sea package or haven't booked Disney's ground transfer, don't tag your luggage until you arrive at the terminal. You wouldn't want your bags collected prematurely. Don't forget to ID every piece of luggage with your own tags, too (use http://www.passporter.com/luggagelog.asp).

Deciding what **clothing** to pack depends a bit on what time of year you're cruising and your itinerary. Cruises in the cooler months require a few more jackets and sweaters, while you'll want to be ready with raingear in the summer. Pack dress clothing for dinner (see page 113) regardless of your itinerary. Guests on the 7-night and longer itineraries will want to add more dress clothing for the formal and semi-formal evenings (see page 312). Everyone may want to consider pirate or tropical garb for the Pirates in the Caribbean evening. Guests on shorter cruises can get by with just one nice outfit.

Packing Tips

Our **packing list** on the next two pages is complete, but for an exhaustive list, visit: http://www.geocities.com/Calgon1/Ultimate_Packing_List.html.

There's no need to over-pack. Unlike some other cruise lines, self-service **laundry rooms** are available onboard, as is valet laundry service.

The air-conditioned public rooms on the ships can be **chilly**, as are the winds on deck. Bring sweaters or jackets.

Pack comfortable **shoes** with non-slip rubber soles for walking around on deck and on shore. You'll also appreciate sandals and water shoes.

While room service is free, delivery is not immediate. If you need snacks on hand, bring packaged **snacks** like crackers or granola bars. You could also bring your own bottled water (it's pricey onboard), but the drinking water tastes fine to most. Note that Disney prohibits personal coolers onboard unless they are for medications, baby foods, or dietary needs. Ice buckets are provided in the staterooms, as are small coolers.

The health-conscious may want to consider a well-stocked **medicine kit**, as trips to the onboard infirmary cost you. Beyond the usual items, consider anti-nausea aids (see page 317), antidiarrheal aids, sunblock, sunburn gel, and "Safe Sea," a sunblock that helps protect against the stinging of most jellyfish, sea lice, coral, and sea anemone (see http://www.nidaria.com).

Two-way radios can be handy for keeping in touch onboard—use the ones with extra subchannels. The radios won't work everywhere due to all the metal in the ship—they only seem to work up to a few decks away.

You can bring your own **stroller** or just borrow one free of charge at Guest Services onboard and/or at Castaway Cay (first come, first served). Wheelchairs can also be borrowed free of charge.

Unlike many other cruises, you can bring your own **alcohol** onboard to save money on drinks. Beer and wine are the best items to bring; you can usually buy hard liquor for great prices on the islands. Note that you won't be able to bring opened bottles home with you at the end of the cruise.

Worried about **lost or delayed luggage**? Don't pack all your items in one bag. Instead, split items between bags. Couples can pack half their things in their suitcases and half in their partner's suitcases to be safe.

Knives, pocket tools, and other **potential weapons** are prohibited onboard. All luggage is inspected, and confiscated items are held until you return to port. This can seriously delay luggage delivery to your room.

Introduction

Reservations

Staterooms

Dining

Activities

Ports of Call

Magic

Index

Packing List

Electronic, interactive worksheet available—see page 350

Packing for a cruise is fun when you feel confident you're packing the right things. Over the years, we've compiled a packing list for a great cruise vacation. Just note the quantity you plan to bring and check them off as you pack. Consider packing items in **bold** in your cruise carry-on (some items may not be appropriate for your airplane carry-on due to security restrictions).

The Essentials

❑ Casual, nice clothing for daytime and late-night wear
___ Shorts ___ Long pants ___ Shirts ___ Skirts/dresses
___ Underwear (lots!) ___ Socks ___ Pajamas ___ Robes

❑ Jacket and/or sweater (light ones for the warmer months)
___ **Jackets** ___ Sweatshirts ___ Sweaters ___ Vests

❑ Formal and semi-formal clothing for special evenings
___ Suits and ties ___ Dresses ___ Jewelry ___ Tropical dress

❑ Comfortable, well-broken-in shoes, sandals, and dress shoes
___ Walking shoes ___ Sandals ___ Dress shoes ___ _____

❑ Swim wear and gear (regular towels are provided)
___ **Suits/trunks** ___ **Cover-ups** ___ Water shoes ___ Goggles

❑ Sun protection (the Caribbean sun can be brutal) 👓
___ **Sunblock** ___ **Lip balm** ___ **Sunburn relief** ___ **Sunglasses**
___ **Hats w/brims** ___ **Caps** ___ **Visors** ___ _____

❑ Rain gear 🐚 (for your port excursions)
___ Raincoat ___ Poncho ___ Umbrella ___ _____

❑ Comfortable bags with padded straps to carry items in port
___ Backpacks ___ Waist packs ___ Shoulder bags ___ **Camera bag**

❑ Toiletries 🪥 (in a bag or bathroom kit to keep them organized)
___ **Brush/comb** ___ **Toothbrush** ___ **Toothpaste** ___ Dental floss
___ Favorite soap, shampoo, conditioner ___ Deodorant ___ Baby wipes
___ **Anti-nausea aids** and **pain relievers** ___ **Band aids** ___ **First aid kit**
___ **Prescriptions** (in original containers) ___ Vitamins ___ **Fem. hygiene**
___ **Makeup** ___ Hairspray ___ Cotton swabs ___ Curling iron
___ Razors ___ Shaving cream ___ Nail clippers ___ **Spare glasses**
___ Lens solution ___ Safety pins ___ Bug repellent ___ Insect sting kit
___ Mending kit ___ Small scissors ___ **Ear plugs** ___ _____

❑ Camera/camcorder and more film 📷 than you think you need
___ **Cameras** ___ **Camcorder** ___ **Film/batteries** ___ **Memory cards**

❑ Money in various forms and various places
___ **Charge cards** ___ **Traveler's checks** ___ **Bank cards** ___ **Cash**

❑ Personal identification, passes, and membership cards
___ **Documents** ___ **Birth certificate** ___ **Driver's license** ___ **Passports**
___ **AAA card** ___ **Travel perks cards** ___ **Discount cards** ___ Air miles card
___ **Other IDs** ___ **Insurance cards** ___ **Calling cards** ___ SCUBA cert.

Tip: Label everything with your name, phone, and stateroom to help reunite you with your stuff if lost. Every bag should have this info on a tag as well as on a slip of paper inside it. Use our Luggage Tag Maker at http://www.passporter.com/luggagelog.asp.

For Your Carry-On

☐ **PassPorter, cruise documentation, ground/air confirmations, multiple photo IDs** (driver's license, passports, birth certificates, and a **pen/pencil!** ✒
  Remember not to pack any sharp or potentially dangerous items in your carry-on.
☐ **Camera** and/or **camcorder**, along with **film/memory/tapes** and **batteries**
☐ Any **prescription medicines, important toiletries, sunblock, sunglasses, hats**
☐ **Change of clothes**, including **swimwear** and **dress clothes** for dinner
☐ **Snacks, water bottle, juice boxes, gum, books, toys, games**
☐ **PassHolder Pouch** for passports, IDs, cash, etc. (see http://www.passporter.com)

For Families

☐ **Snacks** and **juice boxes**
☐ **Books, toys, 🎲** and **games**
☐ Familiar items from home 👇
☐ Stroller and accessories
☐ **Autograph books** and **fat pens**

For Couples

☐ **Champagne** for your send-off
☐ Wine and favorite adult beverages
☐ Portable CD player, speakers, and CDs
☐ Good beach novels
☐ Massage oil

For Connected Travelers

☐ Handheld/Palm organizer
☐ Laptop, cables, extension cord
☐ Chargers
☐ GPS system or compass
☐ Security cable with lock
☐ **Cell phones** and/or **two-way radios**

For Heat-Sensitive Travelers

☐ **Personal fan/water misters**
☐ **Water bottles**
☐ Loose, breezy clothing
☐ **Hats** with wide brims
☐ **Elastics** to keep long hair off neck
☐ **Sweatbands**

Everyone Should Consider

☐ **Penlight** or flashlight (for reading/writing in dark places)
☐ Battery-operated alarm with illuminated face and nightlight (or just open the closet)
☐ Earplugs, sound machine, or white-noise generator (for noisy staterooms)
☐ **Water bottles** and personal **fans/water misters**
☐ Plastic storage bags that seal (large and small) and plastic cutlery for snacks ✐
☐ Address book, envelopes, and stamps (with numeric denominations) ✉
☐ Laundry detergent/tablets, dryer sheets, stain stick, and wrinkle remover
☐ **Binoculars** and a **soft-sided, insulated tote** for going ashore
☐ Currency exchange calculator or card (if you'll be doing a lot of shopping)
☐ Collapsible bag or suitcase inside another suitcase to hold souvenirs on your return
☐ **Small bills and coins** for tipping and quarters for laundry
☐ Photo mailers or large envelope with cardboard inserts (for safeguarding photos)
☐ **Highlighters** (multiple colors for each person to mark activities in your *Personal Navigator*)
☐ Closet organizer (the kind used to hold shoes) to store small items and avoid clutter
☐ **Sticky notes** (to leave your cabinmates messages)
☐ Plenty of **batteries** (and don't forget the charger if you're using rechargeables)
☐ An electrical power strip if you'll need extra outlets for lots of chargers
☐ Something to carry your small items, such as a **PassHolder Pouch** or evening bag

Your Personal Packing List

☐ _____   ☐ _____
☐ _____   ☐ _____
☐ _____   ☐ _____

Introduction
Reservations
Staterooms
Dining
Activities
Ports of Call
Magic
Index

Adventuring!

Here are our tried-and-true cruise traveling tips:

- Any travel delay can sink your plans, so don't let the ship sail without you. Plan to **fly (or drive) in the day/night before** you sail to have a stress-free, early start to your vacation. There are many hotels near both the Orlando International Airport and the Los Angeles-area airports, and good deals can be had by shopping on http://www.priceline.com or the hotel web sites in the weeks before you cruise. In the morning, you can take the hotel's shuttle back to the airport and catch Disney's ground transfer to the port. Or give yourself a full day in port—many hotels offer shuttles (free or low cost) to the cruise terminal.

- "Need to **pack a bottle of alcohol safely**? My bottle-packing solution serves a double purpose. I double-bag the bottle(s) and place them in a plastic bin (shoebox size will work, depending on the size of the bottle). Add some bubble wrap around the bottles, secure the lid on the box, then pack the box in the suitcase. The hard plastic protects the bottles should a heavier suitcase be placed on top. Then, after I've finished the bottle(s), I've now got a fantastic way to bring fragile gifts and souvenirs home—bubble wrap and a plastic box! No more broken or squished mementos!" – *contributed by Disney vacationer Lynn Mirante*

- "If you're driving, look for the **Ron Jon Surf Shop billboards** along the Florida highways—they count down the mileage remaining to their store, which isn't far from the terminal." – *contributed by Dave Huiner*

Magical Memories

- *"When planning our first Disney cruise, I realized my husband had never cruised before. To see if he liked it and would consider a future 7-night cruise, we did a 3-night Disney Wonder cruise after a visit to Walt Disney World. I highly recommend cruising AFTER doing Walt Disney World because we were really able to relax. We had to cut costs to add the cruise, and we made the tough decision to take an interior stateroom, thinking that because we would be exploring the ports, we wouldn't be in the room all that much. We were right! We were so pleased with our category 11 room—it was very large and felt like a regular hotel room to us. Even the non-split bathroom didn't make a difference because it was only the two of us. We were so glad we saved money in this area because it allowed us to do an excursion instead."* ...as told by Disney cruiser Annette Konicek

- *"I prepared my young son for the journey to 'Mickey's Boat' by drawing a treasure map from our home to the airport to the hotel to the ship. We looked at the treasure map and talked about the trip each evening before bed. It really seemed to help him understand the concept of traveling and got him excited about going on the cruise!"*
  ...as told by Disney cruiser Jennifer Marx

Staying in Style in a Stateroom

Style is, indeed, the operative word for Disney Cruise Line staterooms. Every stateroom, regardless of its price, category, or location onboard, is resplendent with warm, natural woods, luxurious fabrics, imported tile, nautical touches, and dramatic lighting. Robert Tillberg, esteemed naval architect, worked with Disney to design the stateroom interiors with more storage space and the innovative split bathrooms available in categories 10 and up. Unlike many other ships, 73% of the staterooms have an ocean view, while 44% of all rooms have private verandahs. Better yet, staterooms on Disney ships have the "luxury of space"—they are substantially larger (up to 25%) than those on many other ships. Many cruise industry insiders consider Disney Cruise Line staterooms to be among the best afloat. You'll actually enjoy being in your stateroom!

Every stateroom has a generous queen-size pillow-top bed that can be converted to two twin beds, ample closet space, shower/tub combination (or roll-in showers in the handicap-accessible rooms), hair dryer, desk/vanity, phone with voice mail, safe, color TV, small cooler, individual climate controls, and room service. Most staterooms also have a sitting area with a desk/dressing table and a sofa that converts into a twin bed, and many also have a pull-down single berth. A curtain separates the sleeping area from the sitting area. Staterooms sleep 2–7 guests, though most sleep 3–4. Staterooms are located on decks 1–2 and 5–8, all of which are above the waterline. Crew quarters are on decks A and B, which are off-limits to guests.

Choosing your stateroom is one of the first things you'll do after you decide to cruise, so we put this chapter before dining and playing. We recommend you read this chapter in conjunction with chapter 2 before you make your cruise reservations. This will ensure you make the best possible choice in staterooms. Different stateroom categories offer different amenities, and there are some special rooms and decks that have an added benefit or two. The ship will be your home away from home for several days. Stateroom changes and upgrades are rarely available once you board, as the ships often sail completely full.

Selecting Your Stateroom

The Disney Cruise Line offers 12 different categories of staterooms on both the Disney Magic and the Disney Wonder. You'll need to specify a category when you make your cruise line reservation, so it is important to know as much as possible about each category in advance.

The most obvious difference between categories is **price**. Category 1 is the priciest, while category 12 is the least expensive. Price may be your only determining factor, and if so, we encourage you to check the current cruise category rates at http://www.disneycruise.com or in your Disney Cruise Line booklet. You can find typical rates on page 44.

Beyond price, we can combine the stateroom **categories** into four groups: outside stateroom suites with verandahs (1-3), outside staterooms with verandahs (4-7), outside staterooms with portholes (8-9), and inside staterooms (10-12). We devote one overview page to each of these four groups, plus one page of delightful detail for each category.

The Disney Cruise Line may offer different "categories," but old-fashioned "classes" are a relic of the past. If you choose a category 12 stateroom, you won't be made to feel like you're in a lower class than any other passenger. You will have **access to all facilities** on your ship and dine in the same style, regardless of your category. We booked our first cruise in a category 12 and never once felt funny about it. (We were later upgraded to category 9, which we loved. For more on upgrades, see page 106.) Guests on a land/sea package stay at different hotels based on their category, however (see chart on the next page). If you want to stay in a nicer hotel, you may be able to upgrade for an additional charge—inquire when reserving.

Another deciding factor may simply be **availability**. This is particularly true of the high and low category staterooms, which are in shorter supply. You can find out what categories are available before you make a decision by calling Disney at 888-325-2500. To learn how to check specific stateroom availability, see page 92. Note that you may be booked into a "guaranteed category" rather than a specific stateroom. This tends to happen when all of the staterooms in a certain category are booked. A guaranteed category means you're guaranteed a room in that category or higher. Guaranteed category guests do occasionally get upgraded.

Each class of stateroom offers its own **charms and drawbacks**. Check our chart of stateroom pros and cons on the next page for an overview of the staterooms, and then turn the page for a more in-depth look.

Staterooms Side-by-Side

Charms and Delights	Issues and Drawbacks
Outside Stateroom Suites With Verandahs (categories 1-3)	
Huge staterooms, two with room for up to 7 people. Total separation of sleeping and sitting areas. DVDs, CD players, duvets, pillow choices, walk-in closets, wet bars, and some whirlpool tubs. Extra-long verandahs. Concierge, 105-day advance reservations, and expanded room service. Guests with land/sea packages stay at the Grand Floridian.	Very expensive and deals are almost never offered on the suites (although per-guest cost is good if you fill it to capacity). Very popular and are often booked far in advance. There are only 22 suites (all on deck 8). Most cat. 3 staterooms have the pull-down bed in the master bedroom. Can be noisy when crew is cleaning deck 9 above.
Outside Staterooms With Verandahs (categories 4-7)	
Verandahs! It's like having a private deck to watch waves or gaze at passing islands. And the wall-to-wall glass adds light and a sense of extra space. Located on decks 5-8, close to all activities. One category (4) sleeps 4-5; the others sleep 3-4. Staterooms are 268-304 sq. ft. Guests with land/sea packages stay at Disney's deluxe resorts, such as the Beach Club.	Still on the pricey side, and may be out of range for many vacationers. Sitting and sleeping areas are in the same room. Category 5-7 layouts and interior square areas are identical to categories 8-9. Verandahs on deck 5 are slightly more shallow than on decks 6-8. Wind and/or bad weather can make the verandah unusable. Category 7 sleeps only 3.
Outside Staterooms With Portholes (categories 8-9)	
Portholes! Some natural sunlight and the ability to see where you are (i.e., already docked in port!) are real blessings. These staterooms are also more affordable. Some rooms sleep up to 4 guests. Category 8 and 9 staterooms feature split bathrooms (unlike category 11 and 12 staterooms). Provides the same access to the ship as higher categories. Portholes on decks 2 and up are picture-window-sized.	No verandahs. Category 9 rooms are on decks 1 and 2, which aren't as accessible as the higher decks. And while category 8 staterooms are on decks 5-7, they aren't in the most desirable of spots, all being located forward in the ship. Sitting and sleeping areas are in the same room. Guests with land/sea packages stay at Disney's moderate resorts, along with category 10-12 guests.
Inside Staterooms (categories 10-12)	
The least expensive staterooms available. Some rooms sleep up to 4. Category 10 has the same square footage as categories 8-9. Some category 10-11 staterooms are on decks 5-7. Six staterooms in category 10 actually have an obstructed porthole (bonus!). Same access to the ship as higher categories. Guests with land/sea packages stay at Disney's moderate resorts, such as Port Orleans or Caribbean Beach Resort.	No windows, making your stateroom seem small, slightly claustrophobic, and dark. Smaller room size (184 sq. ft.) for categories 11-12. Category 12 rooms sleep no more than 3 guests. All staterooms in category 12 are on deck 2, and there are only 13 staterooms in this category (making them hard to get). Categories 11 and 12 don't have split bathrooms (see explanation on page 98).

(see explanation on page 98)

Outside Stateroom Suites
(categories 1, 2, and 3)

The best of the ship's staterooms, these suites (all on deck 8) offer many luxuries. All feature extra-large verandahs, VCRs, DVD and CD players, dining areas, wet bars, walk-in closets, duvets, special pillows, robes and slippers, marble bathrooms, plus concierge and expanded room service.

AMENITIES

Suite guests may get **perks** like priority boarding, a separate waiting area in the terminal, a special planning meeting once you're aboard, a private party with the Captain, personalized stationery, and some special surprise gifts. You may be able to request water and soda delivery for your room. All suites come with **concierge service**. You can make reservations for Palo, childcare, Vista Spa, and shore excursions in advance of non-suite guests, and the concierge will help with other special requests. You can borrow from a library of CDs, DVDs, and games (board and electronic)—check the concierge book in your stateroom for a list. The crew often adds goodies, such as a fruit basket or cookies. Suite guests also get **expanded room service**, meaning you can order a full breakfast in the mornings (same menu as Lumiere's/Triton's breakfast menu—see page 116) and a full dinner from the restaurants during dinner hours—menus are available from concierge, or check our menus in chapter 4. Suite guests can also book massages in their staterooms or on their verandahs.

TIPS & NOTES

The suites are **extremely popular**; if you do not book one far in advance, expect to be put on a waiting list.

Guests with land/sea packages have **first pick of suites**; any suites available 30 days before sailing can be booked by all. No restrictions are placed on the 7-night cruise suites.

Suite guests have online **priority booking** for excursions, Vista Spa, Palo, kids' programming, and babysitting up to 105 days in advance (see page 139). If you have not booked in advance, plan to meet with the concierge staff on your first afternoon to make reservations.

Suites have **duvets on pillow-top beds**, and the choice of a hypo-allergenic, feather, and/or therapeutic memory foam pillow.

Suites have **hand-held blow dryers** in their vanity drawers.

Suite guests have **gold Key to the World cards**, rather than blue.

Note that deposits for suites are **non-refundable**, presumably to discourage bookings "on spec."

Category 1 Staterooms
(Walter E. and Roy O. Disney Suites—sleep 7 guests)

The two **category 1 suites**, known as the Walter E. Disney Suite and the Roy O. Disney Suite, are the height of cruising. The 1,029 sq. ft. (95 sq. m.) suites luxuriate with warm, exotic woods, two bedrooms, 2 ½ bathrooms, whirlpool tub, a media library with a pull-down bed, and a quadruple-wide verandah. Sleep up to 7 guests. Note that the baby grand piano in the Walt Suite has been removed as of December 2007—we don't know if it will return.

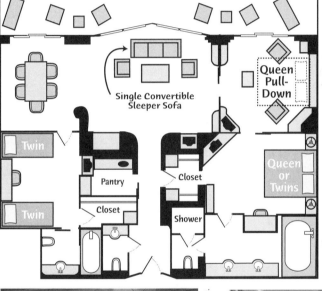

Entryway

The pantry in the Walter E. Disney suite

A view from the media library into the bedroom in the Walter E. Disney suite

Jennifer enjoys the quadruple-wide verandah of a category 1 suite

Introduction | Reservations | Staterooms | Dining | Activities | Ports of Call | Magic | Index

Introduction
Reservations
Staterooms
Dining
Activities
Ports of Call
Magic
Index

Category 2 Staterooms
(Two-Bedroom Suite—sleeps 7 guests)

The **category 2** suites (at 945 sq. ft./88 sq. m.) have two bedrooms, 2½ baths, a whirlpool tub, and a triple-wide verandah. There are just two of these suites onboard, and both sleep up to seven.

Note: Categories 1 and 2 can sleep up to seven guests, but the sixth and seventh guests will require booking an additional resort hotel room at an extra cost (for those on land/sea packages).

Tip: Connecting rooms are great for larger groups. Many of the category 3 suites have connecting doors to a category 3 or 4, which holds four to five more guests. Alas, the category 1 and 2 suites do not have connecting staterooms.

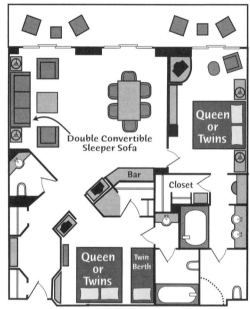

Double Convertible Sleeper Sofa

Queen or Twins

Bar

Closet

Queen or Twins

Twin Berth

The triple-wide verandah of a category 2 suite

A category 2 bedroom

The entertainment center

© MediaMarx, Inc.

Category 3 Staterooms
(One Bedroom Suite—sleeps 4-5 guests)

The 18 stateroom suites in **category 3** (614 sq. ft./57 sq. m.) offer a bedroom separate from the living room and dining room, two baths, a double-size convertible sofa in the living room, and a double-wide verandah. Most category 3 suites have a pull-down twin bed in the bedroom (as shown on the layout). Four suites (#8032, #8034, #8532, and #8534) have a slightly different layout with a bit more floor space and feature the pull-down twin bed in the living room, which guests find more convenient—these four suites are under the Goofy Pool, however, and are noisier. Suites #8100, #8102, #8600, and #8602 are handicap-accessible and have deeper verandahs. Category 3 suites sleep four to five guests (see chart on pages 108-109 to see which suites sleep only four).

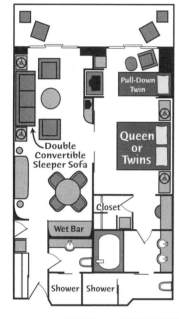

A category 3 bedroom

Dave relaxes in the living room of stateroom 8034 (different layout than pictured above)

Outside Staterooms With Verandahs
(categories 4, 5, 6, and 7)

Welcome to the luxury of a private verandah at just a fraction of the cost of the higher categories! Staterooms with verandahs (categories 4-7) comprise the largest percentage of the ship's staterooms at a whopping 42%, and all have split baths (see page 98). All are located on decks 5-8.

AMENITIES

The main amenity in categories 4-7 is the verandah (balcony). Not only does the verandah offer fresh air and a gorgeous view, but it extends the space of your stateroom considerably. The option to sit outside and enjoy a sunset or read a book while someone else watches TV or sleeps inside is a huge bonus. Verandahs in categories 4-6 are open to the air, covered, and have privacy dividers. Category 7 staterooms (same size as categories 5 and 6) have either a slightly obstructed view from the verandah or a Navigator's Verandah, which offers more privacy by hiding the verandah behind a large, glassless "porthole" (see photos on page 95). All verandahs have exterior lighting that is controlled by an on/off switch inside the stateroom. All the verandah staterooms can sleep at least three guests, and most category 4 rooms sleep up to five guests. See the chart on pages 108-109 for more specific room capacities.

© MediaMarx, Inc.

Most verandahs have a clear, plexiglass-covered railing (shown in the first photo). Others have a solid, metal railing (as shown in the second photo). There are fans of both styles, though we personally prefer the clear railings.

Verandah with plexiglass railing   Verandah with metal railing

---

Which Staterooms Are Available for My Cruise?
Most guests let Disney or their travel agent select their stateroom. If you'd rather have a specific stateroom, find out which staterooms are available by calling Disney (888-325-2500). If you have Internet access, get online and visit Disney Cruise Line (http://www.disneycruise.com) or Travelocity.com (http://www.travelocity.com)— follow the directions to choose your cruise, then continue through the windows to check rates and to see any availabilities. If you have your heart set on a particular stateroom, call Disney or check the Internet to find a cruise with that room available. When you make your reservations, indicate the exact stateroom you want. Confirm that the stateroom you requested is printed in your travel booklet when it arrives.

Category 4 Staterooms
(Deluxe Family With Verandah—sleeps 4–5 guests)

Category 4 is the Deluxe Family Stateroom, which sleeps up to four or five guests (304 sq. ft./28 sq. m.). The room has a pull-down twin bed for the fifth guest, along with a convertible twin sofa bed, a pull-down twin berth, and a queen-size bed that can be separated into twin beds. The 80 **category 4** family staterooms are all on deck 8. Avoid staterooms directly below the Goofy Pool (#8036–8044 and #8536–8544) due to noise during deck parties. Note that staterooms #8092–8094 and #8596–8698 have a solid railing, rather than a plexiglass railing. Access to the verandah is limited when you have the twin bed pulled down.

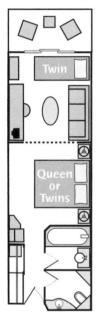

Squidgy the teddy bear naps in a category 4 stateroom (8544)

Desk/vanity area in category 4 stateroom

Another view of category 4

Category 5 & 6 Staterooms
(Deluxe Stateroom With Verandah—sleeps 3-4 guests)

Categories 5 and 6 are the Deluxe Staterooms With Verandahs. These staterooms are identical to category 4 (see previous page) except they are 268 sq. ft. (25 sq. m.), sleep three to four guests, do not have the extra pull-down twin bed, and are missing a handy bench across from the bed. The 114 **category 5** staterooms are located on deck 7, mostly midship and aft. Staterooms to the aft have quick access to a secluded public deck. Staterooms #7130–7138 and #7630–7638 have a solid, four-foot metal railing (as opposed to the plexiglass railing on other verandahs), but the verandahs may be deeper and quieter, too. Avoid #7590 as it is across from a laundry room. **Category 6** staterooms number 138 and are situated on decks 5 and 6. We recommend deck 6 for its slightly larger verandahs. Avoid #6588 as it is across from a laundry room. Staterooms #5142–5150, #5642–5650, #6144–6154, and #6644–6654 have a solid railing.

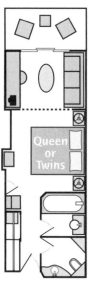

Verandah at sunset

Jennifer enjoys the verandah in our category 5 stateroom (7618)

© MediaMarx, Inc.

Category 7 Staterooms
(Navigator's Verandah—sleeps 3 guests)

There are only 30 **category 7** staterooms (268 sq. ft./25 sq. m.), of which 26 are Navigator's Verandahs (enclosed verandah with open-air porthole). All are located on the quietest decks: 5, 6, and 7. We recommend deck 7 for its easy access to the public deck to the aft. Note that the verandahs on deck 5 are a bit shallower at 42" (106 cm.) than those on upper decks at about 48" (122 cm.). Note that four of the category 7 staterooms (#6134, #6634, #7120, and #7620) were originally category 5 and 6 staterooms—they have plexiglass railings and partially obstructed views due to the hull design, and their verandahs aren't enclosed like the other category 7 rooms.

Disney Magic Navigator's Verandah

Disney Wonder Navigator's Verandah

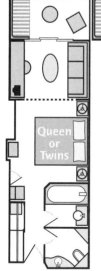

Note that the Navigator's Verandah on the Disney Wonder sports a larger porthole, while the Magic's is a bit smaller. Both have a built-in, padded bench, a chair, and a small table.

Our category 7 stateroom was cozy and comfortable

© MediaMarx, Inc.

The enclosed navigator's verandah

Dave loves the built-in bench

© MediaMarx, Inc.

Introduction · Reservations · Staterooms · Dining · Activities · Ports of Call · Magic · Index

Outside Staterooms With Portholes
(categories 8 and 9)

Affordable elegance is yours if you choose a porthole over a verandah. As one of the most popular categories for cruisers, these rooms make up 27% of the staterooms onboard. They're located on decks 1, 2, 5, 6, and 7.

The only real differences between these two categories are location and price—category 8 staterooms are on higher decks and cost more, while category 9 staterooms are lower in both regards. Their floor space and room layouts are identical. Both categories are considered "deluxe," which simply means they have the split bath (see page 98). Both are approximately 214 sq.ft. (20 sq.m.) and feature the sitting area in the rear of the stateroom. The natural light of the porthole is a real bonus over inside staterooms, especially for kids. We've included the layout for these staterooms on the next page.

Baby Alexander enjoys our category 9 stateroom

Note that the portholes on deck 1 differ from those on the higher decks. Photographs of the two different styles of portholes are shown below. We've stayed in rooms with both types, and we prefer the larger porthole.

Deck 1 portholes

Deck 2 and up porthole

Category 8 and 9 Staterooms
(sleeps 2-4)

There are only 60 **category 8 staterooms**, scattered among decks 5-7 forward. This is due to the hull design of the ship, which features portholes rather than verandahs near the ship's bow. Staterooms on deck 5 are convenient to the kid's clubs. The fact that these staterooms are directly over the Walt Disney Theatre shouldn't be a problem—you aren't likely to be in your room during a show. Staterooms on decks 6 and 7 are excellent, by all accounts. Note that two category 8 rooms are handicap-accessible (#6000 and #6500). **Category 9 staterooms** are limited to decks 1 and 2. In general, we don't recommend deck 1 because it only has access to the forward and midship elevators and stairs, making it harder to get around. Additionally, staterooms #1030-1037 are fairly noisy on port days, which may be bothersome. Perhaps more importantly, the outside staterooms on deck 1 have two small portholes, rather than the one large porthole found on the other decks. We stayed in stateroom #1044 (deck 1) on our first cruise and liked it well enough, but we much prefer the staterooms we've had on deck 2. That said, there are certainly some staterooms that are better than others on deck 2. Due to fairly constant noise and vibration, we recommend you avoid these staterooms: #2000-2004, #2036-2044, #2078-2096, #2114-2129, #2140-2152, #2500-2508, #2586-2600, #2626, and #2630-2653. Unless you need connecting rooms, we recommend you avoid them (38 of the 177 category 9 staterooms are connecting) due to noise from the connecting stateroom. Our family stayed in rooms #2610-2616 on one cruise and we loved them—quiet and convenient (near the aft elevators and stairs).

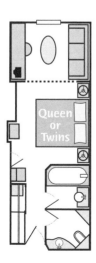

© MediaMarx, Inc.

Relaxing in our category 8 stateroom with a porthole (#7514)

Inside Staterooms
(categories 10, 11, and 12)

Resplendent with the same luxurious decor found in the other staterooms, inside staterooms are smaller and more affordable versions of the higher categories. Inside staterooms make up 29% of the staterooms onboard and are located on decks 1, 2, 5, 6, and 7 (all above the waterline).

AMENITIES

Inside staterooms come in three price categories, but in only two layouts—categories 11 and 12 have identical layouts. Category 10 is the Deluxe Inside Stateroom and is 214 sq. ft. (20 sq. m.) with a split bath (see below). Categories 11 and 12 are the Standard Inside Staterooms at 184 sq. ft. (17 sq. m.). Beyond the size and the split bath, there's little difference. All three categories of staterooms put the sitting area before the sleeping area, presumably because without a window there's no need to have the sitting area at the farthest end of the stateroom. One notable difference between category 10 and 11/12 is the orientation of the bed (see room layout diagrams on following pages). It is also important to note that none of the staterooms in categories 11/12 have connecting rooms, while many of the category 10 staterooms are connecting. The lack of a connecting door makes for a subtle difference in room layout.

The split bathroom found in category 10 (as well as 4–9) is convenient for families.

The toilet/sink room | The shower/tub/sink room

The one-room bathroom in categories 11 and 12 is much more compact. We show two views: a regular bathroom and a handicapped bathroom.

A category 11/12 bathroom | A cat. 11 handicapped bathroom

Category 10 Staterooms
(Deluxe Inside Stateroom—sleeps 4 guests)

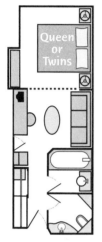

Inside staterooms are scattered over five decks of the ship. The 96 **category 10 staterooms** occupy four decks: 1, 2, 5, and 7. The staterooms on deck 1 are our least favorite because the corridor doesn't run the entire length of the deck, making it harder to reach destinations in the aft of the ship. Many of the staterooms on deck 2 are immediately below noisy places. To avoid noises from above, try for odd-numbered staterooms between #2071-2075, #2571-2575, #2101-2111, #2601-2611, #2629-2635, and #2129-2135. We also recommend the staterooms on deck 7. You should also note that almost half of the category 10 staterooms have connecting rooms, unlike the category 11 and 12 staterooms, which have none. Get a category 10 if you're traveling with a large family or friends and want connecting rooms. If you have booked only one stateroom, however, our advice is to avoid these connecting rooms. Many cruisers have reported that the connecting doors do not dampen noise well. Try to swing a category 10 on deck 5 (#5020, #5022, #5024, #5520, #5522, or #5524) with a partially obstructed, "secret" porthole—see the next page for details. All category 10 staterooms sleep up to four guests.

© MediaMarx, Inc.

A cat. 10 inside stateroom with a round mirror on the far wall

Outside or Inside Stateroom?

There's no easy answer to this question. Each choice affects your cruise experience, but not necessarily in the ways you may think. First off, no matter where you sleep, it won't affect your status with fellow cruisers or staff—everyone receives the same quality of service. What does change is how much time you're likely to spend in your stateroom. Verandahs encourage folks to stay in their staterooms, while inside rooms push you out-of-doors to enjoy the sun, stars, and ocean breezes. With a ship full of attractive public spaces, there's nothing wrong with spending less time in your room. And a cheaper room can mean having more to spend on once-in-a-lifetime shore excursions, the deluxe wine package, or shopping in port. But then there are those magical, early morning moments in your bathrobe on the verandah while everyone else is asleep, reading a good novel and sipping room service coffee. We haven't made your choice any easier, have we? Maybe you can compromise with a picture-window-sized porthole?

Introduction · Reservations · Staterooms · Dining · Activities · Ports of Call · Magic · Index

Special Category 10 Staterooms
("Secret Porthole"—sleeps 4 guests)

Six of the category 10 staterooms (see previous page) have a different layout—and a porthole! Now before you get too excited, the porthole has an obstructed view (see photo below), but most cruisers are delighted with these "secret porthole rooms." We've included the layout for these special staterooms below as well—they were once category 9 staterooms, but were later reclassified as category 10 because of the obstructions. These six special category 10 staterooms are all located on deck 5 (#5020, #5022, #5024, #5520, #5522, or #5524), and all sleep up to four guests.

Getting one of these special category 10 staterooms can be difficult. You can simply try checking with Disney Cruise Line or your travel agent to see if one of these staterooms are available for your cruise (use the

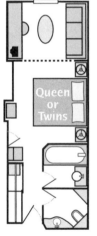

stateroom numbers noted above). You can also use the Internet to find out which staterooms are still available for your cruise—then if you find that one of these coveted secret porthole staterooms is available, book that cruise before someone else books it. See page 90 to learn how to determine which staterooms are still available for your cruise.

If you're considering a "secret porthole" stateroom but aren't sure how you feel about the obstructed view, we refer you to the excellent Platinum Castaway Club web site (http://www.castawayclub.com), which has photos of each of the six "secret portholes" so you can judge for yourself. Just click on the "Secret Porthole Rooms" link in the left column to get the photos and a list of pros and cons to help you make your decision.

© MediaMarx, Inc.

A "secret porthole" stateroom (#5024)   Another view of this category

Category 11 and 12 Staterooms

(Standard Inside Stateroom—sleeps 3-4 guests)

The 147 **category 11 staterooms** are located on decks 5, 6, and 7, making them convenient to many destinations within the ship. We recommend the aft staterooms due to their convenience to food and relative quiet. Families with young children may prefer a stateroom on deck 5 for quick access to the movie theater and Oceaneer Club/Lab. Aft staterooms on deck 7 are just down the hall from a secluded, public deck. Category 11 staterooms are also the only ones in this group to offer handicap-accessible rooms (#6147, #6647, #7131, and #7631—see photos below). Staterooms #6002, #6004, #6502, and #6504 are on the ship's outer side, but they have no portholes. There are 18 category 11 staterooms on decks 5 and 6 which have an alternate, "sideways" layout—some cruisers find them a touch roomier. Category 12 staterooms only sleep up to 3 guests, but you can book them for 4 guests and get an automatic upgrade.

A handicap-accessible, category 11 inside stateroom (6647)

Another view of stateroom 6647, a handicap-accessible category 11 room

Category 12 staterooms (all 13 of them) are on deck 2 forward. While the staterooms closer to the elevators and stairs are convenient, they are also noisier (they are directly below Beat Street/Route 66). Request another stateroom for less noise.

A standard category 11/12 inside stateroom

Stateroom Amenities and Services

Bathrooms—All staterooms have their own bathrooms, while categories 4-10 have innovative split bathrooms with a sink/toilet in one small room, and a second sink plus tub/shower in another room—see page 98. Plush bath towels and bath sheets are provided. We love the split bathrooms—it makes getting ready much easier. Note that the light switches are located outside the bathrooms—remember to turn them on before you enter!

Beds—Every room has a Sealy Posturepedic Premium Plush Euro-top bed with 300 thread-count Egyptian cotton sheets. The comfy queen-size beds can be unlocked and separated into two twin-size beds by your stateroom host/hostess if needed. Most staterooms also have a twin-size, convertible sofa (72"/183 cm. long). Category 3 has a double-size convertible sofa instead. Many rooms have a pull-down, twin-size upper berth (72"/183 cm. long with a weight limit of 220 lbs./100 kg.) with safety rails. Category 4 has an extra twin-size bed.

Closets—Every stateroom has a roomy closet with a clothes rod, a dozen or so hangers, a set of drawers, a safe, your life jackets, and an overhead light (that turns on automatically when you open the closet). If you don't have enough hangers, ask your stateroom host/hostess for more.

Cribs—Portable, "pack-n-play" cribs are available, as are bed safety rails—request when reserving. High chairs are also provided in the dining areas.

Electrical Outlets—Staterooms are outfitted with four standard U.S. 110v, three-pronged electrical outlets: two near the desk/vanity and two behind the TV. Two special outlets—one in each bathroom—are marked "for shavers only" and have a standard

A pack-n-play crib in a stateroom

U.S. 110v, two-pronged outlet along with a European 220v outlet (20 watts/20VA max.). You can't plug your hair dryer into these outlets, but electric toothbrushes should be OK. There's no outlet near the bed, so bring an extension cord or power strip if necessary.

Hair Dryers—Attached to the wall of the bathroom in each stateroom. They aren't terribly high-powered, though, so you may want to bring your own if you are particular about drying your hair.

Internet Access—Wireless Internet access is now available in staterooms onboard, as well as in many public areas. For details, see page 107.

Laundry—Self-service laundries are available, as is valet laundry service, dry cleaning, and pressing. The three laundry rooms onboard are located across the hall from staterooms #2096, #6588, and #7590. Each laundry has several stacked washer/dryers ($1.00), two irons and boards (no charge), detergent vending machine ($1.00), change machine, and table. Estimate $3.00 for a full load of laundry. Use four quarters for the washer (38 minutes), and use eight quarters to get clothes fully dry (48 minutes for $2.00). If you plan to do laundry, pack some detergent and a mesh bag to tote your items. Plan to visit in the mornings—afternoons are very busy. We do not recommend you bring your own iron or steamer as their use is prohibited in the staterooms for safety reasons.

An onboard laundry (the iron is in the back)

Lights—The staterooms are well illuminated, but it can get pitch black in your room when you turn off the lights (especially the staterooms without a porthole). If you need it, bring a nightlight, leave the bathroom light on, or open your closet door a crack to trigger its automatic light.

Luggage—Once you've unpacked, you can store your empty luggage in the closet, slide it under the bed (it has a 9"/23 cm. clearance—lift up the bed and put the luggage underneath if you can't slide it), or ask your stateroom host/hostess if they can store your luggage (this is not always an option). You'll have plenty of drawers to unpack your belongings—we counted more than 20 drawers and shelves in our inside stateroom!

Messages—There are a variety of ways to leave and retrieve messages. First, the phone system allows you to call staterooms directly (dial 7 + the stateroom number) and leave voice mail messages. To check and retrieve your messages, just pick up the phone and press the "Messages" button. If you have messages, the light on your phone will blink until you listen to them. See page 106 for more details on the voice mail. For a lower-tech message system, a decorative fish ornament outside your door serves as a message holder—you may find messages from crew members or fellow passengers. Third, we recommend you pack a pad of sticky notes—these are handy for messages to your cabinmates!

Phones—All staterooms have phones. For the most part, you'll use your phone to call other staterooms, room service, guest services, and other places on the ship. You can call locations off the ship for $6.95/minute at ship-to-shore rates (Disney uses SeaMobile—http://www.seamobile.com). You cannot call toll-free numbers from your stateroom phone, nor can you use calling cards. If someone needs to reach you while you're on the cruise, they can call toll-free 888-DCATSEA (callers from outside the United States can call +1-732-335-3281). Regardless of which number your caller uses, they will be prompted for a major credit card number. Your caller's card will be charged $6.95 for each minute the call is connected. A less expensive option may be to use your cell phone in your stateroom—see page 107 for details. Another possibility is to use your cell phone when in port and when sailing past islands with cell service (you'll need international roaming) or use a pay phone in port (bring calling cards). Castaway Cay has neither pay phones nor cellular coverage, however.

Refrigerator—While it may be best described as a beverage cooler, there is a small refrigerator in the sitting area of your stateroom. It's cool enough to chill your drinks (roughly 55° F/13° C). It is large enough (8"d x 12"w x 16.5"h, or 20.3 cm. x 30.5 cm. x 50 cm.) to store several bottles of water, cans of soda/beer, and a bottle of wine or champagne. It seems to work best when it's 3/4 full. There's also an ice bucket in the room, and you may request ice for it.

© MediaMarx, Inc.

A stateroom refrigerator

Room Service—Free room service is available 24 hours a day for most of your cruise. For details, see page 129. When your food arrives, raise your coffee table (it adjusts like an office chair), and use it as a dining table.

© MediaMarx, Inc.

A stateroom safe

Safes—Every stateroom has its own safe—they are roughly shoebox-sized (9"d x 6.5"h x 14"w, or 22.9 cm. x 16.5 cm. x 35.6 cm.) and located in the closet. To lock the safe, swipe your Key to the World card through the mechanism. Note that you must use the same card to unlock the safe. Tip: Use another card with a magnetic strip (any will work) to lock/unlock the safe, then hide the card in the room so anyone in your party can access the safe.

Stateroom Amenities and Services *(continued)*

Special Needs—Handicap-accessible, barrier-free staterooms (16 total available in categories 3, 5, 6, 8, and 11) are larger—see photos on page 101. Special features include open bed frames, ramped bathroom thresholds, fold-down shower seats, rails, emergency call buttons, and lowered bars. To reserve a handicap-accessible stateroom, call Disney and request the special medical form. Guests with young kids may request bed railings, pack-and-play cribs, and high chairs from the stateroom host/hostess. Strollers are available on a first-come, first-served basis from Guest Services, as are wheelchairs for emergencies. If you need a wheelchair while onboard or in ports, bring your own or rent one through Brevard Medical Equipment with delivery and pickup right at the ship (866-416-7383 or http://www. brevardmedicalequip.com). Beach wheelchairs are available on a first-come basis at Castaway Cay. Much more information on special needs onboard is available in *PassPorter's Open Mouse for Walt Disney World and the Disney Cruise Line* (see page 348).

A roll-in shower with rails, fold-down seat, and call button

Stateroom Host/Hostess—This crew member attends to all of your stateroom needs. Your stateroom host/hostess will tidy your stateroom once during the day and again in the evening while you're at dinner (turndown), but does not bring ice unless you request it. If you want ice, look for a small card from your stateroom host/hostess, tick the appropriate checkbox to request ice, and leave the card out in plain sight. See page 321 for details on gratuities.

A stateroom TV

Television—All staterooms have 13" televisions with remote control, and categories 1 and 2 have multiple televisions. A channel listing with movie schedules is provided in your stateroom upon arrival (see page 156 for a typical channel listing). Channels may change as you sail, especially when you're in port—expect to see some international networks show up on a channel or two. Special channels offer cruise details, such as "What's Afloat" and onboard shows. Recordings of the special talks on golf, shore excursions, shopping, and debarkation are also broadcast on your TV. Check channel 13 to trace your voyage's progress and channel 12 for bridge reports and views, including the current time, weather conditions, etc. You can use the TV as a wake-up "alarm" by setting it to turn on at a certain time—just be sure you set it to a channel that always has sound (avoid the movie channels). Here's how we set the alarm on our stateroom's television: menu → setup → alarm → use volume buttons to set time.

Temperature—Every stateroom has individual climate controls. The thermostat is normally located near the bed, high on the wall. If you get cold at night, there is an extra blanket—it's usually stored in the cupboard above the TV. You may want to consider bringing a small, portable fan, especially if you are staying in an inside stateroom. The staterooms can get very humid and warm when several people take showers in quick succession.

Toiletries—Your stateroom is stocked with H2O Plus Spa products, including Sea Marine Revitalizing Shampoo, Marine Collagen Conditioner, and Hydrating Body Butter, (all in generous 2.7-oz. size containers) plus Spa Facial Bar Soap (1.5 oz). Bath soap, tissues, and toilet paper are also provided. The suites offer upgraded toiletries, including H2O Sea Salt Body Wash and Solar Relief Gel. For details on the products, see http://www.h2oplus.com.

The generously sized toiletries

Towel Animal—Don't be surprised to see a towel imaginatively folded and twisted into the shape of an animal on your bed at the end of the day. Disney's stateroom hosts and hostesses regularly create these "magical touches" for guests to discover in their staterooms. And if you have some props lying around, such as sunglasses, hats, or stuffed animals, your towel animal may become even more embellished. (Towel animal creation is up to the host or hostess, and there may be some that can't make them.) If towel animals interest you, look to see if a towel animal class is being offered in your *Personal Navigator*.

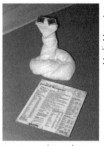

A towel "snake"

Will I Get a Free Upgrade?

Who wouldn't want a free upgrade to a "better" stateroom? It's the kind of perk that everyone wants, and plenty of cruisers look for ways to improve their chances of winning this particular lottery. Unfortunately, in all our time cruising, we've never discovered a foolproof "system." And since upgrades are so unpredictable, our most important advice is this: Never, never book a room you won't be happy to spend your cruise in, should a hoped-for upgrade never materialize.

- Most upgrades occur well in advance of your cruise, as Disney tries to maximize occupancy on the ship. In fact, those upgrades often go completely unheralded. Look closely at your cruise documents when they arrive—if those stateroom numbers don't match your earlier reservation documents, check our chart on the next two pages—you've probably been upgraded! Other cruisers have been delighted to learn they've been upgraded when they check in at the terminal. You may be able to purchase an upgrade at check-in, too—just ask.

- Disney sometimes offers "guaranteed" staterooms—you're guaranteed to receive a stateroom in a particular or better category, but you won't be able to reserve a specific stateroom number or location. In exchange for giving the cruise line the flexibility to locate you wherever they please, you may get an upgrade.

- Disney may want to create vacancies in the lower-priced categories, which tend to sell better at the last minute than the higher-priced rooms. If someone is going to get that vacant verandah stateroom at a bargain price, it'll be someone who booked well in advance. Some folks intentionally "under-book" in the lowest categories in hopes of an upgrade, but again, be sure you'll be happy in a Cat. 12 stateroom.

- On longer cruises, there's higher demand for verandah staterooms and less for inside staterooms, so your chances of an upgrade from inside to outside may be quite low. If they need to "clear space" at all, the upgrade may go from verandah to suite.

- Off-season travelers may hope for an upgrade because there will be more vacancies aboard, but on the flip side, if Disney doesn't have to move you to make room for someone else, then you won't be going anywhere.

Stateroom Amenities and Services *(continued)*

Verandahs—All staterooms in categories 7 and up have a private verandah. A heavy, sliding glass door opens to reveal a deck as wide as your stateroom. Dividers offer privacy from your neighbors and the deck overhead protects you from most of the elements. The sliding door has a child-proof latch that can be difficult to open at first—the trick is to grasp the handle and pull hard without turning. Turn the handle horizontally to lock the sliding door. Two plastic/fabric chairs and a small table are on the verandah, along with an ashtray and two deck lights (the light switch is inside the stateroom, somewhat concealed by the curtains). The deck can be slippery, and the railing can be sticky from salty, moist air. Most verandahs have a clear plexiglass-and-metal railing that you can see through, while some staterooms in the aft have a solid railing—see photos on page 92. If you leave your verandah door open, your room will get warm and muggy quickly. Parents should <u>always supervise children when they're on the verandah</u>. On our recent trip, our three-year-old Alexander was able to climb up onto the arm of a deck chair within seconds—it's a very good thing we were right there to get him down! If you are concerned about kids climbing on the deck furniture, you may ask to have it removed.

Voice Mail—As previously mentioned on page 103, each stateroom has its own voice mail. A red light on your phone will blink when you have message—to check your message(s), just pick up the phone and press the "Messages" button. You can also personalize your outgoing message by following the prompts when you click "Messages." If you are on the phone when a call comes in, the voice mail system still takes your caller's message. We use the voice mail system quite a bit to stay in touch with one another—it's easy to pick up a "house phone" anywhere on board to leave a message with details on where we are and what we're doing. You'll probably get a voice mail from a crew member at the beginning and/or end of your cruise, thanking you for cruising with Disney.

Wake-Up Calls—A clock is provided in your stateroom, but it does not have a lighted dial or numbers. You may prefer to set wake-up calls from your stateroom phone. Try it at least once—Mickey Mouse himself calls you! Alternatives to the wake-up call service are to bring your own travel alarm clock, set the alarm on a portable electronic device you may have brought with you (such as a laptop, iPod, or iPhone), set the alarm on your television (see page 104), or preorder room service for breakfast (a crew member may even give you a reminder call before delivery).

Fitting In

If you're packing a lot of stuff, or just packing a lot of people in your stateroom, you may find yourself a bit crowded. Where do you put all your stuff? We suggest you unpack everything you'll use into the available drawers and cupboards. Use all the hangers in your closet, too. Put your suitcases under the bed, along with anything else you don't need on a daily basis. Need more space? Take the blanket out of the cupboard over the TV, drape it across the sofa, and use the spacious cupboard for storage. You may be able to squeeze a few things on the top shelf in the closet, but don't move the life jackets. If you have something bulky like a car seat, it may fit in the space under the desk area. After this, you can get creative with hanging organizer bags in the closet and on the back of the bathroom door. We also recommend suction cup hooks for hanging items on the back of the stateroom door and in the bathrooms. Strollers can be challenging—we suggest you bring a folding, umbrella stroller and keep it folded in the closet when not in use. You may or may not be able to leave a stroller in the hallway—it depends on where your stateroom is located and if there's space available.

Staying Connected in Your Stateroom

In 2007, Disney Cruise Line made it much easier to stay connected while in your stateroom by adding stateroom wireless Internet access and cell phone usage. We've used both and can offer tips for you to get the most out of your money and time.

© MediaMarx, Inc.

Our laptop connected!

Stateroom Wireless (WiFi) Internet Access— Most staterooms on both the Disney Magic and Wonder now have wireless (wifi) access. In practice, we found the service to be spotty or sluggish, especially during peak usage times. If you need the best connection, you'll still want to go out to one of the "hot spots" (we recommend deck 4 or deck 5 midship)—see pages 158-159 for details. But if you tend to check your mail late at night before bed, stateroom Internet access is extremely convenient. As for which staterooms have the best access, it's hard to say without testing each one. On our recent cruise, we were in stateroom 6634 and we had spotty service. When our reception seemed bad, we walked down one flight of stairs to deck 5 midship, where it was quite strong.

Stateroom Cell Phone Usage— Disney has enabled cell phone usage in your stateroom! Once your ship is 8-10 miles out to sea, the Wireless Maritime Services (WMS) kick in and allow cell phone usage, but only in your stateroom. This "Cellular at Sea" service is generally available with most major cell phone carriers (such as AT&T, Verizon Wireless, Sprint, T-Mobile, Alltel, etc.), and your carrier bills you directly. No cell phone charges will appear from Disney on your cruise bill. If you plan to use your cell phone at sea, call your provider before leaving to check on rates and find out what is needed (such as international roaming). Don't assume that your cell phone won't work without international roaming turned on, however. To avoid any charges you were not expecting, turn off your cell phone and any other wireless devices while you're on your cruise (you could also use "airplane mode"). We tested the service on our recent cruise and discovered that we were able to make a call from our stateroom without having turned on international roaming. When we checked our bill upon returning home, AT&T had charged us $2.50/minute. The charge appeared on our bill immediately, but we have heard that these special usage charges can take up to 90 days to appear on a bill. Note that these cellular services are disabled while in a port, but you may be able to make cell phone calls using the port's cellular networks anyway. Look for a brochure in your stateroom which explains the current Cellular at Sea service in detail.

I Cruise, iPhone

Yes, we have an iPhone ... and we successfully used it on our most recent cruise in December 2007. If you have one of these extremely handy devices, you should know that you probably don't need to specifically enable international roaming to send and receive cell calls while at sea. Thus, put your iPhone in "Airplane Mode" to avoid problems such as incoming calls, e-mail auto-checks, or weather checks. On the other hand, you can use Disney's wi-fi network on your iPhone if you wish—you'll need to take it out of Airplane Mode, turn on WiFi, locate the "MTN-DSI" network and connect to it (don't connect to the crew network—that will cause login problems later), then go to Safari and log in as you would if you were on a laptop. When you're done, put your iPhone back in Airplane Mode. More tips at http://www.passporter.com/iphone.asp.

Stateroom Details

Connecting Rooms	
2038 ⌐ or	2120
2039	**2122** ⌐
2040 ⌐	**2124** ⌐

This chart lists every stateroom, organized by room number, with each room's category and its sleeping capacity. Handicap rooms are marked "H." Connecting rooms are in bold and bracketed. Even numbers are outside rooms; odds are inside. Capacity of rooms marked "3/4" could not be confirmed and may sleep either 3 or 4. Discrepancies exist between this and Disney's cruise brochure, but we've taken pains to make this more accurate. Due to ship capacity regulations, Disney may limit the number of guests in any room at the time of booking, regardless of the room's maximum capacity. However, if your party is booked into a particular room, you can rest assured that room will hold everyone in your party. In the event of confusion, call Disney at 888-DCL-2500.

Room #	Cat.	Sleeps	Room #	Cat.	Sleeps	Room #	Cat.	Sleeps	Room #	Cat.	Sleeps	Room #	Cat.	Sleeps	Room #	Cat.	Sleeps
Deck 1			2028	9	4	2116	9	4	2545	10	4	**2638**	9	4	5514	8	4
1030	9	4	**2030**	9	4	2118	9	4	2546	9	3	2639	10	4	5516	8	4
1032	9	4	**2032**	9	4	2120	9	3	2547	10	4	**2640**	9	4	5518	8	4
1034	9	4	2034	9	4	**2122**	9	4	2548	9	3	2641	10	4	5520	10	4
1036	9	4	2035	10	4	**2124**	9	4	2550	9	3	2642	9	4	**5522**	10	4
1037	10	4	2036	9	4	2126	9	4	2552	9	3	**2643**	10	4	**5524**	10	4
1038	9	4	2037	10	4	2128	9	4	2554	9	3	2644	9	4	5622	6	3
1039	10	4	**2038**	9	4	2129	10	4	2556	9	3	**2645**	10	4	5624	6	3
1040	10	4	2039	10	4	2130	9	4	2558	9	3	**2646**	9	4	5626	6	3
1041	10	4	**2040**	9	3/4	2131	10	4	2560	9	3	2647	10	4	5627	11	3
1042	9	4	2041	10	4	2132	9	4	2562	9	3	**2648**	9	4	5628	6	3
1043	10	4	2042	9	3	2133	10	4	2564	9	3	2650	9	4	5629	11	3
1044	9	4	2043	10	4	2134	9	4	2566	9	3	2652	9	4	5630	6	3
1045	10	4	2044	9	3/4	**2135**	10	4	2568	9	3	2653	10	4	5631	11	3
1046	9	4	2045	10	4	2136	9	4	2570	9	3	**Deck 5**			5632	7	3
1047	10	4	2046	9	3	**2137**	10	4	2571	10	4	5000	8	4	5633	11	3
1048	9	4	2047	10	4	**2138**	9	4	2572	9	3	5001	11	4	5634	7	3
1049	10	4	2048	9	3	2139	10	4	**2573**	10	4	5002	8	4	5635	11	3
1050	9	4	2050	9	3	**2140**	9	4	2574	9	3	5004	8	4	5636	7	3
1051	10	4	2052	9	3	2141	9	4	**2575**	10	4	5005	11	4	5637	11	3
1052	9	4	2054	9	3	2142	9	4	2576	9	3	5006	8	4	5638	7	3
1053	10	4	2056	9	3	**2143**	10	4	**2577**	10	4	5008	11	4	5639	11	3
1054	9	4	2058	9	3	2144	9	4	2578	9	3	5009	11	4	5640	7	3
1056	9	4	2060	9	3	**2145**	10	4	**2579**	10	4	5010	8	4	5642	6	3
1058	9	4	2062	9	3	**2146**	9	4	2580	9	3	5012	11	4	5644	6	3
1060	9	4	2064	9	3	2147	10	4	**2581**	10	4	5013	11	4	5646	6	3
1062	9	4	2066	9	3	**2148**	9	4	2582	9	3	5014	8	4	5648	6	3
1064	9	4	2068	9	3	2150	9	4	**2583**	10	4	5016	8	4	5650	6	3
1065	10	4	2070	9	3	2152	9	4	2584	9	3	5018	8	4	**Deck 6**		
1066	9	4	**2071**	10	4	2153	10	4	**2585**	10	4	**5022**	10	4	6000	8	2H
1067	10	4	2072	9	3	2500	9	4	2586	9	3	**5024**	10	4	6002	11	3
1068	9	4	**2073**	10	4	2502	9	4	2588	9	3	5122	6	3	6003	11	3
1069	10	4	2074	9	3	2504	9	4	2590	9	3	5124	6	3	6004	11	4
1070	9	4	**2075**	10	4	2506	9	4	2592	9	3	5126	6	3	6006	8	4
1071	10	4	2076	9	3	2508	9	4	**2594**	9	3	5127	11	3	6007	11	3
1072	9	4	**2077**	10	4	2509	12	3	**2596**	9	3	5128	6	3	6008	8	4
1073	10	4	2078	9	3	2510	9	4	2598	9	3	5129	11	3	6010	8	4
1074	9	4	**2079**	10	4	2511	12	3	2600	9	3	5130	6	3	6011	11	3
1075	10	4	2080	9	3	2512	9	4	2601	10	4	5131	11	3	6012	8	4
1076	9	4	**2081**	10	4	2513	12	3	**2602**	9	3	5132	7	3	6014	8	4
1077	10	4	2082	9	3	2514	9	4	2603	10	4	5133	11	4	6015	11	3
1078	9	4	**2083**	10	4	2515	12	3	**2604**	9	4	5134	7	3	**6016**	8	4
1079	10	4	2084	9	3	2516	9	4	2605	10	4	5135	11	4	**6018**	8	4
Deck 2			**2085**	10	4	2517	12	3	2606	9	4	5136	7	3	6019	11	3
2000	9	4	2086	9	3	**2518**	9	4	**2607**	10	4	5137	11	3	6020	8	4
2002	9	4	2088	9	3	2519	12	3	2608	9	4	5138	7	3	6022	8	4
2004	9	4	2090	9	3	**2520**	9	3/4	**2609**	10	4	5139	11	3	**6024**	8	4
2006	9	4	2092	9	3	2521	12	3	2610	9	4	5140	7	3	**6026**	8	4
2008	9	4	**2094**	9	4	2522	9	4	2611	10	4	5142	6	3	**6028**	8	4
2009	12	3	**2096**	9	3	2524	9	4	2612	9	4	5144	6	3	**6030**	6	4
2010	9	4	2098	9	3	2526	9	4	2614	9	4	5146	6	3	6032	6	4
2011	12	3	2100	9	3	2528	9	4	2616	9	4	5148	6	3	6034	6	4
2012	9	4	2101	10	4	**2530**	9	4	2618	9	4	5150	6	3	**6036**	6	4
2013	12	3	**2102**	9	3	**2532**	9	4	2620	9	4	5500	8	4	6037	11	4
2014	9	4	**2104**	9	4	2534	9	4	**2622**	9	4	5501	11	4	**6038**	6	4
2015	12	3	2105	10	4	2535	10	4	**2624**	9	4	5502	8	4	6039	11	4
2016	9	4	2106	9	3	2536	9	3/4	2626	9	4	5504	8	4	6040	11	4
2017	12	3	**2107**	10	4	2537	10	4	2628	9	4	5505	11	4	6041	11	4
2018	9	4	2108	9	3	**2538**	9	4	2629	10	4	5506	8	4	6042	6	4
2019	12	3	**2109**	10	4	2539	10	4	2630	9	4	5508	11	4	6043	11	4
2020	9	4	2110	9	3	**2540**	9	3/4	2631	10	4	5509	11	4	**6044**	6	4
2021	12	3	2111	10	4	2541	10	4	2632	9	4	5510	8	4	6045	11	4
2022	9	4	2112	9	3	2542	9	3/4	2633	10	4	5512	11	4	**6046**	6	4
2024	9	4	2114	9	4	2543	10	4	**2635**	10	4	5513	11	4	6047	11	4
2026	9	4				2544	9	3	**2637**	10	4				6048	6	4

Room #	Cat.	Sleeps	Room #	Cat.	Sleeps	Room #	Cat.	Sleeps	Room #	Cat.	Sleeps	Room #	Cat.	Sleeps	Room #	Cat.	Sleeps
Deck 6 (continued)			6303	11	3	6599	11	4	7054	5	4	7540	5	4	8040	4	5
6049	11	4	6305	11	3	6600	6	3	7056	5	4	7541	11	4	8042	4	5
6050	6	4	6307	11	3	6601	11	4	7058	5	4	7542	5	4	8044	4	5
6051	11	4	6309	11	3	6602	6	3	7060	5	4	7543	11	4	8046	3	5
6052	6	4	6311	11	3	6603	11	4	7062	5	4	7544	5	4	8048	3	5
6053	11	4	6313	11	3	6604	6	3	7063	11	4	7546	5	4	8050	4	5
6054	6	4	6315	11	3	6605	11	4	7064	5	4	7548	5	4	8052	4	5
6055	11	4	6317	11	3	6606	6	4	7065	11	4	7550	5	4	8054	4	5
6056	6	4	6319	11	3	6607	11	4	7066	5	3	7552	5	4	8056	4	5
6058	6	4	6321	11	3	6608	6	4	7067	11	3	7554	5	4	8058	4	5
6060	6	4	6323	11	3	6609	11	4	7068	5	3	7556	5	4	8060	4	5
6062	6	4	6500	8	2H	6610	6	4	7070	5	3	7558	5	4	8062	4	5
6064	6	4	6502	11	4	6611	11	4	7072	5	3	7560	5	4	8064	4	5
6066	6	4	6503	11	4	6612	6	4	7074	5	4	7562	5	4	8066	4	5
6067	11	4	6504	11	4	6613	11	4	7076	5	4	7563	11	3	8068	4	5
6068	6	4	6506	8	4	6614	6	4	7078	5	4	7564	5	4	8070	4	5
6069	11	4	6507	11	4	6616	6	4	7080	5	4	7565	11	4	8072	4	5
6070	6	3/4	6508	8	4	6618	6	4	7082	5	4	7566	5	3	8074	4	5
6071	11	4	6510	8	4	6620	6	4	7084	5	4	7567	11	3	8076	4	5
6072	6	3	6511	11	3	6622	6	4	7086	5	4	7568	5	3	8078	3	5
6074	6	3	6512	8	4	6624	6	3	7088	5	4	7570	5	3	8080	3	5
6076	6	3	6514	8	4	6626	6	3	7090	5	4	7572	5	3	8082	4	5
6078	6	3	6515	11	3	6628	6	3	7092	5	4	7574	5	3	8084	4	5
6080	6	3	6516	8	4	6630	6	3	7094	5	4	7576	5	3	8086	3	5
6081	11	3	6518	8	4	6631	11	3	7096	5	4	7578	5	3	8088	4	5
6082	6	3	6520	8	4	6632	6	3	7098	5	4	7580	5	4	8090	4	5
6083	11	3	6521	11	3	6633	11	3	7100	5	4	7582	5	4	8092	4	5
6084	6	3	6522	8	4	6634	7	3	7102	5	4	7584	5	4	8094	4	5
6085	11	3	6524	8	4	6635	7	3	7104	5	4	7586	5	4	8100	3	4H
6086	6	3	6526	8	4	6636	7	3	7106	5	4	7588	5	4	8102	3	4H
6087	6	3	6528	6	4	6637	7	3	7108	5	4	7590	5	4	8500	4	5
6088	6	3	6530	6	4	6638	7	3	7110	5	4	7592	5	4	8502	4	5
6089	11	3	6532	6	4	6639	11	3	7112	5	3	7594	5	4	8504	4	5
6090	6	3	6534	6	4	6640	7	3	7114	5	3	7596	5	4	8506	4	5
6092	6	3	6536	6	4	6641	11	3	7116	5	3	7598	5	4	8508	4	5
6094	6	3	6537	11	4	6642	7	3	7118	5	3	7600	5	4	8510	4	5
6096	6	3	6538	6	4	6643	11	3	7119	11	3	7602	5	4	8512	4	5
6098	6	3	6539	11	4	6644	6	3	7120	7	3	7604	5	4	8514	4	5
6099	11	3	6540	6	4	6645	11	3	7121	7	3	7606	5	4	8516	2	7
6100	6	3	6541	11	4	6646	6	3	7122	7	3	7608	5	4	8518	4	5
6101	11	4	6542	11	4	6647	11	3H	7123	11	3	7610	5	4	8520	4	5
6102	6	3	6543	11	4	6648	6	3	7124	7	3	7612	5	3	8522	3	5
6103	11	4	6544	6	4	6650	6	3	7125	7	3	7614	5	3	8524	4	5
6104	6	3	6545	11	4	6652	6	3	7126	7	3	7616	5	3	8526	4	5
6105	11	4	6546	6	4	6654	6	3H	7127	7	3	7618	5	3	8528	4	5
6106	6	4	6547	11	4	Deck 7			7128	7	3	7619	11	3	8530	1	7
6107	11	4	6548	11	4	7000	8	4	7129	11	3	7620	7	3	8532	3	5
6108	11	4	6549	11	4	7001	10	4	7130	5	3	7621	11	3	8534	3	5
6109	11	4	6550	6	4	7002	8	4	7131	11	3H	7622	7	3	8536	4	5
6110	6	4	6551	11	4	7003	10	4	7132	5	3	7623	11	3	8538	4	5
6111	11	4	6552	6	4	7004	8	4	7134	5	3	7624	7	3	8540	4	5
6112	6	4	6553	11	4	7005	10	4	7136	5	4H	7625	7	3	8542	4	5
6113	11	4	6554	6	4	7006	8	4	7138	5	4H	7626	7	3	8544	4	5
6114	6	4	6555	11	4	7007	10	4	7500	8	4	7627	11	3	8546	3	5
6116	6	4	6556	6	4	7008	8	4	7501	10	4	7628	7	3	8548	3	5
6118	6	4	6558	6	4	7009	11	3	7502	8	4	7629	11	3	8550	4	5
6120	6	4	6560	6	4	7010	8	4	7503	10	4	7630	5	3	8552	4	5
6122	6	4	6562	6	4	7012	8	4	7504	8	4	7631	11	3H	8554	4	5
6124	6	3	6564	6	4	7014	8	4	7505	10	4	7632	5	3	8556	4	5
6126	6	3	6566	6	3	7016	5	4	7506	8	4	7634	5	3	8558	4	5
6128	6	3	6567	11	4	7018	5	4	7507	10	4	7636	5	4H	8560	4	5
6130	6	3	6568	6	4	7020	5	4	7508	8	4	7638	5	4H	8562	4	5
6131	11	3	6569	11	4	7022	5	4	7509	10	4	Deck 8			8564	4	5
6132	6	3	6570	6	4	7024	5	4	7510	8	4	8000	4	5	8566	4	5
6133	11	3	6571	11	4	7026	5	4	7512	8	4	8002	4	5	8568	4	5
6134	7	3	6572	6	3	7028	5	4	7514	8	4	8004	4	5	8570	4	5
6135	11	3	6574	6	3	7030	5	4	7516	5	4	8006	4	5	8572	4	5
6136	7	3	6576	6	3	7032	5	4	7518	5	4	8008	4	5	8574	4	5
6137	11	3	6578	6	3	7034	5	4	7520	5	4	8010	4	5	8576	4	5
6138	7	3	6580	6	3	7035	11	4	7522	5	4	8012	4	5	8578	4	5
6139	11	3	6581	11	3	7036	5	4	7524	5	4	8014	4	5	8580	4	5
6140	7	3	6582	6	3	7037	11	4	7526	5	4	8016	2	7	8582	3	5
6141	11	3	6583	11	3	7038	5	4	7528	5	4	8018	4	5	8584	4	5
6142	7	3	6584	6	3	7039	11	4	7530	5	4	8020	4	5	8586	4	5
6143	11	3	6585	11	3	7040	5	4	7532	5	4	8022	3	5	8588	4	5
6144	6	3	6586	6	3	7041	11	4	7534	5	4	8024	4	5	8590	4	5
6145	11	3	6587	11	3	7042	5	4	7535	11	4	8026	4	5	8592	4	5
6146	6	3	6588	6	3	7043	11	4	7536	5	4	8028	4	5	8594	4	5
6147	11	3H	6590	6	3	7044	5	4	7537	11	4	8030	1	7	8596	4	5
6148	6	3	6592	6	3	7046	5	4	7538	5	4	8032	3	5	8598	4	5
6150	6	3	6594	6	3	7048	5	4	7539	11	4	8034	3	5	8600	3	4H
6152	6	3	6596	6	3	7050	5	4				8036	4	5	8602	3	4H
6154	6	3H	6598	6	3	7052	5	4				8038	4	5			

Rocking to Sleep

Sleeping on a moving vessel can be a magical experience. Make more magic in your stateroom with these tips:

- Bring something from home to **personalize your stateroom**, like a photo in a frame, a bouquet of silk flowers, or a radio or CD player. You can also decorate your stateroom door (see page 314).

- **Make every bit of space count!** After you unpack, stash your empty luggage under the bed and use one (or more) suitcases for your dirty laundry and another for souvenirs.

- Consider bringing a **clear shoe organizer** and hanging it up in your closet or on the back of your bathroom door. It keeps all those little items that can clutter your stateroom organized.

- "When considering which stateroom category to book when traveling with a family, consider **two connecting inside staterooms** rather than a family stateroom (category 4). Two connecting staterooms are much less expensive and are better for naps, plus you can get more space overall! Make sure you bring a bungee cord to tie the connecting doors open—they are a bit heavy to stay open with just the door stoppers." – contributed by Disney cruiser Renee Latta

- "My son was used to having a nightlight in his bedroom. I, however, do not sleep well in a room with any kind of light. Our solution was to **bring along glowsticks**. We put one on the bathroom door so that we could find our way through the dark cabin at night. We also put a glow necklace on one of my son's stuffed animals and placed it at the foot of his bed. The glowstick let off enough light to make my son feel secure but yet not enough light to keep me awake at night!" – contributed by Disney cruiser Michelle Spurrier

Magical Memory

- *"I've been on several cruises, but my brother has not ... yet he's always wanted to try a Disney cruise. My brother is single, however, and it's pricey for a single person to cruise. Yet I have two kids and fill up my stateroom, leaving no room for him to tag along. So as a surprise, I booked a category 3 suite stateroom, which has room for up to five persons. I added my brother to the reservation without telling him, though I did subtly check to see if he had a current passport. For Christmas, I gave him a copy of the PassPorter cruise deluxe edition, with our cruise dates filled in and photos of the sumptuous category 3 stateroom slipped in the pockets. He was SO surprised and happy! Now he can't stop talking about our cruise plans and I can't wait to cruise with my little bro."*

...as told by Disney cruiser Christina Robin

Dining on the High Seas

Introduction
Reservations
Staterooms
Dining
Activities
Ports of Call
Magic
Index

Cruises are famous for food—buffet breakfasts, brunches, snacks, pool-side lunches, high tea, elegant dinners, dessert buffets, and room service! You won't be disappointed by the food on the Disney Cruise Line. Sure, there's plenty of it—we like to say, "If you're hungry, you're not trying hard enough." More important, in our opinion, is the quality of the food. As restaurant critics, we pay attention to food—presentation, preparation, quality, and taste. We would grade virtually every dish we tried during our cruises as a B or B+. There were some disappointments, sure, but in general, we've been very happy cruisers with no rumblies in our tummies.

In all fairness, we have heard a few complaints about the food from other cruisers. Some feel there should be even more food offered, like on some other cruise lines. (Our poor waistlines!) Others feel the food options are too exotic for their tastes (and Disney has since added some simpler choices to the menus). Yet others say the food isn't as "gourmet" as some European lines. Most cruisers, however, rave about the food onboard.

Dining options abound during your cruise. For **breakfast**, try room service (available for virtually all meals, plus snacks—see page 129), Topsider's/ Beach Blanket Buffet (page 124), Lumière's/Triton's (pages 115–116), Parrot Cay (pages 119–120), or Palo's Champagne Brunch (pages 121–122). For **lunch**, try Topsider's/Beach Blanket Buffet (page 124), Pluto's Dog House (page 125), Pinocchio's Pizzeria (page 125), Lumière's/Triton's (pages 115–116), or Parrot Cay (pages 119–120). For **snacks**, try Goofy's Galley (page 125), Pluto's Dog House (page 125), or Pinocchio's Pizzeria (page 125). For **dinner**, you may eat in Lumière's/Triton's (pages 115–116), Animator's Palate (pages 117–118), Parrot Cay (pages 119–120), and Palo (pages 117–118). Topsider's/Beach Blanket Buffet (page 124) may also be open for dinner. Theme dinners and dessert buffets are held on special nights (see page 116 and 123). Whew! Read on to learn about Disney's innovative dining rotations and your delicious choices.

Bon appetit!

Rotation Dining

Unlike other ships that stick you in one dining room throughout your cruise, the Disney ships offer **three uniquely themed dining rooms** for all. Your family rotates together through these dining rooms during your cruise, enjoying a different menu each evening. Best of all, your tablemates and servers rotate with you. You can bypass the regular rotation and choose an adults-only restaurant, one of several snack counters, or room service—a buffet restaurant may also be open. You'll find it hard to do them all!

You learn your **dining room rotation** on your first day—look for a set of "tickets" in your stateroom indicating which dining rooms your party is assigned to for dinner on each day. The tickets are not required to dine, but they do help the servers direct you to your table. To learn your dining rotation a bit earlier, check your Key to the World card for a code (i.e., "PTA," "APPT," or "LAPLAPL"), like the one on page 72. This code indicates your rotation: L or T = Lumière's/Triton's, A = Animator's Palate, and P = Parrot Cay. Your rotation is occasionally based on the ages of guests in your party. Rotation dining only applies to dinner, and breakfast on debarkation day—see page 131 for breakfast and lunch. (Tip: Some readers report that Disney told them their dining rotation when they phoned and asked.)

There are **two dinner seatings**: main (first) seating and late (second) seating. Your seating is noted in your cruise documents. Main seating is typically at 5:30 pm, 5:45 pm, or 6:00 pm. Late seating is at 8:00 pm, 8:15 pm, or 8:30 pm. Check your dining tickets for your assigned time, which will remain constant during your cruise. Dinner takes from $1\frac{1}{2}$ to 2 hours to complete. Guests with main seating watch the evening show after dinner, while guests with late seating see the show first. If you have a seating preference (see page 131 for tips), have it noted on your reservation prior to cruising. Parties with kids tend to get assigned the early seating.

Your **assigned table number** is printed on your dinner tickets and your Key to the World card. Your party has the same table number at dinner in all three of the main dining rooms. Like the dining room assignment, table assignments are determined by factors like age and association (i.e., Disney Vacation Club members may be seated together); your stateroom category does not affect your table assignment. You can request to be seated with your traveling companions—call the Disney Cruise Line well ahead of your departure date and have it noted on your reservation. Table sizes range from four to twenty guests, though most tables seat eight guests. If you want to switch to another table or feel uncomfortable with your assigned tablemates, check your *Personal Navigator* for a Dining Assignment Change session (held on your first afternoon) or see your head server.

....➣

Dressing for Dinner

"How should I dress for dinner?" If we had a nickel for everyone who asks! Whether you itch to relive the elegance of days gone by, or can't stand the thought of being bound into a "penguin suit," you'll find a happy welcome on your Disney cruise. Different itineraries call for slightly different wardrobes, as we describe below, and once you're aboard, you can also refer to your Personal Navigator for the evening's suggested dress.

In keeping with its **guest-friendly policies**, Disney doesn't enforce dress codes for the most part. They won't deny you access if you don't have a jacket, though they will ask you to put on shoes or a shirt. Disney requests that you wear shoes and shirts and refrain from wearing bathing attire in the dining rooms. You should also refrain from wearing shorts at dinner, though jeans are okay everywhere but at Palo and formal night.

Three- and Four-Night Itineraries—In Lumière's/Triton's, Animator's Palate, and Parrot Cay in the evening, men wear casual, open-collared shirts (such as polo or camp shirts) and slacks (such as khakis or Dockers), and women wear a blouse and skirt or casual dress. The exception is the "Dress-Up Night" (third night of the three-night cruise and second night of the four-night cruise), for which dressy attire is suggested. For both "Dress-Up Night" and the elegant setting of Palo, jackets and ties are preferred for men, and the ladies are encouraged to don dresses or pantsuits.

Seven-Night and up Itineraries—Dress code for longer itineraries is the same as for the three- and four-night cruises with the exception of the formal nights. There is one formal and one semi-formal night on the seven-night itineraries—see page 312 for details and tips on formal nights.

All Itineraries—On at least one evening, Disney suggests Pirate or Caribbean style dress for its Pirates in the Caribbean night (see page 123). You'll probably find it easiest to dress in a tropical shirt or dress. If you really want to get into the spirit of the occasion, try picking up pirate gear online, at the parks, or at Treasure Ketch. Other things you could do include eyepatches, temporary tattoos, or a costume like Captain Hook.

Disney requests that guests dress for dinner as it sets a **special atmosphere** in the evenings. The Disney vessels are elegant ships—dressing for dinner shows respect for the occasion, the atmosphere, and your fellow guests. We understand that some guests aren't comfortable in a jacket or suit, and that's okay, too—you'll see a wide range of dress, even on formal night. Don't want to change out of those shorts? Snacks are available on deck 9 (see page 125). Topsider's Buffet/Beach Blanket Buffet (deck 9 aft) may also be open for dinner on some evenings for those guests who don't wish to get dressed up.

Special Diets

Guests with **special dietary requirements** of virtually any type (i.e., kosher, low-sodium, allergies, etc.) are accommodated. When you make your reservation, let the representative know about any requirements. The representative notes the information with your reservation and may instruct you to meet with the Food/Beverage team after you board—they are usually available in Rockin' Bar D/WaveBands (deck 3 fwd) from 1:00 pm to 3:30 pm on your first day—check your *Personal Navigator*. The Food/Beverage team gets details from you and passes it on to your servers. We recommend you remind your server of your requests at your first meal. Jennifer is lactose-intolerant and requests soy milk with her meals—the attention to her request is impressive and she is always offered soy milk.

While Disney excels at these special, pre-cruise requests, we found it **more difficult to get a special dish or variant** ordered at meal time. For example, it generally isn't possible to order a dish from the menu and have sauces or dressings kept on the side. This is because the dishes are prepared *en masse* in the kitchen. However, you can order a plain salad or simple entrée (vegetarian, grilled chicken, etc.) without the highfalutin' extras—ask your server. We note the vegetarian items in the menus later in the chapter. Kosher is only available in the table-service restaurants and you should request it in advance to ensure availability.

Will I Gain Weight on My Cruise?

Short answer: No, you don't have to gain weight on your Disney cruise! Long answer: Cruises are renowned for their ability to add inches to your waistline. All that scrumptious, "free" food can send your diet overboard. But if you're determined to maintain your weight and healthy eating habits, it's not at all difficult to do. Your authors successfully maintain their weight on cruises while still enjoying treats. The first key is **moderation**. Eat well—don't restrict yourself too severely and don't overeat. Not only is it okay to sample a little of everything, it's a good idea—if you deny yourself, you'll likely break down halfway through your cruise and eat everything in sight. Remember that just because the food is included with your cruise doesn't mean you have to overindulge. If the temptation seems too great, grab some of the delicious fruit available at Goofy's Galley (deck 9 aft). If you just can't resist that chocolate ice cream cone, order one, eat half, and ditch the rest. You'll also find that buffet meals may actually be easier for you—there are more food choices. The second key to maintaining your weight is **activity**. Most of you will be more active than usual on your cruise—swimming, snorkeling, biking, and walking around the ports. Take advantage of every opportunity to move your body! You can walk a mile every morning around deck 4 (it takes three laps), take the stairs instead of the elevator, and enjoy free exercise classes at the Vista Spa (deck 9 forward). Check your *Personal Navigator* for a session at the Vista Spa that shows you how to lose weight on your cruise, too.

For more tips, surf to: http://www.passporter.com/wdw/healthyeating.htm

Lumière's/Triton's

Have you ever yearned to dine elegantly in a gorgeous, grand dining room aboard a majestic ocean liner? This is your chance. On the Disney Magic, the grandest dining room is known as Lumière's; on the Disney Wonder, it's called Triton's. Both are located next to the ships' breathtaking lobby atriums on deck 3 midship and serve breakfast, lunch, and dinner. Breakfast and lunch have open seating—just show up when and where you like.

Decor—Lumière's (Magic) has a decidedly French flair, just like its namesake, the saucy candelabra in Disney's *Beauty and the Beast*. Rose-petal chandeliers, inlaid marble floors, and graceful columns set the mood for elegance and romance. Large portholes look out to the sea on one side of the restaurant. A mural depicting a waltzing Beauty and her Beast adorns the back wall. Look for the glass domes suspended from the ceiling—inside each is Beast's red rose. Triton's (Wonder) takes you "under the sea" with Ariel's father from Disney's *The Little Mermaid*. The Art Nouveau-inspired dining room is decorated in soft colors with blue glass-and-iron "lilypads" floating on the ceiling. A breathtaking Italian glass mosaic of Triton and Ariel graces the back wall. The lighting changes during the dinner, casting an "under the sea" effect.

Dinner Dress—Unless the evening is formal, semi-formal, or "pirate" (see 123 and 312), dress is upscale casual: jackets are appropriate (but not required) for men and dresses/pantsuits for women. No shorts, please.

Our Review—The very elegant surroundings are the restaurants' best feature. These are the only restaurants offering full table service at breakfast and lunch. The extra attention and elegance at dinner is a treat. Breakfast here is good, but service is slow and the selection is more limited than at Parrot Cay or at Topsider's/ Beach Blanket Buffet. Lunch is enjoyable, though portions may be a bit smaller than you'd expect. Dinner is very elegant and the food is finely prepared. We highly recommend this restaurant over Parrot Cay and Animator's Palate. Jennifer and Dave's rating: 8/10.

Chatting with Chef Levi at Triton's

Introduction

Reservations

Staterooms

Dining

Activities

Ports of Call

Magic

Index

Lumière's/Triton's Sample Menus

While we can't predict exactly what you'll be offered, we can share the menus from past cruises. We've underlined those menu items we and our fellow cruisers have enjoyed and recommend that you try.

Breakfast at Lumière's/Triton's *(menu does not change day to day)*
chilled juices (orange, grapefruit, cranberry, prune, V-8, apple, tomato); **fresh fruit** (grapefruit, melon, banana, fruit cocktail); **yogurt** (fruit and plain yogurt, assorted low-fat yogurt); **hot cereal** (oatmeal, Cream of Wheat); **cold cereal** (Corn Flakes, Raisin Bran, Rice Krispies, Frosted Flakes, low-fat granola, Froot Loops); **Muesli** (mixture of toasted whole grain flakes, oatmeal, raisins, berries, yogurt, milk, and honey); **lox and bagel** (served with cream cheese); **pastries** (Danish pastries, muffins, croissants, bagels, donuts, English muffins, toast—white, wheat, or rye); **preserves** (assorted jellies, jams, marmalades); **chef's selection** (scrambled eggs, bacon, grilled sausage, oven-roasted potatoes or hash browns); **eggs Benedict; eggs to order** (scrambled, fried, poached, or boiled—with oven-roasted potatoes and your choice of breakfast meat: grilled sausage, grilled ham, or bacon); **omelets** (Denver, ham and cheese, plain, Egg Beaters—with potatoes or hash browns); **hot off the griddle** (buttermilk pancakes, blueberry pancakes, French toast, waffles); **beverages** (coffee—regular or decaffeinated, assorted teas, hot chocolate, milk—whole, low-fat, skim, or chocolate).

Note: Triton's breakfast menu changed just as we were going to press, but it remains pretty much the same in essentials—mostly just fancier names for dishes.

Lunch at Lumière's/Triton's *(menu changes daily)*
starters (shrimp cocktail, chips and salsa, roasted vegetable tart, hummus "chickpea" dip, curried pumpkin soup, Roquette salad, or sesame seed tuna); **main courses** (mushroom risotto, classic Reuben sandwich, traditional American meatloaf, broiled filet of tilapia, oven-roasted chicken, or traditional hamburger); **desserts** (banana cream pie, hot apple 'n' pineapple crunch, double chocolate cake, key lime pie, or chef's sugar-free dessert).

Dinner at Lumière's/Triton's *(for your first rotational visit only)*
appetizers (prosciutto cup, shrimp medley, leek and goat cheese quiche, escargot); **soups and salads** (tomato and basil soup, chilled vichyssoise soup, Normandy salad, mixed garden salad); **main courses** (coquilles St. Jacques, Dijon mustard-roasted beef tenderloin, herb-crusted halibut, braised lamb shank, citrus glazed oven-baked duckling, sirloin steak, roasted chicken breast, salmon fillet, or vegetarian selections—rigatoni pasta provençal and stack of vegetables); **desserts** (honey and cinnamon apple tart, Grand Marnier souffle, crème brûlée, white chocolate domes, ice cream sundae, cheese and crackers, or sugar-free dessert—seasonal fruits, chocolate cheesecake, or sugar-free ice cream).

Tip: No matter where you dine, you'll find simpler choices like steak, chicken, and fish.

Dessert Buffets
You've saved room for dessert, right? On select nights of your cruise (any length), a fruit and dessert spread of monumental proportions is laid out for your gastronomic pleasure. Check your *Personal Navigator* for days, times, and locations. A "midnight" dessert buffet is generally held from 10:45 to 11:15 or 11:30 pm on deck 9 on one night (often "Pirate Night"). The seven-night cruises may feature a Gala Dessert Buffet in Lumière's, typically held at night from 11:15 pm to 12:15 am on the last at-sea day. The line can get long at the dessert buffets—to avoid a long wait, arrive just as it begins. Desserts vary, but typical treats include crepes, cheesecakes, tortes, pies, cookies, and pastries.

Animator's Palate

Disney's true colors shine in this imaginative, $4.3 million restaurant. Animator's Palate—which serves dinner only—is located on deck 4 aft.

Decor—Entering the large, windowless restaurant feels a bit like walking into a black-and-white sketchpad. The tables and chairs are black and white, and the walls are covered in line drawings of classic Disney animated characters. Where's all the color? Don't worry—it's coming, along with your food. As each course is served, color is added to the walls and ceilings, and the characters come to life in full color. There's a colorful surprise at the end, but we won't give it away. This production is limited to the first, second, and third nights; on subsequent evenings, the room remains black and white (this is a good time to visit Palo—see page 121).

Dress—Unless the evening is formal, semi-formal, or "pirate" (see page 123 and 312), dress is resort casual. Polo and camp shirts are fine, but please don't wear shorts in this dining room.

© MediaMarx, Inc.

Animator's Palate on formal night

Our Review—Animator's Palate is a fun place for all ages. The "show" is breathtaking and food is decent. Inventive dishes have an Italian flavor and offer enough choices to please most. Service is fine, though you may feel rushed or stymied as servers need to keep pace with the show. When you arrive at the table, try to pick a seat with a view of one of the video screens on the walls. Jennifer and Dave's rating: 7/10.

Dining Room Etiquette

Don't worry—thanks to Disney's family atmosphere, there's no finicky, starched-up rule of etiquette here. Just remember to arrive on time for dinner, greet your tablemates and servers with a smile, place your napkin in your lap, and have your meal and beverage orders ready for your servers. If the elegant table confuses you, keep in mind that your bread plate is always on the left, your glasses are always on the right, utensils are used from the outside in, and wine glasses are held by the stem for white wine and by the base for red wine. When you get up from the table before you've finished eating, place your napkin on your chair to indicate you will be returning again. At the end of your meal, place your unfolded napkin on the table.

Animator's Palate Sample Menu

Dinner at Animator's Palate *(for your first rotational visit only)*
appetizers (<u>seafood and avocado wrapper</u>, wild garlic mushrooms, smoked salmon, baked stuffed tomato); **soups and salads** (chilled gazpacho, creamy butternut squash soup, confetti tomato salad, Caesar salad); **main courses** (cheese cannelloni, maple-glazed salmon, veal chop encrusted with parmesan, lemon peppered oven baked stuffed chicken, bacon wrapped filet mignon, grilled sirloin steak, roasted chicken breast, salmon fillet, or vegetarian selection—vegetable curry, pasta marinara); **desserts** (strawberry shortcake, Boston cream pie, chocolate and peanut butter pie, double-fudge chocolate cake, ice cream sundae, or sugar-free dessert—seasonal fruits, pound cake, or sugar-free ice cream).

An Armchair Galley Tour

Ever wonder how they prepare all this food and for so many people? Adults on itineraries with at-sea days (four-night and up) usually have the opportunity to take a free galley (kitchen) tour. The 30-minute, adults-only walking tour starts in Lumière's/Triton's, walks through the galley, and ends up on the other side at Parrot Cay. If you won't have the opportunity to experience this behind-the-scenes glimpse into the inner workings, here's a short, armchair version of the galley tour!

The Disney Cruise Line galleys are big, immaculately clean, stainless steel kitchens that gleam with organization. There are six galleys onboard—three main banqueting kitchens, a crew kitchen, Topsider's/Beach Blanket Buffet, and Palo. In these galleys are 9 chefs, 120 cooks, 88 stewards, 12 provision masters, and 150 servers and assistant servers. Galleys are inspected constantly for cleanliness, safety, and temperature requirements— the Captain himself performs inspections. Disney has a shopping list of 30,000 food items for each cruise! When you consider that more than 8,000 cups of coffee and more than 5,000 eggs are served every day, you can imagine how big that grocery bill must be! And all food for your voyage is brought on in your embarkation port—the cruise line is not allowed to take food on in other ports due to FDA regulations.

The first thing you see upon entering the galley are the beverage dispensers—this is how your servers get your drink refills so quickly. Then comes the kids' food station—it's separated from other food prep areas to allow servers to get kids' meals out to the hungry munchkins as soon as possible.

Next we come to the hot food preparation areas of the galley. Did you know that nothing is prepared ahead of time (with the exception of some veggies)? There's a butcher room with four cooks and a fish room with two cooks below decks where the meats are prepared and portioned. The meats are then sent up to the galley to be seasoned and cooked based on each guest's preferences. Once cooked, the plates are cleaned and garnished based on photographs of how each dish should appear (and below each photograph is a list of the dish's ingredients, allowing the servers to spot potential allergens for guests). The servers then come in to pick up the various plates they "ordered" earlier, covering each dish with a warming lid to keep it toasty during its trip to your table. It's quite a production that goes on behind the scenes.

Beyond the hot food prep areas is the pastry prep area. There are four pastry chefs onboard. There's even a 24-hour bakery below decks that keeps churning out fresh baked goods throughout your cruise. And the tour comes to a sweet ending with a chocolate chip cookie for everyone!

© MediaMarx, Inc.

A pastry chef at work

Parrot Cay

This breezy, island-inspired restaurant is the most casual of the three main dining rooms. Parrot Cay (pronounced "key") is on deck 3 aft. The restaurant serves breakfast and lunch, plus dinner with a grillhouse flair. The buffet breakfast and lunch have open seating, often with other cruisers.

Decor—The first thing you may notice is the sound of parrots—they're not real, but they sound like it as you walk through the breezeway and into the restaurant. Inside is a cacophony of colors and sounds, with parrot chandeliers that evoke the Enchanted Tiki Room at Disney's theme parks and lush tropical greens and oranges on the walls and floors. Large portholes line two sides of the restaurant, affording beautiful views.

Dinner Dress—Unless the evening is formal, semi-formal, or "pirate" (see page 123 and 312), dress is resort casual. No shorts at dinner.

Our Review—The grillhouse-inspired menu here is very good and a vast improvement over the old menu. Breakfast and lunch are buffet-style, which just doesn't afford the same elegance you get in Lumière's/Triton's. The food is great, with some stand-out items, and the food variety at the buffet is generous. Most outstanding still, there always seems to be one or two delightful surprises for adventurous diners. They do a good job of keeping the buffet fresh and appealing. A "show" by the servers livens things up at dinner. Alas, Parrot Cay is the noisiest dining room. Jennifer and Dave's rating: 7/10. (This is often the restaurant we skip for Palo.)

© MediaMarx, Inc.

Jennifer enjoys the breakfast buffet at Parrot Cay

Open Seating at Breakfast and Lunch

Breakfast and lunch are usually open seating, meaning you dine where and when you please, and you don't sit at your assigned table—you are seated by a crew member. If you'd like your regular servers at breakfast or lunch, just ask to be seated at their table (if it's available and if they're on duty). Better yet, ask your servers at dinner where they are serving the following day and follow them to that restaurant.

Parrot Cay Sample Menus

Buffet Breakfast at Parrot Cay

You can usually find fresh fruit, cereals (hot and cold), yogurt, smoked salmon, assorted pastries, scrambled eggs, bacon, link sausage, ham, hash browns, pancakes, waffles, or French toast. A made-to-order omelet station is often available.

Character Breakfast at Parrot Cay *(seven-night cruises only; seating at 8:00 or 8:15 am for main seating guests and 9:30 or 9:45 am for those with late seating)*

special Goofy combination plate for children (scrambled eggs, chocolate pancake, Mickey waffle, and Canadian bacon); **chilled juices** (orange, grapefruit, and cranberry); **fresh fruit and yogurt** (sliced fruit, grapefruit, plain and fruit yogurt, and low-fat yogurt); **cereals** (Cream of Wheat, Corn Flakes, Raisin Bran, KO's, Rice Krispie, and Frosted Flakes); **lox and bagel** (served with cream cheese); **pastries** (Danish pastries, muffins, croissants, donuts, and toast—white, wheat, or rye); **express breakfast** (scrambled eggs, bacon, link sausage, and hash browns); **breakfast classics** (scrambled or fried eggs served with hash browns and your choice of bacon, link sausage, or ham); **omelets** (plain or ham and cheese—served with hash browns, Egg Beaters available); **hot off the griddle** (buttermilk pancakes or blueberry pancakes); **beverages** (coffee—regular or decaf, assorted teas, hot chocolate, milk—whole, low-fat, skim, or chocolate); **preserves** (assorted jellies, jams, and marmalades).

Lunch Buffet at Parrot Cay

The buffet on the seven-night cruises changes daily: day one—welcome aboard buffet; day two—Italian buffet; day three—Asian buffet; day four—American buffet; day five—South of the Border buffet; and day six—seafood buffet. On the Disney Wonder, brunch is served until 11:30 am on day two and, on the four-night itinerary, the Oriental buffet is served on day three. On the last day, the menu that is offered at Cookie's BBQ on Castaway Cay is also offered at Parrot Cay onboard the ship (all itineraries).

Dinner at Parrot Cay *(for your first rotational visit only)*

appetizers (quinoa and grilled vegetables, spice island chicken wings, baked crab Martinique, trio of salmon); **soups and salads** (cold cream of mango and papaya soup, cream of sweet onion soup, Parrot Cay salad, mixed island greens, tropical style fruit salad); **main courses** (roasted rib-eye of beef, mixed grill, pan-seared grouper, Caribbean roast chicken, baby back pork ribs, grilled sirloin steak, roasted chicken breast, salmon fillet, or vegetarian selections—gnocchi au gratin with spinach or vegetable strudel); **desserts** (crème brûlée cheesecake, banana bread pudding, lemon meringue pie, chocolate-espresso walnut cake, ice cream sundae, or sugar-free dessert—piña colada bread pudding, cheesecake, or sugar-free ice cream)

Character Breakfast

Seven-night and up cruisers have a special treat—an invitation to a character breakfast in Parrot Cay (see menu above). Typically Mickey, Minnie, Goofy, Pluto, Chip, and Dale show up in tropical garb. The characters put on a show for you and walk through the aisles, but please note that the characters no longer visit each table to greet guests. Expect lots of energy, napkin-waving, character dancing, and loud music. This character meal reminds us of Chef Mickey's at the Contemporary in Walt Disney World. Character breakfasts are offered at two seatings (guests with earlier seating at dinner will have the earlier seating at breakfast). If your dining rotation starts in Animator's Palate, your character breakfast will probably be Sunday morning (Lumière's=Monday morning and Parrot Cay=Thursday morning). Your server may present your tickets on the evening before, or they may be left in your stateroom—bring them with you to breakfast. Your character breakfast's date and time are noted on the tickets.

Palo

Palo is the adults-only restaurant offering Northern Italian cuisine, an intimate setting, phenomenal service, and a 270° view. Unlike the three main dining rooms, adults must secure reservations to dine here and there is a nominal, per-person service charge ($15 for dinner or brunch, $5 for high tea). Palo has its own servers, so be prepared to part with your regular servers for the meal. Palo is on deck 10 aft and serves dinner nightly from 6:00 pm until 9:00 or 10:00 pm. A wine tasting seminar may also be offered here (see page 163), as well as a champagne brunch (four-night and up cruises) and a high tea (seven-night and up cruises—see page 122).

Reservations—Reservations for all Palo meals can and should be made in advance at http://www.disneycruise.com once your cruise is paid in full. Palo reservations can be made from 2 to 75 days in advance for guests in stateroom categories 4-12, from 2 to 90 days in advance for Castaway Club members, and from 2 to 105 days in advance for concierge guests in stateroom categories 1-3 and guests who have reserved the Romantic Escape at Sea package (see page 46). Note that online reservations open at midnight and reservations do go quickly. Only one reservation per stateroom is allowed—we should note this policy may vary from cruise to cruise, as some guests report being able to make a reservation for dinner, brunch, and tea while others (including ourselves) had to choose just one. In the past, you may have been able to dine with guests from another stateroom by reserving a larger table size, but now Disney cross-references you with your friends and will likely block your friends from making their own Palo reservation (this happened to us on our Panama Canal cruise). You may also make reservations and changes on your first afternoon aboard—check the *Personal Navigator* for the time and place. We recommend you send just one person from your party and arrive early—Palo reservations are extremely popular and they go quickly. Know the day(s) you prefer to dine at Palo before arriving (use our worksheet on page 133). Cancel at least six hours before your meal to avoid the charge. If you can't get reservations, get on the wait list and check for cancellations. Guests in suites (cat. 1-3) can ask their concierge to make reservations for them.

Decor—The most striking feature of Palo is its sweeping ocean views—we have fond memories of a meal served just as the sun set. Warm wood paneling, Venetian glass, and smaller tables (yes, you can get a table for two here!) make this the most romantic spot onboard. An exhibition kitchen and wine displays set the stage for a special dining experience. The restaurant also has a private room tucked in the corner for groups.

Dress—Men should wear jackets and ties; women should wear dresses or pantsuits. Formal attire is also welcome. No jeans (this rule is enforced).

Our Review—We simply adore Palo! The servers are friendly, engaging, and incredibly attentive. The restaurant itself is quiet and mellow. The best part of dining at Palo, however, is the food—it's simply outstanding, as items are made or finished to order. We also recommend brunch and high tea. While the service charge is intended to replace the gratuity, an extra tip may be justified. Jennifer and Dave's rating: 9/10.

© MediaMarx, Inc.

Jennifer and Dave dress up for Palo

Introduction

Reservations

Staterooms

Dining

Activities

Ports of Call

Magic

Index

Palo Sample Menus

Dinner at Palo *($15/person service charge; menu doesn't change on repeat visits, but the chefs do try to offer different specials each evening).*

pizzas (margherita, prosciutto, mushroom, white, shrimp, four-cheese, or chef's specialty pizza of the day); **starters and salads** (grilled eggplant, buffalo mozzarella and plum tomatoes, warm shrimp salad, grilled portobello mushroom and polenta, lightly-fried calamari, tuna carpaccio, arugula salad; **soup** (minestrone or traditional fish and seafood soup); **main courses** (grilled salmon, pan-fried tuna, halibut al cartoccio, grilled sea scallops, rack of lamb, chicken breast, beef tenderloin, veal loin, penne arrabbiata, lobster ravioli, pumpkin and broccoli gnocchi, bigoli alla contadina, gnocchi florentina, seafood risotto, wild mushroom risotto, or vegetable and bean casserole); **desserts** (tiramisu, panna cotta, chocolate soufflé with vanilla bean sauce, sweet pizza, chocolate amaretto torte, pineapple and almond ravioli, or assorted gelato).

Special Meals at Palo

In addition to the nightly dinners, Palo hosts two special, adults-only events, primarily on the seven-night cruises. These popular events are by reservation only (see details on making reservations on previous page) and are generally held only on days at sea.

Champagne Brunch *($15/person charge) – also available on the 4-night cruise*
Buffet of assorted traditional breakfast and lunch items: **breakfast items** (cereals, breakfast breads, Danish pastries, specialty eggs, and pancakes); **lunch items** (shrimp, grilled marinated vegetables, Alaskan King Crab legs, smoked salmon & mixed greens, selection of cheeses and meats, pizzas, and garlic roasted tenderloin); and **desserts** (fresh fruit and berries, tiramisu, lemon meringue pie, and cappuccino mousse). One glass of champagne is complimentary, as is fresh-squeezed orange juice. (Tip: If you don't drink, ask for sparkling juice.) Champagne specialty drinks are available for $5.25.

High Tea *($5/person charge)*
traditional teas (Darjeeling, Yunnan Top Grade, Ceylon and Yalta, Lapsaung Souchong); **flavored teas** (California Fields and Black Currant); **herbal and caffeine-free** (Chamomile Citrus, Rainforest Mint, African Nectar); **finger sandwiches** (cream cheese and cucumber, smoked salmon and sour cream, chicken and curry, Norwegian prawn sandwiches); **scones** (available with apricot jam, raspberry jam, or Devonshire cream); **desserts** (English trifle or chocolate eclairs). Specialty coffees, full bar, and extensive wine list also available.

Beverages at Dinner *(all restaurants)*

Don't be surprised if your server learns your drink preferences. We are always impressed when our server remembers what we like after our first dinner. Complimentary beverages include soda (fountain drinks), iced tea, juice, milk, coffee, tea, and tap water. Sparkling water (Perrier or San Pellegrino) is $3.50 for a large bottle. A full bar and wine list is available. If you need suggestions, each menu has a selection of specialty drinks/apéritifs ($4.75) and featured wines ($5.25–$8.25/glass). Each menu also features a themed drink, such as Lumière's French Flag (grenadine, créme de cacao, and blue curaçao), Animator's Palate's Black and White (Kahlúa and layered cream), and Parrot Cay's Island Kiss (Amaretto, Bailey's, and créme de cacao). Specialty drinks are also available without alcohol—just ask your server. If you're a wine drinker, you may be interested in the wine package—see page 128.

Special Dining Themes and Menus

All cruises offer at least one dining theme night simultaneously in the three main dining rooms, and the longer cruises add several more. These theme nights have their own menus and take place on different nights, depending upon your cruise length and destination. For tips on figuring out which night of your cruise you can expect these themed dinners, see pages 132-133. Here are the menus (as of Dec. 2007) for each theme night:

Pirates in the Caribbean *(theme night all cruises; menu on 4+ night cruises)*
This theme night is enjoyed by all Disney cruisers, and all but the three-night cruises have a special menu (guests on the three-night cruises have their regular rotational menu). The special menu is presented on a rolled "treasure map" and all diners are presented with glow-in-the-dark bandanas. For more information, see page 151: **appetizers** (Black Beard's jumbo crab cake, pirate's golden pasta envelopes, buccaneer's sun-ripened pineapple, or pearls of the Caribbean); **soups and salads** (chilled-to-the-bone honeydew melon and mango soup, Caribbean-style vegetable gumbo soup, Hideaway Bay salad, jerk chicken salad, or Mr. Smee's Bib Lettuce); **main courses** (treasure-of-the-seas grilled shrimp and seared scallops, Jack Sparrow's fruit musked smoked pork shank, Castaway Cay's chicken breast rubbed with pirate island spice, Captain Hook's macadamia-dusted mahi mahi, The Black Pearl's oven-roasted beef tenderloin, roasted chicken breast, grilled sirloin steak, baked salmon steak, or vegetarian selections—baked bell pepper or Tiger Lily's grilled eggplant); **desserts** (shiver-me-timbers white chocolate cheesecake, floating island of tropical fruit treasures, walk the triple-layered chocolate gangplank cake, the lost banana treasure, The Calypso ice cream sundae, or no-sugar-added desserts—mango mousse cake or coconut rice pudding).

Master Chef *(all 7+ night cruises)*
appetizers (tomato risotto, cheddar cheese tartlet, tropical fruit cup, spicy tomato bruschetta); **soups and salads** (chilled potato and dill cream, Tuscan tomato soup, beefsteak tomatoes and baby mozzarella, leaves of Boston bib and radicchio); **main courses** (orange roughy, linguine smoked salmon and asparagus, tamarind rubbed roasted pork tenderloin, roasted half chicken, sirloin of beef with truffle jus, grilled rib-eye steak, baked chicken breast, vegetarian selections—lasagna or vegetable biryani); **desserts** (triple chocolate terrine, apple cheesecake, peach flambé, brioche pudding, chocolate mint ice ceram sundae, or no-sugar-added dessert).

Captain's Gala *(all 7+ night cruises)*
appetizers (oysters Rockefeller, grilled shrimp, grilled vegetables and beef prosciutto, or fresh fruit cocktail); **soups and salads** (wild forest mushroom soup, chilled tomato consommé, garden fresh salad, or Californian mixed salad leaves); **main courses** (baked lobster tail, veal roasted with shallots and vin santo, sesame seared tuna loin, grilled venison medallions in Stilton, fettuccine with parmesan crusted chicken, roasted Cornish game hen, sirloin steak, salmon fillet, or vegetarian selection—eggplant parmigiana or blue cheese and asparagus risotto); **desserts** (amaretto cheesecake, cherries jubilee, warm chocolate lava cake, lingonberry cheese pudding, ice cream sundae, or no-sugar-added dessert).

Til We Meet Again *(all 7+ night cruises)*
appetizers (artichoke and garlic dip, chilled tuna roll with caviar, seafood medley, or honey-mustard chicken tenderloins); **soups and salads** (crawfish and lobster bisque, chilled split pea soup, romaine salad, Florida citrus and baby spinach, or bib lettuce); **main courses** (grilled beef tenderloin, chicken and mushroom Wellington, roasted mint pesto crusted sirloin of lamb, seafood linguini pasta, prosciutto-wrapped salmon, rib-eye steak, roasted chicken breast, salmon fillet, or vegetarian selections—puff pastry turnover or risotto with black-eyed peas); **desserts** (banana crème brûlée Napoleon, chocolate decadence, celebration cake, deep-dish apple-cranberry pie, baked Alaska, ice cream sundae, or no-sugar-added dessert).

Topsider's/Beach Blanket Buffet

This casual buffet restaurant (deck 9 aft) is a pleasing alternative to the formal dining rooms. Choices are plentiful and varied, with themes such as seafood, Italian, Mexican, and Asian. The welcome aboard buffet (first afternoon) offers peel-and-eat shrimp, a popular offering with cruisers. Salad and dessert buffets are expansive, and kid-friendly food is always offered. Breakfast offerings are excellent, with hot and cold selections, omelet bar, and a cereal bar—note that breakfast here on the last day is very busy. It's usually open for breakfast (7:30 am to 10:30 am) and lunch (noon to 2:00 pm). Occasionally early-morning pastries, dinner (6:30 pm to 8:30 pm), and a late-night buffet are offered. Seating indoors and outdoors. Drinks include soda, water, fruit punch, iced tea, coffee, milk, and juice.

Decor—Topsider's (Magic) is nautically themed, with bright, nautical flags, teakwood tables, and glass etchings of maritime scenes. Beach Blanket Buffet (Wonder) has a surf's-up feel, with colorful surfboards, beach towels, and beach balls decorating the floors, walls, and ceilings. Both offer indoor and outdoor seating (with and without shade).

Dress—Casual resort wear. You can wear shorts and tank tops for any meal, and dressier clothes are welcome, too. For the sake of other guests, however, do cover up that swimsuit.

Dinner—Dinner works differently than breakfast and lunch—you go to the buffet for your salads and some desserts, but your drinks and other courses are brought to your table by servers. In fact, your main course entrees will probably be the same as those offered in one of the regular restaurants that evening. Note that dinner here may only be offered on select nights of your cruise.

Our Review—An excellent place for a fast yet satisfying breakfast. We generally prefer the other restaurants for lunch (better food, better service, and alcohol can be purchased), but when we've stopped by for a casual dinner, we've always been pleased. It's a great place to feed kids before they go to Flounder's or Oceaneer's. As to whether it's best to eat lunch here or at Parrot Cay on embarkation day, we really prefer Parrot Cay for its service and slightly less crowded atmosphere. Jennifer and Dave's rating: 6/10.

Dave enjoys lunch at Beach Blanket Buffet

© MediaMarx, Inc.

Casual Dining

Need to grab a bite on your way to a movie? Want to avoid the dining room at dinner? Casual dining is your ticket. Disney offers several quick-service options throughout the ship at various times during the day, all at no extra charge. All times noted below are based on previous cruises.

■ Topsider's Buffet/Beach Blanket Buffet   Deck 9 Aft

See previous page for a full description and photo.

■ Pluto's Dog House   Deck 9 Aft

Your not-so-basic burger stand. The menu includes burgers, hot dogs, veggie burgers, chicken sandwiches, tacos, bratwurst, chicken tenders, and fish burgers. All are served with fries. A toppings bar offers standard bun veggies (lettuce, tomatoes, onions, pickles) and condiments. Pluto's may also offer an express breakfast or treats like cheese fries and nachos on select days. Patio tables nearby. Hours vary—usually open from lunch until 8:00 pm or midnight.

■ Goofy's Galley   Deck 9 Aft

Scoops was renovated into Goofy's Galley in October 2005 (Magic) and September 2006 (Wonder). Bakery cases display the daily offerings, which usually include salads, fresh fruit, deli sandwiches, panini, pasta, wraps, ice cream, and cookies. You may even be able to order a special-request sandwich (inquire with the crew members). The ice cream is available in two self-serve machines with vanilla, chocolate, and vanilla/chocolate swirls. Sprinkles, cherries, chocolate topping, and other toppings may also be available. In the morning (7:00 am to 9:30 or 10:00 am), you'll find a selection of pastries (such as croissants, stollen bread, and danish), cereal, fruit, yogurt, and milk. Open daily from 10:30 am to 6:00 or 7:00 pm (ice cream may be available until 11:00 pm).

■ Pinocchio's Pizzeria   Deck 9 Mid

Pizza, pizza, pizza! Get your slice in traditional cheese or pepperoni. Special pizzas like veggie and Hawaiian may also be served at times. Beverages also available here. Generally open from 11:00 am to 6:00 pm, then again from 10:00 pm to midnight. Seating is at patio tables. (Tip: You can order more pizza types from room service—see page 129).

■ Outlook Bar   Deck 10 Fwd

Chicken wings and panini sandwiches are offered here around lunchtime on select days. Check your Personal Navigator or stop up for a visit.

■ Beverage Station   Deck 9 Aft

Breakfast pastries are available early mornings (6:30-7:30 am). Cookies may also be served on select afternoons—look for them on the counters to the aft of the beverage station. Complimentary beverages, including soda, are available 24 hours/day—for more details, see page 128.

Snacks and desserts are liberally sprinkled in other places, too. You'll find snacks in the Cove Café and Promenade Lounge, as well as in Beat Street/Route 66 from 11:00 pm to midnight. Dessert buffets are available as noted on page 116.

Castaway Cay Dining

Two more dining opportunities bear mention, even though they are located off-ship. All Caribbean and repositioning itineraries visit Disney's private island, Castaway Cay, and you'll be happy to learn your food is included in the price of your cruise! The main place to eat is **Cookie's BBQ**, located directly across from the family beach (see island map on page 295). Cookie's typically serves from 11:30 am to 2:00 pm and offers the best selection

© MediaMarx, Inc.

Jennifer's nieces, Megan and Natalie, discuss the nutritional merits of hot dogs vs. burgers at Cookie's BBQ on Castaway Cay

with burgers, BBQ ribs, grilled chicken sandwiches, lobster burgers, hot dogs, potato salad, fruit, frozen yogurt, and big chocolate chip cookies. Food is served buffet-style. Plenty of covered seating is nearby (see photo above). Beverages are also provided (you can get free sodas at the dispensers), or purchase alcoholic beverages across the way at the Conched Out Bar.

Adults 18 and over can eat at the **Castaway Cay Air Bar-B-Q** (see photo below) located at Serenity Bay, the adults-only beach, from about 11:30 am to 2:00 pm. Offerings include burgers, salmon, grilled chicken breasts, steak sandwiches, lobster burgers (not always offered), potato salad, fresh fruit, and fat-free frozen yogurt. Water, soda, and juice is provided, or you can purchase alcoholic beverages at the bar nearby. A half-dozen umbrella-shaded

© MediaMarx, Inc.

tables are located to the left of the food hut, or take your tray down to the beach.

In addition to the two bars already mentioned, there's a third—the Heads Up Bar—at the far end of the family beach. All bars close around 3:30–4:00 pm.

Relax at the Castaway Cay Air Bar-B-Q at Serenity Bay

Tip: If you choose not to visit Castaway Cay, a buffet is served in Parrot Cay, usually from about 8:00 am to 10:30 am and 12:00pm to 1:30 pm.

Kids' Dining

We don't know about your kids, but Jennifer's nieces, Megan and Natalie, won't touch pepper-seared grouper or seafood Creole with a ten-foot pole. Megan, Natalie, and many other kids prefer the kids' menus available at each table-service restaurant (and adults can order from these menus, too!). The **menus vary slightly** and are kid-friendly. Here is a typical menu:

appetizers (chicken noodle soup or honeydew melon boat); **main courses** (Mickey's macaroni and cheese, Minnie's mini burger, crusty cheese pizza, chicken strips, Mickey pasta, roasted chicken, or vegetable croquettes); **desserts** (Mickey ice cream bar, chocolate pudding, caramel custard, or assorted ice cream); **drinks** (milk—whole, low-fat, skim, or chocolate; soda, juice, water). Smoothies are $3.50 each.

And, yes, the menus come with **kid-pleasin'** **activities**, like word searches and connect-the-dots. Crayons are also provided with meals.

If you are the lucky parent of children who will try anything (like we are with Alexander), rest assured that your **kids can choose from the regular menu** if they wish.

Kid-friendly items are **offered elsewhere** outside of the restaurants, too. Pluto's and Pinocchio's are favorites, naturally, and Topsider's/Beach Blanket Buffet has plenty of kids' food.

If your child is checked into **Oceaneer's Club or Lab** at dinnertime, crew members take kids up to Topsider's/Beach Blanket Buffet before or at the start of the first dinner seating. The

Alexander discovers that kids are pampered on Disney cruises, too

eatery reserves one buffet line just for kids. Checking your kids into the Oceaneer's Club or Lab just before dinnertime may be a good idea if you're hoping for a quiet dinner alone some evening.

While lunch and dinner are provided for kids checked into Oceaneer's at mealtimes, **no snacks** are made available. You can check them out and take them to get a snack.

Younger children may find it **hard to sit through a meal** in a table-service restaurant. If you ask your server, you can have your child's meal served at the same time as your appetizers to curb their impatience. And the servers are typically great at entertaining the kids. Of course, you may prefer to do casual dining or room service on some nights.

Babies in **Flounder's Reef** are given apple juice and saltine crackers, as appropriate for their ages—you may also bring food for them. The dining rooms don't have pre-made baby food—you may want to bring a small food grinder to prepare foods for your infant. Formula for infants (Similac and Isomil) is available for purchase in Treasure Ketch (deck 4 mid), but supplies are limited. Disposable bottles are also sold in Treasure Ketch. For older babies, whole milk is available from room service and from the beverage station on deck 9 aft.

Beverages

Your food onboard is included in your fare, but **some drinks are not free**. Sure, you can get tap water, coffee, tea, milk, and juice with your meals and at select locations onboard. Sodas (fountain drinks) are also available for free everywhere except bars and room service. But bottled water, specialty drinks, smoothies, and alcohol come at a price.

✔ **Soda**—Disney offers complimentary soda at all meals, at the Beverage Station (deck 9 aft), and on Castaway Cay. Selection is limited to Coke, Diet Coke, Caffeine-Free Diet Coke, Sprite, Diet Sprite, pink lemonade, fruit punch, ginger ale (not available everywhere). Soda purchased at bars and from room service is priced at about $1.50 each.

✔ **Beers** range from about $3.25 to $4.00 and include tap beers (Bud, Miller Lite, Heineken), canned beers (Bud, Bud Lite, Coors Light, Icehouse, Miller Draft, Miller Lite, Beck's, Guinness, Heineken), and bottled beers (Amstell Light, Bass, Corona). Mixed drinks are $3.00 to $6.00 each, wine is $4.25 and up, and smoothies are $3.50.

✔ A 15% **gratuity is automatically added** to all beverage purchases. There's no need to give another tip, even though there is a space provided for it on your receipt.

✔ **Bring Your Own**—Many guests opt to "BYOB." Pick up some bottled water, beer, wine, and/or liquor and stow it in your luggage. If you run out, pick up more at a port. Unlike other cruise lines, there are no restrictions on bringing beverages aboard so long as fragile items are hand-carried in a day bag (beverage coolers are not permitted onboard). Note that you can only take home one liter of duty-free alcohol per person and it must be unopened. (Warning: Don't expect to restock at the onboard liquor shop—you won't get your booze until the night before you disembark.) The stateroom "refrigerators" keep your beverages chilled (see page 103). If you bring your own wine to the dinner table, expect to pay $17.25 per bottle ($15 corkage fee + 15% gratuity)— ouch! You may bring a glass of poured wine to the dinner table occasionally.

✔ **Beer Mug**—Check the lounges for a 22 oz. refillable, glass beer mug. Cost is $15 for the mug. Get 22 oz. refills at the 16 oz. price. You'd need 10 to 12 refills to break even.

✔ **Beverage Station**—Visit the beverage station on deck 9 aft for complimentary soda, water, coffee, hot tea, iced tea, hot cocoa, whole milk, fruit punch, and lemonade— available 24 hours a day. Orange juice may also be available in the mornings.

✔ **Topsider's Buffet/Beach Blanket Buffet**—Soda, fruit punch, and iced tea are complimentary for lunch or dinner. Hot tea, coffee, and juice are available at breakfast If you want soda at breakfast or hot tea at lunch, the Beverage Station is nearby.

✔ **Wine Package**—Commit to a bottle of wine for each night of your cruise and save more than 25%. You can choose your wine from a list at each meal. The classic wine package is $89 (3-night), $105 (4-night), or $179 (7-night) and the premium package is $139 (3-night), $159 (4-night), or $275 (7-night). If you don't finish an entire bottle of wine at dinner, take it back to your room or ask your assistant server to keep it for you until your next meal. Unopened bottles may be taken home, but they count toward your customs allowance.

✔ **Fairy Tale Cuvée**—This champagne—available for purchase in the dining rooms—was created just for Disney by Iron Horse Vineyard (the White House's purveyor).

✔ **Drinks Come to You**—Servers on Castaway Cay and at the Walt Disney Theatre bring specialty drinks around on trays for purchase so you don't have to get up for them.

Stateroom Dining
(Room Service)

There are no other three words that say "luxury" more than "Hello, Room Service!" It's a sinful extravagance for the filthy rich and people too pooped or love-struck to creep from their rooms. But why feel guilty, when **the cost of room service is included** in the price of your cruise? You want real luxury? Keep your stateroom stocked with oversized chocolate chip cookies from room service throughout your cruise!

Room service is available **24 hours/day** (though it's closed the morning of disembarkation for most guests). Service is quick and punctual—food usually arrives in 20 to 30 minutes. You'll find room service menus in your stateroom, and we've included sample menus at the bottom of this page—please note that menu items and beverage prices may change. Food and basic drinks (coffee, tea, milk, juice) are free, but all other beverages carry an extra charge.

To place an order for room service, fill out the breakfast menu in your stateroom and hang it on your door handle, or simply **press the dining button on your stateroom phone** and relay the items you want. You can also specify a time for delivery if you are ordering in advance, as with the breakfast menu. Coffee drinkers may find it convenient to order a pot of coffee before going to bed and request to have it delivered for a particular time in the morning (its arrival works as a wake-up call). Don't forget to tip your room service steward on delivery. They don't get automatic tips for the food, just the drinks. $1–$2/person is fine.

Tip: Guests going on all-day excursions have been known to order a couple of sandwiches, have them delivered before departing, keep them cool in the refrigerator, and pack them in resealable bags for a midday snack. Be aware that the Disney Cruise Line does not encourage this, it **may be illegal to bring food offboard** in some ports, and you are not allowed to bring cooked/opened food back onboard. We do not recommend it.

Breakfast Menu (7:00 am to 10:00 am) Note: Guests in suites may order full breakfasts (see page 90). *Juices* (orange, apple, grapefruit); **Cold Cereal**, served with whole or skim milk (Corn Flakes, Raisin Bran, Rice Krispies, Froot Loops, KO's, Frosted Flakes, low-fat granola); **Breads and Pastries** (Danish pastries, fruit and bran muffins, croissants, donuts, toast, English muffins, bagel); **Condiments** (selection of jams and honey, butter, margarine); **Beverages** (whole milk, skim milk, chocolate milk, 100% Colombian Coffee, 100% Colombian Decaffeinated Coffee, selection of teas); and **Cocktails**–$4.25 (Mimosa, Screwdriver, Bloody Mary)

All-Day Menu Note: Guests in suites may order from the main dining room menus (see page 90). *Appetizers* (southwestern Caesar salad, blackened chicken quesadilla salad, Mexican tortilla soup, chicken noodle soup, All Hands on Deck—a special selection of international cheeses served with crackers, and fresh fruit bowl); **Sandwiches** (BLT, ham/turkey & cheese, focaccia sandwich with grilled zucchini, portabello mushrooms, and aioli, tuna salad, chicken fajita, and steak sandwich); **All-American Fare** (cheeseburger with fries and cole slaw, hot dog with fries, and macaroni & cheese); **Chef's Specialities** (Mexican fiesta pizza, vegetarian delight pizza, pepperoni pizza, and meat or veggie lasagna); **Desserts** (daily cake selection, an extra large chocolate chip cookie, and an oatmeal raisin cookie); **Beverage Packages** (6 domestic beers for $19.50, 6 imported beers for $22.50, 3 imported and 3 domestic beers for $21, 6 Coca Cola or other sodas for $7.50, or 6 bottled waters for $7.50). Milk is free.

Introduction
Reservations
Staterooms
Dining
Activities
Ports of Call
Magic
Index

Our Recommendations

Your first hours on board can be very chaotic, and it's tough to arrange a proper family meal. We suggest you split up and **grab quick bites** whenever you can—the buffets close before the ship sets sail.

Are you still uncomfortable about wearing a jacket or a suit? Other than formal nights, **a nice shirt and slacks will be fine** at Triton's/Lumière's.

Presuming you love **Disney music** (a fair guess, we think), the soundtrack at Animator's Palate and Lumière's/Triton's takes your meal to a high "sea." You don't get a 16-piece, live, be-tuxed orchestra, but the prerecorded scores are a feast for the ears. This is especially true at Animator's Palate, where the visual extravaganza is choreographed to the music.

You can't keep Dave away from **smoked salmon**, even under "lox and cay." Alas, Disney's smoked salmon is not quite the stuff of dream cruises. It's fine on a bagel with cream cheese, but it's not that firm-but-buttery/velvety, smoky-sweet stuff of his dreams. The salmon at Palo's brunch is a bit better (as is their fresh-squeezed OJ!).

We love **seafood** (especially Dave), and you'll notice that many of our choices in this chapter (all those dishes we've underlined) are seafood-based. We know there are many of you who don't share our love for it, so please rest assured that virtually all the dishes are good—it's just that we've tried the seafood the most often.

The **seating and traffic flow** for Topsider's/Beach Blanket Buffet is the most chaotic on board. It's far better, though, when you enter the buffet using the right-hand doors (port). The indoor seating on that side is also more spacious and relaxing. When the weather's right, we prefer the outdoor tables aft—they're a glorious relief from the indoor chaos.

© MediaMarx, Inc.

Eating outdoors on deck 9 aft

Get to Know Your Dining Room Servers

If you've never had the chance to bond with a good server, try it! Great servers resemble stage actors—they come alive for a good audience. Be generous with your attention and thanks throughout the cruise—don't save it all for the tip. From the start, help them understand your tastes and interests. Listen attentively when they describe dishes, ask for their recommendations (they know what's good), and ask questions while ordering—you may save them several trips to the kitchen. If something disappoints you, break the news gently—but don't suffer in silence, either. Your server likes happy guests, and you'll be even happier with a happy server. You have three crew members on your dinner service staff, all of whom should be tipped at cruise end (see page 321). Your Head Server oversees many tables, supervises your special needs (and celebrations), and should visit your table once per meal. Your Server guides you through your meal, takes your orders, and (hopefully) pampers you beyond belief. Your quiet Assistant Server helps keep your food coming, serves wine and other beverages, and clears the table.

A Melting Pot of Notes

If you're thinking of **bringing any food onboard**, please note that it is against U.S. Public Health regulations to bring aboard any food that is cooked or partially cooked or packaged food that has already been opened. Unopened, commercially packaged foods are fine.

It's a good idea to **pack a change of clothes** for your first night's dinner in your carry-on. While it doesn't happen often, checked luggage may arrive in your stateroom too late to allow an unhurried change for an early dinner seating.

Even parents with **young children may appreciate the late seating**—the kids will be more alert for the early show.

Trying to decide between the **earlier or later seating?** The earlier seating is most popular with families and young children. The earlier seating is also preferred by those who like to get to sleep earlier. Early seating takes about $1\,^1/_2$ hours to complete your meal, while late seating can take as long as 2 hours. As you might have guessed, the later seating is comprised of mostly adults and some older children. The later seating gives you more time on your port days, as you don't need to rush back for an early dinner. Keep in mind that guests with late seating see the show before dinner, so you may need a snack before the show. We prefer the late seating ourselves.

Just can't **finish your meal**? Ask your server if you can take it back to your room. Most servers are happy to accommodate you. Don't be shy about asking for another dish or for seconds, either.

If you are **seated with other guests**, which is likely if you aren't traveling in a large group, enjoy their company and swap tales of your adventures! Most cruisers find it more enjoyable to share a table!

On the **third night** of the four-night cruises, guests return to the restaurant where they dined on the previous night of their cruise. Regardless of what restaurant you're in, you will enjoy the "Pirates in the Caribbean" menu (see page 123) on this evening.

Jennifer's brother-in-law, Chad, enjoys two main entrees

Not sure what evening to **experience Palo**? Personally, we think Parrot Cay is the least interesting of the three dining rooms, and the evening we're in Parrot Cay is generally the evening we prefer to spend in Palo. Be careful, however, that you don't accidentally overlook the "Pirates in the Caribbean" theme night (see next page).

If you want to try **Palo on more than one evening**, don't bother asking your friends or family members to add you to their Palo reservation—Disney cross-references reservations and limits all cruisers to just one reservation. If you really want to do Palo more than once, get on their waiting list once you're aboard and cross your fingers!

Breakfast on disembarkation day is in the same restaurant you were <u>assigned</u> to the evening before (so if you ate in Palo, you need to go the restaurant you would have eaten in if you hadn't gone to Palo). A special "Welcome Home" menu is served—it's virtually identical to the Character Breakfast menu (page 120).

Determining Dining Schedules

Before you read any further, know this: You don't have to figure out your dining schedule ahead of time. If you want to just kick back and relax, all you need to pay attention to is the dining "tickets" left in your stateroom on your embarkation day and the Personal Navigators (the daily schedules left in your stateroom every evening). This approach may make it difficult to decide which night to dine at Palo, however. Should you really want to have a good idea of the what, where, when of your dinners, then read on!

At press time, these are the dining schedules for the various regularly scheduled cruises. If you're on a special cruise, check the bottom of this page. It's important to remember, however, that <u>Disney can and does change these schedules at the drop of a hat</u>. Always, always check your *Personal Navigators* to determine what's really going on for your cruise.

3-Night Cruise Dining Schedule

Day 1	Day 2	Day 3
regular rotation menu (Casual Attire)	Pirates in the Caribbean (Pirate/Tropical Attire)	regular rotation menu (Dress-Up Attire)

4-Night Cruise Dining Schedule

Day 1	Day 2	Day 3	Day 4
regular rotation menu (Casual Attire)	regular rotation menu (Dress-Up Attire)	Pirates in the Caribbean (same restaurant as day 2) (Pirate/Tropical Attire)	regular rotation menu (Casual Attire) Palo Brunch

7-Night Eastern Caribbean Dining Cruise Schedule

Day 1	Day 2	Day 3	Day 4	Day 5	Day 6	Day 7
regular rotation menu (Casual Attire)	regular rotation menu (Formal Attire)	regular rotation menu (Casual Attire)	Pirates in the Caribbean (Tropical/ Pirate Attire)	Master Chef (Casual Attire)	Captain's Gala (Semi-Formal Attire)	'Til We Meet Again (Casual Attire)
	Palo Brunch/ High Tea	Palo Brunch/ High Tea			Palo Brunch/ High Tea	

7-Night Western Caribbean Dining Cruise Schedule

Day 1	Day 2	Day 3	Day 4	Day 5	Day 6	Day 7
regular rotation menu (Casual Attire)	regular rotation menu (Casual Attire)	regular rotation menu (Formal Attire)	Master Chef (Casual Attire)	Pirates in the Carribean (Pirate Attire)	Captain's Gala (Semi-Formal Attire)	'Til We Meet Again (Casual Attire)
	Palo Brunch	Palo Brunch/ High Tea			Palo Brunch/ High Tea	

Note: The character breakfast on the 7-night cruises is on day 2 if your dining rotation starts with Animator's Palate, day 3 if you start with Lumière's/Triton's, and day 6 if you start with Parrot Cay.

The Mexican Riviera cruises will have casual attire on nights 1, 3, 4, and 7; formal attire on night 2; pirate/tropical attire on night 5, and semi-formal attire on night 6. The longer cruises historically have two formal attire evenings (day 3 and day 7) and one semi-formal attire evening (day 9), but schedules may vary greatly based on ports.

Dining Worksheet

Use this worksheet to note your dining preferences and be sure to keep it with you on your first day aboard.

Fill in/circle the following:
We have the **main seating** / **late seating** *(circle the appropriate choice—if you're not sure of your seating, call the Disney Cruise Line and inquire)*

Our Anticipated Dining Rotation: While this rule doesn't work for everyone, in general you can anticipate the following rotations if the occupants of your stateroom include:
  All adults—day 1: **Lumière's/Triton's**, day 2: Animator's Palate, day 3: Parrot Cay, etc.
  Young kids—day 1: **Animator's Palate**, day 2: Parrot Cay, day 3: Lumière's/Triton's, etc.
  Older kids—day 1: **Parrot Cay**, day 2: Lumière's/Triton's, day 3: Animator's Palate, etc.
Note: The exception to the above rotation rule is on 4-night cruises, which repeat the second night's restaurant on the third night, then continue on. See page 131 for details.

Now write in the restaurants you anticipate being assigned to on each day. You may also want to add ports or other notes such as formal/semi-formal nights.

Day 1	Day 2	Day 3	Day 4	Day 5	Day 6	Day 7

Day 8	Day 9	Day 10	Day 11	Day 12	Day 13	Day 14

Now pencil in your first and second preferences for a dinner at Palo, keeping in mind which restaurants/meals you really want to try and which you are less interested in. Guests on the seven-night cruise: Add your preferences for the champagne brunch and/or high tea, if those interest you. Also note your preferences below for easy reference:

My first Palo preference is for _____ at _____ pm
My second Palo preference is for _____ at _____ pm

My Palo brunch preference is for _____
My Palo high tea preference is for _____

You can fill in this worksheet before you leave for your cruise or once you're aboard and are confident about your dining rotation—just be sure to bring this worksheet with you!

A Recipe for Fun

Make the most of your dining experience with these delicious tips:

- Can't decide between the lamb and the cod? Tell your server you'd like to **try both dishes**! You can also order multiple appetizers and desserts if you wish. But take our advice and don't say you want "nothing" for dessert—that's just what you may get (you'll see!).

- How do you **choose between four full-service restaurants** on a three-night cruise? If you can't bear to miss the pleasures of Triton's, Animator's Palate, Parrot Cay, and Palo, try this: Make a late-night reservation at Palo and just have appetizers and/or dessert. Or, eat an early, light meal in your regular restaurant before having a late, full dinner at Palo.

- For easy **room service tipping**, bring an envelope full of $1 bills and leave it by the door in your stateroom. We do not recommend coins.

- Picky eater? Ask your server to **mix and match menu items** so you can get just the meal you want.

- If you've **brought your own wine** or picked up a bottle at a port, you can request a "wine opener" (corkscrew) from room service.

- "One way to cut the **cost of your drinks and snacks** during the shows is to bring your own. Go up to deck 9 to get drinks from the free beverage station and snacks from Pluto's or Pinocchio's. It's completely acceptable to bring your own drinks and snacks into the theaters." – contributed by Disney cruiser Diana Barthelemy

Magical Memory

- *"We just got back from a 7-night Disney cruise and had the most wonderful experiences at dinner with our kids! Our servers were quite attentive to our kids, bringing their food out as early as possible and making fun napkin shapes for them while they waited for dessert. And all the unusual food choices allowed our kids to experiment with new tastes—we'd never have let them try our pricey escargot at a regular restaurant, but here on the cruise we felt free to offer it ... and they tried it! Best of all, the servers seemed to really understand kids as well as their parents. When my food arrived while my toddler was asleep on my shoulder, my server actually cut my food for me so I could eat one-handed. Now that's real service!"*

...as told by Disney cruiser Tom Herman

Playing and Relaxing Onboard

LEARN the basics of having fun on the cruise

DECIDE what to do on your first afternoon onboard

READ your Personal Navigator

DISCOVER activities for kids, teens, and adults

Cruise ships are often called floating hotels, but "mobile resort" is much closer to the truth. Like the legendary "Borscht Belt" hotels of New York's Catskill Mountains, the Disney cruise offers a bewildering array of entertainment, recreation, and enrichment opportunities from sunup way into the wee hours.

The Disney Cruise Line has become legendary for its pacesetting children's and teens' programs, and it may seem like an ocean-going summer camp. With the kids' programs open all day and well into the night, even Mom and Dad get a vacation.

Despite their emphasis on family travel, the Disney cruises are a summer camp for all ages, boasting a full range of adult-oriented activities. The single most obvious omission is the lack of a gambling casino—you'll have to be satisfied with onboard bingo and in-port casinos.

Leave time for relaxation as well as playing. On a cruise, it's just as easy to overplay as it is to overeat. You'll be tempted to fill every available hour with shipboard fun, but you'll have a far more enjoyable cruise by picking only the most tempting morsels. If you shop 'til you drop in port and play 'til you plotz (collapse) onboard, you'll be one very weary vacationer.

We start this chapter with an introduction to the *Personal Navigator*, your cruise's daily gazette. Then it's time to prep you for your first day onboard. There's a lot to do, and it's particularly hectic for first-time cruisers. From there, we move on to describe shipboard activities for families, teens, kids, and adults—this is where you learn about the famous kids' program and adult entertainment offerings. Next, in-depth details are in order—the swimming pools, deck parties, films, stateroom TV, live entertainment, surfing (the World Wide Web), the spa, and lounges all get their moment in the limelight. Finally, now that you're completely exhausted, we help you kick back and relax, and share some insider tips. Shuffleboard, anyone?

Introduction

Reservations

Staterooms

Dining

Activities

Ports of Call

Magic

Index

Your Personal Navigator

We hope this field guide has become your "first mate." If so, we predict the *Personal Navigator* will seem like your very own "cruise director." The *Personal Navigator* is a folded, 4-page sheet that **lists the day's activities**. A new *Personal Navigator* is placed in your stateroom each evening, and there may be special versions for kids and teens, too. While we don't have room to print the full text of *Personal Navigators* here, you can get a peek at previous editions of *Personal Navigators* at http://www.castawayclub.com—this site maintains collections from previous cruisers, and they'll give you an excellent idea of what to expect.

The first time you see a *Personal Navigator*, you may feel overwhelmed. Here's a **capsule review** of what you'll find in the daily Personal Navigator:

Page 1—Date, day's destination, suggested dress, sunrise/sunset times, day's highlights, major events, ship directory, operating hours, important numbers, and trivia
Page 2—Daily activities, character appearances, movies, family activities, etc.
Page 3—Descriptions of the day's activities for kids, teens, families, and adults
Page 4—More things to do, shopping deals and hours, and important reminders

We highly recommend you keep **highlighters** handy (a different color for each person) to mark appealing activities. Finding activities in your *Personal Navigator* later can be tricky—on some days, there are more than 80 activities listed! Obviously, you can't do everything, and that's where this chapter comes in—we introduce many of the activities here, so you'll be better informed when it comes to deciding among all of your choices.

We find that life is much easier when we each have a copy of the *Personal Navigator* with us at all times. Only one copy is left in your stateroom, so stop at Guest Services (deck 3 mid) and **pick up more copies**. (The kids' versions are in Oceaneer Club/Lab and the teen version is in The Stack/Aloft, when available.) How do you keep it with you if you don't have pockets? We fold it and tuck it into a PassHolder Pouch, which also holds our Key to the World card and other small items. See page 313 for a photo of a PassHolder Pouch—you can order one at http://www.passporter.com.

In addition to the *Personal Navigator*, you may receive a highlights sheet covering the entire cruise, a listing of movie showtimes and TV channels, plus a daily onboard shopping flyer. **Port and shopping guides** are distributed when you visit a port—they contain historical overviews, maps, shopping and dining ideas, basic information, and hours.

Note: The Personal Navigator's format changes every couple of years, so don't be surprised if your copy looks different than those pictured here.

Anatomy of a Personal Navigator

To help you get the most out of your *Personal Navigators* once you're aboard your ship, here is a recent sample with the notes on the general location of important information on the **first and second pages**. Please keep in mind this is a sample only—the format of your Personal Navigators may be similar, but they will have different information and activities

First Page

Looking for a place onboard? This ship directory offers the **deck and location** (fwd, mid, or aft) of important services and amenities.

Service operating hours for everything from the art gallery and swimming pools to the health center and guest services.

The day's major "don't-miss" events. On port days, shore excursion departure times are also listed here.

Glance here for the **day, date, and sunrise/sunset times**. On port days, "Ashore" and "All Aboard" times are noted. Evening attire is also noted here, along with the drink of the day.

A quick overview of the **day's lunch and dinner options**. Also included are dining hours for the day, including all restaurant, casual dining, late-night snacks, and bar/lounge hours.

Important **phone numbers**.

First Page Tips:

✔ Upcoming events that require registration or sign-up may appear along with the day's highlighted events, such as a Galley Tour or a Family Talent Show.

✔ On port days, shore excursion meet times and meeting locations are listed on the first page, along with the ship's agent in the port of call.

✔ The evening's suggested attire (formal, semi-formal, dress-up, or cruise casual) is usually listed near the top of the right or left column.

Anatomy of a Personal Navigator *(continued)*

The *Personal Navigator's* second page contains grids which list the day's **entertainment schedule**. The grids are reminiscent of a *TV Guide* schedule, with one grid each for morning, afternoon, and evening activities. The columns across the top of each grid give specific start and end times for each activity. The rows organize the activities into types (family, adult, kids, teens, special, character, movies, etc.), making it easy to find the sort of activity that appeals to you. Refer to pages 3 and 4 (not shown here) for activity descriptions.

Second Page

The top third of the page is devoted to **morning activities**. On embarkation day, this space is reserved for notice of reservations and sign-ups (i.e., Palo).

The middle third of the page lists the **afternoon activities**. This grid can be very dense (and hard to read) on at-sea days—read it carefully.

Evening activities occupy the bottom third of the page. If an event lasts longer than the last time on the grid, a small notation appears to indicate its ending time.

If you feel overwhelmed, note the **activity categories** in the left-most column and concentrate on activites that appeal to you. The "Special" category is for the day's highlights and don't-miss events. The "Character" category refers to character appearances throughout the ship.

Back Page Tips:

✔ In order to fit in all events on busy days, the grid's type size is quite small and narrow. If you find it hard to read small type, consider bringing a magnifying glass.

✔ The activities are generally listed in order of popularity—highlight events are at the top and age-specific activities are at the bottom.

✔ When you find an event that interests you, be sure to cross-reference the other events in the same row (and hence, same time) so you don't overlook something important.

✔ Parents, note that the kids' activities are listed in these grids, making it easy to see what your kids may be interested in or where they already are.

Your First Day Aboard

At last! Are you excited? Many cruisers report feeling overwhelmed and even a little nervous on their first afternoon. The good news is that your first day aboard can be far more relaxing. The Disney Cruise Line web site (http://www.disneycruise.com) lets you make Palo, Vista Spa, Flounder's Reef childcare, and shore excursion reservations online—you can even preregister for the Oceaneer Club and Lab. Reservations can be made online from 3 to 75 days in advance (up to 90 days for Castaway Club members, and up to 105 days for guests in stateroom categories 1–3 or guests who booked the Romantic Escape at Sea package—see page 46), assuming your cruise is paid in full. Look for the "My Disney Cruise" links on the web site. Note that online bookings are limited to one Palo reservation per meal type and no more than 8–10 hours per child in Flounder's Reef, and some Spa treatments (such as haircare and the Rainforest) are not listed. Additional reservations may be available after boarding.

To give you an idea of what to expect on your first afternoon onboard, we've made up a sample **"touring plan."** You probably won't want to do everything in our touring plan, and remember that times/locations may differ. Modify it as needed and use the worksheet on page 141 to record your own plans!

As soon as you can—Smile for the photographer, walk the gangway, and board the ship. Go to Topsider's/Beach Blanket Buffet (deck 9 aft) or Parrot Cay (deck 3 aft) for a seafood buffet. Relax and enjoy—it may get a bit hectic over the next few hours.
12:00 pm (or so)—Send one adult from your party for Palo reservations, if you didn't reserve in advance (be sure to check your *Personal Navigator* for exact time and place).
12:00 pm (or so)—Send one adult to get Vista Spa bookings (including massages on Castaway Cay), if not done in advance. Send another person to your stateroom (usually ready at 1:00–1:30 pm). This is also the time to confirm any special requests you made (visit Guest Relations).
Tip: If you've got kids, they may be getting antsy by now. Let them explore your stateroom, or, if they're old enough, introduce them to the pools and meet up with them later.
1:30 pm—Go to Flounder's Reef Nursery (deck 5 aft), if not reserved in advance.
1:30 pm—Send someone to the Shore Excursions Desk (deck 3 midship) to fill out and drop off order forms, if not reserved in advance. Decide which excursions you'd like in advance.
Lunch—Take a deep breath and slow down. If you haven't eaten or visited your stateroom yet, do so now. The buffet typically closes at 3:30 pm, so don't miss it!
2:30 pm—Make dining assignment changes or special dietary requests, if needed.
2:45 pm—Take kids age 3–12 to Oceaneer Club/Lab (deck 5 midship), if not preregistered.
3:15 pm—Return to your stateroom and get acquainted with it. If you're in need of anything (extra pillows, bed safety rail), request it from your stateroom host/hostess.
3:45 pm—Make sure everyone meets back in the room for the mandatory assembly drill.
4:00 pm—Don your life jackets and walk to your assembly station (see next page).
4:15 or 4:30 pm—After returning your life jackets to your room, go up to deck 9 midship and have fun at the sailaway deck party, and/or explore the ship until it is time to get ready for dinner or the evening's show.
5:30 pm/5:45 pm/6:00 pm/6:30 pm—Enjoy dinner (main seating guests) or the stage show at 6:30 pm (late seating guests).
7:00 pm—The Stack/Aloft (teens) and Oceaneer Club/Lab (kids 3–12) are now officially open. If you haven't yet registered your children, do this now.
8:00 pm/8:15 pm/8:30 pm—Enjoy the show (main seating) or dinner (late seating)

Whew! What a day! Rest assured that it all gets much, much easier from this point forward.

···➤

First Day Tips

Having a plan is the key to staying on course and feeling good. Here are a few helpful tips for your first day:

Check and double-check your **Personal Navigator** as soon as you get it (either at check-in or when you visit your stateroom). Places and times often change, and new activities and opportunities may be available.

Don't forget to eat! It can be hard to sit down together to one big family meal on your first afternoon. It's okay to split up and/or get **nibbles and bites** here and there.

Of course, you can always **kick back and do nothing** on your first day but eat, drink, be merry, and attend the boat drill. If you prefer this tactic, you can try to get those Palo and spa reservations later (if you haven't already), and you may get lucky with cancellations. If you've got someone in your family who just wants to relax once they're onboard, arrange to go your separate ways on this first afternoon—you'll all be much happier.

Lucky guests with **concierge service** only need to attend one meeting to make the various reservations. You'll be told when and where to meet.

Be **flexible**. Make a plan, but then be willing to change it when needed.

Mandatory Boat Drills

It's inevitable that just as you're settling in or about to leave your stateroom for an exploration of the ship, a disembodied voice from the bridge announces the mandatory boat drill. But thanks to this guide, you now know that the drill happens at 4:00 pm on departure day, and all ship services are suspended from 3:30 to 4:15 or 4:30 pm. You'll find bright-orange life jackets on the top shelf of your stateroom closet (if you need a different size, such as an infant jacket, ask your stateroom host/hostess). The life jackets were replaced with significantly more comfortable models in 2005. They have a water-activated light and a whistle—please remind your kids not to blow the whistles. Your Assembly Station location is mapped on the back of your stateroom door. Assembly stations are all on deck 4, but may be outside on deck or inside. If you forget your assembly station designation, it's printed on your life jacket (see the "M" on Dave's jacket in the photo). When you hear the loud emergency signal, put on your life jackets and walk to the assembly station—your attendance is mandatory. Be sure to bring your Key to the World card(s) with you, but leave cameras and other things behind. The life jackets feel strange, but now is the time for everyone (including young kids) to get used to them. Crew members in the hallways will direct you to your assembly station (disabled guests should ask crew members for special instructions on attending drills). Once there, a crew member takes attendance and displays the correct way to wear and use the life jacket. If you miss the drill, you'll receive a sternly worded letter indicating where and when to meet to go over the assembly procedures—don't miss it! When the drill is over, the captain releases everyone back to their staterooms. The drill lasts from 15 to 30 minutes. Keep your life jacket on until you return to your stateroom.

© MediaMarx, Inc.

"Hey, these life jackets aren't half bad!"

First Things First Worksheet

Electronic, interactive worksheet available— see page 350

Use this worksheet to plan those crucial activities that occur during your first day aboard. The chart below includes times (spanning the time period with the most important activities) and two columns each for activities and decks/locations. You may wish to list activities for other members of your party in the second column to coordinate and organize your day, or use the second column for notes or alternate activities.

Time	Activity	Deck	Activity	Deck
10:00 am				
10:15 am				
10:30 am				
10:45 am				
11:00 am				
11:15 am				
11:30 am				
11:45 am				
12:00 pm				
12:15 pm				
12:30 pm				
12:45 pm				
1:00 pm				
1:15 pm				
1:30 pm				
1:45 pm				
2:00 pm				
2:15 pm				
2:30 pm				
2:45 pm				
3:00 pm				
3:15 pm				
3:30 pm				
3:45 pm				
4:00 pm	Mandatory Boat Drill ↓	Deck 4	Mandatory Boat Drill ↓	Deck 4
4:15 pm				
4:30 pm				
4:45 pm				
5:00 pm				
5:15 pm				
5:30 pm				
5:45 pm				
6:00 pm				
6:15 pm				
6:30 pm				
6:45 pm				
7:00 pm				
7:15 pm				
7:30 pm				
7:45 pm				
8:00 pm				
8:30 pm				

Introduction

Reservations

Staterooms

Dining

Activities

Ports of Call

Magic

Index

Activities for Families

When Walt Disney was asked why he created Disneyland, he replied, "I felt that there should be something built where the parents and the children could have fun together." And that's exactly what Disney does for cruising. Family activities outnumber all other activities onboard, helping families have a great time when they're together. By "family" we mean groups of all ages, including all-adult families! Here's a list of what you can expect:

Deck Parties—Celebrate with music and dancing on deck 9 midship (see page 155).

Stage Shows—Disney puts on a different stage show each night of your cruise, and all shows are designed to please both adults and kids. See page 157 for more information.

Movies—Most of the movies playing in the Buena Vista Theatre and at the big outdoor screen over the Goofy Pool are rated G or PG, making them ideal for families. Special matinees may be held in the huge Walt Disney Theatre, too! See page 156 for movie details.

Studio Sea—This "family nightclub" (deck 4 midship) is a working TV studio. The club hosts family dance parties, family karaoke, theme parties, Tea with Wendy (see page 320), and game shows like Mickey Mania (Disney trivia) and A Pirate's Life For Me (see next page). Game shows are oriented toward families with young children, and generally contestant teams include both a parent and a child (see photo to right). Note that in the late evening, Studio Sea may be reserved for teens only.

Family dancing at Studio Sea

Cabaret Shows—Shows for all ages may be held in Rockin' Bar D/WaveBands in the early evening. See page 152 for details.

Promenade Lounge—We think of this as the "family lounge"—it's nonsmoking and families can relax together here in the afternoon and early evening. Watch for many family-friendly events, hosted in the Promenade Lounge. Located on deck 3 aft.

Oceaneer Club/Lab—At special times, families can explore these areas together.

Swimming—Families can swim together in the Goofy Pool (deck 9 midship), where pool games are also occasionally held. See page 154 for more information on the pools.

Games—Board games, shuffleboard, Ping-Pong, and basketball. A special Family Mini Olympics may also be held on deck 10 forward.

Pin Trading—Trading cloisonné pins is a very popular activity for kids and adults alike! Attend one of the trading sessions in the Atrium Lobby or trade casually with other cruisers and crew members. See page 165.

Character Meet & Greets—Plenty of opportunities for kids (or kids-at-heart) to get autographs and for parents to get photos. See page 320 for more information.

Shore Excursions—Most of Disney's shore excursions are great for families with kids ages 12 and up, and a good number of these work for families with kids ages six and up. Quite a few are open to all ages, as well. See chapter 6 for all the details.

Special Events—Try your hand at drawing Disney characters, or compete in a talent show or the "Mickey 200" veggie race—check your *Personal Navigator*.

Tip: Check the entertainment grid on the back side of your *Personal Navigator* for the family activity rows—these list the family-oriented events for the day. Also, there's usually some family-oriented entertainment between dinner and the show, such as the cabaret shows and game shows. Here is a sample of activities taken from recent *Personal Navigators* (keep in mind that not all these activities may be available on your cruise):

✔ A Pirate's Life For Me (a new game show inspired by *Pirates of the Caribbean*)
✔ Pictionary or Scattergories—test your skills against the crew members'
✔ Fun in the Sun Pool Party
✔ Family Dance Parties in Studio Sea
✔ Disney and Family Team Trivia
✔ Karaoke and Talent Show—show-off time!
✔ Mr. Toad's Wild Race (limited to 16 teams)
✔ Who Wants to be a Mouseketeer?
✔ Family Spy Party—fun for all "secret agents"
✔ Animal Towel Folding
✔ Pirate Dance Class
✔ Family Golf Putting Contest
✔ Walk the Plank Game Show
✔ Ping-Pong Tournament
✔ Disney Tune Trivia and Movie Trivia
✔ Family Animation Lesson
✔ Kite Making and Decorating
✔ Wii Golf, Games, and Tournaments

Kim and daughter Natalie dance on deck 10

Families That Play Together Don't Always Have to Stay Together

One of the wonderful benefits of a cruise is that each member of your family can do entirely different things, all while staying within the general vicinity of one another—a cruise ship is not a big place like Walt Disney World. With all the activities on your cruise, you're going to want to go in different directions at times ... and you should feel free to do it! It only makes the time you spend together that much more valuable. When we sail alone, we often split up—one goes to the pool with Alexander, the other to the spa—and we agree on a time and place to meet again. With larger families, including extended families, you can do your own thing in small groups while still feeling like you're "together." The key to making this work is to communicate with one another and set meeting places/times for the next group get-together. Some families bring along two-way radios, which do work to keep one another in touch—keep in mind, however, that the metal bulkheads of the ship can interfere with reception. A much less expensive, low-tech way to stay in touch is by leaving one another notes in your stateroom—or if you're staying in multiple staterooms, leaving them on one another's doors or voice mail. You can keep tabs on one another with a notepad—everyone in your family/group signs in each time they pass through the stateroom. On our last group cruise (MouseFest—see page 315 for details), we made up our own versions of *Personal Navigators* and left them on each other's stateroom doors. During the cruise, folks were able to add new events/times/places to the list by noting them on a magnetic whiteboard on one stateroom door. Sometimes it's as simple as picking up a phone somewhere on the ship (they're everywhere) and letting a family member know where you are (live or via voice mail). So feel free to go your separate ways—just be sure to save some special time to spend together as a family, too!

Activities for Teens

Teens are perhaps the hardest to please onboard, given their widely varying interests and levels of maturity. Some are perfectly happy to swim all day or play in the arcade. Others prefer to hang out with the adults. Still others want to socialize with other teens and party. If your teen prefers more family-oriented activities, we refer you to the previous page. Read on for Disney's teen-oriented places and events:

Note: Disney defines a teen as a 13- to 17-year-old. Older teens (18 and 19) are considered adults (although drinking age is still 21 and up).

Personal Navigators—Teens may have their own version of the daily schedule in the teen club (see below). The teen version lists teen activities for the day and what's coming up.

Teens-Only Club—A teens-only (ages 13 to 17) hangout is located on both ships, but with some decor differences. The Stack (Disney Magic) and Aloft (Disney Wonder) are each located on deck 11 midship (in the spot of the former ESPN Skybox)—they're actually inside one of the ship's stacks! Both clubs are hip and trendy. The Stack has huge windows dominating the large dance floor, flanked by chairs, tables, and a bar. Aloft has more of a big-city loft feel to it, with lots of comfy couches, brick walls, and a big table. Both clubs serve smoothies and non-alcoholic drinks at

The Stack on the Disney Magic

their bars. Tucked in the corner are three Internet terminals (same rates apply—see pages 158-159). Flat-panel screens are scattered throughout the clubs, offering a playlist of music videos that are shown on state-of-the-art TVs (including one giant-screen TV). In the back behind glass doors is an intimate little area with more comfy chairs, video screens, and a great view. Both clubs schedule plenty of parties, games, trivia, and karaoke during the cruise—the *Personal Navigators* list activities and times. The teen-only clubs also serve as an assembly spot for teen activities elsewhere on the ship, such as group events at the pool, group lunches, or a dance at Studio Sea.

Allie at Aloft on the Disney Wonder

Arcade—Quarter Masters is a favorite teen hangout located on deck 9 midship, near Cove Café. There are also a few video arcade games on deck 10 midship, just below the teens-only club. See page 146.

Wide World of Sports Deck—Shoot some hoops alone or with friends on deck 10 forward.

Internet Cafe—Sure, there are Internet terminals in The Stack/Aloft, but sometimes it's just more convenient to come down to deck 3. See pages 158-159.

Ocean Quest—This interactive area on deck 2 midship (Magic) and Oceaneer Lab (Wonder) appeals to younger teens—see page 147 for details on this area.

Vista Spa—Normally off-limits to anyone under 18, teens may be able to sign up for facials/ manicures on port days. $69/hour treatment. See pages 160–162.

Buena Vista Theatre—Teens love free movies! See page 156 for details.

Teen Parties—On special evenings, teens get dance parties, held either in The Stack/Aloft or in Studio Sea.

Teen Shore Excursions—Special teen-only excursions are available at certain ports, such as the "Wild Side" on Castaway Cay. See chapter 6 for details.

Teen Beach—On Castaway Cay, teens get their own beach with activities.

Other Teen Activities—Here is a sample of activities taken from recent teen *Personal Navigators* (keep in mind that not all these activities may be available on your cruise):

- ✔ Brains & Brawns Challenge
- ✔ Masquerade Ball and Homecoming Night Parties
- ✔ Pump It Up—Weight training in the Vista Spa
- ✔ Gotcha!—A day-long game of elimination
- ✔ Teen Karaoke
- ✔ Shooting Stars—Form crews and shoot movies!
- ✔ Lava Flow—Build your own volcano and watch it erupt!
- ✔ Animation Cells—Learn to draw your favorite Disney characters
- ✔ Gender Wars—Girls vs. Boys
- ✔ Bring It—Trivia game show
- ✔ Say What?—Who's lying and who's telling the truth?
- ✔ H2O Splashdown in the Goofy Pool
- ✔ Hold the Phone
- ✔ Capture the Flag—Team vs. team!
- ✔ PS2 and Guitar Hero Challenges
- ✔ Memory Books—Create your own!
- ✔ Ultimate Teen Scavenger Hunt and Video Scavenger Hunt

Tip: Even if you're not sure about all these activities, we highly recommend teens visit the club on the first evening to meet other teens and see what it's all about. This first evening is when many onboard friendships are formed.

Note to Parents of Teens

Teens have virtually the run of the ship, and aside from the times they're with you, in The Stack/Aloft, or at a structured teen activity, they're not chaperoned. Teens may make friends with others from around the country and the world—their new friends' values may be incompatible with your own standards. It's a good idea to know where they are and who they're spending their time with, and agree on what time they should return to the stateroom (some teen activities go late into the night). Talk before you go and remind them that being on vacation is not an excuse to flout our rules about drinking, drugs, or dating. U.S. Customs does not take drug possession lightly and penalties can be severe in other countries, too. Note also that any underage person caught with alcohol on the ship is fined $250 and could get up to three days of "stateroom arrest."

Activities for Kids

A whopping 15,000 sq. ft. (1,394 sq. m.) are devoted to activities just for kids. And there are a lot of kid-oriented activities on these ships. What else would you expect from Disney?

Oceaneer Club/Lab—A fantastic program for kids ages 3 to 12 with activities available daily from 9:00 am to midnight or 1:00 am. We highly recommend you encourage your kids to give these programs a try on the first day aboard. See pages 148–150 for more information.

Celebrate the Journey Farewell Show—Kids registered for the Oceaneer Club/Lab have the opportunity to participate in a special show on the last day of the cruise. All participants get to sing on stage with Mickey and receive a T-shirt and graduation mortarboard hat! Held in the Walt Disney Theatre.

Swimming—We dare you to keep them out of the water! See page 154 for details.

Arcade—Located on deck 9 midship, Quarter Masters is a small arcade offering about 20 video games, plus air hockey and a prize "claw" game. These are straight games, though—no award tickets and no prize redemption. Most games are 50 cents to $1 each and you must use an arcade card to play. An "arcade debit card teller" machine dispenses $10 arcade cards—just use your Key to the World card to purchase. You can also purchase arcade cards at Guest Services. (Note: Keep your arcade card separate from your Key to the World card as they'll de-magnetize if they come into contact.) If you're worried about your kids racking up huge charges for arcade cards, disable the charging privileges on their cards at Guest Services and purchase arcade cards for them. Hours: 8:00 am to midnight (last game at 11:50 pm).

Allie enjoys a game in Quarter Masters

Games—In addition to the arcade, there are often pool games and Ping-Pong on deck 9, board games in the Oceaneer Club/Lab, basketball on deck 10, and shuffleboard on deck 4. There is no charge for these games.

Movies and Shows—Most of the movies playing are kid-friendly! And the stage shows in the Walt Disney Theatre are well-liked by kids, especially "Disney Dreams." See page 157 for details.

Sports—The sports deck on deck 10 forward may be just the thing for your young sport stars.

Deck Parties—The deck parties are very popular with kids! See page 155 for details.

Snacks—The opportunity to eat ice cream and hot dogs without forking over money is a real treat for kids! We don't think it's a coincidence that Goofy's Galley, Pluto's Dog House, and Pinocchio's Pizzeria are right next to the kids' pools. See page 125 for details.

Character Meet & Greets—Disney friends come out for autographs and photos many times during your cruise. For details, see page 320.

Ocean Quest—Did you know that there's a second bridge tucked away on both the Disney Magic and the Disney Wonder? It's called Ocean Quest! And while the bridge isn't real, it is a very fun—albeit scaled down—replica of the real thing, complete with a traditional captain's chair and LCD viewscreens with live video feeds. Kids can pretend they are steering the ship in and out of various ports in a simulator game. There are also computer and video game stations, movies on one of several plasma screen TVs, and arts and crafts. A sitting area with books, magazines, and board games is also here. The area is geared toward kids ages 8–12. The location of Ocean Quest varies—on the Magic, it's on deck 2 midship; on the Wonder, it's inside the Oceaneer Lab on deck 5 midship—and thus its accessibility also differs a bit. On the Magic, guests ages 8 and up are welcome to participate unaccompanied; kids under 8 may participate with their kids program (Oceaneer Club/Lab) and/or with a parent. Do note, however, that the area isn't always open to anyone—a posted schedule will let you know when there's an "Open House" (open to all) or when the area is reserved for certain age groups or for organized children's or teen's programming visits (kids participating in the Oceaneer Club or Lab, as well as The Stack, venture down here as part of their regular programming). There's typically an Open House every day. Ocean Quest's hours of operation vary from day to day, with longer hours on days the ship is at sea. There is no extra cost to use this area, the area is always staffed by at least one crew member, and adults are welcome to try out their navigation skills during Open Houses. Also note that while kids do not need to formally check in, the on-duty crew member does have access to the kids' programming computer and paging system. On the Disney Wonder, the Ocean Quest area is inside the Oceaneer Lab, meaning it's really only accessible to kids participating in the kids clubs.

Here is a sample of kid-pleasin' activities taken from recent *Personal Navigators* (keep in mind that not all these activities may be available on your cruise):

✔ Kite Making Activity—Make your own kite for Castaway Cay (no extra charge)
✔ Paper Plane Making
✔ Goofy's Fun Fitness Pool Party
✔ Board Games in the Promenade Lounge

Wondering about letting your **kids roam free** onboard? It depends on their age and maturity. A general guideline is that kids 8–9 may be given some onboard freedom, while kids 10 and up can move about independently. These are in line with Disney's policies at the Oceaneer Club and Lab. If you let your kids loose, set down ground rules, such as no playing in elevators, keeping in touch, and set meeting times for meals, shows, and family activities.

Activities for Toddlers

While the rate for your toddler to cruise with you is a great deal, the variety of toddler-friendly activities onboard isn't as favorable. We've spent more than five weeks onboard with a toddler (our son Alexander) in the last two years alone, and here's what we've found to do: Go "swimming" in the shallow Mickey ear wading pool on the Disney Magic, or in the Toddler Splash Zone on the Disney Wonder (see page 154). Take your toddler to Oceaneer Club (see pages 148–150) to play on the climbing toys or even participate in activities—your toddler is always welcome as long as a parent remains with the child (just check in at the desk for name tags). Watch a movie (see page 156)—you may want to sit in the back of the theater near the aisle for easy escapes, however. Go for supervised treks down the hallways and up and down staircases—our son Alexander learned to walk independently while exploring the ship this way. Your toddler may or may not sit through stage shows or enjoy Flounder's Reef, but both are worth trying.

Introduction
Reservations
Staterooms
Dining
Activities
Ports of Call
Magic
Index

Playing at Oceaneer Club/Lab

Oceaneer Club and Oceaneer Lab are special areas on deck 5 midship **designed just for kids**. The Oceaneer Club is for potty-trained kids ages 3 to 4 and 5 to 7, while the Oceaneer Lab is for older kids ages 8 to 9 and 10 to 12. The four age groups primarily play independently. Kids may participate in an older age group if they are within one month of the minimum age for that group, but older kids cannot join younger groups (though exceptions may be made for children with special needs). Participation in the Club and Lab is included in your cruise fare.

The Club and Lab provides fun, **age-appropriate activities** throughout the day and into the evening. Some kids spend virtually their entire cruise in these areas, while others drop in now and then. Some prefer to spend their time with their families or just playing with other kids elsewhere. Typically, the kids that visit the Club or Lab on their first evening (when friendships are being formed) are more likely to enjoy the experience.

To participate in the Club or Lab, you may **preregister in advance online** (see page 121). Preregistering online means you can skip the Club open house on embarkation day—just pick up your child(ren)'s wristbands and your pager in the cruise terminal before you board. If you don't pre-register, drop by the Club or Lab on your first afternoon to take a look around and register your kid(s). To register, you'll need to fill out a participation form indicating name(s), birthday(s), age(s), special considerations (such as allergies, fears, and/or any special needs), and give your authorization for first aid if necessary. While there are maximum occupancy limits for the Club and Lab, Disney Cruise Line is very careful about booking and ratios—it's extremely rare that the Club or Lab fills up.

Once registered, your kids may **partake of Club/Lab activities as often as desired**—there's no need to sign up for blocks of time, no reservations for activities, and no worries. Kids ages 3 to 7 must have their parents sign them in when they enter the Club and the parents must return to sign them out later. Parents of kids 8 to 9 can indicate whether their kids can sign themselves in and out of the Lab or if the parents must sign them in and out. Kids ages 10 to 12 can sign themselves in and out by default. Each family is given one pager for the duration of the cruise. Each child gets a wristband—they should keep the wristband on for the duration of the cruise. Name tags are applied to children upon each visit to the Club/Lab. Parents are welcome to drop in and observe at any time.

The **Oceaneer Club** (see photo to right) is a big, fanciful, Neverland-themed playroom with a pirate ship to climb on and slide down and computers to play games on—it's also equipped with tables and chairs, a dress-up room, and a stage. Floors and furniture are kid-friendly. It's a big hit with the 3 to 7 crowd. On the Disney Wonder, the Club was revamped and now offers more hands-on, interactive activities, as well as additional PlayStation and computer stations. Jennifer's niece Megan fell in love with it at first glance. Our son Alexander now enjoys playing here, too!

© MediaMarx, Inc.

Alexander was captivated by the treasure chest TV at the Oceaneer Club

The **Oceaneer Lab** (see photo on right) looks just like it sounds—a kids' lab! It has lots of tables and cupboards, along with computer game stations, activity stations, and board games. Allie's visit here (at age 9) is one of her best memories of the cruise—she loved making "Flubber"! Allie at age 12, however, felt it was too young for her and she refused to go. (Your mileage may vary!)

The computer game stations at the Oceaneer Lab

Pick up a **Personal Navigator** at the Club or Lab for the appropriate age group(s)—you'll find a great number of group activities planned, including games, crafts, movies, dancing, and theme parties (see sample activities below). Here is a sample of activities taken from recent kids' *Personal Navigators* (keep in mind that not all of these activities may be available on your cruise):

Sample Activities for Ages 3-4
✔ Stormin' the Club—Arts & crafts and playtime with new friends
✔ Nemo's Coral Reef Adventures—Join Nemo for a magical puppet show!
✔ Do-Si-Do with Snow White—Learn the "Dance of the Seven Little Dwarves"

Sample Activities for Ages 5-7
✔ Professor Goo's Magical Experiments—Make your own Flubber!
✔ So You Want To Be a Pirate?—Learn how to play pirate with Captain Hook!
✔ Animation Antics—Learn how to draw Mickey Mouse

Sample Activities for Ages 8-9
✔ Bridge Tour—Get a tour of the ship's control center
✔ Disney Game Show—Test your Disney knowledge
✔ Goofy Files—Enter the invisible world of forensics and crack a case

Sample Activities for Ages 10-12
✔ Animation Hour—Write and create your very own commercial
✔ Mysterious Islands—Share scary stories of lost ships and vanishing islands
✔ Cranium Crunchers—Test your knowledge and bring your team to victory

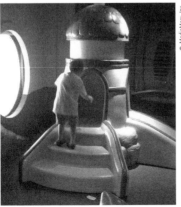

Fanciful climbing toys at Oceaneer Club

A huge video game station at Oceaneer Lab

Introduction | Reservations | Staterooms | Dining | Activities | Ports of Call | Magic | Index

Oceaneer Club and Lab *(continued)*

Tips and Notes

The **first activity** on the Disney Wonder typically starts at 6:30 pm or 7:00 pm on your first night aboard. On the Disney Magic, the entire first night is "Family Time" and if children want to visit this evening, a parent must accompany their child in the Club/Lab (kids who can check themselves in and out do not need to be accompanied by a parent). Family night gives kids a chance to acclimate to the new surroundings with the security of parents nearby.

Trained **counselors** keep kids active and safe while checked in. The counselor-to-kid ratio is 1:15 (ages 3 to 4) and 1:25 (ages 5 to 12). Counselors are mostly female, college grads, and from English-speaking countries (Canada and the United Kingdom are popular). You may rest assured that counselors are trained in how to evacuate children in the event of an emergency.

If your kids are checked in during **mealtimes**, they'll generally be taken up as a group to Topsider's/Beach Blanket Buffet for a trip through a special kid-friendly buffet. At times, younger children may remain in the Club for meals, at the discretion of the counselors. Other than that, no food or drink (other than a water fountain) is provided here.

If your child is very **recently potty-trained**, have a special talk with them before leaving them alone at the Club. All that first-day excitement may give them upset tummies, and they may not know what to do without you there to help. Show them where the toilet is, explain to them that they will need to use the toilet by themselves (the crew members cannot help them nor will they regularly prompt them to use the toilet), and remind them that they can ask a counselor to contact you if they have a problem. Rest assured that the toilets and sinks in the Oceaneer Club are kid-sized, not adult-sized. If a child has an accident, you will be paged and they may be asked not to revisit the Club for 24 to 48 hours in the event their accident was the result of an illness. Pull-up diapers are not allowed unless you are dropping off your child in their pajamas in the evening hours, as it is understood that young children may sleep in pull-up type diapers at night and will probably be sleeping when you pick them up.

Do you have a **toddler under three** who is already potty-trained? If so, the counselors may allow your child to join the Oceaneer Club on a trial basis. Your child must be fully potty-trained, however, from deciding when to go, finding the toilet, closing the door, removing clothing, going potty, wiping, redressing, and washing up. If you have a fully potty-trained child, and you feel your child is ready for this type of environment, talk to the counselors and politely inquire if your child can be accommodated.

Kids may stay in the Club or Lab while you go **play in port**. Just be sure to let the counselors know where you are, and be aware that your pager won't work if you go too far afield. Also check that the Club/Lab opens early enough for your shore excursion meeting time.

If a child gets **sleepy** while at the Club, they can nap on a sleep mat, which is usually placed near the check-in desk or in a quiet corner. If kids are still in the Club around 10:00 pm, counselors will bring out sleep mats to rest on while watching movies.

When Allie cruised at age 9, her 10-year-old cousin Nina was also along. Alas, the 8 to 9 group and the 10 to 12 group have different activities. Allie and Nina found it frustrating that they couldn't stay together. Allie asked us to remind you that if you have siblings or cousins in these **different age groups**, let them know in advance that they may be separated so it's not such a huge disappointment.

Activities for Adults

Kids, keep out—this page is just for grown-ups! Disney may be family-focused, but rest assured Disney hasn't forgotten your adult needs. There are **plenty of adult-oriented and adult-only activities** onboard, including an entire entertainment district (see next page). If you're worried you'll be bored, it's unlikely—we never have enough time to do what we want, with or without kids. Here's a list of specifically adult-oriented activities:

Bingo—If you're not a bingo person, you may want to pass this one up, but it is surprisingly popular and fun! Bingo is the only gambling onboard and attracts mostly adults. (Kids often attend and play, but you must be 18 or older to claim any winnings.) Bingo is held once a day in Rockin' Bar D/WaveBands (and occasionally in the Promenade Lounge) and a special "Snowball" jackpot rolls over each day until won. Cards are about $15 for a single pack (5 cards, one per game), $25 for a value pack (15 cards, three per game), or $35 for a super pack (30 cards). Your odds of winning are higher earlier in the cruise, when fewer people are playing. Prizes (cash and gifts) are awarded daily at each game. Yeah, baby!

Dance Lessons—Learn the basics of ballroom dancing—check your *Personal Navigator*.

Beer, Margarita, and Wine Tastings—There are beer and margarita tastings in Diversions (check your *Navigator*). There's also a wine tasting seminar (about $12)—only adults can participate. Make reservations at Guest Services.

Captain's Receptions—Meet the captain at various functions, including receptions and Disney Navigator Series seminars (see page 163).

Sports—Shoot hoops or play volleyball on the Wide World of Sports deck (deck 10 forward), play shuffleboard or run laps on deck 4, or try your hand at Ping-Pong (deck 9 mid). And don't forget the exercise classes in the Vista Spa (see pages 160–162).

Pin Trading—Bring along your pins and trade with others. Special pin trading sessions are generally held in the Atrium Lobby—check your *Personal Navigator*.

Games—Play chess or backgammon in Diversions or start up a Scrabble game in Sessions/Cadillac Lounge. There may also be pool games at the Quiet Cove pool. Check your *Personal Navigator* for details.

Live Auctions at Sea—Fun to bid or just watch others bid! See page 165 for details.

Cocktail Hours—Held in the Atrium (deck 3 midship) or in Sessions/Cadillac Lounge (deck 3 forward) on certain days. Alas, the beverages—alcoholic or not—aren't complimentary, with the possible exception of the Captain's Reception.

Seminars and Tours—Get the low-down on shopping, shore excursions, and debarkation procedures with talks held in the Buena Vista Theatre (note that these talks are broadcast on your stateroom TV if you can't make it). And on the 7-night and longer cruises, adults can learn the art of entertaining, get behind-the-scenes peeks, and more. See page 163.

In addition to the above, you'll also enjoy these **adult-only places**: Palo restaurant (see pages 121–122), Vista Spa (see pages 160–162), the Quiet Cove pool (see page 154), the Cove Café (see page 153), Signals bar (deck 9 forward), the adult entertainment district (see next page), and Serenity Bay Beach on Castaway Cay (see page 295). And while it's not adults-only, the Buena Vista movie theater in the late evenings is mostly adults (see page 156).

Tip: Check your *Personal Navigator's* grid for the "Adult" row with adult activities.

Adult Entertainment District (Beat Street/Route 66)

After all those adults-only activities, you may want an adults-only place to wind down the day, too. Beat Street (on the Disney Magic) and Route 66 (on the Disney Wonder), both on deck 3 forward, are exclusively for adults 18 and older after 9:00 pm. The names and decor of the clubs and lounges may differ a bit on the two ships, but after a recent renovation on the Wonder they offer essentially the same venues. On both ships you can expect to find a dance club; a relaxing, adult lounge; a pub; and the ship's duty-free liquor shop. Here is a description of each club:

Dance Club—Rockin' Bar D (Magic) and WaveBands (Wonder) are the ships' largest clubs, offering Top 40 and Golden Oldies dance music, DJs, karaoke hours, and cabaret acts featuring entertainers from the stage shows. Typically, a special event is held each evening around 10:30 pm or 11:00 pm, such as the Match Your Mate game show, Decades, Krazy Karaoke, Rock Star, One Hit Wonders, and so on. Many cruisers report a preference for the 70s night, and would pass up the 80s night. Guests are selected from the dance floor to participate in some shows—if you want to be picked, get up and be wild! The Match Your Mate game show works like the Newlywed Game. Crew members choose three couples who've been together for various durations as contestants. Unmarried couples will enjoy watching it, but we've been on cruises where only married couples are invited to play. A DJ or live band generally precedes and follows these events. Hours are usually from 7:30 pm to 2:00 am. Smoking is allowed in the rear, but poor ventilation can make the entire club smoky.

© MediaMarx, Inc.

Dave gets drafted to play one of the Village People during 70s Disco Night

Smoking Onboard

Unlike most other cruise ships, Disney restricts smoking to limited areas on the ship, and enforces their rules. Smoking is allowed in part of the adults-only lounge, bar area at Diversions, outside Cove Café, and open-air guest areas such as decks 4, 9, and 10 (port side only) and stateroom verandahs. The Mickey Pool area is an exception, as it is all non-smoking. No smoking is allowed in any of the staterooms. We've had no problems with smoke on our cruises. And smokers report that the accessibility of smoking areas meets their needs, though it is sometimes tough to find an ashtray (try deck 10). You can purchase cigarettes ($16/carton) in the liquor shop on deck 3 forward. For those interested in Cuban cigars, you can purchase them in virtually all of the ports except Key West. At the time of writing, cigar smoking was allowed only in the usual open-air guest areas (decks 9, 10, and stateroom verandahs). Sometimes there is a cigar and cognac night at Cove Café. Keep in mind that you cannot bring Cuban cigars back into the U.S., so smoke 'em while you can.

Introduction

Reservations

Staterooms

Dining

Activities

Ports of Call

Magic

Index

Adult Lounge—This lounge is always adults-only. On the Disney Magic, it's called Sessions and it has a jazzy feel. On the Disney Wonder, it's called Cadillac Lounge and has a vintage auto theme. Relax in low, comfy chairs, listen to the pianist or recorded music, and get mellow. Music listening stations are available along the wall with the large portholes if you want to listen to something different (though cruisers report they aren't always functioning). This is a dim, mellow lounge—perfect for pre-dinner or pre-show drinks and romantic interludes. It's not uncommon to find fruit and cheese platters in here between 7:30 pm and 8:30 pm. Hours are usually from 4:30 pm to midnight or 1:00 am. Smoking is permitted at the bar and in the rear of the lounge only, but it can still get smoky.

Diversions—Formerly a dueling piano club, renovations in September 2003/2004 opened the space up into Diversions, an all-purpose pub and sports bar. The lounge now has huge portholes, spilling light into a clubby room filled with comfy chairs. Warm wood tones create a relaxing atmosphere, as do large chess/backgammon tables in the center of the room. The lounge still has a piano off to the side, as well as a long bar in the back of the room. A small selection of books and magazines are available for those who want a quiet

Diversions on the Wonder

respite during the day. What can you do here besides drink and relax? Check your *Personal Navigator* for sporting event broadcasts (shown on the numerous televisions in the back), beer tastings and trivia, and a British Pub Night. Smoking is allowed at the bar only.

Beverages of all kinds are served at all clubs. See page 128 for details on availability and prices. Snacks may be available out in the hallway from 11:00 pm to midnight. There's a duty-free liquor shop (see page 311), but purchases cannot be consumed onboard.

Cove Café

A cozy adults-only area is available on both the Disney Magic and Disney Wonder: Cove Café on deck 9, beside the adults-only pool. It took the place of the Common Grounds teen club, which moved up to deck 11 at the same time. Cove Café is a cozy coffeehouse, lined with books and magazines and filled with light from huge portholes and sliding glass doors. Several music listening stations are here. The area immediately outside the café has comfortable padded lounge chairs. Wireless Internet access is available here, both inside and immediately outside. An extensive specialty coffee menu is available—expect to pay $2.00 for espresso, $2.50 for cappuccino and café mocha, and $4.75 for coffee drinks laced with liquors. Teas ($3.75) are also available, as is champagne, wine, port, martinis, and a full bar. Light snacks such as pastries and sandwiches may be available, too. Open until midnight. This is a delightful expansion of the ship's adults-only territory.

Cove Café

Swimming in the Pools

Cruise ship pools aren't exactly sized for Olympic competition, but while your ship's three pools are best described as "cozy," it doesn't stop them from being some of the busiest places onboard. What makes Disney's pools especially nice is that they're fresh water, not salt; that kids, families, and adults each get their own pool; and that they have a little extra magic.

Quiet Cove Adult Pool—the largest pool onboard—is on deck 9 forward. This is one of the five areas on the cruise where adults can go for child-free relaxation. Pool depth is 48" (122 cm). No jumping or diving is permitted. Adjacent are two whirlpools (Caution: The water can be hot!), Vista Spa, Cove Café, an open shower, and the Signals pool bar. On the Disney Wonder, waterfalls cascade into the whirlpools and deluxe lounge chairs with comfy cushions are arranged on the teak deck.

Amidship is **Goofy's Family Pool** featuring an image of Goofy snorkeling at the bottom of the pool. Alongside Goofy's pool are two whirlpools, an open shower, and Pinocchio's Pizzeria (see page 125). Pool depth is 48" (122 cm). No jumping or diving is permitted. At the other end of the pool is a stage where the crew and Disney characters join the guests for the deck parties (see next page). A hideaway deck may be pulled out to completely cover the pool during deck parties.

The sight to see on deck 9 is **Mickey's Kid's Pool** (see photo below). True to Disney style, a regular wading pool and slide is transformed into Mickey Mouse. His face is the main part of the pool with a depth of 18" (46 cm). Mickey's ears (with a depth of 11"/28 cm) are for

the very little ones. This is a very busy place on sea days. The centerpiece of Mickey's Kid's Pool is the water slide supported by Mickey's gloved hand. To use the slide, the kids must be from ages 4 to 14 and between 32" and 64" tall (81 to 162 cm). The slide is staffed by crew members, but there are no lifeguards. Health regulations require that kids be potty-trained—swim diapers are not allowed in the pools. Infants with swim diapers are allowed in the starboard "ear" on the Disney Magic, which is a fountain play area. On the Disney Wonder, kids in swim diapers can use a 385-sq. ft. "Toddler Splash Zone" under the Mickey slide with star- and moon-shaped interactive fountains. Pluto's Dog House as well as Goofy's Galley (see page 121) are nearby.

© MediaMarx, Inc.

A quiet day at the Mickey Pool

Typical **pool hours** are from 6:00 am to 10:00 pm for Mickey's Pool and 6:00 am to midnight for the other pools. Goofy's pool closes during deck parties and other events that use the extending deck. Mickey's slide is usually only open 9:00 am to 6:30 pm.

Tip: When is a good time to use the pools? With a lot of guests and small pools, the pools can get very crowded. This is especially true on hot afternoons at sea. The trick is to think differently—go when your fellow guests are busy elsewhere, like in port or during meals. Immediately after you embark is a good time, but be ready to make it to your assembly station by 4:00 pm. Other good times are in the evenings and early in the morning, as the pools open at 6:00 am.

Living It Up at Deck Parties

Every Disney cruise, regardless of its length, has at least one of Disney's famous deck parties. These high-energy parties are held on and around the family Goofy Pool on deck 9 midship. No, you don't have to dance on water—the pool is covered by a large, retractable dance floor during the parties. You can expect to be entertained by some or all of the following: a live band, DJ, dancers, fireworks, a dessert buffet, big video screen, and "party animals" (Disney characters). Here are descriptions:

Bon Voyage Sailaway Celebration—Every cruise enjoys this celebration, held as your ship pulls away from the dock. This is probably the first time you'll meet your cruise director, who is joined by Disney characters and either a live band or a DJ. As the ship gets underway, the ship's whistle plays the first seven notes of "When You Wish Upon a Star." We highly recommend this party—it really gets you in the mood (see the photo on page 19). Tip: Celebrate your sailaway by bringing bubbles to blow or a small flag to wave! (Party typically starts at 4:15 pm or 4:30 pm and lasts for about 30-60 minutes.)

Pirates in the Caribbean Party—Ahoy, ye landlubbers! This fun deck party is offered to all Disney cruisers, regardless of cruise length. On the three- and four-night cruises, it's held on your second to last evening; on the seven-night cruises, it's held on day 4 or 5 (see page 132 for schedule). The party starts around 9:45 pm on deck 9 midship, after the Pirate-themed dinner earlier that evening (see page 123). Expect lots of infectious music, dancing, and visits from crew members and Disney characters (watch out for Captain Hook!). You are treated to a Pirate buffet around 10:45 pm with desserts and "pirate fare" such as chili, fajitas, and turkey legs. You may even get fireworks! We've experienced this party twice ourselves and it's a not-to-be-missed experience—it's better than the Tropical deck party it replaced. Pirate or Caribbean dress is encouraged (we dressed up and loved it!). The party lasts for about 30 minutes.

© MediaMarx, Inc.

Pirates on Deck!

The **music** at the deck parties is quite loud and is geared toward older kids, teens, and young adults. If you don't want to be in the thick of things, you may enjoy watching from deck 10 midship. We recommend you visit deck 10 during the sailaway party—it's the best place to enjoy the party while watching the ship pull away (see sidebar below).

To find out exactly what deck parties are offered, check the **Personal Navigator** upon arrival. Note: In inclement weather, the deck parties are held in the atrium (deck 3 mid).

Sailing Away From Port Canaveral

One of the most exciting experiences of your cruise is when your ship pulls away from the pier and makes its way down the channel, heading for the ocean. You don't want to miss it. Make time to go up to deck 10 around 5:00 pm and watch the scenery slide by as you leave port. Look for the crew members at the terminal—they don huge Mickey gloves and wave the ship off. One of the best places to watch your ship's progress is from deck 10 forward, near the Wide World of Sports courts. Or visit deck 9 forward to watch the bridge crew on the wing. Look for the escort of security boats as your ship moves through the channel, too!

Introduction
Reservations
Staterooms
Dining
Activities
Ports of Call
Magic
Index

Watching Movies and TV

The Walt Disney Company all started with a mouse projected on a movie screen, and its cruise line takes those beginnings seriously. From the sumptuous **Buena Vista movie theatre** on deck 5 aft with its 268 stadium-style seats and two-story screen, to the giant 24-by-14-foot outdoor screen on decks 9 and 10, the free, round-the-clock Disney movie channels on your stateroom TV, you'll never lack filmed entertainment on a Disney cruise.

You can expect to see recent Disney animated classics and first-run movies from Disney's motion picture divisions. You may also see some popular, non-Disney movies a few months after they've been released—cruisers were treated to the "Da Vinci Code" on 2006 cruises. Films are rated G and PG (with some PG-13 and R in the Buena Vista Theatre only) and are shown in that order throughout the day. Movies are free, there's no need to reserve seats, and they start as early as 9:30 am—the last show usually starts between 10:00 pm and 11:00 pm. Check your *Personal Navigator* or the theater for a **list of movies** during your cruise. Matinees on at-sea days are popular—arrive early for a good seat. Wondering

what will be playing on your cruise? About a week before you cruise, you can call 888-325-2500, choose the "reservations" option, then ask the representative what movies will be showing. Tip: If you like to snack during your movies, a stand outside the theater sells packaged snacks, bagged popcorn, and beverages. To save money, order room service and bring it with you or take a detour up to deck 9's snack counters.

© MediaMarx, Inc.

Buena Vista Theatre

The **big-screen outdoor movies on the "Ariel View Television"** (seen on page 19) are always rated G or PG and have recently included favorites like "Finding Nemo," "The Little Mermaid," "Miracle," and "Pirates of the Caribbean." Movies are displayed on a large, bright screen affixed to the stack above the Goofy Pool (deck 9 midship). Movies play in afternoons and evenings, but are generally limited to one or two showings per day.

Your **stateroom TV** has plenty to watch, too ... and it is all free! Below is a recent channel guide (channels and stations may vary). Use the TV for Disney background music while you're in the stateroom. We enjoy watching movies on it at the end of the day. Check your stateroom for a movie list. Anticipate about 12–15 distinct movies to be showing on TV—movies repeat frequently. The "all movies, all the time" channels (31–36) start a new movie every two hours, beginning at midnight. The Animated Classics channel (37) also starts a Disney animated movie every two hours, beginning at 1:00 am. Both movie channels go around the clock. Tip: You may be able to watch taped performances of the stage shows like *Golden Mickeys* and *Disney Dreams* on your stateroom TV—look between 6:30 pm and 10:30 pm on show nights.

10	Entertain. Guide	15	Time/Special Events	20	CNN	30	Sitcoms
11	View from Bridge	16	What's Afloat	21	Time/ESPN Intl.	31–36	All Movies
12	Bridge Report	17	Shore Excursions	22	ESPN	37	Animated Classics
13	Voyage Map	18	ABC	23	ESPN2	38	Animated Features
14	Shoppping	19	CNN Headline News	24	Disney Channel		

Enjoying the Shows

Depend on the world's greatest entertainment company to deliver the **best live shows** on the seven seas. Disney turned to Broadway and Hollywood for inspiration (rather than Las Vegas), and delivers shows that the whole family enjoys. Live shows are presented in the Walt Disney Theatre on deck 4 forward, a 975-seat theater that fills the ship from decks 3 to 7. State-of-the-art sound and lighting systems (there are nearly 400 stage lights!) and a very talented cast combine to entertain you.

On all of the cruise itineraries, you can expect to see three shows: *Golden Mickeys, Disney Dreams*, and either *Twice Charmed* (Disney Magic) or *Toy Story—The Musical* (Disney Wonder). The 4-night cruises add a Variety Show. The 7+-night cruises add the *Welcome Aboard Variety Show*, a first-release film, an entertainer (such as a juggler or magician), and the *Farewell Variety Show*. Shows are held **twice nightly** at roughly the same times as the dinner seatings (see page 110), so if you have the early seating, you'll see the "late" show (and vice versa). Shows are 50 to 55 minutes long. Arrive about 15 to 30 minutes before showtime to get a good seat. Disney doesn't allow videotaping, flash photography, or the saving of seats in the theater. Preludes Lounge (located just in front of the theater) sells beverages and snacks (such as candy bars), or you can bring your own. Smoothies and beverages are sold in the theater before the show.

Toy Story–The Musical (Disney Wonder)—Replacing the long-running *Hercules the Muse-ical*, this new show follows the heartwarming storyline of the first Toy Story movie. The stage adaptation features eight new songs, inflatable costumes, and rear-projection sets.

Twice Charmed–An Original Twist on the Cinderella Story (Disney Magic)—This creative show picks up where the traditional Cinderella story ended. What would happen if an Evil Fairy Godfather turned back time to stop Cinderella from fitting into the glass slipper?

The Golden Mickeys—This delightful, Hollywood-style award show features favorite musical scenes from Disney films, just as you might see at the Oscars or Tonys. Flanking the stage are two movie screens that show a wide range of documentary film clips, presentations by celebrities like Roy Disney and Angela Lansbury, and excerpts from the animated films.

Disney Dreams—The must-see show for Disney fans! Anne-Marie is visited in her dreams by characters from her favorite Disney stories. It's wonderfully sentimental and the special effects at the end are not to be missed. Every Disney fan will be at least a little misty-eyed by the end of this "bedtime story." Being the most popular show aboard, Disney Dreams is often crowded. Check your *Personal Navigator* for an extra performance in the afternoon.

Variety and Cabaret Shows—Featuring guest performers who do a short sampling of the shows they'll perform later in the Rockin' Bar D/WaveBands club. Because Disney switches guest entertainers mid-cruise on the 7-night itinerary, the Farewell Variety Show features different performers than the Welcome Aboard Variety Show.

Notes: The **Who Wants to Be a Mouseketeer?** show that was previously held in the Walt Disney Theatre is now only held in Studio Sea. In this game show (based on the popular show "Who Wants to Be a Millionaire?"), contestants are selected at random from the audience and the "phone a friend" panel is also selected from the guests. Prizes are limited-edition Disney merchandise, much smaller than the one million dollars offered on television.

Introduction

Reservations

Staterooms

Dining

Activities

Ports of Call

Magic

Index

Surfing the Internet

While it isn't as fun as a message in a bottle, the Internet is an easy, quick way to keep in touch with family, friends, and clients while you're cruising. Internet access is available on both the Magic and Wonder at computer terminals and as wireless access (wifi) in most areas of the ships.

Terminal Access—Computer terminals are available to guests in two locations onboard: Internet Cafe (main location, eight terminals, open to everyone), and The Stack/Aloft (two terminals, teens only)—The Internet Cafe (located at the aft end of the Promenade Lounge on deck 3 midship) is open 24 hours a day and boasts about 8 terminals (flat panel screens, keyboards, mice, headphones, and video cameras) with reasonably comfortable chairs. Typically at least one, if not several, terminals are available at any given time. All terminals are installed with web browsers and America Online. Your e-mail provider may offer a web-based interface to check your e-mail—inquire about this before you leave home and bring any necessary web site addresses, login names, and passwords with you (see worksheet on the next page). Note that if you can access your e-mail through America Online (AOL) or the web, you avoid the CruisEmail rates noted later (see Pricing on the next page)—just be sure not to send e-mail through the "E-Mail" option on the terminal and use AOL or the web instead. AOL Instant Messenger users can use the AOL application to access their buddy list and send Instant Messages. Note that if you log in to any e-mail, message boards, or other sites that require a login name and password during your time on the cruise, be sure to log off before you leave the terminal. If you do not, the next person who uses those same sites could find themselves able to access your account or post under your user name on a message board. SeaMobile (http://www.seamobile.com) provides reliable Internet access. If you have questions once you are onboard, you can check with one of the Internet Cafe managers, who are on duty during the day and early evening. There may be a printer available, though it may also incur an additional, per-page fee—inquire with the manager on duty. Note that the Internet Cafe is not always open the morning of disembarkation.

© MediaMarx, Inc.

One of Jennifer's hangouts, the Internet Cafe

Wireless Access—Wireless Internet access is available on both the Magic and the Wonder in select locations on the ship. To use it, you'll need to bring your own laptop (which must be wireless-ready) and power cables. Once onboard, look for the Wireless Internet information sheet at the Internet Cafe or from Guest Services (deck 3). Next go to a wireless "hot spot" on the ship—at press time, the "hot spots" include most public areas, guest staterooms, and the open areas on decks 9 and 10. While wireless access now reaches to staterooms (see page 107), your signal strength may not always be ideal. When we were unable to get a good signal in our stateroom, we preferred to use our laptop while sitting in the comfortable chairs on deck 4 or 5, overlooking the atrium. As for ease of use, we had to fiddle a bit with our settings at first on our first cruise, but all subsequent cruises with a variety of devices (including an iPhone!) have been smooth sailing. Instructions for both PC and Mac users are provided on the information sheet from Guest Services. Note that printing is not available with wireless access. Note: VOIP (Voice Over Internet Protocol) services are reportedly blocked on the Disney ships.

Pricing—Alas, Internet usage is not free. Expect to pay 75 cents a minute for access (either terminal access or wireless access). If you expect to surf for more than an hour total, you can pre-purchase your minutes for less: 50 min./$27.50, 100 min./$40 and 250 min./$75 (extra-long cruises may offer 500 min. for $125). Your minutes can be used for both terminal access and wireless access. Alas, there is no longer an unlimited minutes package offered for either terminal or wireless access. Everyone in your stateroom can use your minutes, but only one person can be logged in at a time. Note that you are "on the meter" from the moment you log in until you log off. It's very important that you specifically log off as directed when you use wireless access, or you may continue spending your minutes! With terminal access, you can send special "CruisEmail" ($3.95 each) or "Video Email" ($4.95 each), but note that the basic Internet usage fees are tacked on top of these rates. "CruisEmail" is an unnecessary expense—save money by using a free e-mail service such as Hotmail (http://www.hotmail.com) or Yahoo! Mail (http://mail.yahoo.com). All Internet usage fees are automatically billed to your onboard account. Parents who don't want their kids to use the Internet can contact Guest Services to disable their Internet accounts. Note that no credit is given for unused time plan minutes. If you feel you have fewer purchased minutes remaining than you expected and suspect an error, visit Guest Services (deck 3) to discuss it.

Logging In—Expect to enter a login name—it's typically the first initial and last name of the person under whose name the cruise reservation was made, plus the stateroom number (e.g., jmarx2612). Passwords are also required, and may initially be the birthdate of person who made the cruise reservation.

Access—If you've pre-purchased a block of minutes, only one member of your family/group can be online at any one time. Note that if another family member is online somewhere else, you won't be able to get online until they log off. While there are computers in the Oceaneer Club and Lab and Ocean Quest, the kids can not surf the Internet from them.

Off-Board Internet Access—There are cafes with Internet terminals offering lower rates in various ports of call. In Nassau, "Tikal Tees & Tokens" has Internet access at 10 cents/min. In St. Maarten, there's an Internet Cafe at the end of the pier for 20 cents a minute. In St. Thomas, "Soapy's Station" in front of the Havensight Mall offers access at 10 cents/min. In Key West, check out the "Internet Isle Cafe" on 118 Duval Street for 25 cents/min. In Cozumel, the "C@fe Internet" near Ave. 10 and Calle 1 has access at 10 cents/min. You can usually find Internet Cafes very near the pier—just browse or ask around.

Web Site Addresses—E-mail your favorite web site addresses to yourself before you cruise or visit http://www.passporter.com/dcl/porthole.htm once onboard for helpful links.

My E-Mail: _____

_____

Account	Login Name	Password	Notes

Tip: Use some system to disguise your passwords here, just in case your PassPorter is seen by someone else.

Rejuvenating at the Spa

The Vista Spa & Salon on deck 9 forward offers world-class spa treatments, a hair salon, an aerobics studio, and a fitness room. The large spa is **exclusively for adults** (with the exception of special teen days—see your *Personal Navigator*). The expansive spa on both the Magic and the Wonder measures in at an astounding 10,700 sq. ft. Like most cruise ship spas, the facility is operated by Steiner (http://www.steinerleisure.com) and the spa staff tends to be female and young. The spa is typically open from 8:00 am to 10:00 pm. Most spa reservations can be made in advance online (see page 139).

If the spa interests you, we recommend you visit during the **open house** on your first afternoon (check your *Personal Navigator* for specific start times). This is also the best time to make reservations for spa treatments, if you haven't booked online already. Read this section well so you have a good idea of what spa treatments you may want to reserve (see next page). Reservations must be canceled at least 24 hours in advance to avoid a 50% fee.

The **hair salon** offers a variety of services—reservations are necessary and they fill up quickly for formal and semi-formal evenings. The hair stylists specialize in European styles and all the basics. Prices: blow dry ($30 to $45); woman's hair cut with wash, cut, and style—$52 to $70 (depends on hair length); man's cut and style—$23; highlights ($79 to $99); permanent color (roots)—$64 to $79; and permanent color (full head)—$84 to $104. You can also get nail services: A 40-minute manicure is $40 and a 55-minute pedicure is $55.

The **aerobics studio** is where many of the fitness classes and seminars are offered. Activities are listed in the *Personal Navigator* as well as on a schedule available in the Vista Spa. Expect complimentary hair consultations, metabolism seminars, fatburner aerobics, detoxification seminars, skin care clinics, introduction to Pilates, de-stress techniques, Step Magic, and cardio kickbox. You are encouraged to sign up in advance for the free classes and seminars, which last about 30 to 45 minutes each. Group personal training may be offered on your cruise for $75/60 minutes. Or get a Body Composition Analysis to measure your body's metabolic rate, water, fat, and lean tissue—price is $30 and includes analysis from a fitness instructor. Zone diet consultation (which includes the body composition analysis) is available for $75/45 min. Preregistration is required for the personal training sessions, body composition analysis, and diet consultations.

The **fitness room** has a panoramic overlook on both ships. The fitness room recently doubled in size by expanding over the bridge, and it now overlooks the ship's bow. The expansion also brought more fitness equipment, an area for spinning classes, and private salons for Pilates instruction. On both ships, the fitness rooms offer guests the use of free weights, Cybex weight machines, treadmills, stair-steppers, ab-rollers, and stationary bikes. No fees or reservations are needed to use the fitness room, though there may be a waitlist for a treadmill during peak times. The fitness room is more crowded on at-sea days. Open from 7:00 am to 8:00 pm.

Tip: Walk (or jog) all around the perimeter of deck 4—the "promenade" deck. One lap around the deck is $1/3$ of a mile (535 m.); three laps is one mile (1.6 km). Note that the jogging direction is counter-clockwise to avoid collisions. Want to walk with others? Check your *Personal Navigator* for instructor-led "Walk a Mile" morning sessions.

Spa treatments are given in one of twelve private treatment rooms or in the private "spa villas." Separate men's and women's locker rooms are available with restrooms, delightful showers, saunas, steam rooms, and lockers. Some people prefer the showers at the spa to the showers in their staterooms—there's more room, the water pressure's better, and the showerhead is luxurious. Present your Key to the World card at the check-in desk to get a robe and locker key at no charge.

Spa Treatments—A variety of treatments are available at prices ranging from $26 to $288. We've underlined the spa treatments we've tried and would do again! A menu of treatments is available in the spa, but here's a sneak peek: Spa Taster (massage and facial for $109/50 min. total or $242 for couples massage); Aromaspa Ocean Wrap with Well Being Back Massage ($176/75 min.); Ionithermie Algae Super-Detox ($145/50 min.); Aromastone Therapy ($175/75 min.); LT Oxygen Lifting Facial ($109/55 min.); Elemis Pro Collagen Facial ($130/50 min.); Well Being Massage ($109/50 min. total or $242 for couples massage); Lime & Ginger Salt Glow ($178/75 min.); 4-Hand Massage ($219/50 min.); Gentle Touch Teeth Whitening ($199/45 min.); and Cabana Massage at Castaway Cay ($139/50 min. or $278 for couples massage). Let's not forget the Tropical Rainforest, the Exotic Rasul, and the Spa Villas—read on for more details!

Tropical Rainforest—An innovative, relaxing "thermal suite" with a dry sauna, a chamomile-essence sauna, a eucalyptus steam room, and special showers that spray water overhead and on the sides. The main room has four heated, tiled loungers (see photo on right)—loll about on one then cool off in a fog shower. Jennifer loves this! The Tropical Rainforest is open from 8:00 am to 10:00 pm. It's very popular and can host upwards of two dozen people—men and women—at any one time. Quietest times are on the first day of the cruise and on port days. On busy days, the four tiled loungers are usually occupied and waiting for one to open can be frustrating. Swimsuits are required. Cost is $15/day (just $8 if you're having a "hands-on" spa treatment) or $35/3 days, $75/week, or $120/10 days.

Jennifer relaxes in a heated lounge chair in the Tropical Rainforest

© MediaMarx, Inc.

Exotic Rasul (formerly known as Surial Ritual Chamber)—This unique treatment is inspired by the Rasul cleansing rituals performed in the Sultan's harems during the Ottoman Empire. You are escorted to the tile-lined ritual chamber, which is a suite with a sitting area, steam room, and shower. Exfoliating mud is in a small bowl—smear the mud on yourself or on each other (if you're with a friend) and relax in the steam room to absorb the minerals and trace elements from the mud. Afterward, shower off and apply complimentary lotions and scrubs. This is very popular with couples. We loved it ourselves! Be warned that it does get very hot. Bring some bottled water—you'll probably get quite thirsty—and extra towels. Cost is $83 for 1 to 3 people for 50 minutes.

Rejuvenating at the Spa *(continued)*

Spa Villas—The spa's expansion in 2006 included the creation of singles and couples spa "villas" with special spa treatments. The villas are private, Mediterranean-themed treatment rooms with their own verandahs, complete with whirlpool tubs, open-air showers, and luxurious lounge "beds." All spa treatments in the villas include a tea ceremony, a bathing ritual of your choice, and a foot cleansing ceremony—and you can spring for a bottle of champagne and strawberries or add an extra spa treatment. Treatments available in the single villas (for one person) include Alone Time (50-min. spa treatment of your choice—$199/105 min.); Body Purifying (100-min. body wrap with full body massage and dry float bed—$245/155 min.); and Sensory Awakening (facial and deep tissue massage—$295/155 min.). Treatments in the couples villas include Romantic Hideaway (50-min. spa treatment of your choice—$449/120 min.); Couples Choice (75-min. spa treatment of your choice—$475/130 min.); and Ultimate Indulgence (facial and deep tissue massage—$589/130 min.). If you do the math, you'll see that each of these treatments has 55-70 minutes of extra time included so you can enjoy your spa villa's amenities in privacy, though we should note that this extra time is not in one uninterrupted block but rather a bit before your treatment and the rest after. And if you need more privacy than the open-air verandah provides (remember, that is where your whirlpool tub and shower are located), there are two curtains you can use—one offers privacy for the shower, the other offers privacy for the tub. These curtains may not provide complete protection when it's windy or when in port (just something for the shy to keep in mind), though we didn't have difficulties in our Spa Villa experience. We absolutely adored our Spa Villa and found it infinitely relaxing and luxurious. We highly recommend it!

Yes, the Spa Villas really are this relaxing!

Special Treatments—Check your *Personal Navigator* or visit the spa to learn about special treatments offered during your cruise. We've seen Teen Days for hair and nails, Ladies Mornings/Nights, and a Mid-Cruise Booster Package. The Ladies Morning/Night package is a massage, foot massage, and facial in a private room, plus a trip to the Tropical Rainforest where you can enjoy champagne and sweets. Cost is $150 for 120 minutes.

Cabana Massages—Get a private or couples massage in one of the delightful, open-air cabanas on Castaway Cay. Note that the treatments in the cabanas are a bit more expensive than the same ones on the ship. Prices are $139 for a single massage and $278 for a couples massage (choose from Spa Taster or Well Being Massage). Reserve early as they book up quickly. We recommend you avoid the first or second appointment of the day, just in case the ship docks late. Also, keep in mind that the oils they massage into your skin can make your skin more likely to burn later in that Castaway Cay sunshine—bring hats and coverups as well as extra sunscreen. Also see page 298.

Spa Products—The spa personnel may push their spa products during treatments, which is uncomfortable for some guests. The products are Elemis (http://www.elemis.com) and are good, but pricey. If you don't want to buy a product, just say "no thank you" and be firm. You could also indicate on your health form that you don't want to purchase products.

Tipping—It's customary to tip 15%, though really good service may deserve 20%. 10% is fine for treatments like the Exotic Rasul that require minimal staff time or treatments like the spa villas that have extra private time. Just write the amount you wish to tip on your bill and it will be charged to your onboard account.

Learning Through Seminars

We keep saying that nobody has to be bored, even on a long cruise, and here's more proof! Disney produces a full schedule of shipboard tours, seminars, and programs for guests 18 and older. You don't even have to register or pay extra in most cases.

Disney's Art of Entertaining—These presentations showcase a senior chef who prepares a dish, allowing you to sample it. They also include tips on place setting, decorating, and napkin folding. Some have wine sampling. Programs include Great Expectations: The Appetizer, Dazzling Desserts, and Signature Entrée. Available on 7-night and longer itineraries only.

Galley Tour—Enjoy an adults-only guided tour of the main galley between Lumière's/Triton's and Parrot Cay. Available on both the Magic and Wonder. See page 119 for more details.

Disney Behind the Scenes—Presentations by a Disney historian, actor, or artist (either a special guest or regular crew member), usually presented in the Buena Vista Theatre. These presentations vary in length and by topic but they are all entertaining and well worth the time. Programs include a Stage Works Tour (meet the stage production crew members—they demonstrate some of the stage effects, answer questions, and allow you to go up on the stage and take a look around at the set and props); Costuming Tour (see and even wear some of the costumes used in the show); and a Q&A session with the Walt Disney Theatre cast (hear stories and get answers to questions). This program is offered on the Magic and on the 4-night cruise on the Wonder.

Disney's Navigator Series—Programs include "The Making of the Disney Magic" (the captain presents a video on the history of the Disney Magic from concept to construction to maiden voyage and then answers questions) and Captain's Corner (a Q&A session with the senior staff covering just about everything involving the cruise and the ship—it's very impressive, informative, and fun). Available on 7-night and longer itineraries only.

Wine Tasting Seminar—This is a good place to mention the "Stem to Stern" Wine Tasting Seminar held on all cruises in either Palo or one of the lounges. For $15/adult (21 and up only), the Cellar Master introduces you to wine types, gives you tips on identifying wines, and shows you how to properly taste a wine. Seminar includes tastings of four to six wines. You may also receive a commemorative pin for attending the seminar. (Pin traders take note!) Reservations are required—stop by Guest Services to make reservations. Available on both the Magic and the Wonder.

Beer Tasting—Check your *Personal Navigator* for a beer tasting session held in Diversions (deck 3 forward).

Towel Animal Folding—Find out how to make those cute animals they leave in your stateroom each night—check your *Personal Navigator* for time and place.

Art of the Disney Magic Self-Guided Tour—The Walt Disney Company was founded by an artist, so it's natural that its beautiful ships are full of art—original as well as reproductions. The Art of the Disney Magic tour is a self-guided tour of the art found everywhere on the Disney Magic (sorry, the tour is not available on the Disney Wonder). Pick up a tour booklet at Guest Services—it leads you around the ship, describing and explaining the artwork. Get the booklet early in the cruise so that you can read about the art in the restaurants as you dine in each. If you'd like to see photos of the various stops on the tour, visit http://www.castawayclub.com/dmtour.htm.

Kicking Back and Relaxing

This chapter would not be complete without a few words on how to get the most out of your "down time" on the cruise. You know—relax, bum around, sunbathe, or whatever. This is one of the benefits of cruising, after all!

Relaxing on Deck—Looking for the best place to loll about in a deck chair? Deck 9 is great if you want to be near the pools or people-watch, but it gets very crowded. Try the deck aft of Topsider's/Beach Blanket Buffet after dinner—almost no one goes there. Deck 10 has lots of sun. Deck 7 aft has a secluded and quiet deck. Deck 4 has very comfy, padded deck loungers and lots of shade (see photo below). The lounge chairs on decks 7–10 are made of plastic and metal and recline in several positions, including completely flat. Disney requests that you not reserve the lounge chairs, so don't drape a towel over a chair to use later. If you see loungers being saved with towels, don't be shy about using them. There are also tables and chairs on deck 9 that are mostly in the shade and protected by windows, but decks 4 and 10 can get very windy. Alas, only the larger verandahs at the very aft of the ship are large enough for lounge chairs, but regular deck chairs are on each verandah.

Sunbathing—Sunworshippers typically prefer deck 10. Deck 7 aft works well, too. Decks 4 and 9 are typically too shady. Don't forget sunscreen—the Caribbean sun is harsh.

Reading—With all the things to do onboard, you might not think to bring a book. But if you enjoy reading, you'll absolutely adore reading in a deck chair on your verandah, on deck 4 (our personal favorite), or deck 7 aft. Cove Café (page 153) has a small lending library, too!

Strolling—Haven't you always dreamed of perambulating about a deck? Deck 4, also called the Promenade Deck, allows you to walk all around the perimeter of the ship (3 laps = 1 mile). Decks 9 and 10 are also options, though they can get crowded during the day. Deck 10 gets very windy and wet in the evenings, but if you can handle that, it makes for fun walks.

Napping—There's nothing like a good nap, especially while cruising. It's something about the lulling effect of the waves. Your stateroom is a great place for a nap, but you may also catch some zzz's in a quiet spot like deck 7 aft.

People-Watching—It's hard to find a spot where you can't people-watch on a ship with this many people! Deck 9 and deck 4 overlooking the atrium are particularly good spots, though.

Spa—The Tropical Rainforest in the Vista Spa (see page 161) is a relaxing spot to spend time.

Shopping—Why not? See page 311.

© MediaMarx, Inc.

Relaxing on deck 4

Lost & Found

Did you leave your half-finished book on your lounge chair before heading to lunch? Report it to Guest Services on deck 3 midship. If you discover you left something behind after disembarking, check with Lost & Found in the terminal or call Disney Cruise Line after returning home. Don't forget to ID all your important items—just in case!

Overlooked Attractions Aboard

Disney is renowned for its attention to detail, and the Disney Cruise Line is no exception. There are any number of smaller, overlooked attractions and activities that may interest you. Here's a list of our favorites:

Hidden Mickey Hunt—How many Mickeys can you find onboard? The internationally recognized Mickey Mouse head (one big circle and two smaller circles for the ears) has been hidden in murals, railings, footstools—you name it! We know of more than 25 on the ships, including one in the dinner plate at Palo. Ask at Guest Services for the Hidden Mickey Challenge—it's a fun activity geared toward kids, but still fun for adults. To see the photos of the hidden Mickeys, visit http://www.castawayclub.com/hmick.htm.

Listening Stations—Listen to your favorite tunes in the adults-only lounge (Sessions/Cadillac Lounge) and the Cove Café. Just check the playlist for the music, punch in the code on the pad, and put on the headphones.

Pin Trading—This popular activity that started at the parks has migrated to the cruises! You can buy all sorts of enamel, cloisonné-style pins on the cruise (there are about 500 unique cruise pins) to trade with others. Or bring pins from the parks or from home. Check your *Personal Navigator* for trading sessions. The shopping supplement distributed daily highlights the featured pin for the day (see page 311 for shopping). There's even a PassPorter enamel pin, though you can't trade it for Disney pins—see our web site.

Live Auction at Sea—Unlike the silent auctions on Disney cruises previously, the new live auctions allow cruisers to bid on up to 500 pieces of Disneyana and high-priced artwork. Opening bids can range from $40 to more than $10,000. Here's how it works: Cruisers register in advance (free) to receive a bidding card with a number. Auction items are displayed for preview prior to the auction, and you can mark the pieces you are interested in to ensure they are brought out for bidding. This is followed by the live auction itself, which is open to everyone and quite exciting in its way, even for spectators. The auctions are typically held on sea days in the Promenade Lounge, though we've also seen them in the Lobby Atrium. In addition to the auctions, special artist exhibitions may go on display—check your *Personal Navigator*. If you win an auction, your purchase may be available to take home immediately (especially if it is a low-ticket item), but more likely it will be shipped to you in 6–8 weeks. Payment is made at close of auction. Live auctions are run by Park West at Sea (http://www.parkwestgallery.com), which does live art auctions on many other cruise lines.

Off-The-Beaten-Path—A thorough exploration of the ship reveals several little nooks and crannies. Explore hallways, elevator lobbies, and staircases for art. The secluded deck on deck 7 aft (open from 7:00 am to 11:00 pm) is great for sunbathing. Check out deck 6 behind the midship elevators—you can walk through for a closer look at the mural. Deck 8 aft also has a small deck that is sometimes open. And how about that view from the fitness center?

Religious Services

Seven-night cruisers can attend an interdenominational service in the Buena Vista Theatre on Sunday at 8:30 am. Erev Shabbat (Jewish Sabbath Eve) services are held on Friday at the appropriate time. Or attend services in Cape Canaveral on Sunday—see http://www.marinersguide.com/regions/florida/capecanaveral/churches.html. Western Caribbean cruisers can attend afternoon services on Sunday in Key West—see http://www.marinersguide.com/regions/florida/keywest/churches.html.

Overlooked Attractions *(continued)*

Lounges—There are many quiet spots where you can relax with a tropical drink or a glass of wine. Besides the lounges we described on pages 152–153, you'll find Preludes (deck 4 forward), open from 6:00 pm to 9:30 pm for pre-show and afterglow drinks—all ages welcome; Signals (deck 9 forward) is next to the adult pool so it's limited to ages 18 & up—it's typically open until 7:00 pm; Outlook Bar (deck 10 forward) overlooks the adult pool and seems a bit removed from the hustle of the lower decks—all ages welcome; and the Promenade Lounge (deck 3 midship) offers games in the day and live entertainment in the evenings for all ages—it's usually open to midnight.

© MediaMarx, Inc.

The Disney Magic's Promenade Lounge

Captain's Photo Sessions and Signings—It's always good to meet the Captain! If you're willing to wait in line, you can usually get a handshake and a photo with the Captain. And let's not forget that the Captain's signature is a great souvenir! The Captain typically appears at one of the shops on deck 4. Check your *Personal Navigator* for times and places.

Guest Entertainer Workshops—Seven-night and up cruises have entertainers onboard for the variety shows, and sometimes these entertainers give demonstrations and/or workshops in magic, ventriloquism, juggling, etc. Check your *Personal Navigator*.

Napkin Folding/Towel Animal Folding/Ice Carving Demonstrations—See how each of these amazing creations comes about. Check your *Personal Navigator*.

Coffee or Lunch With the Crew—Have a chat with crew members and learn about life onboard. Various sessions may be offered, some for just singles, some for just adults, and some for everyone.

Treasure Hunts—We just love hunting for "treasure," those little-known bits of trivia and hidden details throughout both the Magic and the Wonder. You may even have the opportunity do a scavenger hunt on Castaway Cay (see page 299). And you can certainly make your own treasure hunts to challenge your friends and family. We have hosted treasure hunts during our MouseFest cruises in December and plan to do a big one on our "Decade of Dreams" cruise in 2009 (see page 347). To top it off, we published a book of treasure hunts at Walt Disney World and on the Disney Cruise Line—it's filled with ready-made hunts for all skill levels (see page 348).

Photo Surfing—While you're onboard, you'll probably have your photo taken by Disney's professional photographers many times. Kids in particular get lots of shots. Regardless of whether you plan to actually buy any of the photos, it's fun to just stop by Shutters and "surf" the photos on display. It's fun to look at photos of other cruisers, too! (And if you find a dreadful photo of yourselves that you'd rather make disappear, feel free to drop it in one of the containers for unwanted photos.)

Art Browsing—If you enjoy art, take a stroll around the ship to appreciate the various prints, paintings, and sculptures that fill the Disney ships. Stairways contain a good share of the artwork onboard but are often overlooked because many people prefer elevators. And don't forget the Live Auction at Sea items (see page 165), which are placed on display for preview much of the time. Disney Magic guests may also enjoy the "Art of Disney Magic Self-Guided Walking Tour" on page 163.

Hair Braiding—For that authentic "I've been to the islands" look, how about cornrows or braids, ladies? Get the "look" early in the cruise from the braiders up by the pools on deck 9. Hair braiding is also available on Castaway Cay—see page 298.

Dolphin Spotting—Did you know dolphins sometimes frolic in the waters around the ship? The best time to spot dolphins is within the first hour of leaving a port, particularly as you're leaving Port Canaveral. For optimum spotting, you'll want to be looking over either the port or starboard side of the ship, toward the bow. Dolphins like to hitch rides on the bow waves of moving ships. We recommend the big windows on deck 3 or outside on deck 4 for the best views, but deck 10 also offers good views. Taking pleasure in spotting dolphins is an old tradition—Ancient Greek sailors considered dolphin escorts a good omen for a smooth voyage.

Talent Show/Karaoke—If you've got an exhibitionist streak, you may enjoy the opportunity to show your stuff in a talent show or karaoke session. Guest talent shows aren't available on all cruises, but we have recently spotted them on the 7-night and longer cruises—they are typically held in Rockin' Bar D on the last day of the cruise. Look for an announcement in the *Personal Navigator* regarding sign-ups. Crew talent shows are hilarious—if you spot one of these in your *Personal Navigator*, make it a point to attend. Karaoke is much more common and is available for most age groups. Of course, watching other people perform can be almost as much fun as doing it yourself!

Meeting Internet Friends—You may have friends on your voyage and not even know it. If you're a member of an Internet community, just let others know when you're sailing and try to arrange a "meet" or two while you're onboard. Two good places to hook up with fellow cruisers are PassPorter's message boards (http://www.passporterboards.com) and DIS (http://www.disboards.com).

Learning More—Want to know the latest inside scoop on Disney Cruise Line? The single best place to pick up tidbits is at the Navigator's Series Captain's Corner session (see page 163) where the Captain answers cruiser questions. Beyond this, chatting with crew members can yield interesting news, but you'll need to take their unofficial buzz with a grain of salt.

'Til We Meet Again—On the last night of your cruise, the Disney characters and Walt Disney Theatre performers put on a sweet little show along the grand staircase in the lobby atrium. The characters "meet and greet" after the show so you can get that last "kiss" goodnight. It's typically held at 10:15 pm, but check your *Personal Navigator*.

Stuck in Your Stateroom?

Caring for a young one? Feeling queasy? It's not uncommon to be "stuck" in your stateroom for a while and unable to get out to enjoy all these wonderful activities. If you find yourself in this predicament, the stateroom TV is your obvious means of entertainment—note that many onboard talks and even some shows are recorded and later broadcast on the TV during your cruise. If you can't stomach all-TV-all-the-time, reading material is available for purchase in Treasure Ketch. Cove Café also has a supply of magazines and books that you can borrow. If you have a verandah, spend as much time outdoors as you can—it'll vastly improve your mood. Here are some other ideas: take a bath at sea • listen to music on the TV (several of the channels play music non-stop) • request a Mickey Bar from room service • try your hand at folding a towel animal • record a personal greeting on your stateroom phone • decorate your stateroom door • use the Disney Cruise stationery in the desk drawer to write letters or keep a journal. Most importantly, keep this in mind: If you had to get stuck in a room somewhere, a pleasant stateroom is a good place to get stuck.

Introduction
Reservations
Staterooms
Dining
Activities
Ports of Call
Magic
Index

Playing Your Way

If you've read this chapter, you know just how much there is to do aboard a Disney ship. Here are some tips to help you make the most of it all:

- To help you **navigate the ship**, remember this general rule: We had <u>Fun</u> in the <u>Forward</u> (front of ship) and we <u>Ate</u> in the <u>Aft</u> (back).

- Keep in mind that there is **way more to do** on the ship than you can fit in—even on days you visit ports. So don't expect or try to cram in every activity, or you'll be disappointed in the end.

- "The first time we saw the *Personal Navigator*, we were so overwhelmed with what we should do that day and always filled up the day with activities. We learned that we really had no time to relax and do anything other than go from activity to activity. On our second cruise we were well prepared for this—we found it more relaxing and enjoyable to **carry the *Personal Navigator* around** with us. That way, we could do whatever we wanted without feeling like we were following a schedule all day. We still highlighted one or two activities we really wanted to do and tried to go to those."
  — contributed by Disney cruiser Grant Torre

- "If you want/need an **extra copy of the daily *Personal Navigator***, ask your stateroom host(ess) if they can leave you two copies each night. This way you have one to mark up and one for your souvenir collection/scrapbook." — contributed by Disney cruiser Jeff D.

Magical Memories

- "Before we left on our recent 7-night cruise, I picked up 100 glow bracelets. We got our bracelets from Target, but they can be purchased from OrientalTrading.com or party stores. The night of the Pirates in the Caribbean party, my daughters and I wandered through the crowd before the party started, handing them out to other children. Their faces would light up with extra smiles as we spread our glowing 'pixie dust.' It was a wonderful memory for my daughters and I as we watched the glow of the bracelets in the darkness, knowing that we'd helped bring some 'magic' onboard."
  ...as told by Disney cruiser Dawn Dobson

- "On my most recent cruise, I took many photos of the stage shows with my new iPhone. After the Golden Mickeys, we met a family in the elevator who mentioned that their son had been one of the dwarfs on stage. I pulled out my iPhone, found the photo I'd took, and found I had a great photo of their son. I was able to e-mail the photo to them right away thanks to the Internet wireless access on my iPhone!
  ...as told by Disney cruiser Jennifer Marx

© MediaMarx, Inc.

Putting Into Port

LEARN the basics of having fun in port

GET where you want to go easily

DECIDE what ports to visit and which excursions to do

DISCOVER the ports and attractions of the Caribbean

Land, ho! For many, the promise of visiting new places is the big appeal of cruising. The Caribbean and Mexican Riviera are worlds away from what most of us are familiar with, and the lure of exotic lands is great. This chapter was written with your needs in mind. We hope to help you determine which ports you'd most like to visit (and hence which cruise itinerary to choose) and what you can do while you're in each port.

Each and every port on the 2008 Disney cruise itineraries—including the home port of Port Canaveral, the private island of Castaway Cay, and the special itinerary ports—is represented by a "port guide." Each port guide is four to eight pages long and includes general information (time zone, currency, climate, etc.), ambience, history, transportation, safety, walking tour, layout, attractions, sports, beaches, and shopping. In addition, we add one of our own maps of the port and a detailed listing of the shore excursions offered through Disney (if shore excursions are not yet announced, we list typical excursions Disney is likely to offer). These port guides are by no means comprehensive. (That would require an entire book for each port.) Rather, they focus on what's possible and practical during the short hours you'll have in port and should give an excellent overview.

For those of you who've "been there and done that" or simply don't want to venture off the ship, feel free to stay onboard while the ship is in port. Disney offers plenty of activities onboard during port days, and you'll enjoy the slower pace and quieter atmosphere of the ship. Do note that the onboard shops will be closed while you're in port, and some places (like Flounder's Reef) will have shorter operating hours.

On all four-night and longer itineraries, you'll have a day (or two, or more—see pages 32–36) when you visit no ports at all. These are called "at-sea" days, and most passengers adore them. The crew offers more stuff to do onboard than usual, and the ship hums with activity. Plus, there's just something special about "being underway" during the day, instead of at night as is more typical on port days.

Introduction

Reservations

Staterooms

Dining

Activities

Ports of Call

Magic

Index

Island Daze

Feeling adventurous? There's a whole world to explore off-ship. Each of the ports, many of which are islands (even Port Canaveral, which is on a barrier island), offers fun things to do and explore. Here are the details:

If you wish, you can **get off the ship** at each port (guests under 18 will need to be with an adult or have the permission of a responsible adult to go alone) and there is no additional fee to simply visit the ports—Disney folds the port fees into your cruise price. It does cost extra to book shore excursions (see next page), and if you plan to eat ashore anywhere other than Castaway Cay, that cost is also your responsibility.

It's fun to watch as the **port slides into view**. Check your *Personal Navigator* for the arrival/departure times and observe from deck 4, deck 10, or from your verandah.

While the ship and Castaway Cay have a cashless system, you'll need to **bring cash, major credit cards, and/or traveler's checks** to pay for anything at the other ports. You will also want to have small bills to tip excursion operators, too. Note that there is no ATM (cash machine) on the ship, but there are ATMs at

Allie watches the ship come into port

the ports (except Castaway Cay). Keep in mind, however, that ATMs will give you cash in the local currency—this can be good if you're planning to use it immediately, but a drawback if you are taking out any extra or don't understand the local currency-to-dollar rates well enough. So if you're looking for U.S. currency from an ATM, you'll generally only find it at ports that use the U.S. dollar as their main currency—check for this in the small chart at the bottom of the first page of each port description in this chapter.

Some of the ports attract merchants aggressively **hawking their wares or services** near the dock. If this makes you uncomfortable, avoid eye contact and keep walking. Most travelers find that hawkers will respect a polite, but firm, "No thank you."

Some guests like to bring **drinks and snacks** with them during their time onshore (see page 129). Be aware that you can't bring open containers of food back on the ship.

Changing facilities may not always be handy for those **planning to swim** or get wet. We suggest you "underdress" your swimsuit (wear it under your clothing) before going ashore.

Some guests **never get off the ship** at the ports, preferring to stay onboard and enjoy the ship's amenities. We've done this ourselves on non-research cruises. The decision to stay onboard or explore the port is a personal one, however, and no one way is right for everyone. If this is your first visit to a port, we suggest you at least get off and look around for an hour, or book a shore excursion. If you decide you like it, you can explore more!

Disney **does not guarantee** that you'll visit all ports on an itinerary. Bad weather or rough seas can prevent docking, and you may spend the day at sea or at an alternate port instead. Although you will not receive a refund of cruise fare if this happens, you will not be charged for the canceled Disney shore excursions, either. In addition, you may have port charges for the port you missed refunded to your stateroom account. In any case, Disney will do what they can to make your extra onboard time fun.

Shore Excursions

Disney offers many shore excursions at each port, with the exception of Port Canaveral. These activities incur an additional, per-person fee, anywhere from $6 for Castaway Cay float rentals to $325 for the Baja 1000 Test Track in Cabo San Lucas. In most cases, the excursions are not run by Disney but by outside companies. The good news is that if you book one of these excursions through Disney, virtually all details are taken care of for you. All you need to do is reserve the shore excursion, pay the fees, and show up at the designated meeting point to go ashore. Here are the details:

A **variety of shore excursions** are available, from sightseeing, walking tours, and beach visits to snorkeling, scuba diving, and kayaking. Check the last few pages of each port guide in this chapter for a list of the shore excursions offered at the time of writing. You'll also receive a shore excursion guide with your cruise documentation, and you can check http://www.disneycruise.com (click "Ports of Call") for a list of the excursions and prices. Note that the excursion details, times, and prices given in this guidebook may change.

Once you've read this chapter carefully, choose and **reserve your excursions in advance**. Some excursions are popular and get booked quickly. To make advance reservations from 2 to 75 days before your cruise (up to 90 days for Castaway Club members and up to 105 days for guests in stateroom categories 1–3), reserve at http://www.disneycruise.com or call 877-566-0968 (see page 139 for more details). (Note: You cannot make reservations until your cruise is paid in full.) You can also e-mail excursion requests to dcl.shore.excursion@disneycruise.com, or fill out the form that comes with your cruise documentation and fax to 407-566-7031. You can alter your shore excursion requests any time up to two days prior to sailing. After that time, all excursion reservations are considered final and cannot be changed or refunded. If you do not pre-reserve shore excursions, you can visit the Shore Excursion Desk (deck 3 mid) to check availability and reserve excursions. Use the worksheet on page 303.

When you pre-reserve your excursions, fees are billed to your onboard account and your **excursion tickets** are waiting in your stateroom upon arrival. If you book excursions onboard, you'll receive your tickets in your stateroom the night before the excursion. When you get your tickets, check the time and meeting location printed on it. With each ticket is an excursion waiver form, which you should fill out and sign ahead of time.

On the day of your excursion, bring both the ticket(s) and the signed waiver(s) to the **meeting location** at the assigned time, where they are collected. You'll receive a color-coded sticker to wear, identifying yourself as a member of the excursion group. When ready, a crew member leads the group off the ship and to the excursion.

You can usually book the same excursions offered by Disney for less if you **do it on your own**. The excursion operators are locally known and most have web sites. You'll need to find your own transportation to and from the excursion, but in return you'll have more flexibility and you can take side trips if you wish. Weigh these benefits against the peace of mind you'll have when booking through Disney. We offer tips to do an excursion "On Your Own" at the end of most excursion descriptions in this chapter. Then why book with Disney Cruise Line? First, it's simple and easy. One call and everything is arranged. Second, Disney books blocks of excursion tickets, sometimes entire excursions—so you might have trouble getting a ticket on your own. Third, if a Disney excursion is delayed, they'll hold the ship for you—do it yourself, and the ship may sail without you.

Understanding the Shore Excursion Description Charts

We describe each of Disney's shore excursions with our custom-designed, at-a-glance charts. Each chart includes a description, tips, typical meeting times, our reviews (when available), cruiser reviews in summary form (when available), information on how to do the excursion on your own, a reader rating, and more! We've organized this array of information into a consistent format so you can find what you need quickly. Below is a key to our charts, along with notes and details.

Key to the Excursion Chart:

[1] **Excursion Name** [Disney's Code Number]	Rating: # ☀ 🛍 📷
Description offering an overview of the excursion, what to expect (without giving too much away, of course), historical background, trivia and "secrets," our recommendations and review (if we've experienced it), tips on getting the most out of the excursion, height/age restrictions, typical meeting times, things you should and shouldn't bring with you, a summary of cruiser reviews we've received, and contact information if you want to do the excursion (or something similar to it) "On Your Own"—note that doing it on your own will often be with a different tour operator, however.	Type[4]
	Activity Level[5]
	Ages[6]
	Prices[7]
	Duration[8]

Reader Rating[2]   Icons[3]

[1] Each chart has an empty **checkbox** in the upper left corner—use it to check off the excursions you want to take (before you go) or those you've taken (after you return).

[2] When available, we note a reader rating from a scale of 0 (bad) to 10 (excellent). These ratings are compiled from the shore excursion reviews we receive (see sidebar below).

[3] Icons indicate what you should (or can) bring along. The sun icon ☀ suggests plenty of sunscreen and a hat. The bag icon 🛍 means you can bring a totebag or backpack along on the excursion. And the camera icon 📷 indicates you can bring a camera or camcorder.

[4] The type of activity you can expect on the excursion, such as Sports, Beach, or Tour.

[5] The physical activity level, such as "Leisurely" (a mild level of activity), "Active" (a moderate level of activity), and "Very active" (a whole lot of activity).

[6] The age requirements for the excursion. Some excursions are for "All ages," while others are for certain ages and up. A few are for teens only.

[7] Prices for adults (and kids, if available). Kids prices are for kids up to 9. Most tours that do not involve a boat transfer will allow kids under 3 to go free. Prices subject to change.

[8] The approximate duration of the excursion. If we offer a range, it's more likely that the excursion will take the maximum time noted, in our experience.

About Our Cruiser Reviews

Excerpts from our cruiser reviews are summarized in each shore excursion description. These reviews are submitted by cruisers via an online form. Excursions without ratings mean we haven't received enough reviews from cruisers. To submit your own review of a shore excursion, visit us at http://www.passporter.com/dcl and click the "Shore Excursion Survey" link. We'd love to hear from you!

All Ashore! All Aboard!

If you decide to take a shore excursion or simply explore the port on your own, you'll need to get off the ship and onto the shore. Here's how:

To find out what time you can **go ashore** at a given port, look for the "All Ashore" time in your *Personal Navigator*—we also give typical times in each of our port guides. This time is typically the earliest you can disembark in the port. (You don't have to go ashore if you prefer to stay onboard.) Ports that put more limitations on disembarking (such as Grand Cayman) may require that guests not on shore excursions meet in the Walt Disney Theatre before going ashore. If this is necessary, the details will be listed in your *Personal Navigator*.

At most ports, the ship **pulls up right alongside the dock** and guests step out right onto the pier. When this isn't possible, guests must be ferried ashore in "tenders." Boarding a tender isn't difficult—you simply step off the ship and onto the tender and enjoy the ride to the shore. If the seas are rough, you are more likely to feel the effects while on the tender. At the time of writing, the only regular port that always requires tenders is Grand Cayman—other ports may require tenders if Disney cannot secure a berth or if rough seas inhibit docking.

Before you go ashore, pack a day bag with bottled water, sunscreen, hat, raingear, a watch, and any other necessities you may need. You may also want to "underdress" your bathing suit so you don't need to find changing facilities in the port. And make sure everyone has their Key to the World card and, for those over 18, photo ID. (If you lose your Key to the World card, go to Guest Services on deck 3 midship.)

To go ashore, follow the signs in the passageways to locate the specific **"tender lobby"** from which you'll disembark. There are two of these, both located on deck 1 (see page 5). Remember, however, that deck 1 passageways don't extend the length of the ship, so you'll need to take the proper elevator to deck 1 to reach the correct lobby—the signs won't lead you wrong. Note that if you booked a shore excursion through Disney, you'll disembark with the other guests going on the shore excursion. See page 171 for more details.

Once you're in the tender lobby, have your **Key to the World card** (and photo ID) in your hand so the crew may swipe your card and allow you to disembark. Guests under 18 must have an adult accompany them to the gangway to go ashore anywhere other than Castaway Cay. Once you're cleared to go ashore, simply step out onto the dock or into the tender. On Castaway Cay, watch for a crew member handing out towels for use ashore (towels are bath-size, not beach-size). If they run out of towels at the gangway, the crew members will invite you to take towels from the pool areas on deck 9.

While you're onshore, **keep an eye on the time**—you don't want to miss the boat! The "All Aboard" time is noted in your *Personal Navigator*. If you are late, the ship won't wait for you and it is your responsibility to get to the next port to reboard the ship. The exception to this rule is for guests on one of Disney's own shore excursions—if their excursion makes you late, Disney will hold the ship's departure for you.

Reboarding is simple. Just return to the dock area, present your Key to the World card (and photo ID) to security personnel to enter the dock, show your ID again to the Disney crew to either board the ship or board the tender (which then takes you to the ship). You will need to put your belongings through a security scanner once you're onboard and have your Key to the World card scanned again (so Disney knows you're back on the ship). Don't bring restricted items onboard, such as opened food and black coral.

Introduction · Reservations · Staterooms · Dining · Activities · Ports of Call · Magic · Index

Shopping Ashore

For some cruisers, shopping is a major reason to visit an exotic port of call. Not only can you find things you can't get at home, but prices on certain luxury items can be remarkably good.

If you plan to shop on shore, pick up the **Shopping in Paradise** port guide at the gangway. It lists recommended stores at which to shop, though keep in mind that these stores are included because they have an advertising relationship with the publishers of the shopping guide. The good news is that if you purchase from one of those listed stores, you'll receive a 30-day guarantee on repair or replacement of an unsatisfactory item (but the guarantee doesn't help if you change your mind about an item). Regardless of this guarantee, you should always ask about return policies before you make a purchase. If you have questions, a knowledgeable crew member is stationed at the gangway or at the Shore Excursion Desk on deck 3 midship. If you need to make a claim after you return from a cruise (and within 30 days of purchasing the item), you must contact the merchant directly and send a copy of your correspondence along with the store name, date of purchase, copy of receipt, and a written description of the claim to Onboard Media, 960 Alton Road, Miami Beach, FL 33139. For more information, visit http://www.onboard.com or call 800-396-2999.

Live presentations on shore excursions and shopping are held during the cruise (freebies may be given out to lucky attendees at the shopping presentation) and later broadcast on your stateroom TV. Check the *Personal Navigator* for times. Stop by the Shore Excursion Desk on deck 3 midship for port and shopping information and excursion brochures (see examples at http://www.castawayclub.com). Desk hours are listed in the *Personal Navigator*, too.

Certain luxury items can be had for less in **particular ports**. Here's where your fellow cruisers have found good deals:
  Alcohol: St. Thomas
  Cigars: Everywhere but Key West
  Cosmetics: St. Thomas, St. Maarten
  Jewelry: St. Thomas, St. Maarten (Philipsburg), Grand Cayman, Cozumel
  Perfume: St. Martin (Marigot)
  Quirky/Artsy stuff: Key West
  Silver jewelry: Cozumel
  T-shirts: Key West (though all ports sell t-shirts, of course)
  Watches: St. Maarten (Philipsburg), St. Thomas

Here are some **smart shopping tips** for great deals and quality merchandise:
  · Be prepared. Know what you're looking for before you venture out. And be familiar with the typical prices of the items you're interested in so you know whether or not you're getting a good price.
  · If you want to deal but aren't successful at initiating it, walk out of the store—this usually gets the clerk's attention.
  · If you're shopping for jewlery, ask to go out in the sun to look at it—you may notice flaws in the sunlight that you could not see in the store.
  · Check out other stores with similar goods before you buy. And before you leave the store, ask the clerk to write down the item you are interested in along with the price on the back of the shop's card in the event you decide to return.
  · Don't settle for something you don't really like.
  · Keep your receipts in a safe spot—you'll need them for customs declarations.

Port Canaveral and Cocoa Beach
(All Bahamas/Caribbean Itineraries—Home Port)

Far more than just a place to park a cruise ship, Port Canaveral offers an exciting extension to your Disney cruise vacation. This is Florida's Space Coast, home to the Kennedy Space Center, 72 miles (116 km.) of prime Atlantic beachfront, the Merritt Island National Wildlife Refuge, ecotourism, water sports, sport fishing, etc. Do you have an extra week?

© MediaMark, Inc.

Cocoa Beach at sunrise

Thundering rockets, crashing surf, and the total peace of an empty beach come together in the Port Canaveral area. You won't find built-up beach resorts like Daytona or Fort Lauderdale here, though crowds do rise for space shuttle launches. There are just a relative handful of hotels and beachfront condos—so quiet that this is where endangered sea turtles choose to nest! Whether you unwind here prior to your cruise or wind up your vacation with a visit to the astronauts, this can easily be one of the best ports you ever visit.

AMBIENCE

You'll either want to drive your own car or rent a car to get around (taxis are not abundant). A list of area transportation companies is at http://www.portcanaveral.org/portinfo/groundtrans.htm. The Space Coast region stretches from Titusville in the north to Melbourne in the south (see map on page 179). I-95 runs north/south on the mainland, paralleled by U.S. 1 for local driving. Many attractions are on the barrier islands to the east, across the Banana and Indian Rivers, and the Intercoastal Waterway. SR A1A is the principal route for beach access. Commercial airlines serve Melbourne International Airport and Orlando International. Port Canaveral is just south of Kennedy Space Center, and Cocoa Beach is immediately south of Port Canaveral, roughly halfway between Titusville and Melbourne. See chapter 2 for full details on travel to and from Port Canaveral and the Disney Cruise Terminal.

GETTING AROUND

Facts	
Size: 72 mi. long (116 km.) x 15 mi. wide (24 km.) (Brevard County, Florida)	
Temperatures: Highs: 72°F (22°C) to 91°F (33°C); lows: 50°F (10°C) to 73°F (23°C)	
Population: 476,000 (Brevard)	**Busy Season:** Mid-February to April
Language: English	**Money:** U.S. Dollar
Time Zone: Eastern (DST observed)	**Transportation:** Cars and taxis
Phones: Dial 911 for emergencies, local pay phone calls = 50 cents	

FACTS

(Side tabs: Introduction, Reservations, Staterooms, Dining, Activities, Ports of Call, Magic, Index)

Exploring Kennedy Space Center and the Astronaut Hall of Fame

KENNEDY SPACE CENTER

It just wouldn't be the Space Coast without the **Kennedy Space Center** (KSC), located 12 miles from Cocoa Beach. The huge gantries and Vehicle Assembly Building dominate the horizon for miles around. Those aren't high-rise condos along the beach; they're the historic launch towers of Cape Canaveral!

The new and very fun Shuttle Launch Experience simulator ride at Kennedy Space Center

You can easily **spend two days** at the KSC Visitor Complex exploring the history and future of the U.S. space program. The new Shuttle Launch Experience simulator, two IMAX theaters, live talks with veteran astronauts, hands-on exhibits, historic spacecraft, and the sobering Astronaut Memorial make the **main visitor complex** an all-day experience. The complex also has a kid's play area and souvenir shops. Seven eateries include the Orbit Cafeteria, New Frontier Café, and Mila's, a full-service restaurant. Board a bus to tour the working Space Center (allow three more hours). The bus stops at the huge **Apollo/Saturn V interpretive center**, displaying a Saturn V rocket, an Apollo command module, and Lunar Module, plus several theaters, Apollo Launch Control, a snack bar, and a shop. Visit the **Launch Complex 39** observation gantry, a four-story launch tower affording sweeping views and even more interpretive exhibits.

ASTRONAUT HALL OF FAME

View historic spacecraft and memorabilia, and experience astronaut-training simulators at the **Astronaut Hall of Fame** in nearby Titusville, which is part of the KSC Visitor Complex. Here you can learn about past NASA astronauts and take a ride in various flight simulators to find out just what it is like to be an astronaut. Mission:SPACE fans take note: The G-Force Trainer is a longer, faster cousin of the simulator ride at Epcot—and at four times the force of gravity (4 Gs), it's not for the faint of heart! Almost half of the Hall of Fame is dedicated to hands-on experiences, and all exhibits and motion simulators are included in the price of admission. The Hall of Fame is a nine-mile drive from Kennedy Space Center, but it's worth the trip and good for at least an afternoon's enjoyment.

Exploring Kennedy Space Center and the Astronaut Hall of Fame

Two-day admission (Maximum Access Badge) to KSC and the Astronaut Hall of Fame: $38/adult and $28/child age 3–11. Single-day admission is no longer available. Tickets for the Astronaut Hall of Fame alone are $17/$13. **Two special tours**, NASA Up Close and Cape Canaveral: Then and Now, may be available, too. These tours go even farther, with an expert guide to bring you into restricted areas omitted from the regular tour. The tours last about three hours, each costs an extra $21/$15, and they're well worth it! Also available on most days of the week is a chance to **dine with an astronaut**. These meals add $23/adult, $16/child age 3–11 to the price of admission.

Another program is the **Astronaut Training Experience (ATX)** available for guests 14 and older at $250/person—it's held from 10:00 am to 4:30 pm at the Astronaut Hall of Fame. This is an in-depth, immersion program that includes motion simulators, exclusive tours, firsthand experiences with veteran NASA astronauts, gear, and lunch. Guests under 18 must be accompanied by an adult. Some simulators have height/weight restrictions. Advance reservations are required—call 321-449-4400.

The Visitor Complex also sells **tickets to space shuttle launches**, when KSC is closed to private vehicles. For $28 to $61 you get off-site parking, a ride to the viewing area, and Visitors Complex admission (optional). The official Kennedy Space Center launch schedule is at http://www.kennedyspacecenter.com (click on "Launches").

Directions to Kennedy Space Center: From Cocoa Beach/Port Canaveral, take SR 528 west to SR 3 north, and follow the signs for the Visitor Complex. From the mainland, take I-95 or US 1 to Titusville, then take SR 407 east. Visit http://www.kennedyspacecenter.com or call 321-449-4444 for **more information**. Tickets are available on-site and online. Open every day but Christmas. Normal hours: 9:00 am–5:30 pm. The last tour bus departs at 2:15 pm, so be sure to start your day early!

Directions to the Astronaut Hall of Fame: From Kennedy Space Center, take SR 405 west across the Indian River and follow signs to the Astronaut Hall of Fame. From Cocoa Beach/Port Canaveral, take SR 528 to US 1 (Titusville exit), then turn right onto Vectorspace Blvd. From the mainland, take I-95 or US 1 to Titusville, get off at SR 405, and follow signs. Normal hours: 10:00 am–6:30 pm.

ADMISSION

DIRECTIONS

Introduction

Reservations

Staterooms

Dining

Activities

Ports of Call

Magic

Index

Exploring Port Canaveral and Cocoa Beach

PLAYING

Some of Florida's **best beaches** line the Space Coast. Cocoa Beach offers miles of soft, white sand and rolling surf. Beach access is easy, with public access points every few blocks. There's metered parking at the public accesses, or walk from the nearby motels. Cocoa Beach Pier at 401 Meade Ave. offers a variety of on-pier restaurants. For a back-to-nature experience, Canaveral National Seashore's **Playalinda Beach** is located just north of the Kennedy Space Center boundary line. It offers a long, gorgeous beach protected by a tall sand dune and great views of the Kennedy Space Center gantries. It's closed for shuttle launches and landings and closes at 6:00 pm at all times. Entrance fee is $3/person ages 16 & up. Camping on the beach is allowed November–April (permit required). Take I-95 to Titusville exit 220 then SR 406 east to the park. For additional information, call 321-867-4077 or visit http://www.nps.gov/cana.

Endangered species such as bald eagles, manatees, and sea turtles call this area home. **Merritt Island National Wildlife Refuge**, just north of the Space Center, offers hiking trails and incredible wildlife viewing. On your way in, stop by the Wildlife Refuge Visitor Center for information and some museum-style exhibits featuring the wildlife—there's also a delightful boardwalk over a freshwater pond in the back. The seven-mile Black Point Wildlife Drive offers views of many kinds of birds, alligators, river otters, bobcats, and snakes. We visited the wildlife refuge just before sunset one December and were treated to beautiful panoramas and the sight of many birds roosting for the evening. A special manatee viewing platform is located at the northeast side of Haulover Canal. Located on the road to Playalinda Beach (see above), the refuge closes for shuttle launches and landings. Call 321-861-0667 or visit http://merrittisland.fws.gov.

Black Point Wildlife Drive

© MediaMarx, Inc.

This is the biggest **sea turtle nesting area** in the U.S. Nesting season runs May–August. Turtle encounters are organized at Canaveral National Seashore, Melbourne, and Sebastian Inlet. Call the Sea Turtle Preservation Society at 321-676-1701. More ecotourism opportunities exist, including kayak tours, airboat rides, and guided nature encounters. For listings, visit http://www.nbbd.com/ecotourism or http://www.space-coast.com, or call 800-936-2326.

Dining in Port Canaveral and Cocoa Beach

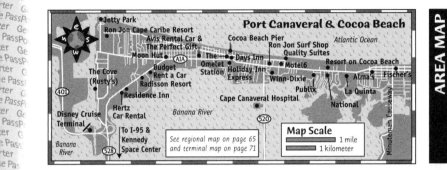

Looking for a place to eat? There are plenty of **chain restaurants**—in Port Canaveral, you'll find a 24-hour McDonald's and a Subway, and in Cocoa Beach, there's a Wendy's, Taco Bell, Denny's, International House of Pancakes (IHOP), Blimpie Subs, and a Waffle House (Perkins has been replaced by The Omelet Station). Over on Merritt Island, you'll also find Applebee's, Chili's, Outback Steakhouse, Olive Garden, Red Lobster, and Hooters. If you're looking for something nicer and more "local," here are the restaurants we've tried:

Alma's Seafood & Italian Trattoria—A quirky, moderately-priced Italian restaurant with hometown charm, decent food, and Space Coast memorabilia. 306 N. Orlando Ave., Cocoa Beach • 321-783-1981

Cactus Flower Mexican Restaurant—A delightful, atmospheric cafe serving excellent Mexican cuisine. You can dine in or take out. 1891 E. Merritt Island Causeway, Merritt Island • 321-452-6606

Fischer's Seafood Bar & Grill—The moderate restaurant in the trio owned by the Fischer family (see next page). It offers decent seafood for reasonable prices. Info at http://www.geocities.com/bernardsseafood. 2 S. Atlantic Ave., Cocoa Beach • 321-783-2401

Grill's Seafood Deck & Tiki Bar—A fun spot right on the harbor—the menu is equally fun and the food is great. http://www.visitgrills.com. 505 Glen Cheek Dr., Cape Canaveral • 321-868-2226

Zachary's—A basic diner, serving satisfying American and Greek food. 8799 Astronaut Blvd., Cape Canaveral • 321-784-9007

Rusty's Seafood & Oyster Bar—Overlooking the port and harbor, this scenic restaurant serves quality seafood. Also owned by the Fischer family. 628 Glen Cheek Dr., Cape Canaveral • 321-783-2033

The Omelet Station—A new eatery offering breakfast and lunch buffets. http://www.theomeletstation.com. 5590 N. Atlantic Ave., Cocoa Beach • 321-783-1038

DINING

Dining

Activities

Ports of Call

Magic

Index

Playing in Port Canaveral and Cocoa Beach

ACTIVITIES

Fishing (both saltwater and freshwater) is huge in this area. Charters and fishing camps are easy to find, maybe harder to choose from. Check out Coastal Angler Magazine at 888-800-9794 or visit them at http://www.camirl.com.

Lodging rates in this area are reasonable, especially in the off-season (May–December). See pages 68–70 for our lodging suggestions.

Port Canaveral Tips: For seafood, boating, and fishing charters, visit **The Cove**, a waterfront development a stone's throw from the cruise terminals. We had great meals and sunset views at Rusty's and Grill's (see previous page). To get there, exit SR 528 one exit east of the cruise terminals, turn left on George J. King Blvd., turn left on Dave Nisbet Dr., and take it to Glen Cheek Dr. • **Jetty Park** is a perfect spot to watch space launches, fish, camp, or watch the cruise ships—to get there, exit SR 528 one exit east of the cruise terminals, turn left (northeast) on George J. King Blvd., and follow it to Jetty Park.

Cocoa Beach Tips: No trip to the Space Coast is complete without a visit to **Ron Jon Surf Shop** on SR A1A, souvenir T-shirt capital of Central Florida. This large, very pleasant store does sell surfboards and other serious water sports gear, but most visitors exit with items from the huge selection of swimwear, T-shirts, and other outdoor apparel. And it's open 24 hours! • Route A1A in Cocoa Beach varies between pleasant neighborhoods and somewhat seedy sections filled with cheap eats and budget motels. For the most part, though, it's very nice, and the beach is just a few blocks to the east (see photo on page 175). • The Fischer family, who also owns Rusty's in Port Canaveral, runs three fish restaurants under one roof at 2 S. Atlantic Ave. (SR A1A) in Cocoa Beach: Rusty's is cheapest and most informal, Fischer's is the mid-range choice (see previous page), and Bernard's Surf is the most upscale. • Aging sitcom fans might want to follow A1A south and look for "I Dream of Jeannie Lane," in Lori Wilson Park.

Web Cams: Several web cams offer a sneak peek. Try http://www.twopalms.com or http://bestwesterncocoabeach.com/beachcam.cfm.

Other Space Coast Tips: Farther South, Melbourne is home to a wonderful planetarium and observatory, live theater productions, Montreal Expos Spring Training, and the Brevard County Zoo. Call 800-872-1969 or visit http://www.space-coast.com.

Introduction

Nassau
(3- and 4-Night Itineraries—First Port of Call)

Two-thirds of all Disney cruisers visit Nassau on New Providence Island in the Bahamas, one of the cruising world's most fabled ports. If you've heard the song Sloop John B ("Around Nassau town we did roam, drinkin' all night, got into a fight"), you might think twice about stepping ashore, but you can have an enjoyable day in this busy capital city if you do your homework.

© MediaMarx, Inc.

A statue of Columbus greets visitors to Government House in Nassau

Many cruisers feel uncomfortable walking around Nassau's wharf area, where they're likely to encounter aggressive, enterprising locals intent on their piece of the tourist pie. Hair wrappers, cab drivers, street vendors, and tour hawkers swarm the seedy wharf area—hardly the squeaky-clean welcome Disney crowds prefer. But this large, attractive island boasts a long, British colonial heritage. Historic buildings, large casinos, and attractive beaches await travelers willing to take an excursion or strike out on their own.

AMBIENCE

Bahamian history starts with the first voyage of Chris Columbus. He called the area "baja mar"—low (shallow) sea—and the name stuck. The Spaniards left in search of gold and the native inhabitants were decimated by disease before the British arrived in the 1600s. Nassau, which was originally called Sayle Island, was a favorite port for fabled pirates like Blackbeard and Anne Bonney, until the islands became a Crown Colony in 1718. Governor Woodes Rogers, a former buccaneer himself, cleaned house and created a town plan that—more or less—remains in effect to this day. The islands became a haven for British loyalists fleeing the American Revolution, and for Southerners during the U.S. Civil War. Trade revived during the Prohibition era, when rum running became a major stock in trade. The islanders voted for and received independence on July 10, 1973, making the Bahamas a member of the British Commonwealth.

HISTORY

Size: 21 mi. long (34 km.) x 7 mi. wide (11 km.)	
Climate: Subtropical	**Temperatures:** 70°F (21°C)–90°F (32°C)
Population: 211,000	**Busy Season:** Mid-February to April
Language: English	**Money:** Bahamian Dollar (equal to U.S. $)
Time Zone: Eastern (DST observed)	**Transportation:** Walking, taxis, and ferries
Phones: Dial 1- from U.S., dial 919 for emergencies, dial 916 for information	

FACTS

Reservations

Staterooms

Dining

Activities

Ports of Call

Magic

Index

Introduction

Reservations

Staterooms

Dining

Activities

Ports of Call

Magic

Index

Getting Around Nassau

GETTING THERE

Your ship berths at **Prince George Wharf** in the heart of the port. Paradise Island is across the water. A short walk puts you in the heart of town. Disembarkation starts at around 9:45 am (check your *Personal Navigator* for going ashore details), and be sure to bring photo ID—wharfside security is tight these days. Enjoy the view from deck 10 to note major landmarks before going ashore, including the Water Tower at the top of the hill, the towering Atlantis resort on Paradise Island, and the arching bridge to Paradise Island. Check your *Personal Navigator* for the all-aboard time, usually at 7:00 pm.

GETTING AROUND

Nassau is a **good port for walking**, but several popular attractions, including Paradise Island and Cable Beach, are best reached by taxi, jitney, or water taxi. The taxi stand is to the right as you leave the wharf, beyond the hair braiders stand. • As you leave the pier, you'll pass through a pierside welcome center, with a tourist information booth (get free tourist maps here), post office, ATM, telephone/Internet facilities, and a small, pleasant shopping mall. • As you leave the wharf, you'll find Woodes Rogers Walk, which parallels the waterfront. One block inland is the main shopping district, Bay Street. To your left, you'll find the grand government buildings near Rawson Square, while a right turn on Bay Street will take you toward the Straw Market. The streets follow a rough grid, and the town is built on a slope. If you get disoriented, just walk downhill to the waterfront. • Small jitneys provide local bus service. The fare is $1 (exact change). Taxi fares are negotiable, but expect to pay $8 for a trip for two to Paradise Island, $12 to Cable Beach, and about $6 for shorter trips. The fare is good for two people, with a $3 surcharge for each extra passenger. Note that the passenger in the front seat may be required to pay the bridge toll. • When crossing streets and if you rent a car or scooter, note that Nassau follows the British tradition of driving on the left-hand side of the road.

STAYING SAFE

Safety is often a state of mind, and that's especially true here. Downtown Nassau is **reasonably safe**, but it can be intimidating, with busy streets near the wharf and many locals hustling aggressively. The streets can be empty a few blocks beyond the wharf, so you'll feel better (and be safer) walking with a companion. You can't hide the fact that you're a tourist, so relax, look self-assured, stay alert, keep valuables out of sight, and use your big city street smarts. Panhandlers may offer their "services" as tour guides. Be firm, and don't get sucked in. Carry a few dollars, just in case it's needed to tip a guide.

Touring Nassau

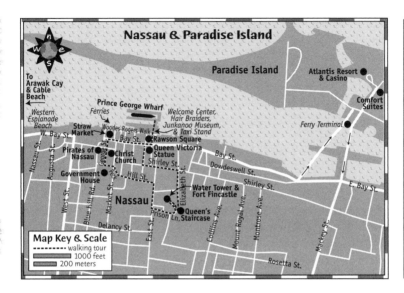

Nassau & Paradise Island

NASSAU MAP

WALKING TOUR

A **self-guided walking tour** around Nassau is a break from the ordinary. Grab one of the free tourist maps distributed on the wharf, play connect-the-dots with your choice of highlighted sights, and trace a route around the perimeter of the downtown district. Allow at least two hours for a nonstop walk or more if you want to spend time exploring. Finish before 5:00 pm, when the streets get empty. Here's our suggested walking tour (highlighted on map above): Leaving Prince George Wharf, turn right onto Bay St. Near the corner of Bay and George St. is the famous (or infamous) Straw Market. Turn left up George St. to continue our tour, or follow Bay St. west to the beaches of Western Esplanade and the seafood vendors of Arawak Cay. On George St., you'll soon pass Christ Church and the Pirates of Nassau attraction. Follow George St. to its end, and peer through the gates of Government House (see photo on page 181). Turn left again, cross Market St., and make your way uphill on winding Peck Slope to Hill St. for a commanding view of the port. Follow Hill St. to its end, turn right on East St. to Prison Lane, and follow the lane up to the Water Tower and Fort Fincastle. The tower can be climbed for free, or pay a fare to take the elevator. Exit via the remarkable Queen's Staircase and follow Elizabeth St. down the hill. Turn left onto Shirley St., then right onto Parliament St. to view the Library (Old Jail) and the statue of Queen Victoria in Parliament Square. From there, it's a short walk back to the wharf.

ACTIVITIES

Playing in Nassau

Bay St. is lined with **shops** offering the typical selection of upscale luxuries and downscale knickknacks, but Nassau is probably best-known for its Straw Market. There was a time when nobody could leave the port without a straw hat, basket, or handbag, but not every visitor is enchanted by the experience. The stalls and crafters of the market fill a city block between Bay St. and the waterfront—its narrow quarters are shaded by a huge, temporary awning.

The soft, white sands of Nassau are a major attraction. The nearest **public beach** to the wharf is Western Esplanade, along West Bay St. Famed Cable Beach, with its hotels, casino, and water sports, is more attractive and just a few miles farther down the road. Paradise Island has many first-class beaches, best visited as part of a shore excursion. Remote South Ocean Beach is a $33 cab fare from the wharf, or rent a car. Its quiet beauty may be worth the journey.

Casino action centers on Paradise Island's fancy Atlantis Casino and the older Crystal Palace Casino on Cable Beach. A day in either spot offers beach lounging, water sports, and similar distractions for those family members too young or disinclined to gamble. Water taxis serve both destinations from Prince George Wharf.

The **Atlantis Resort** offers aquariums and sea life exhibits to go along with the casino, recreation, and dining. All-day admission is $25/adults, $19/kids 3–12, and includes a guided tour, but does not include their water park—for that, you need to do the Atlantis Aquaventure excursion (see page 188) or get a room at Comfort Suites Paradise Island that includes use of the resort's facilities for up to 4 guests/room (http://www.comfortsuites.com, 800-330-8272).

Nassau offers too many scuba, snorkeling, boating, and sea life encounters to list here, but the Wonder's shore excursions (see next page) offer a good **cross-section** of these activities. Golf, tennis, fishing, and other sporting opportunities abound for those willing to do it on their own. Fortunately, you have a long day in Nassau. For details, visit the Bahamas' official site at http://www.bahamas.com.

"Goombay" and "Junkanoo" have become well-known Bahamian catchwords. Goombay is a local musical style that gets its name from the African term for rhythm. The Bahamas famed Junkanoo parades take place when your ship is out of port, but you can view a Junkanoo exhibit right on Prince George Wharf.

Embarking on Shore Excursions in Nassau

■ Ardastra Gardens and City Tour [N16]   Rating: 7

First visit the jungle gardens of the Ardastra Gardens, Zoo, and Conservation Centre, famous for its marching Caribbean Flamingos. After an hour and a half at the gardens, enjoy a city tour in air-conditioned van. A fair amount of walking is required. Typical meeting time is 12:45 pm. Cruiser reviews are mostly positive: The excursion offers "variety" and a way to see a lot in a "short amount of time." Kids enjoy the "zoo" and the animals and birds are "great." The tour's worth "depends on your tour guide." Overall, most "enjoyed it" though a few felt it would have been better to "take a taxi" and do "on your own." (On Your Own: Ardastra Gardens at http://www.ardastra.com, 242-323-5806)

Tour
Active
All ages
$38/adult
$29/child 3-9
2.5-3 hours

■ Atlantis Beach Day [N07]   Rating: 6

*Spend the day lolling about on the beach on Paradise Island. The excursion includes a 25-minute bus ride (to and from Paradise Island) and a meal coupon. Upon arrival, enjoy your reserved spot on the beach, complete with chair and towel. You can explore the resort's casino and shops, but this excursion **does not include access to the Atlantis water park or aquarium**. Typical meeting time is 9:00 am. Ferries return every 30 min. from 1:30 pm to 5:30 pm. Cruiser reviews are uniform: The bus ride to Paradise Island was "bad" and travelled through a "not-so-nice area of Nassau." The highlight was the "private beach for cruisers," which is "wonderful" with "beautiful" water "so blue" and with "so many fish." On the beach you are "provided with a towel and chair," and the chair "has an umbrella." The meal coupon left a bit to be desired, as you could only get "certain items" and the food "was not that great." If you want to buy something else, it can be "difficult to pay with cash." And cruisers felt it was unfortunate that they "can't use any of the pools at Atlantis." In sum, the beach is "beautiful" but the rest is just so-so. (On Your Own: Atlantis Resort, http://www.atlantis.com, 888-528-7155)*

Beach
Active
All ages
$65/adult
$47/child 3-9
4-7 hours

■ Blackbeard's Cay Beach & Stingray Adventure [N17]   Rating: 9

Take a 20-minute boat ride through Nassau Harbour to a private island to snorkel with stingrays, relax on the beach, and enjoy a lunch buffet (included in price). Snorkel equipment and food to feed the stingrays is provided. There's time for swimming and shopping in the little gift shop, too. Typical meeting time is 9:45 am. Cruiser reviews are mixed: The "crowded and hot" ferry ride to the "beautiful little island" with its "pretty beach" is "pleasant." The time with the "stingrays in the penned area" lasted "10 minutes tops" and some kids are "scared," while others "dove right in and started snorkeling" and "loved feeding" the stingrays. Some reported that the "food stunk"—you have your choice of "a burger, a hot dog, or chicken sandwich"—but more recently, we've heard that the "food was very good." Cruisers advise you "bring sunscreen" and "bottled water because the only drinks available are soft drinks with lunch." If you're in the mood to shop, visit the gift shop early as "the stringray-themed sourvenirs sell out quickly." Most everyone agrees that the beach area is "beautiful" and "great for the kids." Overall, some found the excursion "a waste of time" and "not worth the money," but more felt it was "very relaxing and fun for all" with "friendly stingrays." (On Your Own: ShoreTrips.com at http://www.shoretrips.com)

Sports
Active
Ages 3 & up
$47/adult
$35/child
4.5-5 hours

See page 172 for a key to the shore excursion description charts and their icons.

Embarking on Shore Excursions
in Nassau *(continued)*

☐ Caribbean Queen Snorkel Tour [NO4]   Rating: 9

Like the *Sunshine Glass Bottom Boat* excursion, this trip cruises Nassau Harbour before heading off to Athol Island. Unlike the *Sunshine Glass Bottom Boat* excursion, you WILL get wet! Snorkel equipment and instruction is provided for your open-water snorkeling adventure. Freshwater showers and cash bar available onboard the 72-foot boat. Typical meeting time is 1:30 pm. Cruiser reviews are consistently good: The "great" excursion crew offers some "sightseeing" along the way to the island. Once there, the snorkeling is "awesome" and there was a "great variety of fish." Younger children and "uptight" people may be "a little frightened at first" but the "crew is wonderful at relieving fears." Chips and beverages ("local beer" plus soda and water) are available for sale on the boat. In sum, "it was great" and cruisers would "do it again." (On Your Own: Stuart Cove's Aqua Adventures at http://www.stuartcove.com, 800-879-9832)

Sports
Very active
Ages 6 & up
$37/adult
$27/child
2–3 hours

☐ Catamaran Sail & Reef Snorkeling [N14]   Rating: 8

Set sail on a comfortable, 65-foot catamaran with a large sundeck and shady lounge deck. After a brief tour of Nassau Harbour, you'll sail to a coral reef for snorkeling (equipment provided). Sodas and water are served during the sail, as are snacks and alcoholic beverages after snorkeling. Typical meeting time is 9:00 am. Cruiser comments are mostly positive: The 20-minute sail is "enjoyable" and "relaxing." The snorkeling is "wonderful" though some felt it was in "pretty deep water for beginners" and you cannot "touch bottom." Most report seeing "plenty of fish." Overall, most "loved it!" (On Your Own: Flying Cloud at http://www.bahamasnet.com/flyingcloud, 242-363-4430)

Sports
Very active
Ages 5 & up
$45/adult
$31/child
3.5–4 hours

☐ Discover Atlantis [NO5]   Rating: 6

This excursion begins with a 20-minute bus ride to the Atlantis resort, where you receive a guided tour of the resort and aquarium on Paradise Island. We did this excursion in 2002 and we enjoyed it—be aware that you will do a lot of walking. Typical meeting times are 11:00 am or 1:00 pm. Buses return every half-hour from 1:30 pm to 5:30 pm—don't miss it, or you'll have to pay for a taxi. Cruiser reviews are mixed: This very popular excursion begins with a "capacity-filled" ride to Paradise Island, during which the tour with "very little narrative" could not be "heard or understood over the roar of the engines." Once on the island, you are taken in "smaller groups" to the "stunning" Atlantis Resort, but the walk to it is "boring" because there is "nothing to see." Inside you may "spend a lot of time touring the retail areas," but then are led to the "breathtaking" aquarium. After the aquarium, some felt you were "left somewhere to find your own way back" while others enjoyed the "free time to explore." Expect to "spend the entire tour walking." Overall, some cruisers felt the excursion was "awesome" while others felt it "takes way too much time" and "wasn't interesting at all." (On Your Own: Atlantis Resort, http://www.atlantis.com, 888-528-7155)

Tour
Active
All ages
$39/adult
$26/child
3–5 hours

☐ Nassau Harbour Cruise   Rating: n/a

This recently introduced excursion offers a relaxing ride through Nassau Harbour and around Paradise Island on a state-of-the-art, custom-built catamaran (the "Ballyhoo"). You'll need to walk 15 minutes to get to the boat. During your cruise on the yacht, your guide will narrate the sights while you enjoy comfy seats and island music. Note that there are no restrooms available on the yacht. Typical meeting times are 10:15 am and 2:00 pm.

Tour
Leisurely
All ages
$25/14 (3-9)
1.5 hours

Embarking on Shore Excursions
in Nassau *(continued)*

Blue Lagoon Island Dolphin Encounter [N21]   Rating: 9

Despite the hefty price tag, this is the most popular excursion and it typically sells out quickly. Everyone wants the chance to cavort with a friendly dolphin! Guests stand on a platform set at a few feet under the water and play with bottlenose dolphins. (If you want to actually swim in the water with the dolphins, you'll need to book that excursion on your own—see below.) This excursion includes a cruise to the private island of Blue Lagoon (Salt Cay)—a calypso band plays during your ferry trip. Once there, you can swim, sunbathe, and play—water sport equipment rentals are available—in addition to your dolphin encounter. A voucher for lunch is included in the price of the excursion. Professional photos of your dolphin encounter are $8-$35/each and movies are $40-$60/each. Typical meeting time is 9:15 am. Cruiser ratings are mostly positive: The excursion starts with a long, "45-minute" ferry ride that some felt was "slow" and "miserable" while others found it "a lot of fun." At the dolphin encounter area, small groups of "10-12" guests stand around a "small pool" and watch a "skit" between the dolphin and "informative handlers." You stand in the "cold" water for about "20 minutes" to "hug, kiss, and dance with" the dolphins, but you only get about "2-3 minutes with a dolphin personally." Cruisers recommend you "wear water shoes" for ease and comfort. All loved the "unbelievably intelligent animal" and the "expertise, friendliness, and humor of the trainers." Some were put off by the "expense" of the photo; others wanted them but "did not know to bring enough money." Overall, most felt it was "exactly as advertised" or "better than expected," though a few felt it was "neat but not worth that much money." (On Your Own: Blue Lagoon Island at http://www.dolphinencounters.com, 242-363-1003)

Sports
Active
Ages 3 & up
$99/adult
$84/child
4-4.5 hours

Blue Lagoon Island Dolphin Observer [N22]   Rating: 8

Just want to go along for the ride with your family or friends to the Nassau Dolphin Encounter (described above)? You can for a reduced price! You get all the same benefits except you don't interact with the animals and you don't get wet. Tip: Bring your camera so you can take photos of your loved ones playing with the dolphins! Typical meeting time is 9:15 am. (On Your Own: Blue Lagoon Island at http://www.dolphinswims.com, 242-363-1003)

Tour
Leisurely
All ages
$35/for
ages 3+
4-4.5 hours

Nassau Historic City Tour [N06]   Rating: 6

Board an air-conditioned van for a guided tour of historic points of interest in Nassau. The tour visits historic buildings and famous sites, stopping at Fort Charlotte, Fort Fincastle, the Water Tower, and the Queen's Staircase. A good overview without a lot of walking. Typical meeting time is 10:00 am. Cruiser reviews are uniform: Aboard "not very comfortable" but "air-conditioned" vans you see historic sights around Nassau. The driver may not "talk very much" or offer enough "commentary" during the tour, but you will see "much of the city" in a "short time" and stop a few times to "take some photos." Most cruisers enjoyed the climb up to the Water Tower for the "view at the top," but felt it was "more physical activity" than expected. Cruisers were dismayed at the "begging" for tips and "peddlers." Overall, most felt the excursion was a way to see "a lot of things" without a "lot of walking." (On Your Own: Bahamas Experience Tours at http://www.bahamasexperiencetours.com, 242-356-2981, or Henry's Mobile Tours at 242-356-2981)

Tour
Leisurely
All ages
$23/adult
$18/child
2 hours

Introduction
Reservations
Staterooms
Dining
Activities
Ports of Call
Magic
Index

Embarking on Shore Excursions
in Nassau *(continued)*

☐ Scuba Dive Adventure at Stuart Cove [N20] Rating: 3

If you're a certified diver, this excursion offers an exciting look at the coral reefs and marine life that make their home here. Price includes basic dive equipment (regulator, tank, weight belt, buoyancy control device, mask, snorkel, and fins—wet suits are available for an extra fee). Note that guests ages 12–17 must be accompanied by parent or guardian to participate. Typical meeting time is 11:45 am. Don't forget that underwater camera. Cruiser reviews are uniform: The Disney scuba excursion is "OK" but not "great." The dive takes them "windward" and the waters can be "very rough"—rough enough that most cruisers report that they were able to do only "one of the two dives." The excursion does "provide all equipment," but you may only go "10 to 15" feet deep. The best thing about it is that you don't have to worry about "getting there or back" since it was all arranged through Disney. Overall, the dive was "disappointing" and most felt it would be best to "arrange your own scuba dive" through an outfit like Stuart Cove's. (On Your Own: Stuart Cove's Aqua Adventures at http://www.stuartcove.com, 800-879-9832)

Sports
Very active
For certified divers only
Ages 12 & up
$99/adult
4.5–5 hours

☐ Sunshine Glass Bottom Boat [N02] Rating: 3

Curious about what's under that aquamarine water? Take this excursion and you won't even have to get wet. The 70-foot boat has one sundeck, a covered deck, restrooms, cash bar, and (what else?) a glass bottom. You'll cruise the Nassau Harbour, then head off to the coral reefs—if the weather permits, you see a shipwreck, too. Typical meeting times are 10:30 am and 2:30 pm. Cruiser reviews are mostly negative. It is a "bit of a walk from the ship to the pier" where the glass bottom boat is moored. Once on the boat, the "scratched up" glass bottom was "way too small" and you may have to stand to see. On the other hand, it "wasn't too expensive" and the "kids really enjoyed it." Overall, the experience was a "complete and total" waste of money for some, while others thought it was a "nice little ride."

Tour
Leisurely
All ages
$25/adult
$17/child
1.5–2.5 hours

☐ Atlantis Aquaventure Rating: n/a

New! Enjoy the new 63-acre water park at the famous Atlantis Resort. The excursion begins with a 25-minute bus ride to Paradise Island. Once here, you can explore the aquarium, relax on the many beaches, and dive into the amazing, well-themed water park. The park features nine thrilling water slides that utilize "master blaster" water jet technology, pushing you both uphill and downhill. The water park also has a mile-long "lazy river" with underground tunnels, churning rapids, waterfalls, and conveyers to water slides. Complimentary light lunch, towels, and life jackets included. Lockers and other water rentals are extra. Typical meeting time is 9:15 am. Guests must be at least 48" tall to ride all water slides.

Beach/ Sports
All ages
$155/adult
$105/3–9
5–9 hours

☐ Atlantis Dolphin Cay & Aquaventure Rating: n/a

New! Take the above Atlantis Aquaventure and add a hands-on, interactive dolphin experience at the 11-acre Dolphin Cay. You'll receive instruction, put on a provided wet suit, and get in waist-high water to meet a dolphin. You'll have the opportunity to touch and play with the dolphin, but this is not a swim with the dolphins experience. The 2-hour Dolphin Cay visit is first, followed by the Aquaventure water park access and free time to explore the resort's beaches, shops, and casino. Typical meeting time is 9:15 am.

Sports
Ages 3 & up
$285/adult
$245/3–9
6–8 hours

See page 172 for a key to the shore excursion description charts and their icons.

⟶

St. Maarten/St. Martin
(Eastern Caribbean Itineraries—First Port of Call)

The Dutch say Sint Maarten, the French say St. Martin, but what's in a name? Where else can you visit **two countries** this easily, dine so lavishly, shop so extravagantly, and sun so beautifully? Two nations share this bit of paradise, but if we must take sides, we'll take the French. Alas, the Disney Magic docks on the Dutch side.

Dave and Allie on Pinel Island, St. Martin

With the Atlantic to the east, the Caribbean to the west and a lagoon in between, St. Maarten's 37 beaches offer **everything** from roaring surf to gentle ripples, and brisk trade winds keep the island cool. Its 37 square miles (96 sq. km.) include tall, luxuriantly green mountains, two capital cities, hundreds of appetizing restaurants, a dizzying array of shops, and a dozen casinos. Philipsburg, the bustling Dutch capital, hosts up to four cruise ships daily, and offers handy, excellent shopping. Picturesque Marigot, the French capital, offers a lot more charm and sophistication for cruisers willing to go the extra distance.

The **history** of this island begins with the Arawaks, seafaring Indians who discovered salt on the island. Later, Columbus named and claimed this island as he sailed past on the Feast of St. Martin. After harassing the Spanish for some years (New Amsterdam's Peter Stuyvesant lost his leg here), the Dutch and French moved in and carved it up in 1647. Relations are friendly now, but the border moved several times during the next 200 years. Sugar cane was the cash crop until slavery was abolished, and sea salt was produced in Philipsburg's Salt Pond, but this was a very quiet place until tourists came to call. And despite this long history, there's still a strong difference in culture and architecture between very French St. Martin and commerce-focused Dutch Sint Maarten.

Size: 12 mi. long (19 km.) x 8 mi. wide (13 km.)	
Climate: Subtropical	Temperatures: 80°F (27°C) to 85°F (29°C)
Population: 77,000	Busy Season: Late December to April
Language: English, French, Dutch	Money: Euro or Florin (U.S. dollar accepted)
Time Zone: Atlantic (no DST)	Transportation: Taxis and cars
Phones: Dial 011- from U.S., dial 22222 for emergencies	

Sidebar tabs: Introduction · Reservations · Staterooms · Dining · Activities · Ports of Call · Magic · Index

AMBIENCE · HISTORY · FACTS

Making the Most of St. Maarten/St. Martin

GETTING THERE

Your ship docks at the **Captain Hodge Wharf** in Philipsburg in Dutch St. Maarten, at the east end of Great Bay. Taxis and tour buses leave from the wharf, and a water taxi makes two stops along Front Street ($5 buys a pass good for unlimited trips, all day long). A walkway provides direct access to the beach and the shops, casinos, and restaurants of Front Street. It's about a 10- to 15-minute walk to the near end of Front St., and about a mile (1.6 km) from one end of Front Street to the other. The wharf hosts a tourist information booth. Disembarkation time is typically 8:00 am with an all-aboard time around 7:00 pm.

GETTING AROUND

As with many ports, the real pleasures are found outside of town. Most destinations are within a half-hour drive of Philipsburg, and a **rental car** is the way to get there. Research and book your rental in advance, as rates skyrocket for on-site rentals. All major agencies are represented, but only five have pierside offices. • The island is really two rocky land masses. A pair of sand spits connects the roughly circular main bulk of the island with the small western portion, Terre Basses (the Lowlands). Between the sand spits is Simpson Bay Lagoon. • The French side occupies 21 sq. miles (54 sq. km.) of the northern part of the island, the Dutch 16 sq. miles (41 sq. km.) of the south. A picturesque range of mountains runs north to south, further dividing the island. From Philipsburg, nearly every point of interest, including Marigot, can be reached by driving around the perimeter of the island. • **Taxis** use a government-controlled rate chart. The base fare is for two persons, and each additional person costs about 1/3 the base fare. Sample fares from Philipsburg: Marigot, Orient Beach, Dawn Beach, Maho Resort, all $15; Grand Case, $20. An island tour is $50. • **Public buses** travel between Philipsburg and Marigot. The fare is around $3, U.S. funds are accepted. • Once you're in Philipsburg, Marigot, or any other community, everything will be within walking distance.

STAYING SAFE

There's nothing too unusual about staying safe on "The Friendly Island." No place is crime-free, but St. Maarten does very well. Be wary when carrying parcels, of course. Don't bring valuables to the beach. American and Canadian drivers will be happy, as the island follows U.S. driving practices (right-hand side), but beware of **speed bumps** through towns and resorts. The breeze may fool you into forgetting the sun—be sure to apply plenty of sunblock, especially if you'll be more exposed than usual (if you catch our drift).

Touring St. Maarten/ St. Martin

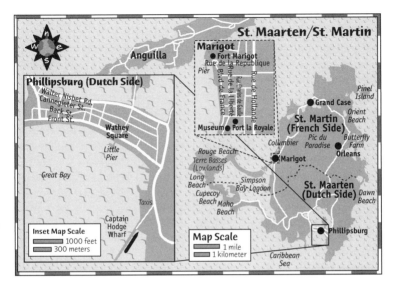

ST. MAARTEN/ST. MARTIN MAP

Walking Around in Philipsburg: Philipsburg is a narrow sand spit, just four streets deep and about a mile long (1.6 km.). Front Street runs the length of the town and supplies most of the town's shopping and dining. Back Street is one block over. If you take the water taxi from the wharf you'll arrive at old Little Pier, where the cruise ships' tenders used to dock. Great Bay Beach is right at hand, as are many locals, plying the tourist trade. Leave Little Pier and you'll be in Wathey Square, with its landmark Dutch courthouse. (If you walk from the ship, you'll be at the east end of Front Street, and Wathey Square will be about three blocks west.) You'll find shops, restaurants, and casinos no matter which way you turn. Just walk west until you've had your fill, then retrace your steps.

Walking Around in Marigot: The heart of Marigot is a rough rectangle, bordered on the west by the harbor. On the north, Rue de la Republique offers upscale shopping, with the local pier at its west end. From the pier, head north to climb to the ruins of Fort Marigot, or head south on restaurant-lined Boulevard de France to the Creole graveyard and small museum at the south end of town. Also on the south side, about a block inland, is Port la Royale, a marina surrounded by restaurants and shops—a perfect spot for lunch. Afterward, head back north on shady Rue de la Liberté or shop-filled Rue Charles de Gaulle.

ACTIVITIES

Introduction

Reservations

Staterooms

Dining

Activities

Ports of Call

Magic

Index

Playing in St. Maarten/ St. Martin

Great Bay Beach is a short walk from the ship along a new, beachfront promenade. The surf is gentle, and food and shopping are right behind you on Front Street. To the north, **Orient Beach**, with its long crescent of soft white sand and gentle surf, is called the "French Riviera of the Caribbean," but it achieved fame as the island's official nude beach. Beachfront restaurants and resorts have dressed the place up, but bathers at the south end of the beach are still very undressed (not that you have to be). **Maho Beach**, **Mullet Bay**, **Cupecoy Beach**, and **Long Beach** are way out west by the big resorts, past Juliana Airport. All are very pleasant, with Maho offering full resort amenities. Other beaches include remote Rouge Beach (one of Dave's favorites) and Grand Case Beach. Note: With the possible exception of Great Bay beach, you're likely to encounter European-style beach attire (topless women, men in thongs).

The brisk trade winds make the island very popular for **sailing**. For convenience, take one of several "shore" excursions described on the next four pages. Excursions are also available at the marinas near the wharf in Philipsburg. For **snorkeling**, Dawn Beach, several miles to the northeast of Philipsburg, is a top choice.

The island is a **diner's paradise**, with fabulous French, Creole, Indian, Vietnamese, and Indonesian restaurants (and KFC). You'll have no trouble finding a meal along Front Street in Philipsburg, but you'll do better in "France." In Marigot, head toward charming Port la Royale Marina, which is encircled by more than a half-dozen bustling bistros. Note: Many restaurants automatically include a 15% service charge (tip), so watch that bill carefully before you tip.

Twelve **casinos** dot the Dutch side. Four are within walking distance of the wharf, on Front Street in Philipsburg. The largest (and most elegant) casino is the Princess Casino at Port de Plaisance.

The **luxury goods shops** on both sides of the island present a staggering array of French perfumes and cosmetics, crystal, fine porcelain, jewelry, clothing, liquors, and wines. Philipsburg offers many of the French brands you'll find in Marigot at equal or lower prices, but somehow it feels better to shop in Marigot. The huge Little Switzerland luxury goods chain has shops in Philipsburg and Marigot. Cigar fans can find good Cubans, but be sure to smoke them before you arrive back home.

Embarking on Shore Excursions in St. Maarten/St. Martin

Pinel Island Snorkel Tour [SMO1]   Rating: 6

Sports
Active
Ages 5 & up
$37/$31 (5–9)
3 hours

Pinel Island, which is often called St. Martin's best-kept secret, is an uninhabited island in Orient Bay (French side). You'll take a bus ride, then a water taxi to reach the island. Price includes snorkeling instruction and equipment, with plenty of time to snorkel, swim, sunbathe, or shop. We visited on our own a few years ago and absolutely loved the island. Typical meeting times is 8:00 am. Cruiser reviews are mixed: Some feel the bus ride is "short," while others say it "seems like hours." All agree that the island itself is "very beautiful" with a "sandy beach" and "gradual drop-off." The snorkeling "leaves something to be desired" as it's "often windy" with "poor visibility." Some felt if you visited to "just go swimming" it would be better—others had a "great time."(On Your Own: Scuba Fun at 599-542-2333, ext. 3160)

Shipwreck Cove Snorkel Tour [SMO2]   Rating: 5

Sports
Active
Ages 8 & up
$41/$34 (8–9)
3.5 hours

Experienced snorkelers may enjoy this boat trip to Shipwreck Cove to hand-feed the fish that swim among sunken ships and coral reefs. Instruction and snorkel equipment provided, but this excursion is not recommended for non-swimmers. Refreshments, Calypso music, sun decks, and restrooms onboard the boat. Cruiser reviews are mixed: Most felt the snorkeling was "lackluster" in "murky water," while a few others enjoyed "very clear water." The "shipwrecks are real," but some say the were "relocated from somewhere else" and "were intentionally sunk for the tourists." In general, most cruisers do "not recommend it," while some "couldn't stop talking about how wonderful it was." Chances are your experience "depends on the weather," which is often windy. Typical meeting time is 1:00 pm.

Golden Eagle Catamaran [SMO3]   Rating: 9

Sports
Active
Ages 5 & up
$71/$41 (5–9)
4–4.5 hours

Enjoy a half-day jaunt to Tintamar—a real deserted island—aboard the majestic Golden Eagle. The luxurious, 76-foot catamaran sails at up to 30 knots! The excursion price includes pastries, an open bar, and complimentary use of beach floats and snorkel equipment. Typical meeting times are 7:45 am and 1:00 pm. Cruiser reviews are very positive: The ride over is "fun" and "not too fast for kids to enjoy," while the crew "friendly and courteous." The "deserted island" is a "great place to snorkel or just relax on the beach." The "beautiful" beach is "scenic" with "very clear" water. There is "music and singing" during the cruise. All cruisers report that they would "do it again," but some would be sure to "take seasickness medicine" first. (On Your Own: Eagle Tours at http://www.sailingsxm.com or 599-543-0068)

12-Metre Regatta [SMO4]   Rating: 10

Sports
Very active
Ages 12 & up
$75
3 hours

Become a crew member aboard one of the famous America's Cup yachts, such as the "Stars and Stripes." You'll compete in an actual race on a shortened version of the America's Cup course. You may get to "grind a winch" or "trim a sail"—no experience is necessary. Wear soft-soled shoes. Typical meeting time is 8:15 am. Cruiser reviews are overwhelmingly positive: This excursion lets you be "as active" as you like—some cruisers were "captain" while others were "in charge of the beverage chest." The "exciting" race is "great fun" with "friendly competition." Cruisers enjoyed the option to purchase a "great photo" of their team. While the seas are "not rough," this is not for anyone "prone to motion sickness." Overall, this excursion is a "highlight of the cruise" and "a blast!" (On Your Own: America's Cup at 599-542-0045)

See page 172 for a key to the shore excursion description charts and their icons.

Embarking on Shore Excursions
in St. Maarten/St. Martin *(continued)*

▪ Island Drive & Explorer Cruise [SM05]   Rating: n/a

Drive along the Atlantic coast of the island on a guided tour, then board the "Explorer" pleasure boat for a 30-minute cruise to Marigot (the island's French capital). Cash bars onboard. There's time for shopping and sightseeing before you return to Philipsburg. Typical meeting time is 1:15 pm. Cruiser reviews for this excursion were not submitted; it appears it is not very popular. (On Your Own: Eagle Tours at http://www.sailingsxm.com or 599-543-0068)	**Tour**
	Leisurely
	All ages
	$47/$24 (3–9)
	4 hours

▪ Under Two Flags Island Tour [SM06]   Rating: 7

Board an air-conditioned bus for a scenic, narrated tour of both the French and Dutch sides of the island—you'll see much of the island. The bus makes short 15-minute stops for photos, plus a 45-minute stop in Marigot (the French capital) so you can shop or explore. The tour ends back in Philipsburg. Typical meeting time is 8:45 am. Cruiser reviews are mixed: Most cruisers enjoyed the island drive in a "comfortable, clean bus" with a "friendly driver," though a few did not like to see the "ramshackle houses" along the way. There are several "photo op stops" on "both sides of the island," plus a "French market shopping stop." Most feel this is an "informative," "get acquainted tour" that is "short enough," but some felt the "shopping time is too short" and "kids will be bored out of their skulls." (On Your Own: n/a)	**Tour**
	Leisurely
	All ages
	$22/$17 (3–9)
	3 hours

▪ French Riviera Beach Rendezvous [SM07]   Rating: 8

Enjoy a beach day at Orient Bay, which has been called the "French Riviera of the Caribbean." You'll receive a guided tour on your way to the beach, where you'll be welcomed with a complimentary beverage and a full-service lunch. Then it's off to your reserved beach chair for relaxation. One end of this beach is clothing-optional. Typical meeting time is 9:15 am. Cruiser reviews are mostly positive: The "20–30 minute" bus ride is informative, filled with "facts regarding the island," though some cruisers were uncomfortable with the "visible poverty" on the island. At Orient Beach, you get a "padded lounge chair" to use and a complimentary "fruit punch" with "optional rum." Lunch is "good" with "ribs, chicken, and fish." Cruisers report "topless" bathers and "full nudity," but "forgot about it" after a while. Most felt this excursion is an "adventure" and a "fun experience." (On Your Own: Just take a taxi to Orient Beach!)	**Beach**
	Leisurely
	All ages
	$57/$40 (3–9)
	5 hours

▪ St. Maarten Island & Butterfly Farm Tour [SM09]   Rating: 8

Board a bus for a narrated tour through Philipsburg to the famous Butterfly Farm on the French side of the island. After the farm you'll stop at Marigot for shopping and exploration. Tip: Wear bright colors and perfume if you want the butterflies to land on you. Typical meeting time is 8:00 am. Cruiser reviews are mostly positive: The "great island tour" with "narration" from the "entertaining driver" gave insight into the "rich history" of St. Maarten. The "best part of the trip" was the Butterfly Farm, which "should not be missed" and good for "kids under 12." Most had not seen "so many butterflies so close" and were enchanted when they "landed" on them. Most felt this was a "great overall tour," but some said there are "better butterfly farms at zoos." (On Your Own: The Butterfly Farm at http://www.thebutterflyfarm.com or 599-544-3562)	**Tour**
	Leisurely
	All ages
	$34/$28 (3–9)
	3.5–4 hours

© MediaMarx, Inc.

The Butterfly Farm

See page 172 for a key to the shore excursion description charts and their icons.

Embarking on Shore Excursions
in St. Maarten/St. Martin (continued)

See & Sea Island Tour [SM10] Rating: 6

Explore the best of both worlds—land and sea—on this guided tour. First you'll take a narrated bus tour to Grand Case. Then you'll board the "Seaworld Explorer"—a semi-submarine—for an underwater glimpse of sea life. Afterwards, there's an hour for shopping and exploring in Marigot. Typical meeting times are 8:15 am and 1:15 pm. Cruiser reviews are mixed: The bus driver is "knowledgeable" and "personable," but the ride was "slow" and "harrowing" at times as the roads are very narrow. The "sea portion" aboard the "semi-sub" was "interesting" and "educational," and the "kids really loved seeing the fish." Some reports suggest that "the sea life is minimal." Overall, some cruisers liked seeing "pretty much all" of the "pretty island," while others felt there were "better ways" to see the island. (On Your Own: Seaworld Explorer at 599-542-4078)

Tour
Leisurely
All ages
$51/$36 (3–9)
3.5 hours

"BUBBA" Fishing Adventure Tour [SM11] Rating: n/a

Take a five-minute drive to Doc Maarten Marina and hop aboard the custom-built fishing boat for a 45-minute cruise along the St. Maarten coast. At the "secret fishing spot" you'll drop anchor for two hours while you bottom fish for Snapper, Snook, African Pompano, Triggerfish, Barracuda, Grouper, and more. This is a "catch and release" experience with a high-tech rod and reel (provided). Also note that the motion of the boat can be rocky and those who are prone to motion sickness should come prepared. Complimentary beverages are offered during the trip. An opportunity to shop in Philipsburg is available after the cruise. Typical meeting time is 8:15 am. No cruiser reviews are available yet.

Tour
Leisurely
Ages 6 & up
$90/$77
4–4.5 hours

St. Maarten Certified Scuba [SM13] Rating: 8

Certified scuba divers enjoy visits to some of St. Maarten's famous dive sites. Dive sites are chosen on the day of the dive according to weather and sea conditions. You must have your scuba certification and have completed at least one dive in the past two years to participate. Typical meeting time is 8:45 am. Cruiser reviews are limited but generally positive: The "two-tank" dive is "great," with "one divemaster per six divers." The tour operators "handled all the equipment" and "took plenty of time" at each location. Even though "St. Maarten isn't the greatest place to dive" due to "choppy waters," once you're underwater it is "beautiful." Those "prone to motion sickness" should take the "appropriate meds" before going. Overall, most felt it "couldn't have been nicer." (On Your Own: Dive Safaris at http://diveguide.com/divesafaris, 599-542-9001 or Aqua Mania at http://www.stmaarten-activities.com, 599-544-2640)

Sports
Very active
Ages 12 & up
$94
4.5 hours

Lotterie Farm Hidden Forest Tour [SM17] Rating: n/a

Are you ready for a challenging hike up to Pic du Paradise, St. Martin's tallest mountain at 1,400 feet (427 m.)? After an air-conditioned bus ride to the Lotterie Farm Hidden Forest, you'll begin your 1 ½-hour hike through a lush rainforest. After your hike you'll enjoy an open-air lunch and a brief stop in Marigot. Bring good walking shoes and water. Typical meeting time is 8:15 am. No cruiser reviews were received for this excursion. (On Your Own: n/a)

© MediaMarx, Inc.

Jennifer on Pic du Paradise

Sports
Very active
Ages 8 & up
$80/$48 (8–9)
4.5–5 hours

See page 172 for a key to the shore excursion description charts and their icons.

Embarking on Shore Excursions in St. Maarten/St. Martin (continued)

Mountain Bike Adventure [SM19]   Rating: n/a

Need some exercise? This excursion outfits you with a mountain bike and safety gear, then takes you for a bumpy on- and off-road bike tour. You'll ride along the coastline, through the village of Colombier, and encounter at least one steep hill. After your exertions, take 30 minutes to relax and swim at Friar's Bay Beach—includes a complimentary beverage. Typical meeting time is 7:45 am. We received no cruiser reviews for this excursion. (On Your Own: n/a)

Sports
Very active
Ages 12 & up
$72
3.5 hours

Rhino Rider and Snorkeling Adventure [SM18]   Rating: 9

This excursion offers a chance to zoom about on your own, two-person inflatable boat (the "Rhino Rider") in Simpson Bay. After your cruise, you'll have the opportunity to snorkel (equipment provided). When your adventure is over, you can relax with a complimentary beverage. Note that each boat holds two people maximum, and only those 13 or older can drive. Typical meeting times are 7:45 am and 1:45 pm. Cruiser comments are positive: After a bus ride out to Simpson Bay, guests get a "brief explanation" on using the "two-seater mini boats." Take a "30-minute" ride with "great views" to the "good" snorkeling location. Most cruisers agree the excursion is "worth it" and offered a "great time." (On Your Own: Atlantis Adventures at http://www.atlantisadventures.com, 599-542-4078)

Sports
Very active
Ages 10 & up
$84
3.5 hours

Afternoon Beach Bash Tour [SM23]   Rating: n/a

Here's your chance to relax on a beautiful beach on Orient Bay. Bask in the sun, swim in the ocean, or explore the coastline. Allow 3.5 to 4 hours. Afterward, take a 30-minute drive to St. Maarten for some rum or fruit punch. Mmmm!

Beach
All ages
$37/20 (3-9)

Tiki Hut Snorkel [SM26]   Rating: n/a

New! Board a tender boat for a 15-minute journey to a "floating island" in Little Bay. From this vantage point, you can snorkel and swim in clear waters or just relax in the floating lounge. You can return after two hours (return boats leave every hour) or stay as long as a half day. Note that while snorkel equipment is provided, food and drinks are not (but you can buy them—bring cash). (On Your Own: ExcursionWorld at http://www.excursionworld.com/tours/569.htm)

Sports
Active
Ages 5 & up
$59/$42
2-5 hours

Seaworld Explorer—Coral Reef Exploration [SM27]   Rating: n/a

New! You'll begin with a 30-minute bus ride to Grand Case on the French side, where you'll board the semi-submarine to see beneath the waters. The fully submerged sub ride is 45 minutes long and includes a diver who encourages underwater creatures to move within sight of the sub's windows. You'll enjoy a complimentary glass of fruit punch or rum punch. (On Your Own: Seaworld Explorer at http://www.atlantissubmarines.com, 599-542-4078)

Tour
Leisurely
All ages
$39/$29
2.5 hours

The Ultimate Charter Choice [SM28]   Rating: n/a

New! Would you like to charter your own private yacht? Here's your chance! Your yacht excursion includes a Captain and first mate, onboard lunch (cold cuts, cheeses, bread, beer, soda, and water), snorkel equipment, and life vests. Choose your own itinerary or let the Captain make recommendations. Only your traveling party has the use of the yacht, but there is a maximum guest limit of 10. Download and submit the special form from the Disney Cruise web site.

Tour
Leisurely
Ages 5 & up
Price varies
8-8.5 hours

See page 172 for a key to the shore excursion description charts and their icons.

Introduction · Reservations · Staterooms · Dining · Activities · Ports of Call · Magic · Index

St. Thomas & St. John
(Eastern Caribbean Itineraries—Second Port of Call)

Welcome to pretty St. Thomas, the **busiest cruise ship port** and duty-free shopping haven in the Caribbean! Pirates once roamed freely here, but your visit will be far tamer, thanks to its status as a U.S. Territory. Shopping not your cup of tea? The neighboring island of St. John is a prime, back-to-nature getaway.

The Disney Magic in St. Thomas
(view from Paradise Point)

St. Thomas boasts beautiful beaches like many Caribbean islands, but its **rugged mountain terrain** gives it a distinctive look. St. Thomas is shaped like an elongated hourglass and is about 28 square miles (72 sq. km.) in size, making it the second largest island in the U.S. Virgin Islands (St. Croix is the largest). Shoppers throng the narrow lanes and old, stone buildings of St. Thomas' downtown Charlotte Amalie, a duty-free port since the 1700s. The neighboring island of St. John is just a ferry ride away, home to the hiking trails, wildlife, and remote beaches of 7,200-acre Virgin Islands National Park. Your day in port is brief, so a trip to St. John will take most of your day.

Adventurers from many nations visited St. Thomas, but none put down roots until Denmark colonized in the late 1600s. The Danes made the island's prime harbor a **safe haven** for pirates, cashing in on this early "tourist" trade. They also operated sugar plantations, a thriving seaport, and one of the busiest slave markets in the Americas. Charlotte Amalie's waterfront is still lined with old stone buildings from its commercial heyday. The economy crashed after slavery was abolished in the mid-1800s, so by 1917 the Danes were happy to hand the islands to the U.S. for $25 million (it's now a U.S. Territory). Then in 1956, Laurence Rockefeller donated 5,000 acres on St. John to create the Virgin Islands National Park (and not incidentally, to ensure an attractive setting for his Caneel Bay resort).

Size: St. Thomas: 13 mi. (21 km.) x 4 mi. (6 km.) /St. John: 7 mi. (11 km.) x 3 mi. (5 km.)	
Climate: Subtropical	**Temperatures**: 77°F (25°C) to 85°F (29°C)
Population: 51,000 & 4,000	**Busy Season**: Late December to April
Language: English	**Money**: U.S. Dollar
Time Zone: Atlantic (no DST)	**Transportation**: Walking, taxis, cars
Phones: Dial 1- from U.S., dial 911 for emergencies	

Introduction

Reservations

Staterooms

Dining

Activities

Ports of Call

Magic

Index

AMBIENCE

HISTORY

FACTS

Making the Most
of St. Thomas and St. John

Introduction
Reservations
Staterooms
Dining
Activities
Ports of Call
Magic
Index

GETTING THERE

Your ship docks near **Charlotte Amalie**, capital of the U.S. Virgin Islands, normally at the West India Company pier in Havensight, 1.5 miles (2.4 km.) from downtown. Occasionally, guests must be tendered ashore (if this happens, you'll arrive in Charlotte Amalie rather than Havensight). All ashore is typically at 8:00 am, with all aboard around 4:00 pm. All guests must meet with U.S. Immigration officials onboard the ship, regardless of whether you plan to go ashore (see page 322). No guests may disembark until <u>all</u> guests have met with immigration, so there's no sleeping in today (meeting times vary—refer to the letter placed in your stateroom the night before). Visitors traveling to St. John should either book a shore excursion, or take a taxi to the Red Hook ferry on the eastern end of the island—round-trip ferry fare is $6/adults, $2/kids (15- to 20-minute ride). There's also a ferry from downtown Charlotte Amalie for $14/adults, $6/kids, but again you'll have to take a taxi to the ferry.

GETTING AROUND

There's **plenty of shopping near the pier**, or take a cab into town or to other destinations. Havensight Mall, right next to the cruise pier, offers more than 60 shops, and several other malls are within walking distance. • The Paradise Point aerial tramway ($19/$9.50) is a short walk from the pier, and offers panoramic views of the island. • There's far more shopping in downtown Charlotte Amalie (1.5 miles/2.4 km.). A taxi will cost about $3 (no meters, get the rate in advance). • Car rentals are available at the pier, but taxis and mini-buses are generally a better idea. • Maagens Bay, several miles from Charlotte Amalie on the island's north shore, is a beautiful and well-known beach. Nearby is Mountain Top, famed for its views and banana daiquiris. A half-mile west of Charlotte Amalie is the picturesque fishing village of Frenchtown, known for its restaurants and bars. • If you want to visit **St. John**, Disney offers shore excursions to most of St. John's most famous spots, and with the day's tight schedule, they make sense. If you want to explore on your own, Hertz and Avis both have agencies in Cruz Bay, and taxi fares to the major sights are $3–$9. Ferries arrive in Cruz Bay, and the National Park interpretive center is a short walk away. • The beach at Trunk Bay is most popular. • History buffs may enjoy the ruins of Annaberg Sugar Plantation ($4 day use fee).

SAFETY

Pickpockets and beach theft are the most notable crime problems you'll encounter, so **leave your valuables on board**, and safeguard your purse or wallet while shopping. Drinking water is collected in cisterns from rain water, so you may prefer to drink bottled water.

Touring St. Thomas and St. John

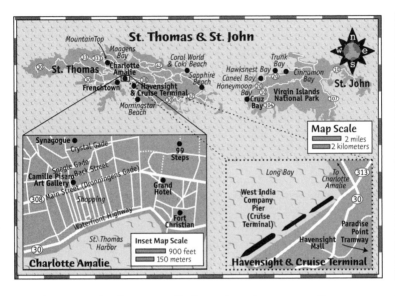

St. Thomas: Charlotte Amalie is a nice place to stroll on steep, narrow streets with Danish names. Most sights are found on the island's many shopping streets, which are within three blocks of the waterfront. Waterfront Highway provides a harborfront promenade. One block inland is Main Street (Dronningens Gade), followed by Back Street, Snegle Gade, and Crystal Gade. More than a dozen Alleys, Gades, Passages, Plazas, and Malls run between Main Street and the waterfront, all lined with shops. Strollers will find historic Fort Christian and the Virgin Islands Museum at the southeast end of downtown. A tourist information center is located nearby, in the former Grand Hotel. One of the New World's oldest Jewish congregations in a charming, 1833 synagogue can be found three blocks inland, near the corner of Crystal Gade and Raadets Gade. Toward the west side of Main Street is the Camille Pissaro Art Gallery, named for the impressionist painter, a St. Thomas native, and featuring works by local artists. Walkers will also enjoy the many brick staircases, including the 99 Steps, that connect the steep streets in the northeast corner of downtown.

St. John's tiny port town of Cruz Bay is good for a short stroll among its cluster of shops and restaurants. The Virgin Islands National Park Visitor Center is a short walk from the dock, and several hiking trails depart from there.

Playing in St. Thomas and St. John

ACTIVITIES

There are no **beaches** within walking distance of the wharf. Morningstar Beach is the closest, and includes all the comforts of the Marriott resort. Maagens Bay ($3/day for adults) is famed for its beauty, but will be thronged with fellow cruise visitors. Sapphire Beach out on the east end offers full, resort-based recreation rentals, and nearby Coki Beach is convenient to Coral World (see below). • On **St. John**, there's a small beach right at the ferry dock in Cruz Bay, but the real attractions are elsewhere. Caneel Beach is a short ride from Cruz Bay, and part of the Caneel Bay resort (stop at the front desk on your way to the beach). Along St. John's north shore, Hawksnest Bay, Trunk Bay, and Cinnamon Bay are easily accessible, offer food, recreation, and other amenities, and are all part of the national park. Trunk Bay ($4/day) is very beautiful, most popular, and features a snorkeling trail. Cinnamon Bay has great windsurfing. • **Snorkeling** equipment can be rented at many beaches. The early departure time makes fishing excursions impractical.

Shopping is St. Thomas' biggest attraction. Shopping is duty-free, sales-tax-free, and is conducted in U.S. dollars. As always, while prices can be excellent, know what you'd pay back home for the same goods. Not everything is a "deal." Some shopkeepers will bargain with you. Just ask, "Is that your final price?" With as many as eight cruise ships in port per day, it takes hundreds of shops to absorb the throngs. We suggest you head into Charlotte Amalie and start exploring. If your time is short, the malls and shops in and around the cruise wharf will be most convenient.

Visitors to St. John will find the **Virgin Islands National Park** web site very helpful, with a detailed map of the island including its 22 hiking trails. Get more info at http://www.nps.gov/viis.

Coral World Marine Park and Undersea Observatory on St. Thomas' east end (adjacent to Coki Beach) offers underwater observation areas, aquariums, exhibits, stingray encounters, nature trails, and the "Sea Trek" adventure where you get to walk the sea bottom (extra $64/adult and $57/child 8 & up, reservations suggested). Admission is $19/adults and $10/kids 3–12, or $75 for a family of two adults and up to four kids. Visit http://www.coralworldvi.com or call 888-695-2073.

For one of the most informative and well-laid-out **web sites** for the U.S. Virgin Islands, visit http://www.vinow.com.

Embarking on Shore Excursions
on St. Thomas and St. John

■ **St. John Trunk Bay Beach & Snorkel Tour** [ST01]	**Rating: 6**	
Travel by sea and land to Trunk Bay, where you'll have 1.5 hours to swim, snorkel (equipment provided), and relax in this beautiful national park. Typical meeting time is 7:15 am. Cruiser comments are mixed: Most report that the "ferry ride" over was "long" and "boring." Once at Trunk Bay, however, cruisers found it to be "one of the most beautiful" and "breathtaking" beaches. There is a "marked snorkel trail" and some cruisers have seen a "lot of fish," "stingrays," and "sea turtles." Most felt this was the "highlight of their cruise," while some "were not impressed." (On Your Own: Take a taxi to Red Hook, a ferry to St. John, and then a taxi to Trunk Bay)	**Sports**	
	Active	
	Ages 5 & up	
	$48/$34 (5-9)	
	5-5.5 hours	

■ **St. John Island Tour** [ST02]	**Rating: 9**	
Take a boat ride to St. John, then board an open-air safari bus for a guided tour through the unspoiled beauty of this island. Includes a stop at Annaberg Ruins and many stops for photo ops. For all ages. Typical meeting time is 7:15 am.	**Tour**	
	Leisurely	
	All ages	
	$42/$31 (3-9)	
	5-5.5 hours	

We took this excursion in May of 2003 and absolutely adored it. Cruiser reviews are uniformly positive: Most enjoyed the "boat ride" to "beautiful" St. John, though it was "long." The "very good driving tour" "makes a lot of stops for pictures" and the driver is both "entertaining" and "knowledgeable." Some of the roads are "very curvy," which could bother some. Overall, the tour is a "great way" to "see a lot" of the island.

© MediaMarx, Inc.

Dave stops for a panoramic photo on St. John

■ **St. John Eco Hike** [ST03]	**Rating: 8**	
Take a ferry to Cruz Bay, where you'll embark on a 90-minute guided hike (1.2 miles). You'll stop at Lind Point Lookout and Honeymoon Beach for swimming. Typical meeting time is 7:15 am. Cruiser reviews are positive: This "wonderful way to see this island" starts with "long ferry ride" then a short walk through the city to meet your "knowledgeable guide." The "very easy" hike is "informative," with a look at "local flora and fauna" ("bring bug spray!"). At the end of the "hot" hike, you get 30 min. to "frolic" in Honeymoon Bay ("wear your swimsuit under your clothes").	**Sports**	
	Very active	
	Ages 6 & up	
	$60/$50 (6-9)	
	5.5 hours	

■ **5-Star St. John Snorkel & Beach Adventure** [ST04]	**Rating: 7**	
Board the 115-foot "Leylon Sneed" in St. Thomas and cruise to Trunk Bay to snorkel (equipment provided), swim, and sunbathe. Includes a complimentary beverage. Typical meeting time is 7:00 am. Cruiser reviews are mixed: Most cruisers appreciated the cruise on the "1939 Chesapeake Bay Oyster Buy Boat replica," but found the trip "long" (45 minutes) and "a little crowded." Those cruisers that made it to Trunk Bay thought it "simply beautiful" with "great snorkeling," but a significant number of reviews noted that they were "detoured to St. James" island because of "rough seas," and this was "disappointing."	**Beach**	
	Active	
	Ages 5 & up	
	$48/$34 (5-9)	
	4-4.5 hours	

See page 172 for a key to the shore excursion description charts and their icons.

Embarking on Shore Excursions on St. Thomas and St. John *(continued)*

☐ Maagens Bay Beach Break [ST27] Rating: 9

Relax and swim at the beautiful white sandy beaches of Maagens Bay. Take a 25-min. scenic drive, stopping at Drake's Seat along the way for photos and great views. A beach chair and bottled water are included in the price of the excursion. Typical meeting time is 9:00 am. Cruiser reviews are positive: Those visiting Maagens Bay found the beach "wonderful" and "absolutely beautiful." They also "enjoyed the ride from the pier" as "some of the views going over the mountain were absolutely	**Beach**
	Leisurely
	All ages
	$44/$33 (3–9)
	4–4.5 hours

gorgeous." "Restrooms and a snack bar" are available. Most cruisers recommend you "do the excursion on your own" because "it's so easy to do and much cheaper than paying what Disney charges per person for the same thing." (On Your Own: Take a taxi from the pier to Maagens Bay for about $6/person each way, and then pay $3/person admission to the beach.)

☐ Atlantis Submarine Adventure [ST06] Rating: 5

Climb aboard the "Atlantis XV" and dive down to 90 feet (26 m.). Typical meeting times are 8:45 am, 10:15 am, and 12:15 pm. Guests must be 36 in. tall. Cruiser reviews are mixed: This "expensive" excursion takes place in a "fairly spacious" sub which you "board in water (no dock)" "after a choppy 30-minute ride." It has portholes "running along the sides." Two people need to "share a porthole" to gaze out at the "cloudy water" with "some sea life" but "nothing spectacular." A	**Tour**
	Leisurely
	Ages 4 & up
	$89/$57 (4–9)
	2.5 hours

"knowledgeable guide" points out specifics along the way. Most cruisers "enjoyed it" but probably wouldn't "do it again." (On Your Own: http://www.atlantisadventures.net or 340-776-5650)

☐ Doubloon Sail & Snorkel [ST08] Rating: 9

Help hoist the sails of the 65-foot "Doubloon" schooner and cruise to Turtle Cove on Buck Island. Snorkel (equipment provided) and swim. Includes snacks and drinks. Typical meeting time is 7:15 am. Cruiser reviews are positive: This "fun" excursion with a "heavy pirate theme" is fun for "kids and adults alike." While it's not a "major sailing experience," it is "enjoyable" and the "crew is attentive." Snorkeling at Buck Island is "good," though you may not be able	**Sports**
	Active
	Ages 5 & up
	$49/$32 (5–9)
	3.5 hours

to walk on the beach due to "nesting birds." "Rum punch," "beer," and "soda" are served. Overall, most cruisers "recommend it."

☐ St. Thomas Island Tour [ST11] Rating: n/a

Take an open-air safari bus tour to St. Peter's Great House and Mountain Top, the highest point on the island. The bus does make some stops for photo opportunities. Typical meeting times are 7:15 am and 12:30 pm. Cruisers visiting Mountain Top on their own claim it is "amazing" how you can "see so much!" Allow 2.5 hours.	**Tour**
	Leisurely
	All ages
	$35/$24 (3–9)

☐ Buck Island Catamaran Sail & Snorkel [ST29] Rating: n/a

Sunbathe on the deck of the catamaran or check out the beautiful coral formation that teems with exotic fish. You'll also be given the opportunity to snorkel above a sunken ship. Typical meeting time is 7:15 am. Allow 3.5 hours.	**Sports**
	Ages 5 & up
	$50/$35 (5–9)

☐ Kayak, Hike, and Snorkel of Cas Cay [ST32] Rating: n/a ☀ 🎒 📷

A 20-minute van ride brings you to the Virgin Islands Eco Tours Marine Sanctuary where the fun begins. There you board a two-person kayak and enjoy a guided tour of Cas Cay. Then hike through the tropical ecosystem to see a marine tidal pool and a blowhole along a coral beach. Now strap on snorkel gear for a guided tour. End with a 15-minute kayak trip. Typical meeting time is 8:00 am.	**Sports**
	Ages 8 & up
	$69
	4–4.5 hours

See page 172 for a key to the shore excursion description charts and their icons.

Embarking on Shore Excursions
on St. Thomas and St. John *(continued)*

Coral World Ocean & Island Drive [ST12]   Rating: 7

Take a guided tour to Mountain Top (highest peak) and Coral World in St. Thomas. Typical meeting times are 7:45 am and 11:45 am. Cruiser reviews are mostly positive: Coral World is a "wonderful adventure," a bit like "Sea World" but "more science-oriented." "Kids love it," and "see all kinds of sea life" and "pet a shark." The disappointments were the drive which was "not well narrated," and the length of time at Coral World ("only an hour and a half"). Cruisers did enjoy Coral World, but many suggested they'd "do it on their own" next time. (On Your Own: See page 200 to save money and see Coki Beach, too!)

Tour
Leisurely
All ages
$41/$30 (3–9)
3.5 hours

Water Island Mountain Bike Adventure [ST13]   Rating: 10

Enjoy a short boat ride to Water Island where you'll explore the terrain by mountain bike. Includes all necessary equipment. Includes a beach stop. Typical meeting time is 12:15 pm. Cruiser reviews are overwhelmingly positive: Get a ride to Water Island on a "large pontoon boat" and listen to the "history" of the island. Once on the island, you get a "quick how-to" on the bikes, "fit you for your helmet," and you're off. Most of the ride is "downhill," but it does cover ground with "gravel and loose rocks." After reaching Honeymoon Bay, you can "beach it" or "keep biking" a mostly "uphill trail." Cruisers of "all shapes and sizes" enjoyed this excursion.

Sports
Very active
Ages 10 & up
$69
3.5 hours

Golf at Mahogany Run [ST15]   Rating: 10

Play a round of golf at this 6,022-yard course designed by George and Tom Fazio. Price includes greens fees, golf cart, and transportation. Rental clubs are additional (about $20). Typical meeting time is 7:15 am. Cruiser reviews are very positive: The excursion "includes transportation" to and from the "beautiful course" with "awesome views." Players are "matched by handicap" and play in "foursomes." Some cruisers report that the course is "challenging," but "lots of fun." Other cruisers suggest you "carry your own golf shoes" to ensure a "comfortable fit." (On Your Own: Mahogany Run Golf Course at http://www.mahoganyrungolf.com)

Sports
Active
Ages 10 & up
$189
6 hours

Certified Scuba in St. Thomas [ST16]   Rating: 9

Certified scuba divers can take a two-tank dive to a maximum depth of 60 feet. Equipment and transportation are provided; wet suit not included. Typical meeting time is 7:45 am. Cruiser reviews are limited: Most cruisers enjoyed this "well-organized" tour and had a "great dive." In general, most agree that St. Thomas is a "far better location for diving" than St. Maarten. (On Your Own: Coki Beach Dive Club at http://www.cokidive.com, 800-474-2654)

Sports
Very active
Ages 12 & up
$94
4 hours

St. John Barefoot Sail & Snorkel [ST21]   Rating: 7

After a 20-minute scenic drive in an open-air taxi, you'll board a boat and sail to St. John, where you'll swim, snorkel, and sunbathe. Snacks, snorkel gear, and open bar included. Typical meeting time is 7:45 am. Cruiser reviews are mostly positive: This "great sailing trip" "over and back to St. John" is "excellent." The crew is "terrific" and served "drinks and snacks" both coming and going. Snorkeling at Honeymoon Bay is "very good" with "clear water, lots of fish, and even stingrays," but be aware that if you just want to lounge on the beach you'll need to "swim a short way from the catamaran to the beach." Overall, this excursion is "highly recommended" but a few would "do something else next time."

Sports
Active
Ages 5 & up
$75/$55 (5–9)
4.5 hours

Embarking on Shore Excursions
on St. Thomas and St. John *(continued)*

Historical St. Thomas Walking Tour [ST22] — Rating: 5

Explore the quaint town of Charlotte Amalie—along the way you'll admire a stunning vista of the town and visit Notman's Manor. Wear comfy walking shoes. Typical meeting time is 7:45 am. Cruiser reviews are mixed: Guests board a "van" and "drive up to the highest point" on the tour. From there, you "walk downhill" and listen to your "knowledgeable tour guide" point out sites and divulge the "history of the island." This is an "interesting tour" if you are a "history buff," otherwise it is a "bit dry." There are a "lot of stairs" and the tour is boring for "young kids."

Tour
Leisurely
All ages
$31/$20 (3–9)
3.5 hours

Skyway to Paradise Point [ST23] — Rating: 7

Enjoy a great view (see photo on 197) in this suspended tram. Bird shows are held twice daily. You can do this excursion anytime after 9:00 am. Jennifer tried this and found it a fun diversion with great views, but not a don't-miss. Cruiser reviews are mostly positive: The tramway is an "easy 10- to 15-minute walk" from the pier (but if you tender in, it's a "$3/person taxi from town" instead). The view from the tram is "just amazing" and you get a "great view of the Disney Magic." The "birds are cute" (shows are at "10:30 am and 1:30 pm") and there are some "nice shops" to browse. There is also a quarter-mile "nature walk" and a "little cafe." Most cruisers simply walked over (you can see the tramway from the pier) and purchased tickets on their own ($19/$9.50). (On Your Own: http://paradisepointtramway.com)

Tour
Leisurely
All ages
$18/age 13+
$9/age 6–12
(0–5 free)
1 hour

Captain Nautica's St. John Snorkeling Expedition [ST25] — Rating: 9

Enjoy a speedboat ride to two different snorkeling sites. Price includes snorkeling equipment, snacks, and beverages. Typical meeting times are 7:15 am and noon. Cruiser comments are very positive: The "adventurous" speedboat ride is "pretty fast" and "lots of fun." The crew is "friendly" and "helpful." The reported snorkeling sites are either "Turtle Cove off Buck Island" or "Christmas Cove," plus "Honeymoon Bay." Snorkeling is "wonderful" with "many colorful fish." The only complaint reported was with the snacks, which "weren't all that great." Overall, cruisers "loved it" and "would do it again." (On Your Own: http://www.captainnautica.com)

Tour
Active
Ages 8 & up
$69/$57 (8–9)
4 hours

Butterfly Secrets & Mountain Views [ST35] — Rating: n/a

New! Board an open-air safari bus and drive to Mountain Top, where you'll enjoy stunning views and have an opportunity to shop or try the famous banana daiquiris (extra cost). Then you'll visit Butterfly Farm for a guided tour through the gardens. Typical meeting time is 8:00 am. Note that if you simply want to visit the Butterfly Farm, you can book the "Butterfly Anytime" excursion (ST36) for $15/$9, which gives you admission to the farm anytime during the day.

Tour
Leisurely
All ages
$35/$24 (3–9)
3 hours

Tortola Dolphin Encounter [ST37] — Rating: n/a

New! Begin with a ferry across the bay to Tortola in the British Virgin Islands, then take a one-hour bus ride with an island tour guide before arriving at Dolphin Discovery. Here you'll receive an orientation, then submerge in waist-deep water for a 30-minute, hands-on "meet and greet" with real dolphins. You'll have the opportunity to touch and kiss the dolphin. A buffet lunch is included. Note that the excursion includes a 30-minute immigration stop. If you want to simply observe, sign up for the Tortola Dolphin Observer excursion (ST38) for $129/$101. Typical meeting time is 7:00 am.

Sports
Active
Ages 3 & up
$188/10 & up
$162 (3–9)
8–8.5 hours

See page 172 for a key to the shore excursion description charts and their icons.

Key West
(Western Caribbean Itinerary—First Port of Call)

Casually hanging out at the tip of the fabled Florida Keys, Key West is the southernmost point in the continental U.S., famous for Ernest Hemingway and Jimmy Buffett (and their bars), charming homes, sunsets, sport fishing, historic spots, and a way-laid-back lifestyle. You won't be in town long enough to waste away, but you sure can try.

© MediaMarx, Inc.

Key West's Mallory Square at sunset

As Florida's southernmost landfall, Americans feel more secure wandering Key West than other ports. The charm of its century-old buildings and the small-town air put you right at ease. Most attractions are a short stroll from the pier, and streets head off in (mostly) straight lines. To visit the sights, just start walking!

Spaniards called this flat, sun-drenched outpost "Cayo Hueso" (Island of Bones). The English (some buccaneers among 'em) were soon mispronouncing it "Key West." The U.S. Navy banished the pirates and has been stationed here ever since. Nearby, treacherous reefs sank countless vessels in the New Orleans trade, making salvage crews fabulously rich. A lighthouse turned that boom into a bust, and the town has been reborn again as a capital for spongers, cigar rollers, a President, treasure seekers, wealthy vacationers, artists and writers (James Audubon, Tennessee Williams, Robert Frost, Ernest Hemingway, and Thornton Wilder), and generations of dropouts from the rat race. Islanders declared the Conch Republic in 1982 to protest a federal roadblock that choked access to the Florida Keys. They soon had enough media attention to restore free passage, but the Republic's flag still flies high. Hurricane Wilma flooded most of Key West in October 2005, but it has now recovered well.

Size: 4 mi. (6.5 km.) wide x 2 mi. (3 km.) long	
Climate: Subtropical	**Temperatures**: 72°F (22°C) to 82°F (28°C)
Population: 24,832	**Busy Season**: Mid-February to April
Language: English	**Money**: U.S. Dollar
Time Zone: Eastern (DST observed)	**Transportation**: Walking, scooters
Phones: Dial 1- from U.S., dial 911 for emergencies	

Introduction

Reservations

Staterooms

Dining

Activities

Ports of Call

Magic

Index

AMBIENCE

HISTORY & CULTURE

FACTS

Getting Around Key West

GETTING THERE

Your ship docks around noon right at the **Hilton Marina** (Pier B), which is an easy five-minute walk to Mallory Square and Front Street. Tendering is not necessary, unless the ship is unable to dock (rare). You should be able to disembark by 12:30 or 1:00 pm (check your *Personal Navigator* for going ashore details). The marina is on the northwest corner of the island, looking out to the Gulf of Mexico. For those exploring on foot, most of the major destinations are within easy reach of the marina. Check your *Personal Navigator* for the all-aboard time, usually 7:30 pm.

GETTING AROUND

This is one of the **easiest ports to navigate**, thanks to its small size and pedestrian-friendly streets. Most visitors here just **walk**, and even many of the residents don't bother with cars. Almost all of Key West's streets near the docks run on a grid, making it easy to get around with a map. If you'd rather not walk, try one of Key West's famous **tram tours**. The Conch Tour Train (described on page 211) is $27/adults, $13/kids 4–12 (3 & under free)—board the tram near Mallory Square. If you'd prefer to get off and look around, the Old Town Trolley makes nine stops (see page 211) for $27/adults, $13/kids 4–12 (3 & under free)—board near the dock. • The Key West **bus system** is less expensive than the trams at just 75 cents/adults and 35 cents/kids and seniors (kids 5 & under are free). There are always two buses running—one goes clockwise around the island, the other goes counterclockwise. Call 305-293-6435 for bus info. • **Taxis** are also available—the meter starts at $1.40 and adds 35 cents per quarter mile. You can get taxis near the dock—if you need to call for one, try Florida Keys Taxi (305-284-2227). • Need your own transportation? Try a **scooter** rental. Adventure Scooter (601 Front Street, 305-293-9933, http://keywest.com/scooter.html) rents scooters for about $24/day—see the coupon at their web site.

STAYING SAFE

The "key" to **staying safe** in Key West is simple common sense. The biggest potential dangers here are overexposure to sun (bring that sunscreen and hat) and overindulgence at a local bar. Key West is very laid-back—we didn't encounter any street hawkers on our visit and we felt secure walking around on our own. If you rent a scooter, be sure to wear your helmet. If you swim, note the color-coded flags that indicate swimming conditions at the beach: blue = safe, yellow = marginal, and red = dangerous and prohibited. If you walk, wear comfortable, well-broken-in walking shoes. And bring a watch so you don't lose track of time and miss the boat!

Touring Key West

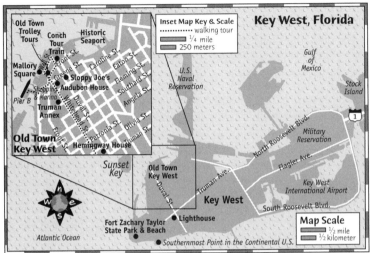

Key West is one of the best ports for a **casual walking tour**. Take along our map or pick one up at the Chamber of Commerce at 402 Wall Street. We've marked a walking tour on the map above. From the pier, you first reach the Truman Annex waterfront shopping area. Near the junction of Front and Greene Streets is the brick 1891 Custom House and its Museum of Art and History. Turn left onto Front Street, passing the U.S. Customs House (and Post Office) and the Naval Coal Depot building. At the corner of Front and Whitehead is the Key West Art Center, showcasing local artists. Nearby are the Key West Shipwreck Historeum ($11/adult, $5/kids 4–12) with its 60-foot lookout tower, and the Key West Aquarium ($11/adult, $5/kids 4–12), Key West's oldest tourist attraction. Turning onto Wall St. you'll find the Chamber of Commerce (free maps and info), and famous Mallory Square (see next page for sunset viewing tips). Continue along Wall St., rejoining Front St., where you can board the Conch Tour Train (see previous page), or stroll another block along Front to the Historic Seaport boardwalk. Follow Front St. back toward the ship, crossing Duval St. then turn onto Whitehead for its charm and many museums. Stop where you will, but if you're in a walking mood, follow Whitehead nine blocks to the Lighthouse and Hemingway House. When you've had enough, retrace your steps toward the waterfront to explore Duval and nearby side streets, or re-board the ship. For a more directed tour, try the "Presidents, Pirates & Pioneers" shore excursion (see page 212).

Introduction

KEY WEST ISLAND MAP   Reservations   Staterooms   Dining

WALKING TOUR   Activities   Ports of Call   Magic   Index

ACTIVITIES

Introduction | Reservations | Staterooms | Dining | Activities | Ports of Call | Magic | Index

Playing in Key West

Sloppy Joe's isn't the original Hemingway hangout; that's Captain Tony's, which used to be Sloppy Joe's. Captain Tony's gave Jimmy Buffett his first place to waste away, but now Jimmy can afford his own Margaritaville. Got all that? Regardless of your choice, these and many other atmospheric bars are a short crawl from the ship.

One of the joys of Key West is its **architecture**. Walk along Whitehead Street and turn down a few of the side streets. The old, clapboard homes, trimmed with Victorian gingerbread and surrounded by flowering foliage and white picket fences, are a delight. Household eaves are painted sky blue to ward off bugs, demons, or some such.

This isn't really a **beach zone**. The rocky bottom isn't swim-friendly. Fort Zachary Taylor State Park offers an attractive, nearby place to sun (enter via the Truman Annex gate on Thomas St.), but be careful of the sharp shells (wear sandals).

Your day in port is too short for an all-day **fishing or diving trip**, but a half-day may work. Plan in advance. Visit the Florida Keys & Key West Visitors Bureau at http://www.fla-keys.com or call 800-FLA-KEYS for information and lists of charter operators.

Want some authentic **Caribbean junk food**? Try hot, greasy, conch fritters for a fair price at the stand by the Aquarium entrance. For seafood and Key Lime Pie, just follow your nose.

The daily **Mallory Square sunset ritual** gathers thousands of revelers to watch the legendary sunset. We surveyed the superb scene from deck 10. Go to http://floridakeyswebcams.tv for web cam previews. Sunset time is printed on the front of your *Personal Navigator*, or visit http://www.usno.navy.mil and click on "Sun Rise/Set."

Key West has too many **museums** for a brief cruise ship visit. Choose just one or two. Whitehead St. is the equivalent of Museum Mile, with nearly every attraction listed here either on the street or a block away. For glimpses inside beautiful historic homes, visit Audubon House, Harry S. Truman Little White House, Hemingway House, and/or Oldest House. All charge admission.

Key West and **t-shirts** seem to go together. Nearly every bar sells its own, Hog's Breath Saloon, Sloppy Joe's, and Margaritaville among 'em. Try the Conch Republic Store for local color. Brand luxuries can be had at U.S. prices, but you'll also find items by local designers.

Embarking on Shore Excursions in Key West

As of January 2008 Disney offers 11 shore excursions in Key West, all of which are described below and on the following pages. Note that the Key West Beach Break excursion previously offered is no longer available. We don't think you need to go on one of these shore excursions to enjoy your time in Key West, but in general they are excellent. If you want to try one of these activities on your own, we also offer information on arranging your own tours and excursions at the bottom of each description.

Sail, Kayak, & Snorkel [K01]	Rating: n/a
This is the "smorgasboard" of shore excursions, offering three different adventures in one. You'll start with a sail in a two-masted schooner to mangrove islands. At the islands, you'll hop into kayaks and paddle about the backcountry mangrove creeks for an hour. When you're done, its time to don snorkeling equipment (provided) and explore underwater for 45–60 minutes. Top it all off with a refreshing snack of fruit, chips, salsa, and beverages back at the pier. Meeting time is typically 12:15 pm. Bring an extra pair of dry shorts for the return trip. Unfortunately, we received no reviews for this excursion, nor could we find anyone who'd experienced it. Most cruisers preferred the Back to Nature Kayak Tour or the Key West Catamaran Sail & Snorkel Tour, described later. (On Your Own: JavaCat Charters at http://www.keywestkayak.com, 305-797-3460)	**Sports** Very active For more experienced snorkelers Ages 10 & up $79/person 5–5.5 hours

Key West Butterfly & Nature Conservatory [K14]	Rating: 6
Take a trip through a state-of-the-art nature conservatory to observe some of the most exotic creatures the tropics have to offer. See butterflies, birds, and exotic fish. The Key West Aquarium is the next stop and admission is included in the price. Find out what makes up the ecosystem of the Islands of Key West, watch stingrays feed, and if you're lucky, pet a shark! Cruisers think this is a "neat experience" with "butterflies landing on you," and it is "great for families with young kids." Typical meeting time is 12:30 pm.	**Tour** Leisurely All ages $36/$25 (3-9) 3 hours

Pirate Scavenger Hunt [K16]	Rating: 8
Ready to find your inner pirate? A short journey to the Pirate Soul museum is needed to start your adventure. At the museum you're given everything needed for the pirate scavenger hunt. Throughout your adventure, you'll encounter loads of old artifacts and fun audio presentations. After the hunt, rewards such as Pirate Soul bookmarks are given as your booty. Typical meeting times are 1:50 and 2:40 pm. (On Your Own: Pirate Soul at http://www.piratesoul.com, 395-292-1113 or http://www.keywesthunt.com, 305-292-9994)	**Tour** Leisurely All ages $23/$13 (3-9) 1.5 hours

White Knuckle Thrill Boat [K17]	Rating: 7
Have the need for speed? Yes? This excursion is for you. A short 20-minute bus ride lands you at the dock. Board a jet boat with 11 other people and hang on for the next half-hour. Sudden stops, sharp power slides, and complete 360° turns are sure to get your heart pumping! Listen as the tour guide gives lessons on the Island of Key West. Typical meeting time is 12:15 pm. Plan to spend two hours.	**Sports** Active Ages 8 & up $65/$55 (8-9) 2 hours

See page 172 for a key to the shore excursion description charts and their icons.

See page 172 for a key to the shore excursion description charts and their icons.

Embarking on Shore Excursions
in Key West *(continued)*

☐ Back to Nature Kayak Tour [K03]   Rating: 8 ☀ 🛡 🔘

	Sports
Looking for wildlife beyond Duval Street? Take a boat to the Key West Wildlife Preserve and paddle around in two-person, stable kayaks. Your tour guide leads you through the protected salt ponds and points out the many species of birds and marine life in their natural habitat. Typical meeting times are 12:15 pm and 1:50 pm. Bring an extra pair of dry shorts for the return trip—cameras and binoculars are a good idea, too. Water and soft drinks are provided. Cruiser	Very active
	For beginners and all levels
	Ages 10 & up
	$59/adult
	3–3.5 hours

comments are positive: You start with a 20-minute boat ride ("board at the pier") to a mangrove wash called "Archer Key." From here you board yet another boat to "receive a short lesson on using the two-person kayaks." You then kayak "beside the mangroves" and down "some passages." The "interesting guide" points out the "local birds and sea life," plus "natural history." The kayaking "is not difficult," except for those cruisers who experienced "stiff winds."

☐ Key West Catamaran Sail & Snorkel Tour [K05]   Rating: 6 ☀ 🛡 🔘

	Sports
Set sail on a comfortable 65-foot catamaran with large sundecks, shady lounge deck, restrooms, and a fresh-water shower. The catamaran takes you about 6.5 miles (10 km.) south of the harbor to the only living coral reef in the continental U.S. Snorkeling equipment is provided for you to explore the reefs. Bring an underwater camera. Sodas and water are served, as are complimentary beer and white wine after snorkeling. Typical meeting time is 12:30 pm. Cruiser reviews are mixed: The "great crew" motors the "super clean" sailboat out of the	Active
	For all levels
	Ages 5 & up
	$47/adult
	$27/child
	3–3.5 hours

harbor, though a few cruisers report "no sailing, just motoring." The snorkeling location "feels like the middle of the ocean" with depths of "20 feet or so." Some cruisers report that "snorkeling is great" with "plenty of coral and fish," while others note that "surge can be strong" and "kids may be afraid to snorkel" in the "bobbing water." Overall, most "enjoyed it" but "probably wouldn't do it again." (On Your Own: Fury Catamarans at http://www.furycat.com, 305-294-8899 or 800-994-8898)

See page 172 for a key to the shore excursion description charts and their icons.

© MediaMarx, Inc.

A famous Key West sunset as seen from deck 10 of the Disney Magic

Embarking on Shore Excursions
in Key West *(continued)*

■ Conch Republic Tour & Museum Package [K08]   Rating: 4 ☀ 🛍 📷

Yes, you can do this all on your own, but if you'd prefer a more directed tour at a slightly steeper price, this is for you. First take an hour-long tour aboard the Conch Tour Train or the Old Town Trolley (see below). After the tour, you'll disembark at Mallory Square to visit the Aquarium and Shipwreck Museum on your own. Wear comfortable walking shoes and bring a camera. Typical meeting time is 12:40 pm. Cruiser reviews were uniform: The "city tour" is "great," conveying a "lot of info" in a "short amount of time" (good enough that some say it "made them want to visit Key West in the future"). The downfall seemed to be the Shipwreck Historeum, for which you "have to wait outside for the group before entering" and "then listen to a guide" before you are "free to explore on your own." The Aquarium is "ok" but many have "seen better at home." In general, this excursion has "too much waiting around." (On Your Own: See pages 207-208.)

Tour
Leisurely
All ages
$50/adult
$25/child
2-2.5 hours

■ Pirate Soul and Shipwreck Historeum [K07]   Rating: 5 ☀ 🛍 📷

New! This museum package gives you admission to both the Pirate Soul Museum (http://www.piratesoul.com) and the Shipwreck Historeum (http://www.shipwreckhistoreum.com, see page 207). Once you've got your admission, you can explore these two museums at your own pace. Cruisers report that the museum is just a "quick walk" from the dock with "interactive" exhibits like "mystery sniffing boxes" and a "pirate audio show" in a "pitch black room." Note that scavenger hunt maps are "free for the asking." The Shipwreck Historeum has "practically everything there is to know about shipwrecks" with "artifacts" and "the view from the top of the tower is worth the price of admission." Typical meeting times are 12:30 and 1:00 pm. Most cruisers visit these museums on their own.

Tour
Leisurely
All ages
$33/adult
$18/child
age 3-9
Varies

■ Old Town Trolley or Conch Train Tour [K09]   Rating: 6 ☀ 🛍 📷

A great way to get an overview of Key West and learn something on the way. The one-hour tour (either the trolley or the train) passes 100 points of interest and your tour guide offers historical and cultural commentary. We've done the Conch Tour Train and recommend it to first-time visitors as a friendly overview of Key West. Bring a camera. Young kids may get bored. Typical meeting time is 1:00 pm. Cruiser reviews are mostly positive: The "informative" tour is a "lot of

Tour
All ages
$29/adult
$14/child
1-1.5 hours

fun." A complete circuit of the tour route "takes about an hour," which is "good for kids who can sit still long enough." The "friendly tour guide" "driver" provides "plenty of information about the history and architecture" of "Key West." The downfall to booking this excursion through Disney is that "you cannot get on and off it" like you can when you book it yourself (which is useful when you want to use it as transportation as well as a tour). (On Your Own: There's not much reason to book this one with Disney—see page 206 for more information.)

© MediaMarx, Inc.

The Conch Tour Train

See page 172 for a key to the shore excursion description charts and their icons.

Embarking on Shore Excursions
in Key West *(continued)*

☐ Glass Bottom Boat Tour on the Pride of Key West [K10] Rating: 1 ☀ 🛡 📷

If you'd like to see the underwater world of Key West but don't want to get wet, this catamaran is your ticket. The catamaran boasts an air-conditioned viewing area and an upper-level sun deck. Your guide delivers a narrated eco-tour as you visit the continental U.S.'s only living coral reef about 6.5 miles (10 km.) south of Key West. Typical meeting time is 1:20 pm. Cruiser reviews were mostly negative: The boat's "bottom viewing window" is "way too small for everyone to use." And while the viewing area is air-conditioned, the sun deck is "miserably hot" with "no shade." The only refreshments were "sodas for a buck a pop." Some cruisers also report that they did not visit the reef because "the tide was too strong." Overall, most cruisers "were not impressed." (On Your Own: Key West Famous Glassbottom boats at http://www.seethereef.com, 305-289-9933)

Tour
Leisurely
All ages
$39/adult
$18/child
2-3 hours

☐ Presidents, Pirates, & Pioneers [K18] Rating: n/a ☀ 🛡 📷

New! This 2-hour walking tour meanders through Old Town, passing Truman's Little White House and the birthplace of Pan Am. Along the way you'll hear history of this remarkable place. The tour concludes in Mallory Square, where you are treated to complimentary conch fritters and bottled water. Afterward, admission to the Shipwreck Historeum is included so you can explore Key West's rich history in wrecking. Wear comfy walking shoes and bring your camera. Typical meeting time is 1:15 pm. (On Your Own: See page 207)

Tour
Active
Ages 3 & up
$35/adult
$23/child
2 hours

See page 172 for a key to the shore excursion description charts and their icons.

Key West On Your Own

Many cruisers prefer to embark on non-Disney excursions in Key West. While we don't have experience with these tour operators ourselves, here are some popular options: The **Sunset Watersports** allow you to drive your own speedboat through the back country mangrove channels, with time for snorkeling and swimming. For more information, visit http://www.sunsetwatersports.net or call 888-382-7864. • Another fun option is to rent a funky-yet-fun electric car from a place like **Tropical Rent a Car** for about $60 for two hours (2-seater) or $80 (4-seater). They also rent scooters and bicycles. They are located at 1300 Duval St. For more information, visit http://www.tropicalrentacar.com or call 305-294-8136. • We've also heard good things about the Southernmost Scavenger Hunt, which is best done with a group of cruisers. Cost for the classic scavenger hunt is about $20 and takes about three hours. For details and availability, visit http://www.keywesthunt.com or call 305-292-9994. • A visit to the Kino Sandal Factory is popular with shoppers—the sandals are good quality at good prices. Visit http://www.kinosandalfactory.com or call 305-294-5044. Note: The Bone Island Shuttle previously noted in our guidebook as alternate transportation is now only available for charters—if you're interested, call them at 305-293-8710.

© MediaMarx, Inc.

The Southernmost Point Marker

Grand Cayman
(Western Caribbean Itinerary—Second Port of Call)

In these days of corporate scandals, the Cayman Islands have come to symbolize shady dealings hidden by offshore banks. Cruise visitors find a different pleasure waiting offshore; some of the most spectacular coral reefs in the Caribbean. Whether you snorkel, scuba, tour by submarine, or swim with the fishes at Stingray City, Grand Cayman is the perfect island for **watery recreation**.

© MediaMarx, Inc.

Dave plays with stingrays in Grand Cayman

Of all Disney's ports of call, Grand Cayman seems the **quaintest**. Visitors arrive at a small pier, adjoining a relatively modest shopping street. We find scattered, freestanding buildings and several outdoor malls. The real action is taking place offshore, where fleets of excursion boats help visitors enjoy the island's sea life and fabled coral reefs. Alas, Grand Cayman was hit hard by Hurricane Ivan in September 2004, but the island is now restored—in fact, new buildings and shopping centers have reinvigorated its appearance.

A wayward breeze pushed the Cayman Islands onto the map in 1503, when Columbus stumbled upon these essentially flat outposts. He named them "**Tortugas**," for the plentiful local sea turtles, but soon the islands were renamed the Caimanas, after some other local reptilians (either crocodiles or Blue Iguanas, depending on who you ask). For centuries nobody bothered to settle here, but many ships visited to gather fresh turtle meat for their crews. Famed pirates visited frequently, but eventually the islands were ruled from British Jamaica. Still, with the exception of some mahogany-logging operations, there was little development here until well into the 20th century, and its famous banking industry didn't arrive until the 1950s. When Jamaica voted for independence from Great Britain in 1962, the Cayman Islanders chose to remain a British Crown Colony.

Size: 22 mi. (35 km.) long x 8 mi. (13 km.) wide	
Climate: Subtropical	**Temperatures**: 78°F (25°C) to 84°F (29°C)
Population: 37,000	**Busy Season**: Mid-February to April
Language: English	**Money**: Cayman Islands Dollar (= $1.25 US)
Time Zone: Eastern (no DST)	**Transportation**: Walking, taxis, cars
Phones: Dial 1- from U.S., dial 911 for police, or dial 555 for an ambulance	

Sidebar tabs: Introduction · Reservations · Staterooms · Dining · Activities · Ports of Call · Magic · Index

AMBIENCE · HISTORY & CULTURE · FACTS

Making the Most of Grand Cayman

GETTING THERE

Currently, this is the only Disney Cruise Line destination that regularly **requires tendering** (when finished, a new cruise ship pier will make tenders obsolete). The ship anchors a short distance offshore of George Town, Grand Cayman—capital of the Cayman Islands. Tenders ferry guests to the pier in a matter of minutes, and run continuously throughout the day. Tenders returning to the ship depart from the South Terminal pier. A notice in your stateroom outlines tendering procedures. A taxi stand is just a few steps from the dock, and the island's duty-free shopping district is tightly clustered within several blocks of the pier. The nearest beach is Seven Mile Beach, a short drive north of George Town. The first tender ashore is typically 7:30 am, with the last tender around 4:30 pm.

GETTING AROUND

Grand Cayman is **shaped like a sperm whale**, with its capital of George Town where a whale's "fluke" would be (see map on next page). It's easy to get around on foot in town. • Grand Cayman hardly overflows with sights to see, so while car rentals are available, we don't suggest them. Shore excursions can take you to nearly every sight, and taxis are fine for those who want to tour on their own. Taxis use a rate chart that is posted at the taxi stand by the cruise pier. Most car rental agencies are at the airport. Reserve in advance and arrange to have the car waiting at the pier for you. • Due north of George Town are Seven Mile Beach and the settlement of West Bay, home to the Cayman Turtle Farm and a tourist trap named Hell. Just to the east, kettle-shaped North Sound takes a big bite out of the north shore. A long coral reef guards the entrance to this bay, and just south of the reef, miles from shore, is "Stingray City," where excursion boats gather and guests cavort with the gentle stingrays (see photo on previous page). • The resort-and-beach destination of Rum Point is at the easternmost extreme of North Sound. • A single road follows the perimeter of the island (except for a huge gap between West Bay and Rum Point) connecting the island's many scuba dive destinations. • One of the most famous dive sites is Wreck of the Ten Sails, just beyond the village of East End.

SAFETY

For water-based excursions, **leave your valuables** (and change into your swimwear) on the ship. Lockers aren't easy to come by on the island. Wear cover-ups, as local customs are sedately British, and carry lots of sunscreen. As always, know your prices before you shop, and agree to taxi fares in advance (fares are posted at the pier's taxi stand).

Touring Grand Cayman

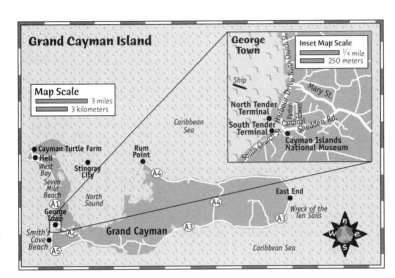

There are **many shops** but few sights to see in George Town. After several hours of walking and shopping you'll be ready to head back to the ship. Your tender arrives at South Terminal pier, a few steps from a tourist information center, the taxi stand, and tour bus loading area. North Terminal pier is just across the tiny harbor. A single road, known alternately as North Church St., Harbour Drive, and South Church St., lines the waterfront. As you face inland, North Church will be to your left, and South Church to your right. Cardinal Ave., opposite North Terminal, heads directly inland from the waterfront into the heart of the shopping district. Shops and malls line Cardinal and wrap around onto Panton St. and Edward St. You'll find the Post Office at the corner of Cardinal and Edward. The shops of Anchorage Centre can be reached from Cardinal or Harbour Drive, directly across from the docks. The worthy Cayman Islands National Museum ($5 U.S./adults, $3/children) is across from the terminal, at the corner of South Church and Shedden Rd. Follow Harbour Drive a block northward to reach Blackbeard's Rum Cake shop, and two blocks beyond, Cayman Auto Rentals and the Nautilus undersea tours. Follow South Church southward to reach Atlantis Submarines and a cluster of shops and restaurants including the local Hard Rock Cafe, Blue Mountain Cyber Cafe, and the Tortuga Rum Cake Bakery. A long walk or short cab ride along South Church brings you to small Smith's Cove Public Beach, the closest sunning spot to the pier.

ACTIVITIES

Introduction

Reservations

Staterooms

Dining

Activities

Ports of Call

Magic

Index

Playing in Grand Cayman

The **shopping** is passable in this duty-free port, offering the usual selection of jewelry, luxury goods, and island wares. Serious shoppers report less-than-wonderful experiences, but if you know your prices and can cut a bargain, you may do fine. The principal "native" item is rum cake (yo ho, yo ho). Many visitors stock up on small sampler packages, perfect for gift-giving. Turtle and coral-based items cannot be brought into the U.S., so don't buy them!

Certified scuba divers may be tempted to bring their own gear on the cruise and make their own dive arrangements. The Cayman Islands Department of Tourism at http://www.divecayman.ky has a useful online guide. Several shore excursions also exist for divers who don't want hassles. Snorkeling excursions are a good choice for those lacking scuba credentials.

While several **beaches** can be found around the perimeter of the island, we suggest you take an excursion to either Seven Mile Beach or Rum Point. Seven Mile Beach starts a short cab drive north of the port, with most of its length dominated by resorts and condos. A public beach with restrooms is found toward the beach's north end. Small Smith's Cove Beach at the south end of George Town also has restrooms, and is a long walk or short cab ride from the pier.

Unless the island's legendary coral reefs draw you elsewhere, you may want to consider an excursion that includes **Stingray City**, a submerged sand bar out in the middle of a huge bay. Guests climb from the boat right into the waist-high water for an encounter with friendly stingrays. We were instructed to "Stingray Shuffle" (shuffle your feet in the sand—the rays only sting if you step on them), and members of the crew introduced us to their aquatic protégé. While the rays are wild creatures, they've become willing partners in this enterprise—anything for a free handout (think pigeons in the park). On the ride to the sandbar, one of our crew members spent his time cutting bait (frozen squid). The rays will swim right up to (or even into) a wader's arms for a snack, and the boat's crew shows us how to snuggle up with the rays (see photo on page 213). Silky-soft rays swim among the guests, brushing past legs, sucking bait out of loosely closed hands, and tolerating all sorts of petting zoo behavior. While the squeamish need some time to get used to the activity, eventually everyone becomes captivated by this up-close and personal encounter with these very gentle, odd creatures.

Embarking on Shore Excursions on Grand Cayman

Grand Cayman's shore excursions offer jaunts to less-than-sterling tourist sights and several attractive water-based activities.

Thriller Sand & Sea Adventure [G23]　　Rating: 7

See some of Grand Cayman's most popular tourists attractions, from the Grand Cayman Turtle Farm to the shores of Sea Grape Beach, as you cruise past them at speeds of 50–60 mph aboard the Grand Cayman Thriller boat. You journey to a beach where you have an hour to lounge in the sun or play in the water. Enjoy a complimentary beverage at the beach. Afterward, you will be whisked back in the boat to George Town Harbour. Typical meeting time is 9:20 am.

Sports
Active
Ages 5 & up
$69/$49(5–9)
1.5–2 hours

Two-Tank Dive Tour [G03]　　Rating: 9

Certified scuba divers can take this two-tank dive. The first dive will be along the Cayman Wall, followed by a shallow dive of 50 ft. (15 m.) or less. All equipment is provided. Typical meeting time is 8:00 am. This excursion is very popular (Grand Cayman is an excellent diving spot) and has been known to fill up more than 30 days in advance. If you find this excursion is full, here are some other scuba operators used by Disney cruisers: Bob Soto's Reef Divers at 800-262-7686 (from the U.S.) or 345-949-2022 • Abanks Scuba Diving Diving Center, http://caymanislandsdiscounts.com/AbanksDiveCenter.htm, 345-946-6444 • Don Foster's Dive Cayman at http://www.donfosters.com, 800-833-4837 (from the U.S.) or 345-949-5679. Note that Red Sail Sports (http://www.redsailcayman.com) is the exclusive dive operator for Disney Cruise Line, but they prefer you do not book directly with them.

Sports
Very active
Ages 12 & up
$135
4 hours

Nautilus Undersea Tour and Reef Snorkel [G07]　　Rating: 8

Board a semi-submarine for a peek at shipwrecks and the Cheeseburger Reef, then spend some time snorkeling (equipment included). Typical meeting time is 7:40 am. Cruiser reviews are positive: This excursion is "great if you have both snorkelers and non-snorkelers in your group." The "tour is short" and "you stay close to the shore." Snorkeling is "great" and "views are phenomenal," with "fish," "plants," and a "wreck." (On Your Own: http://www.nautilus.ky or 345-945-1355)

Beach
Leisurely
Ages 5 & up
$49/$43 (5–9)
3 hours

Sea Trek Grand Cayman [G24]　　Rating: 9

Using a specially designed diving oxygen helmet, you'll be up close and personal with tropical fish. But don't worry—you'll receive full instructions before donning your helmet. Once outfitted and instructed, you are submerged into the water for a 30-minute guided underwater tour. No swimming skills are needed. The helmet even keeps your hair dry! Typical meeting times are 8:30 am and 1:15 pm. (On Your Own: http://www.seatrekcayman.com or 345-949-0008)

Sports
Active
Ages 10 & up
$85

Seven Mile Beach Break [G22]　　Rating: 7

This relatively new beach is perfect for loads of relaxation in the warm Caribbean sun. Choose one of the inviting beach chairs and sip on an island beverage. If you are so inclined, go for a swim in the waters just a few feet from your chair. Typical meeting times are 7:45 and 11:30 am. Allow 4.5 hours.

Beach
Leisurely
All ages
$36/$26(3–9)

See page 172 for a key to the shore excursion description charts and their icons.

Introduction

Reservations

Staterooms

Dining

Activities

Ports of Call

Magic

Index

Embarking on Shore Excursions
on Grand Cayman *(continued)*

☐ Stingray City Snorkel Tour [GO8]   Rating: 9   ☀ 🏛 🔲

Enjoy a ride in a double-decker catamaran to snorkel with the stingrays in 3 to 6 feet of water, depending on the tide, along a natural sandbar (see photo on page 213). All snorkeling equipment is provided. Complimentary water and lemonade served after snorkeling. If you want to see stingrays, this is the excursion we recommend. Cruiser reviews are very positive: You start with "hot," "20-minute van ride" to a harbor, where you board the "great" catamaran. The cruise to Stingray City is "fun," with "great scenery." The stingrays are "amazing," but be aware that "some kids may be afraid at first" and the "water may be over their heads" if it's "high tide." Overall, this "unique" excursion is one "the whole family can participate in." Typical meeting time is 10:00 am. (On Your Own: Captain Marvin's—see page 220 or Native Way Water Sports at http://www.nativewaywatersports.com, 345-916-5027)	**Sports**
	Active
	Ages 5 & up
	$47/$36 (6-9)
	3.5 hours

☐ Seaworld Explorer Semi-Submarine [G10]   Rating: 9   🏛 🔲

Take a ride on this semi-submarine to discover shipwrecks and sea life. A marine expert is on board to provide narration and answer your questions. Note that this excursion is very similar to the Nautilus Undersea Tour (see below). Cruiser reviews are very positive: This "short" excursion takes you down "five feet below the water" to view "Cheese Burger Reef" and two "shipwrecks," with "coral reefs" and "many fish." The "viewing windows" are "generous" and "clear." Cruisers note that it's the same price to "book this one on your own ($39/adult)." Overall, a "fun time for the whole family!" Typical meeting times are 8:30 am and 10:30 am. (On Your Own: Atlantis Adventures at http://www.atlantisadventures.com/cayman or 345-949-7700)	**Tour**
	Leisurely
	All ages
	$39/$29 (0-9)
	1-1.5 hours

☐ Atlantis Submarine Expedition [G11]   Rating: 6   🏛 🔲

This submarine dives down to 90 feet (27 m.). Guests must be at least 36 in./ 91 cm. tall. Typical meeting times are 9:15 am and 1:15 pm. Cruiser reviews are very similar to those on the same excursion in St. Thomas (see page 206), but it gets a slightly higher rating thanks to the better views and visible sea life. (On Your Own: http://www.atlantisadventures.com/cayman or 345-949-7700)	**Tour**
	Leisurely
	Ages 4 & up
	$89/$57 (4-9)
	2.5 hours

☐ Nautilus Undersea Tour [G12]   Rating: 8   🏛 🔲

Cruise on a semi-submarine with a marine expert. The Nautilus glides like a boat and never entirely submerges. This excursion is very similar to the Seaworld Explorer described earlier, except that your craft does not go down as deep (which one you choose to do may depend on your comfort level). Typical meeting time is 9:15 am. Cruiser comments are positive: The "view is phenomenal" and cruisers loved seeing "actual wrecks," "sea creatures," and "water plants." The "friendly" crew identified the wrecks and sealife. The "comfortable" boat was "a lot of fun." (On Your Own: http://www.nautilus.ky or 345-945-1355)	**Tour**
	Leisurely
	All ages
	$42/$31 (0-9)
	2 hours

☐ Rum Point Beach Adventure [G13]   Rating: 6   ☀ 🏛 🔲

Enjoy a relaxing half-day at a secluded beach. Includes lunch and a soft drink. Watersport rentals available for extra fee. Cruiser reviews are mixed: Take a "long journey" (first a bus then a 45-min. ferry) to reach the "nice" but "small" beach. Cruisers suggest you "try to secure beach chairs as soon as you arrive." Lunch is "good" with a "variety of food." Overall, some cruisers enjoyed "being able to relax" while others felt "herded like cattle." Typical meeting time is 8:20 am.	**Beach**
	Leisurely
	All ages
	$54/$46 (0-9)
	5-5.5 hours

Embarking on Shore Excursions
on Grand Cayman *(continued)*

■ Rum Point Beach Adventure & Stingray City Tour [G14] Rating: 7

Add a visit with the stingrays to the previous excursion for $23–$25 more. After playing at the beach, you'll board a glass bottom boat and cruise out to Stingray City to snorkel. Cruiser reviews were mixed but very similiar to those for Rum Point Beach Adventure and Stingray City tours on the previous page—basically the big winner is the stingrays. Typical meeting time is 8:20 am.	**Sports**
	Active
	Ages 5 & up
	$89/$79 (5–9)
	5.5 hours

■ Shipwreck and Reef Snorkeling [G15] Rating: 9

Explore one of the Cayman's most famous shipwrecks, the "Cali," where you'll learn a history of the ship and snorkel. You'll also visit a coral reef for more snorkeling. Includes snorkel gear and soft drinks (water and lemonade). Cruiser reviews are very positive: This "great" excursion is "good for beginners." Some cruisers report snorkeling "within sight of the Disney Magic," where they explored the "way cool" "shipwreck" which rests in about "15 to 20 feet of water." Then move about a "quarter mile" down to snorkel among "protected reefs" and see "awesome" sea "critters." Overall, cruisers "loved" this "fun excursion." Typical meeting times are 7:45 and 10:30 am.	**Sports**
	Active
	Ages 5 & up
	$37/
	$31 (5–9)
	2–2.5 hours

■ Island Tour & Snorkeling With Stingrays [G19] Rating: 7

Take in the island's sights on an air-conditioned bus—you'll stop and visit the Cayman Turtle Farm (see photo below) and Hell (a prehistoric rock formation). Then head out to sea on a 45-minute boat ride to meet the stingrays at	**Tour**
	Leisurely
	Ages 5 & up
	$63/
	$52 (5–9)
	4.5 hours

© MediaMarx, Inc.

the Stingray City sandbar. Snorkeling equipment and instruction is provided so you can swim with the stingrays in 3–6 feet deep water. Only stingrays—and no fish—will be seen while snorkeling. We tried this excursion—we loved the stingrays, but we didn't care for the island tour. See the cruiser reviews on the island tour portion below. Typical meeting time is 9:15 am.

Turtles at the Cayman Turtle Farm

■ Grand Cayman Island Tour [G17] Rating: 7

Take an air-conditioned bus tour through the streets of George Town, past the Gingerbread House, on through Hell, and to the Cayman Turtle Farm. This is very touristy—we personally didn't enjoy it much and felt like it was mostly a tour of souvenir shops, but other cruisers liked it. Cruiser reviews are mostly positive: A "nice overview" of the island in "cool" air-conditioned "buses." The tour guide is "informative" and "friendly." The turtle farm is "the best part"	**Tour**
	Leisurely
	All ages
	$29/
	$24 (3–9)
	2 hours

and "fun for the kids" (ask if you can "hold a turtle"), though some may be "appalled by the crowding of the turtles in the tanks." Hell was "not a favorite" and "didn't impress" most cruisers, however. Highlights are the "low price" and "learning the history in a short time;" downfalls are the "short stops" and "no interaction with locals." Overall, most cruisers felt it "worth their time" even though is "isn't a sophisticated" excursion. Typical meeting times are 8:15 and 11:30 am.

See page 172 for a key to the shore excursion description charts and their icons.

Embarking on Shore Excursions
on Grand Cayman (continued)

Stingray City Reef Sail and Snorkel [G09]   Rating: 8

Yet another stingray excursion, this one featuring a nice, seven-mile sail in a 65-foot catamaran. For details on the stingray experience, see pages 216, 218 and 219. Includes snorkel equipment and beverages (water and lemonade). We have no cruiser reviews to offer yet. Typical meeting time is 12:40 pm. 3.5 hours.

Sports
Active
Ages 5 & up
$58/$45 (5-9)

Aquaboat & Snorkel Adventure [G20]   Rating: 9

Here's an excursion with an exciting twist—piloting (or riding) in your own, two-person inflatable motorboat. You'll cruise along Grand Cayman's shores, then explore an uninhabited island (Sandy Cove). Then it's off to Smith's Cove to swim and snorkel (equipment provided). On your way back, you'll stop at the Cali shipwreck. When it's all done, enjoy a complimentary beverage (fruit or rum punch) at Rackams Bar on the dock. Note that guests must be 13 or older to pilot a boat, and must be accompanied by a parent or guardian. Typical meeting time at 12:00 pm.

Sports
Active
Ages 10 & up
$84
3 hours

Island Tour & Butterfly Farm [G21]   Rating: 6

This excursion is very similar to the Grand Cayman Island Tour described on the previous page, but it also adds a visit to the Grand Cayman Butterfly Farm. The butterfly farm is operated by the same folks who run the St. Maarten butterfly farm (see page 194), which we recommend. For more information on the butterfly farm, visit http://www.thebutterflyfarm.com. Includes a visit to a rum cake factory. Typical meeting times are at 8:00 am and noon.

Tour
Leisurely
All ages
$59/$43 (3-9)
3.5-4 hours

Boatswain's Beach Adventure Marine Park [G26]   Rating: n/a

New! Take an air-conditioned mini-bus ride to the 23-acre Boatswain's Beach (pronounced "Bo-suns Beach"), which contains the famous turtle farm. Snorkel equipment is provided to explore a 1.3-million-gallon lagoon filled with tropical fish. Typical meeting time is 9:20 am. 4.5-5 hours.

Sports
Active
All ages
$92/$52 (3-9)

Pirate Encounter [G09]   Rating: n/a

New! Take a small boat out to explore one of the world's last wooden brig ships, the "Valhalla." Onboard you'll encounter pirates, who comandeer the brig for a 45-minue cruise to Seven Mile Beach. Here you'll drop anchor, come ashore, and enjoy the beach. Typical meeting times are 9:30 am and 12:45 pm. 2.5 hours.

Sports
Active
Ages 3 & up
$35/$25 (3-9)

See page 172 for a key to the shore excursion description charts and their icons.

Grand Cayman On Your Own

Grand Cayman is another port where you find cruisers going on non-Disney excursions. Here are some popular options, though please note that we have no experience with these tour operators: **Captain Marvin's Watersports** is a very popular and well-liked outfit that offers snorkeling, island tours, and fishing charters at great prices, fewer crowds, and excellent service—visit http://www.captainmarvins.com or 866-978-4554. Another option is **Captain Bryan's Stingray City Sailing Charters**, which offers nicer boats with large sundecks and restrooms—better than the typical excursion boats. For details, visit http://www.cayman.org/captainbryan or 345-949-0038. A third option, also popular, is **Native Way Water Sports**—they have excursions to Seven Mile Beach and Coral Gardens in addition to Stingray City. Visit http://www.nativewaywatersports.com or 345-916-5027.

Cozumel
(Western Caribbean Itinerary—Third Port of Call)

Welcome to **Mexico**! The island of Cozumel, just off the northeastern tip of Mexico's Yucatan peninsula and a bit south of Cancun, offers the Disney Cruise Line's primary taste of the Caribbean's Hispanic heritage. You can stay on the island, or visit the Mayan ruins on the mainland. Cozumel offers a wide range of enticing activities and Mexican handcrafted goods.

© MediaMarx, Inc.

Relaxing on the beach on Cozumel

Cozumel is a **destination of contrasts**. For some, it's a crowded shopping port, intimidatingly foreign to some, exciting for others. It can be a jumping-off point for a visit to ancient ruins, or a gateway to some of the world's greatest reef diving. A unique nature park offers underwater and jungle adventure, and white, powdery beaches offer sheltered, resort/upscale experiences on the western shore, or remote, raucous rolling surf on the eastern shore.

With a history as a **religious destination** dating back to Mayan pre-history (the name Cozumel derives from the Mayan for *island of swallows*), this is one port where you can visit ruins that actually pre-date Christopher what's-his-name. The island's substantial population was destroyed after the Conquistadores' brutal arrival, and its many coves and inlets served as hideouts for pirates such as Jean Lafitte and Henry Morgan. Settlers returned in the mid-1800s and cultivation of rubber here and on the mainland made this once again a trading center. The island's beautiful beaches made it part of the State of Quintana Roo's "Mexican Riviera." Undersea explorer Jacques Cousteau really put the island on the tourism map in the 1960s, thanks to the island's prime coral reefs, part of the second-largest coral reef formation in the world. Hurricane Wilma hit Cozumel hard in October 2005, but the island is 100% restored.

Size: 30 mi. (48 km.) long x 9 mi. (16 km.) wide	
Climate: Subtropical	**Temperatures**: 75°F (24°C) to 90°F (32°C)
Population: 65,000	**Busy Season**: Mid-February to April
Language: Spanish, English	**Money**: Nuevo Peso ($10 Pesos = $1 U.S.)
Time Zone: Central (DST observed)	**Transportation**: Walking, taxis, scooters
Phones: Dial 011- from U.S., dial 060 for emergencies, dial 20092 for police	

Introduction   Reservations   Staterooms   Dining   Activities   Ports of Call   Magic   Index

AMBIENCE   HISTORY & CULTURE   FACTS

Making the Most of Cozumel

GETTING THERE

Your ship docks at the new **Punta Langosta** pier in the city of San Miguel de Cozumel, on the island's western shore. Tendering is not required. You can see Playa del Carmen on the mainland—the channel is just two miles (3 km.) wide. The typical all-ashore time is 9:45 am, with all aboard at 6:30 pm. A tourist information office is at the end of the pier, as is the glitzy Punta Langosta shopping plaza. The plaza is reached via a pedestrian bridge over Avenida (Avenue) Rafael Melgar, and provides a convenient, secure shopping and dining destination. There is no beach within walking distance.

GETTING AROUND

You disembark the ship near the **center of town**, about five blocks south of Muelle Fiscal, the city's central plaza and ferryboat dock (ferries to the mainland). Several miles to the south are the International and Puerta Maya piers, in the resort hotel district. The waterfront road, Avenida Rafael Melgar, goes right past the pier, and leads to most of the sights in town and on the island's west shore. Just five blocks north you'll find Avenida Benito Juarez, which heads directly to the San Gervasio ruins and the beaches of the eastern shore. Drive south on Avenida Rafael Melgar to reach Chankanaab National Park, San Francisco Beach, Playa Del Sol, and Palancar Reef. • Car and scooter rentals are advisable for those who wish to set off on their own, but taxis ($4 for up to four passengers) are more convenient for in-town travel. Four wheel drive vehicles are especially useful if you head for the eastern beaches. Executive Car Rental (529-872-1308) is located in the Punta Langosta Mall, and several other agencies are nearby. Note that cars are driven on the same side of the road as in the United States.

STAYING SAFE

Safety is always, in part, a **state of mind**. Certainly the crowds of sprawling San Miguel will put most travelers on the defensive, as may the dominant, Spanish language (though most shop owners speak some English). Take typical big-city precautions, then try to relax and enjoy. A polite, friendly attitude toward the locals will ease your way—it always helps to treat your host with respect. "Do you speak English?" is a good way to start your conversations. Drinking water and food safety are a classic concern for visits to Mexico. Be sensible. Drink bottled water and commercially prepared beverages, and think twice about dining from street vendors. However, most restaurants will be well up to stateside health standards. As always, sunblock is a must. Dress according to your planned activities—changing rooms are hard to find at the beach.

Touring Cozumel

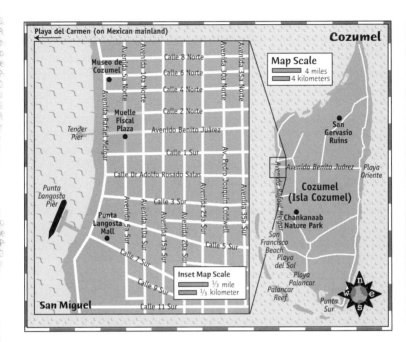

Cozumel

Playa del Carmen (on Mexican mainland)

Museo de Cozumel

Calle 8 Norte
Calle 6 Norte
Calle 4 Norte
Calle 2 Norte

Avenida 5a Norte
Avenida 10a Norte
Avenida 30a Norte
Avenida 35a Norte

Map Scale
4 miles
4 kilometers

Muelle Fiscal Plaza
Avenida Benito Juárez

Tender Pier

Avenida Rafael Melgar

San Gervasio Ruins

Calle 1 Sur
Calle Dr. Adolfo Rosado Salas

Av. Pedro Joaquín Coldwell

Avenida Benito Juárez
Playa Oriente

Punta Langosta Pier

Punta Langosta Mall

Calle 3 Sur
Calle 5 Sur
Calle 7 Sur
Calle 9 Sur
Calle 11 Sur

Avenida 5a Sur
Avenida 10a Sur
Avenida 15a Sur
Avenida 20a Sur
Avenida 25a Sur
Avenida 35a Sur

Avenida Rafael Melgar

Cozumel (Isla Cozumel)

Chankanaab Nature Park

San Francisco Beach
Playa del Sol
Playa Palancar
Palancar Reef
Punta Sur

Inset Map Scale
⅓ mile
⅓ kilometer

San Miguel

n w e s

COZUMEL ISLAND MAP

Introduction
Reservations
Staterooms
Dining
Activities
Ports of Call
Magic
Index

WALKING TOUR

There's not much to see on a **walking tour** other than Punta Langosta Mall. Just across the street from the cruise pier, the mall is brand new, with stylish architecture reminiscent of fashionable stateside malls (it reminds us a bit of Downtown Disney in Orlando). You'll find upscale souvenir and luxury shops, the popular bars Carlos 'n' Charlie's and Señor Frog's, a Tony Roma's Steakhouse, and a Burger King. While the Punta Langosta Mall offers a secure experience, you'll get a better taste of the town by taking a short stroll or cab ride five blocks north to Muelle Fiscal, the town's central plaza. A six-block area has been converted to a pedestrian mall, featuring many restaurants, shops, and a large souvenir and crafts market. Three blocks farther north on Avenida Rafael Melgar is the island's museum, Museo de la Isla de Cozumel ($3 admission), which features two floors filled with archaeological and ecological exhibits and a very popular rooftop restaurant (Del Museo), which is open until 1:30 pm. Most tourist-oriented restaurants and shops are clustered along a ten-block stretch of Avenida Rafael Melgar between Punta Langosta on the south and the museum on the north. However, if you're bargain-hunting, the shops on the side streets and a block inland may offer better deals.

ACTIVITIES

Playing in Cozumel

The best of the island's and mainland's **play spots** and attractions are featured in shore excursions on the next four pages, which we recommend for most visitors. Many are day-long experiences. Serious divers may prefer to make their own arrangements.

The island does not produce much in the way of local crafts, but you can find a wide range of silver, carved wood and stone, and other Mexican specialties, imported from the mainland. **Shops** near the cruise pier will tend to be the most expensive. Know your prices, and be prepared to bargain. Silver items are typically sold by weight, and black coral cannot be brought back into the United States.

White, powder-soft sands and clear, turquoise waters make the island's **beaches** very attractive. The strong undertow found on the east coast beaches, such as Playa Oriente, can be perilous for swimmers, but the big surf, dunes, stretches of rocky coastline, and small crowds are very tempting. Playa Oriente is at the far eastern end of the central, cross-island road, and others can be found by turning right and following the paved road southward. Several of these beaches offer restaurants and watersport rentals. The safe, gentle beaches on the sheltered west side of the island are generally built up, offering a wide variety of recreational and dining opportunities. Top picks (all south of San Miguel) include San Francisco Beach, Playa del Sol, Playa Francesa, and Playa Palancar.

Palancar Reef, at the island's southwest corner, is probably at the top of most serious divers' list, but dozens more **dive sites** dot the map. Visit http://www.travelnotes.cc/cozumel/links/scuba.html for a good introduction to Cozumel diving, listings, and reviews.

Chankanaab Park offers first-rate snorkel, nature, and wildlife encounter opportunities. • On the mainland, the **Xcaret** Eco-Archaeological Park offers many unusual opportunities (book an excursion for either of these). The island's archaeological sites are quite minor, with the most developed at San Gervasio, near the island's center. Archaeology buffs should book an excursion to Tulum Ruins, about 80 miles (128 km.) away on the mainland. Alas, famed Chichen Itza is a bit too far for a day trip.

Your schedule allows for both **lunch and dinner** ashore. Carlos 'n Charlie's is a town fixture, relocated to Punta Langosta Mall. In the center of town, Casa Denis and La Choza offer regional specialties.

Embarking on Shore Excursions on Cozumel

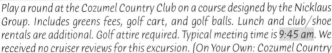

☐ Cozumel's Golf Excursion [CZ01] — Rating: n/a

Play a round at the Cozumel Country Club on a course designed by the Nicklaus Group. Includes greens fees, golf cart, and golf balls. Lunch and club/shoe rentals are additional. Golf attire required. Typical meeting time is 9:45 am. We received no cruiser reviews for this excursion. (On Your Own: Cozumel Country Club, http://www.cozumelcountryclub.com.mx, 987-872-9570)	**Sports**
	Active
	Ages 10 & up
	$145
	5–6 hours

☐ Certified Scuba Tour [CZ02] — Rating: 9

Certified divers enjoy two dives—first to Palancar Reef (70–80 ft. or 21–24 m.) and then to a shallower dive (50–60 ft. or 15–18 m.). Includes equipment, fruit, and drinks. Typical meeting time is 9:45 am. Cruiser reviews are positive: Two "drift dives" offer the opportunity to see more "unique underwater life" than in many other ports. Palancar Reef is "phenomenal" and the reef wall is "very deep" with "lots to see." Visibility is "incredible." (On Your Own: Eagle Ray Divers, http://www.eagleraydivers.com, 987-872-5735)	**Sports**
	Very active
	Ages 12 & up
	$94
	4–4.5 hours

☐ Dolphin Discovery Cozumel [CZ04] — Rating: 7

This popular excursion takes you to Chankanaab National Park, where you'll encounter dolphins in waist-deep water. Afterward, stay and enjoy the park. If you want to swim with the dolphins, you will need to book that separately. Typical meeting times are 9:45 am, 10:45 am, 11:45 am, and 12:45 pm. Cruiser comments were mixed: Listen to a "brief training session," don "bulky life jackets," then enter	**Encounter**
	Leisurely
	Ages 3 & up
	$110/$96
	3–3.5 hours

one of five "water areas" where you stand in the water. Several cruisers report that the "waist-high" water was in fact "chest-high" or even "chin-high" instead, and that it could be over the heads of guests under 7. Most cruisers loved being able to "touch and interact" with the "amazing" dolphins. Cruisers note that you cannot wear "water shoes." Some feel this excursion isn't really great for cruisers "under 12" due to the depth of the water.

☐ Dolphin Discovery Observer [CZ25] — Rating: 6

New! This excursion is for those with friends or family on the Dolphin Discovery Cozumel excursion who wish to observe and not interact with the dolphins. While your friend or family member is getting their orientation and interaction, you'll be observing from an unshaded area approximately 50 feet away. Also note that the taxi ride to and from the facility is in a non-air-conditioned vehicle. Observers may stay to enjoy the park, which includes a beach. Typical meeting times are 9:45 am, 10:45 am, 11:45 am, and 12:45 pm.	**Tour**
	Leisurely
	All ages
	$40/ages 3 & up
	3–3.5 hours

☐ Mayan Frontier Horseback Riding Tour [CZ05] — Rating: 5

Giddyup! Mosey on down a Mayan trail on horseback, passing ruins on your way. Afterward, visit a ranch. Includes complimentary soft drinks and beer after riding. Typical meeting time is 10:15 am. Cruiser reviews were mediocre: The "very friendly staff" is "helpful," but the "saddles are old and unpadded." The horses are also "over the hill" (which could be a good thing as they are more sedate than younger horses). Cruisers also note that some of the "ruins and artifacts" are "not real." Younger guests "enjoyed it," but most cruisers were "not impressed."	**Sports**
	Very active
	Ages 12–65
	$85
	4 hours

See page 172 for a key to the shore excursion description charts and their icons.

Embarking on Shore Excursions
on Cozumel *(continued)*

Power Snorkel Treasure Hunt [CZ31] — Rating: n/a

Take the opportunity to go under the water and search for lost treasures. A 20-minute taxi ride takes you to Aqua Beach, where all necessary snorkel equipment is available. From this point, go with a professional divemaster on a quest for buried treasure coins. After a 45-minute dive you'll be treated to a light snack. Typical meeting time is 11:45 am. Allow 3 hours for this excursion.

Sports
Active
Ages 12 & up
$59

Speed Boat Beach Escape [CZ32] — Rating: n/a

Power off to a tropical getaway in your very own mini speedboat! Take a short 20-minute ride to the instruction center. You're given a briefing on speedboat safety and operating instructions, then handed the keys. Once aboard, cruise through the beautiful Cozumel waters to Hideaway Beach, a short 30-minute ride. Later you are taxied back to the pier. Typical meeting time is 10:45 am.

Sports
Active
Ages 10 & up
$85
5 hours

Jeep Exploration [CZ09] — Rating: 7

Drive a four-person, standard-shift, 4x4 vehicle through the "tropical" scrub. After bump-bump-bumping along the dirt roads, enjoy a yummy lunch on the beach and explore some low-key ruins. If you're a party of two, you'll share a vehicle with another couple and take turns driving. Cruiser reviews are mostly

Tour
Active
Ages 10 & up
$85
4.5 hours

positive: After a "long walk," you get into your "open air" vehicle ("no air conditioning") and "take a fun drive" through town. Once on the dirt roads, it's "very bumpy and dusty" but "adventuresome." Lunch at a "beautiful beach" is "very good," though the ruins are "unimpressive." Overall, most cruisers enjoyed the "entertaining tour guides" and "had a good time." We tried it and enjoyed it! Typical meeting time is 12:20 pm.

© MediaMarx, Inc.

Our Jeep safari

Xcaret Eco-Archaeological Park [CZ10] — Rating: 9

This mainland park is a favorite—it's like a natural water park. Swim, visit an aquarium, and see ruins. Includes transportation, lunch, and entrance fee. Bring cash to buy souvenirs. Regular sunscreen is not allowed; you will be provided with environmentally friendly sunscreen upon arrival. Cruiser reviews are very positive: While the "travel time is long" (about "1.5 hours"), the "beautiful nature park" is "well worth the journey." A favorite feature is the "unique underground fresh water river" that you "float through" (but beware that it is "cold water"). There are also "good spots for snorkeling" with "lots of fish." Many cruisers feel this excursion is the "highlight of their trip." Typical meeting time is 9:15 am.

Tour
Active
All ages
$99/$77 (0–9)
7-7.5 hours

Dune Buggy & Beach Snorkel Combo [CZ23] — Rating: n/a

Drive a dune buggy along the eastern coast of Cozumel, see where the locals call home in the town of San Miguel, and drive through the busy hotel district. Upon reaching your destination, play in the sand and snorkel to your heart's content. Then pile back into the dune buggy and make your way back to town. Must be at least 18 years of age and have a driver's license to drive a dune buggy. Typical meeting time is 10:45 am. Plan to spend 4–4.5 hours on this excursion.

Sports
Active
Ages 10 & up
$90

Embarking on Shore Excursions
on Cozumel *(continued)*

■ Fury Catamaran Sail, Snorkel, & Beach Party [CZ12]   Rating: 10

Board a 65-foot catamaran and cruise out to snorkel in 3-20 ft. (1-6 m.) of water. Afterward, party on the beach with free soft drinks, margaritas, and beer. Typical meeting time is 12:45 pm. Cruiser reviews are overwhelmingly positive: Enjoy a 35-minute sail on a "large," "unexpectedly smooth" catamaran with an "exceptional" crew. Then snorkel for 45 minutes in a "beautiful" area with "many fish and coral." Hop aboard for "short," "20-minute" sail to a "gorgeous beach" with "plenty of shady areas." The food served at the beach is "very good" (about "$8/person"). Then it's back onboard for a "30- to 45-minute" sail back, with "music" and "dancing." "Plenty of free drinks." "Bring cash" for food and tips. Note that you "do need to be mobile to exit and reenter the catamaran at sea." Overall, cruisers had a "great time" and would "do it again." (On Your Own: Fury Catamaran at http://furycat.com,

| **Sports** |
| Active |
| Ages 5 & up |
| $49/$28 (5-9) |
| 4.5-5 hours |

■ Clear Kayak & Beach Snorkel Combo [CZ24]   Rating: n/a

Paddle in transparent kayaks over the unspoiled beauty of coral reef formations, watching tropical fish swim right under your kayak. Afterward, don the provided snorkel equipment to get an even closer look at the underwater world. Then relax on Uvas Beach. Weight limit of 350 lbs. per two-person kayak. Includes fruit and two complimentary drinks (soda, water, beer, margaritas, or daiquiris). Bring biodegradable sunblock. Typical meeting time is 11:45 am.

| **Sports** |
| Active |
| Ages 10 & up |
| $61 |
| 3.5 hours |

■ Cozumel Beach Break [CZ15]   Rating: 8

Bum around the Playa del Sol Beach. Price includes taxi fare to and from the beach, admission, use of pool and beach, open bar (mixed drinks, beer, soda, and juice), water toys, recreation, entertainment, and lunch buffet. Typical meeting time is 10:10 am. Cruiser comments were mostly positive: The beach has a "family party atmosphere" with "lots to do," including "water trampolines" and "a climbing iceberg" (though these are "pretty far out in the water"). Keep in mind that while the drinks may be free, they are also "watered down." Lunch is "good" by most accounts, though you have to "contend with vendors" to get to the food area. (On Your Own: Playa Sol at http://www.playasol.com, or Mr. Sanchos—see end of section)

| **Beach** |
| Leisurely |
| All ages |
| $59/$46 (3-9) |
| 4.5-5 hours |

■ Caverns Exploration and Beach Tour [CZ18]   Rating: n/a

Take an all-day journey via a 45-minute ferry and air-conditioned bus to the Mexican mainland to explore natural caverns in Playa del Carmen. Afterward, relax on the beach with your own beach chair. Includes a Mexican lunch and beverages. Note that there are rocky areas and rough terrain; strollers are not allowed. Typical meeting time is 9:15 am. We received no cruiser reviews for this excursion.

| **Tour/Beach** |
| Active |
| Ages 6 & up |
| $88/$63 (6-9) |
| 7.5 hours |

■ Cozumel Ruins & Beach Tour [CZ19]   Rating: 3

Tour the San Gervasio Ruins, then off to Playa Del Sol Beach for an hour and a half of relaxation. Includes soft drinks (food is extra). Watersports available for extra fee. Typical meeting time is noon. Cruiser reviews were mostly negative: While the "water is beautiful," there "wasn't enough time" to spend at the beach. The food at the beach "didn't seem fresh." Most of your time is spent at the "ancient sites" which are "interesting," but not "spectacular." "Bring bug spray!" Overall, cruisers were not impressed and "do not recommend it."

| **Tour/Beach** |
| Leisurely |
| Ages 5 & up |
| $49/$33 (5-9) |
| 4-4.5 hours |

See page 172 for a key to the shore excursion description charts and their icons.

Introduction · Reservations · Staterooms · Dining · Activities · Ports of Call · Magic · Index

Embarking on Shore Excursions
on Cozumel (continued)

Atlantis Submarine Expedition [CZ20] Rating: 6 ☀ 🔒 📷

Board the "Atlantis" submarine and dive up to 110 ft. (33 m.), viewing tropical fish and 30 ft. (9 m.) coral heads. Includes beverages. Height restriction of 36 in./ 91 cm. minimum. Typical meeting times are 10:45 am and 12:45 pm. Cruiser reviews are very similar to those on same excursion in St. Thomas (see page 202), but it gets a slightly higher rating thanks to the better views and visible sea life.	**Tour**
	Leisurely
	Ages 4 & up
	$89/$57 (4-9)
	2.5 hours

Discover Snorkel [CZ21] Rating: n/a ☀ 🔒 📷

Take a taxi to Playa Corona, where you get to snorkel the beautiful waters of Cozumel. Snorkel gear, instruction, and transportation provided. This is a good excursion for beginners as you enter the water from the beach. Typical meeting time is 10:45 am. We received no cruiser reviews for this excursion. (On Your Own: Bring your snorkel gear and take a taxi to Playa Corona.)	**Sports**
	Active
	Ages 5 & up
	$32/$23 (5-9)
	3 hours

Ocean View Explorer Tour [CZ22] Rating: 5 ☀ 🔒 📷

Explore the coral of Paradise Reef in this semi-submersible. Typical meeting time is 10:45 am. Cruiser reviews on this excursion are limited, but those we received were mixed: Some felt it was a good "compromise" between the Atlantis sub and a snorkeling excursion, while others felt it was "boring" and would not do it again. Compared to the Atlantis, it is less expensive and allows kids 0-3. (On Your Own: AquaWorld at http://www.aquaworld.com.mx)	**Tour**
	Leisurely
	All ages
	$42/$31 (0-9)
	2 hours

Jungle Bike Adventure [CZ29] Rating: n/a ☀ 🔒 📷

A 30-minute bus ride leads you to the Santa Rita Ranch where you learn about the tour and get fitted for a bicycle. Cycle behind the tour guide through several Mayan ruins and learn about ancient and modern Mayan civilizations. Max. weight is 250 lbs. Typical meeting time is 10:45 am. Allow 4.5 hours.	**Sports**
	Ages 10 & up
	$52

Jungle Hike Expedition [CZ30] Rating: n/a ☀ 🔒 📷

A 30-minute bus ride takes you to the point of your hike, where you receive hiking essentials, backpack with binoculars, compass, granola bar, water, and an explorer booklet. Your guide takes you on a tour through two miles of jungle and several Mayan ruins. Then jump on the bus and head back to the ship. Typical meeting time is 10:45 am. Allow 4 hours for this active excursion.	**Sports**
	Active
	Ages 10 & up
	$58

Tulum Ruins and Beach Tour [CZ06] Rating: 9 ☀ 🔒 📷

An all-day adventure to the mainland for a visit to the sacred ruins. Includes a beach visit, drinks, and sandwiches. Note that there is an extra fee if you bring a camcorder. Typical meeting time is 9:15 am. Cruiser reviews are positive: The "boat to Mexico" is "large and comfortable," though a "little bouncy." The "fantastic" tour guides are "knowledgeable," making the ruins "way more interesting than you'd expect." The "beautiful" beach is "perfect," but be aware there are "no changing rooms." Overall, a "worthy" and "fun" excursion.	**Sports**
	Active
	Ages 5 & up
	$97/adult
	$72 (5-9)
	7-7.5 hours

As noted on page 223, Cozumel operates on Central time. The Disney Magic will change its ship time to match the port time. You will be reminded of this fact in your Personal Navigator. This is true of other ports with time zone changes, too!

Embarking on Shore Excursions
on Cozumel *(continued)*

Mexican Cuisine Workshop and Tasting [CZ33] Rating: n/a

New! After a 25-minute ride to Playa Mia Grand Beach Park, you are met by a chef who introduces you to authentic Mexican cuisine. You'll prepare a full-course meal together over the course of the next two hours, then enjoy your fine food with a glass of good wine. After the meal, you'll have time to enjoy the private beach. Cooking utensils and ingredients are provided. Typical meeting time is 10:45 am.	**Workshop**
	Leisurely
	Ages 14 & up
	$69
	5-5.5 hours

Eco-Park & Snorkel [CZ34] Rating: n/a

New! Take a 35-minute ride in an open-air ATV to Punta Sur Ecological Park at the southernmost point of the island. At the park, you'll take in its wild beauty, traveling the unpaved roads alongside the sea and through the jungle. Along the way you'll stop at Columbia Lagoon filled with salt-water crocodiles, a small Mayan temple ruin ("El Caracol"), and the Punta Sur Lighthouse Museum. Be	**Sports**
	Active
	All ages
	$49/$34 (3-9)
	4.5 hours

sure to climb the lighthouse tower to take in the magnificent view. After the tour, you'll have the chance to relax on a white-sand beach—sunbathe, swim, or snorkel! Snorkel equipment is provided, as are beverages. Note that guests must be at least 8 years of age to snorkel. Typical meeting time is 10:45 am. (On Your Own: You could take a taxi for about $50-$60 roundtrip and pay $10/person admission to the park, known locally as Parque Punta Sur, but the Disney excursion is actually less expensive than all this!)

Four Elements—A Mayan Adventure [CZ35] Rating: n/a

New! Journey to the Mexican mainland to Chikin-Ha, a natural sanctuary near Playa del Carmen. On your adventure you'll experience four unique adventures, each representing the four Mayan primal elements: earth, water, wind, and fire. Appreciate the earth as you pedal over it on your bike. Immerse yourself in water as you swim or snorkel through natural sinkholes filled with water (cenotes). Embrace the wind as you fly on zip-lines over the jungle canopy.	**Sports**
	Active
	Ages 10 & up
	$99
	7 hours

And come face to face with fire through a Mayan purification ceremony. You'll also have a complimentary lunch with Yucatecan dishes. Note that the max. weight for the zip-line is 240 pounds. Typical meeting time is 9:15 am.

Discover Mexico and Chankanaab [CZ36] Rating: n/a

New! Enjoy two famous parks in one excursion. Discover Mexico is a 10-minute ride away from the pier, offering a cultural and historical look through gardens, displays, and museums. After 75 minutes at Discover Mexico, you journey to Chankanaab Park, an ecological reserve and excellent swim/snorkel location. Snorkel equipment and lunch is provided during the three hours at Chankanaab. Typical meeting time is 10:30 am.	**Sports**
	Active
	Ages 5 & up
	$69/$49 (5-9)
	5 hours

Luxury Yacht Charter [CZ37] Rating: n/a

New! Would you like to charter your own private yacht? Here's your chance! Your yacht excursion includes a Captain and first mate, lunch (lobster, pasta, white wine, beer, tequila, and kids meals upon request), snorkel equipment, and life vests. Choose your own itinerary or let the Captain make recommendations. Only your traveling party has the use of the yacht, but there is a maximum guest limit of 10. Download and submit the special form from the Disney Cruise web site.	**Tour**
	Leisurely
	All ages
	Price varies
	4-4.5 hours

See page 172 for a key to the shore excursion description charts and their icons.

(side tabs) Introduction · Reservations · Staterooms · Dining · Activities · Ports of Call · Magic · Index

Embarking on Shore Excursions
on Cozumel *(continued)*

☐ **Dolphin Swim at Dolphinaris** [CZ38]   Rating: n/a   ☀ 🛍 ⭕

New! A mere five-minute ride from the pier is Dolphinaris, a newly-built dolphin facility created with families in mind. Cruisers who book the Dolphin Swim begin with a short dolphin presentation to learn about their behavior, then don a life jacket and proceed to a waist-deep submerged platform to get a closer look at the dolphins and their anatomy. After this, you'll head out to deeper waters to touch and kiss the dolphins and enjoy a belly ride with a dolphin! You'll then have 30 minutes to swim freely among the dolphins (snorkel mask is provided). Minimum height is 53 in. (134 cm.), though smaller children can be held by a parent in the water. Cameras, jewelry, and sunscreen are not permitted in the water. This excursion is very new, but we are hearing preliminary positive reports on it. (On Your Own: Dolphinaris at http://www.dolphinaris.com, 987-872-9060)	**Sports** Active Ages 5 & up $160/$145 (5-9) 3 hours

☐ **Dolphin Kids @ Dolphinaris** [CZ39]   Rating: n/a   ☀ 🛍 ⭕

New! A special dolphin interaction program just for kids ages 5-9 is offered at Dolphinaris (see above description). This excursion is similiar to the one above, but there is no free swim time with the dolphins. Kids receive a special commemorative souvenir. A parent or guardian must accompany a child as a Dolphin Observer (see the excursion below), but the parent is not allowed in the water. Note also that kids must be able to swim.	**Sports** Active Ages 5-9 $105 3 hours

☐ **Dolphin Trainer for a Day** [CZ40]   Rating: n/a   ☀ 🛍 ⭕

New! Live your dream job and work alongside the dolphin trainers at Dolphinaris! Your day begins with a 50-minute orientation and snack. You'll then put on a snorkel and mask to explore the waters. Next, assist the Dolphinaris trainers in every aspect of their work including feeding and behavioral training techniques like hand signals and the use of positive reinforcement. You can expect kisses and rides, too! Finish with a complimentary lunch at the Dolphinaris restaurant before heading back.	**Sports** Active Ages 10 & up $285 5.5 hours

☐ **Dolphin Observer at Dolphinaris** [CZ41]   Rating: n/a   ☀ 🛍 ⭕

New! This excursion is for those with friends or family on a Dolphinaris excursion (see above) who wish to observe and not interact with the dolphins. While your friend or family member is getting their orientation and interaction, you'll be observing from a scenic area with some tables.	**Tour** Leisurely All ages $25/(3 & up)

Cozumel On Your Own

Want to set out on your own? There are several popular tour operators and destinations preferred by Disney cruisers. While we haven't tried these outfits ourselves, we offer the information here for your reference: **Mr. Sancho's Cozumel Beach Club** is a nice alternative to the Cozumel Beach Break excursion—just take a taxi to Mr. Sancho's and enjoy a less expensive day at the beach with plenty of amenities should you wish to use them. For more information, visit http://www.mrsanchos.com. **Wild Tours ATV** is an adventurous excursion during which you can tool around the "jungle" in an ATV, go kayaking, then do a bit of snorkeling. For more information, visit http://gocozumel.com/wild-tours-atv or call 987-872-2244. And for those that want something more familiar, try **Cozumel Mini-Golf** with a fun, tropical course just a short distance from the pier. For more information, visit http://czmgolf.com or call 987-872-6570.

Costa Maya
(Special 7-Night Western Caribbean Itinerary)

Ruins and coral and beach, oh my! The port of Costa Maya isn't even on most maps. Development in this **quiet corner** of Mexico's Yucatan coast began in 2000, headed by the same group that made Cancun what it is. The nearby village of Majahual is dwarfed by this, the first Mexican port created for the cruise industry.

© Corel

Costa Maya's port complex

The port of Costa Maya and its **"Mayan Pavilion Park"** are more like Disney's Castaway Cay and Downtown Disney than a traditional port. That can be reassuring—virtually no signs of poverty, no uncomfortable encounters with the locals—just shopping mall-style commerce; clean, safe swimming; free entertainment; and excursions to exciting Mayan ruins. It has everything a Western Caribbean vacationer can expect of a 10-hour port visit, with the exception of a dolphin encounter (it's probably on its way). If "adventure" calls, a short walk brings you to the beachfront village of Majahual.

Native American empires have risen and fallen in the southeast corner of Mexico's Yucatan, but all has been quiet for many centuries. The 80-mile-long **"Costa Maya" (Mayan Coast)** is dotted by some 800 Mayan historical sites (mostly unexcavated) and small villages peopled by Mayan descendants. Such was the village of Majahual (population 200) until the year 2000, when developers seized on the area as the next big thing. To the north is the huge Sian Kaán Biosphere Park, which buffers this region from Cozumel and Cancun. Scant miles to the south is the ecotourism-friendly nation of Belize. Promised to be eco- as well as tourist-friendly, Costa Maya has become a popular stop for most major cruise lines, providing "private island" conveniences on the Mexican mainland. Virtually untouched by the hurricanes that ravaged Grand Cayman, Cozumel, and Cancun, Costa Maya has provided alternate accommodations to displaced cruise ships.

Size: 1 mile long by ¹/₂ mile wide	
Climate: Subtropical	**Temperatures**: 80°F (26°C) to 87°F (30.5°C)
Population: 2,000	**Busy Season**: Mid-December to April
Language: Spanish	**Money**: Mexican Peso (11 Pesos = $1 U.S.)
Time Zone: Central (DST observed)	**Transportation**: Walking, taxis
Phones: Dial 011- from U.S., dial 060 for emergencies, dial 20092 for police	

Side tabs: Introduction · Reservations · Staterooms · Dining · Activities · Ports of Call · Magic · Index

AMBIENCE · HISTORY & CULTURE · FACTS

Making the Most of Costa Maya

GETTING THERE

Costa Maya's pier can berth three large cruise ships (even the huge Queen Mary II docks here). Visitors are shuttled down the long quay in Disney-style trams, directly to the **modern port complex** (see photo on previous page). From there, it's a short walk to your tour bus, or you can "hang" in a complex that includes 70,000 sq. ft./6,500 sq. m. of shopping, a crafts market, a salt water pool, live entertainment, cultural presentations, and several restaurants. The swimming, lounge chairs, and entertainment are all free, included in the port fees paid by Disney Cruise Line. Water sports rentals are available, too. Independent tour operators can be found just outside the complex's gates. The "New" Majahual, a planned town with a target population of 20,000, is growing just beyond the pier facilities, and the village of Majahual is about a half mile to the south (left as you leave the port). The Disney Magic typically docks at 7:30 am and departs at 5:30 pm.

GETTING AROUND

Until recently, only a rutted, dirt road served Majahual and nearby villages. With planned development comes a few paved roads, but we strongly recommend that you **stick to the shore excursions** if you want to venture far afield. An anti-smuggling government roadblock guards the road out of town. We haven't located a local car rental agency. The nearby airport has been under development, but service is slim, so if you're stranded when the boat leaves, you may have an adventure on your hands. The Uvero Beach excursion includes unlimited use of shuttle buses that depart every 35 minutes. If you have the urge to abandon tourist heaven and find the "real" Majahual fishing village, it's about a half mile south of the pier area. Taxis and shuttles are available for $2–$3 per person each way, or you can walk.

STAYING SAFE

Costa Maya is about as **safe as any port can be**. Access to the port area facilities are well guarded, and let's face it, anyone who doesn't belong is going to be pretty conspicuous. Much the same can be said for all the shore excursion destinations. Still, leave valuables on board and take advantage of the port facilities to shuttle purchases back to your room. As always, sunscreen is a must, and insect repellent is a very good idea, especially on excursions that venture near the jungle or visit ruins.

Touring Costa Maya

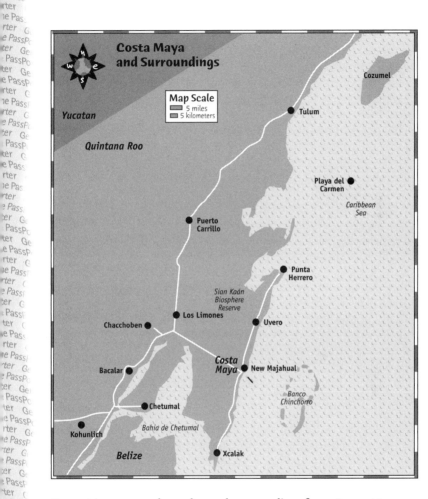

Costa Maya and Surroundings

Map Scale
- 5 miles
- 5 kilometers

Yucatan

Quintana Roo

Cozumel

Tulum

Playa del Carmen

Caribbean Sea

Puerto Carrillo

Punta Herrero

Sian Kaán Biosphere Reserve

Los Limones

Uvero

Chacchoben

Costa Maya

New Majahual

Bacalar

Banco Chinchorro

Chetumal

Kohunlich

Bahia de Chetumal

Belize

Xcalak

Costa Maya **stretches along the coastline** from Punta Herrero to Xcalak, as shown in the map above. You can see how close it is to Belize—it's not even all that far from Cozumel. You'll want to use excursions to do any venturing outside of the port area, however, as roads are not well maintained and rental car agencies aren't popular, as we've already mentioned. The pier complex is just about 200-300 yards from where the Disney Magic is docked.

Playing in Costa Maya

ACTIVITIES

With the growth of cruise ship tourism, the **village of Majahual** has begun to compete with the port's offerings. Parasailing, jetskiing, scuba, snorkel, and fishing excursions are all available without reservations once you leave the confines of the Costa Maya port facilities (see page 232 for tips on how to do this).

A **beachfront of sorts** has developed near the village, with water sports operators, restaurants, bars, and shops popping up, but it still has small-town charm and is far less "touristy" than the main port area.

So far, there's not a Carlos 'n Charlie's or Señor Frog's (the Mexican equivalents of TGIFridays and Bennigan's) in sight, at either the port or in the village. Cruisers report happy experiences at the **locally run eateries**, which focus on fresh seafood.

There are also no sites of significant historical or cultural interest near the port. The shore excursions take you to historic sites that are under development to serve Costa Maya. The excursion that takes you to the **state capital of Chetumal** will give you the best glimpse of "urban" culture. The city of 120,000 retains old-time charm, has a decent history museum, and like the rest of this corner of Mexico, has so far been relatively untouched by the tourist trade.

You can **swim** within the secure arms of the Costa Maya complex in a free-form salt water pool, but the nearby beach is for sunning only. "Downtown" Majahual has a better beach, with part roped off to protect swimmers from power boats. Uvero Beach is 15 miles up the coast and is a very popular "beach break" excursion with cruisers. The beach is beautiful, the facilities are modern, and water sports rentals are plentiful. Food is optional on the excursion.

Scuba and snorkel are popular activities, thanks to the same huge barrier reef that makes Cozumel so famous. Banco Chinchorro, 18 miles off shore, is the Northern Hemisphere's largest coral atoll. No organized excursions go here (it's an hour each way by boat), but you can make arrangements on your own, either on the spot or from several dive operators that are listed on the web.

Embarking on Shore Excursions in Costa Maya

Here are offerings from 2006 (2008 details not available at press time).

4 x 4 Jeep Safari [CM12]	Rating: n/a	
Drive (or ride in) a 4x4 vehicle through the fishing village of Majahual, into the tropical Mexican jungle, and past ocean vistas. Drivers must be 21 years of age and have a valid driver's license. The ride is bumpy and we do not recommend it for guests who have back or neck problems or those who are pregnant. The excursion includes a barbeque lunch. This appears to be very similar to the Tropical Jeep Safari Tour on page 236. Typical meeting time is 11:00 am.		Tour
		Active
		Ages 10 & up
		$85/person
		3.5-4 hours

All-Terrain Truck Expedition [CM09]	Rating: n/a	
Board a special all-terrain, military-style truck and go off road into the coastal jungles of Costa Maya. A bilingual tour guide does the driving along the bumpy terrain. Your destination is a beach where you can swim, play volleyball, or even kayak for an hour and a half. A light snack and soft drinks/bottled water are provided at the beach. This excursion is not recommended for pregnant women or guests with back problems. Typical meeting time is 12:00 pm.		Tour
		Active
		All ages
		$75/adult
		$55/child
		3.5-4 hours

Beach Snorkel Adventure [CM07]	Rating: n/a	
Beginner and intermediate snorkelers can experience an ecosystem with parrotfish, butterfly fish, and angelfish visible at depths from 3 to 15 feet. Your adventure starts from the beach, so you can snorkel at the depth that is most comfortable for you. The excursion includes equipment and basic snorkel instruction. It's not clear if snacks or soft drinks are provided, so bring them if needed. Typical meeting time is 10:30 am.		Sports
		Active
		Ages 5 & up
		$45/adult
		$35/child
		4-4.5 hours

Bike and Kayak Adventure [CM08]	Rating: n/a	
Explore the Costa Mayan coastline in two ways—by bike and kayak. After donning safety gear, you're off on a 30-minute ride along a dirt road to the village of Majahual. Next, board two-person kayaks and paddle along the reef. After kayaking, you bike back along a different route. This excursion is not recommended for guests over 6 feet tall. Typical meeting time is 11:00 am.		Sports
		Very active
		Ages 10 & up
		$45/person
		2.5-3 hours

Catamaran Sail and Snorkel [CM01]	Rating: n/a	
Hop aboard a catamaran at Fisherman's Pier for a delightful cruise along the virgin coast of Costa Maya. Mid-point through the cruise, the catamaran will drop anchor so you can snorkel for about 45 minutes. Equipment (mask, fins, and float jacket) and instruction are provided. Transportation to the pier and a soft drink is provided with the excursion. Time to shop is provided back at the pier. Typical meeting time is 1:30 pm.		Sports
		Active
		Ages 5 & up
		$48/adult
		$38/child
		3-3.5 hours

Chaccohoben Mayan Ruins [CM03]	Rating: n/a	
Board a bus to explore the Mayan ruins of Chacchoben deep in the jungle near Belize. Chacchoben, which means "the place of red corn," is believed to have been settled around 200 B.C. The 10-acre site is mostly unexcavated, but there is a grand pyramid and several temples. A lot of walking over uneven ground is required, as well as stair climbing. Bring cash for the $3 camera tax and snacks. Time to shop is provided back at the pier. Typical meeting time is 12:00 pm.		Tour
		Active
		Ages 5 & up
		$69/adult
		$59/child
		4.5-5 hours

Introduction · Reservations · Staterooms · Dining · Activities · Ports of Call · Magic · Index

Introduction

Reservations

Staterooms

Dining

Activities

Ports of Call

Magic

Index

Embarking on Shore Excursions in Costa Maya

Chetumal Mayan Museum & Spanish Fort [CM04] · Rating: n/a ☀ 🛍 📷

Immerse yourself in Mexican history as you learn about the great Mayan empire and the fateful arrival of the Spanish conquistadors. The excursion begins with a ride in an air-conditioned bus to the Museum of Mayan Culture, which is filled with artifacts and stone carvings. Then it's off to a restored Spanish fort in the city of Bacalar overlooking the Lagoon of Seven Colors. A cold soft drink is served enroute. Typical meeting time is 10:15 am.

Tour
Active
All ages
$85/adult
$75/child
6.5 hours

Clear Kayak and Beach Break [CM10] · Rating: n/a ☀ 🛍 📷

Want to peek underwater without getting wet? This excursion allows you to experience the beautiful underwater world in a two-person, transparent acrylic ocean kayak. You'll glide over colorful reef and coral formations. After your adventure, relax with fresh fruit and a soft drink on the beach. All necessary equipment and basic kayaking instruction is included in this excursion. Typical meeting time is 11:30 am.

Sports
Very active
Ages 10 & up
$59/person
3–3.5 hours

Dune Buggy Exploration [CM11] · Rating: n/a ☀ 🛍 📷

If the Jeep and all-terrain truck don't push your buttons, how about a four-person, customized dune buggy convertible? Bump along dirt roads as a driver or a rider. Enjoy the beach halfway through your drive. Drivers must be 21 years of age and have a valid driver's license. The ride is bumpy, and we do not recommend it for guests who have back or neck problems or who are pregnant. Typical meeting time is 11:00 am.

Tour
Active
Ages 10 & up
$85/person
3.5–4 hours

Horse Back Adventure [CM05] · Rating: n/a ☀ 🛍 📷

Saddle up for a trek through the Costa Mayan prairie and through lush jungles. After a safety briefing and basic riding instruction, your guide leads you and your horse to a neighboring horse ranch. A cold drink awaits you at the end of the trail. Guests should wear long pants and closed footwear. Maximum weight limit is 250 lbs.; guests who have back/neck injuries or who are pregnant may not participate. Typical meeting time is 11:00 am.

Sports
Very active
Ages 12 & up
$82/person
3.5 hours

Jungle Beach Break [CM02] · Rating: n/a ☀ 🛍 📷

Board a bus for a 30-minute trip to Uvero Beach, a popular beach with white, powdery sand, palm trees, and plenty of beach activities. The beach can get crowded, but if you venture farther down the beach, you can find quiet spots. Food and shopping is nearby. You decide when you're ready to leave and board the appropriate shuttle in the parking lot. Typical meeting time is 10:30 am.

Beach
Leisurely
All ages
$55/adult
$45/child
4–4.5 hours

Kohunlich Mayan Ruins [CM06] · Rating: n/a ☀ 🛍 📷

Travel by air-conditioned bus to a secluded jungle near the border of Belize to reach these famous ruins. A broad range of architectural styles in a naturally beautiful setting await you, including the Temple of the Large Masks. A soft drink is served onboard the bus. The tour includes a lot of walking on uneven terrain and stair climbing. If you bring your video camera, expect to pay a $5–$8 fee to use it (no tripods allowed). Typical meeting time is 10:00 am.

Tour
Active
All ages
$85/adult
$75/child
6.5 hours

See page 172 for a key to description charts and their icons.

Port of San Pedro (Los Angeles)
(West Coast Itineraries)

If you are anything like us, you may stay in San Pedro (also known as the Port of Los Angeles) for a day or so before or after your West Coast or Panama Canal cruise. If you don't head up to Disneyland, you can stay in this convenient port town and partake of its **museums, shops, and eateries**.

© MediaMarx, Inc.

San Pedro's Thomas Bridge and S.S. Lane Victory

AMBIENCE

Thanks to the natural harbor, the bustling port, and a revitalized downtown, San Pedro is the classic **port town**. Add to this its location at the edge of the Palos Verdes Peninsula with its majestic ocean vistas and cliffs, and you've got a scenic town that enjoys excellent weather year-round. In fact, San Pedro is a popular movie set location—"Pearl Harbor" was filmed here in 2001.

HISTORY & CULTURE

Before the arrival of the Portuguese, the San Pedro area was a **hunting ground for Indians**. When Juan Rodriguez Cabrillo arrived in 1542 and saw the smoke from Indians rising over the hillsides, he named the natural harbor here "Bahia de los Fumos" (Bay of Smokes). The area remained quiet until 1769, when the Spanish arrived to exploit the coastline and natural resources. San Pedro Bay prospered as a result of cargo shipping, though most of the cargo the ships carried was being smuggled. In 1848, the Americans stepped in to boost the cargo capacity of the harbor to meet the growing needs of Los Angeles. In fact, the San Pedro port is credited with bringing in most of the products needed to build Los Angeles. San Pedro continued to enjoy a booming trade until the Depression. World War II brought the port back to life as ship and aircraft builders manufactured more than 15 million tons of war equipment. Since the war, the Port of Los Angeles has grown into the largest cargo port in the U.S., handling both containers and passengers.

FACTS

Size: 7.7 sq. mi. (20 sq. km.) (water area is 18.5 sq. mi./47.8 sq. km.)	
Climate: Mediterranean	**Temperatures**: 66°F (19°C) to 76°F (24°C)
Population: 72,000	**Busy Season**: Summer
Language: English	**Money**: U.S. Dollar
Time Zone: Pacific (DST observed)	**Transportation**: Walking, cars, taxis
Phones: Dial 911 for emergencies; local phone call = 35 cents	

Introduction

Reservations

Staterooms

Dining

Activities

Ports of Call

Magic

Index

Exploring San Pedro

GETTING AROUND

You may be surprised to learn there's a fair amount to see and do in San Pedro. And whether or not you have a rental car, you should check out the **Big Red Car**, which stops along the length of Harbor Blvd. These replica train cars resurrect a part of the original Pacific Electric San Pedro Line that took passengers to the piers. Movie fans may recall the Red Car from "Who Framed Roger Rabbit." The cars now make four stops on their 1.5-mile run—the cruise terminal, downtown, Ports O' Call Village, and the marina. An unlimited, one-day pass is $1.00 for ages 7+ (you'll need exact change as you board). The cars operate from 10:00 am to 6:00 pm, Friday through Monday (with operation on select Tuesdays, Wednesdays, and Thursdays when cruise ships are in port). Details are at http://www.sanpedro.com/spcom/redcar.htm or phone 310-732-3473. A Red Car ticket is transferable for free rides on the San Pedro Electric Trolleys (described below). The **San Pedro Electric Trolley** is a turn-of-the-century style, enclosed electric trolley that covers a six-mile route between downtown San Pedro and Ports O'Call Village. It costs just 25 cents and operates from 10:00 am to 6:00 pm, Thursday through Monday.

HIGHLIGHTS

Downtown San Pedro is considered to be the rectangle formed by 6th Street and 7th Street between Harbor Blvd. and Pacific Ave. Here you'll find a variety of restaurants and boutique shops. Highlights include The Whale & Ale pub, Williams' Book Store, and the Sixth Street Bistro. On the waterfront is the Los Angeles **Maritime Museum** in an old ferry terminal. The 75,000 sq. ft. museum focuses on the maritime history of coastal California, featuring more than 700 ships, boat models, and equipment. It's open every day except Monday, from 10:00 am to 5:00 pm (opens at noon on Sundays). Adults are $3, teens and seniors are $1, and kids are free. For more information, visit http://www.lamaritimemuseum.org. Next door is **Fire Station #112**, which houses a classic, 99-foot-long fireboat and various fireboat-related exhibits. Admission is free.

The **Ports O' Call Village** is a New England-style seaside mall with shops and restaurants. Quaint cobblestone streets connect the buildings, which are spread out over 15 acres. There's also a boardwalk along the waterfront. It's so picturesque that the TV show "Providence" was often filmed on location here.

For more information, visit http://www.sanpedro.com.

Exploring San Pedro
(continued)

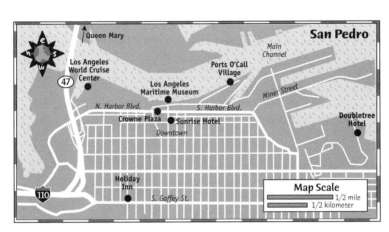

San Pedro is a great place for a walking/train/trolley tour! We suggest you **begin your tour downtown**—drive or take a Red Car to the downtown stop and begin walking west along 7th St. This is a great place to stop for coffee and pastries. When you get to Pacific Ave., turn north (right) and walk one block to 6th St. and turn right again. Right here at the corner is the Warner Grand Theatre, a recently restored performing arts and film center. At the end of 6th St. is the U.S.S. Los Angeles Naval Memorial with a mast and anchors from the battleship/cruiser U.S.S. Los Angeles. Next door is the Maritime Museum, described on the previous page. Turn left and walk north along Harbor Blvd. Along the way you'll discover the Fishing Industry Memorial and the Liberty Hill Memorial. Use your Red Car ticket to hop on the San Pedro Electric Trolley now and take it to the end of the line (north). Walk over to the SS Lane Victory, a World War II cargo ship/museum dedicated to the seamen who lost their lives at sea (see photo on page 237). Get back on the Electric Trolley and take it south to Ports O' Call Village. Pick a nice spot for lunch or an early dinner, browse the shops, and soak up the atmosphere. When you're done, you can reboard the Red Car if you like. If you have more time, take the Electric Trolley to 7th St. and Pacific Avenue, then catch the #446 Metro Bus—get off at 38th Street and walk two blocks north on Pacific to the **Cabrillo Marine Aquarium**. The sprawling aquarium features local marine animals in 38 saltwater displays—there's even a "touch tank" to get up close with live animals. The aquarium is open daily from noon to 5:00 pm (open at 10:00 am on weekends). Admission is free (but they ask for a donation of $5); parking is $2/hour (max $15/day). For details, visit http://www.cabrilloaq.org.

SAN PEDRO MAP

WALKING TOUR

Introduction

Reservations

Staterooms

Dining

Activities

Ports of Call

Magic

Index

ATTRACTIONS

Beyond San Pedro

One of the great things about San Pedro is that virtually every Southern California attraction is within a **30-mile radius**. San Pedro is located at the end of the Harbor Freeway (110) and affords easy access to the entire Southern California Freeway system. Here are some places we expect you may want to visit:

Disneyland Resort—We know many of you will pay Disneyland a visit—it's a mere 20 miles from San Pedro. If you don't have a car, we suggest you use a shuttle service (see page 75). You'll find our award-winning *PassPorter's Disneyland Resort and Southern California Attractions* guidebook very helpful in making travel, hotel, and touring plans (see page 48). For official Disneyland information, visit http://www.disneyland.com or call 714-781-4565.

Sleeping Beauty Castle at Disneyland Park

© MediaMarx, Inc.

RMS Queen Mary—This famous cruise ship is permanently berthed in Long Beach, San Pedro's next door neighbor (take Hwy. 47 east). You can take guided "shipwalk" tours, explore historical exhibits, have a meal, and even sleep aboard this historic, Art Deco ocean liner. Hotel rates begin at $149/night for an inside stateroom up to $700+/night for a Royalty Suite. For more information, see our detailed description on page 77.

Catalina Island—You can catch the Catalina Express (800-805-9201, http://www.catalinaexpress.com), for a 1 hour and 15 minute boat trip to the beautiful, 76 sq. mi. Catalina Island. There's plenty to explore here, including The Casino (not a gambling casino, but rather a museum and art gallery), plus diving, golf, eco-tours, parasailing, snorkeling, and swimming. For more information, visit http://www.visitcatalina.org.

What else is within a **reasonable distance**? Knott's Berry Farm, Universal Studios, Venice, Malibu, Beverly Hills, Hollywood, the Los Angeles Convention Center, the Rose Bowl, and Dodger Stadium. All are described in more detail in *PassPorter's Disneyland Resort and Southern California Attractions* guidebook (see page 348).

Puerto Vallarta
(Mexican Riviera and Repositioning Itineraries)

The romance of the Mexican Riviera awaits you in sun-drenched Puerto Vallarta, the quintessential Mexican beach resort town. As the sixth most popular travel destination in the world, it boasts world-class resorts, palm-fringed beaches, lush tropical vegetation, and the Sierra Madre mountains. Despite its popularity and size, it manages to retain the **charm of Old Mexico** with cobblestone streets, white-walled houses, wrought-iron balconies, and red tiled roofs.

© Corel

The town clock in Puerto Vallarta

Puerto Vallarta is nestled along the shores of the second largest bay on the North American continent, Bahia de Banderas. It enjoys more than 300 days of sunny weather each year, offering visitors an array of activities along its **100 miles of coastline** and around the majestic Sierra Madre Mountains. The romance of Puerto Vallarta is realized with a stroll down The Malecón, a mile-long oceanfront boardwalk—it begins near the first hotel built in the 1940s and ends at "Los Arcos," an open-air theater.

Unlike many other ports with long, rich histories, Puerto Vallarta's recorded history goes back only as far as 1850 when Guadalupe Sanchez began farming here. It was known as "Puerto las Peñas" until 1918 when it was officially designated as a municipality and named after Don Ignacio Vallarta, a state governor. For the next 30 years, it remained a **sleepy little fishing village** without any inroads—the only access was by boat or air. After World War II, American G.I.s relocated to the area, setting up businesses or retiring. But it was Hollywood that put Puerto Vallarta on the map when John Huston filmed "The Night of the Iguana" with Ava Gardner and Richard Burton in nearby Mismaloya Beach in 1963. After the movie, tourism dollars poured in and first-class hotels were constructed. Today, the city sees more than two millions tourists each year.

Size: 670 sq. miles/1735 sq. km.	
Climate: Semi-tropical	**Temperatures**: 71°F (22°C) to 83°F (28°C)
Population: 350,000	**Busy Season**: November to May
Language: Spanish, English	**Money**: Mexican Peso (11 Pesos = $1 U.S.)
Time Zone: Central (DST observed)	**Transportation**: Walking, taxis, buses
Phones: Dial 011- from U.S.; dial 060 for emergencies; dial 2220123 for police	

Introduction
Reservations
Staterooms
Dining
Activities
Ports of Call
Magic
Index

AMBIENCE
HISTORY & CULTURE
FACTS

Making the Most of Puerto Vallarta

GETTING THERE

Your ship docks at the **Terminal Maritima** (Maritime Terminal) three miles north of downtown. The Disney Magic pulls right up to the pier. Mexican Riviera cruises are scheduled to arrive at 7:15 am and depart at 7:30 pm. The westbound repositioning cruise arrives here at 7:30 am and departs at 4:45 pm, while the eastbound cruise arrives at 9:30 am and departs at 11:30 pm. There's not too much you can do right at the pier other than shop—believe it or not, Wal-Mart and Sam's Club are right across the street if you need to pick up some familiar essentials.

GETTING AROUND

Taxis charge about $2/person for the 15-minute ride to downtown Puerto Vallarta. You can also rent a car—a Dollar Rental Car agency is right at the port. Buses are the least expensive way to move around, and they are really quite easy. A bus ride is just 4 pesos (50 cents) and drivers accept American currency. You can catch a bus going to "Centro" (downtown) at the stop just outside the port entrance. Buses are owned by individuals rather than a company, so don't be surprised to encounter some quirky but amusing bus decor. The Puerto Vallarta region encompasses a large area—much too large to show on our map. Pick up a regional map at a tourist information center once you're off the ship. Beyond downtown, popular spots to visit include Mismaloya (John Huston's film site and spectacular views) and Old Vallarta (also known as the Romantic Zone, it evokes that ol' Mexican charm)—these are both within taxi distance, though you may feel more comfortable booking one of the many excursions.

STAYING SAFE

Crime in Mexico has been rising in recent years due to a faltering economy. Take the same precautions you would in any large U.S. city, keeping valuables out of sight and your money secure. You may be accosted by kids selling "Chiclets" (gum) or other items. Don't buy from them or give them money—they are being exploited by their parents. Support programs are in place for these children to help get them off the street. There are **bilingual tourist police in the downtown and resort areas**—they are dressed in white and wear pith helmets or black baseball caps. Don't hesitate to approach them if you need assistance. The water in Puerto Vallarta has consistently exceeded World Health Organization's criteria for drinking water for several years in a row, but bottled water is also plentiful. Observe warning flags on beaches—if black flags are up, don't go in the water.

Touring Puerto Vallarta

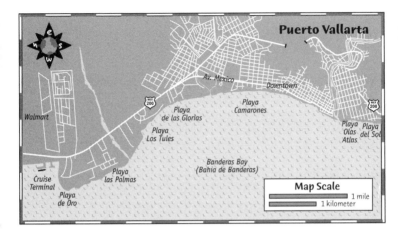

PUERTO VALLARTA MAP

WALKING TOUR

Introduction
Reservations
Staterooms
Dining
Activities
Ports of Call
Magic
Index

You can begin a good walking tour of **"Viejo Vallarta"** (old downtown Vallarta) by taking a taxi or bus into town and starting at Hotel Rosita, Puerto Vallarta's first hotel. The Malecón boardwalk (which, interestingly, has no boards) begins here—follow it to enjoy the beautiful ocean views and shops lined up across the street. Along the boardwalk are some famous sculptures, including "La Nostalgia" (a sculpture of a man and woman gazing off toward the ocean) and "The Seahorse." At the end of the Malecón you'll find Los Arcos, an outdoor amphitheater with four arches. Turn left here and cross the street to the "Plaza Principal" (Main Square)—you'll see City Hall on one side, banks and shops on the other, and a large gazebo where you can sit and listen to the Mariachi musicians who hang out at the square. From the square, walk one block east to Hidalgo, where you can see the gorgeous Church of Our Lady of Guadalupe—from here, turn left onto steep Zaragoza and climb up to Casa Kimberley at Zaragoza 446, the house Richard Burton bought for Elizabeth Taylor (check out the bridge!). This area is known as Gringo Gulch because it's where many foreigners settled in the "old" days post-World War II. Keep walking along Zaragoza to Miramar, then walk one block to Libertad to find the "Mercado Municipal" (City Flea Market) with plenty of t-shirts, silver, and trinkets. When you're done shopping, walk back along Miramar, turn left on Guerror (lots of shops here), then left again onto Hidalgo. The street becomes Guadalupe Sanchez—several landmarks are here, including the Café des Artistes restaurant and Casa de la Torre. Turn left at Allende, walk two blocks, and you'll be back at the Malecón. Walk back along the Malecón or take a taxi back to the pier.

ACTIVITIES

Playing in Puerto Vallarta

Wondering about those **famous golden beaches**? There are more than a dozen sandy beaches fringed with palm trees bordering Banderas Bay. The closest beach to the pier is Playa de Oro, which is a wide sandy beach with a few rocky areas—it's popular with both locals and tourists. Puerto Vallarta's most popular beach is Playa de los Muertos, south of the downtown area in "Zona Romantica" (Romantic Zone). There are plenty of services here, including restaurants, shops, and tube and toy rentals. While you're here, walk to the east end of Calle Pulpito for a lookout over the bay.

There are seven **golf courses** within 18 miles of the city—the closest course to the pier is Marina Vallarta Club de Golf (221-0073). There's also the new Vista Vallarta Golf Club about 10–15 minutes away, with courses by Jack Nicklaus and Tom Weiskopf. For more information, visit http://www.golfinvallarta.com.

You can do some good **deep-sea sportfishing** for marlin, snapper, and sailfish. Fishing boat charters can be hired at most beaches, or take an excursion.

Diving is also available in Banderas Bay and in the Marietas Islands wildlife reserves. We recommend you take the Disney excursion or go through Vallarta Adventures (see description on page 250).

We hear that **shopping** isn't quite as good here as in other ports, but it certainly is available nonetheless. Beyond the beach vendors, there's the City Flea Market (see previous page) and plenty of little shops downtown and along the Malecón. The galleries in Puerto Vallarta are particularly good, and the local artists are plentiful.

If you're looking for a **good lunch or early dinner**, try Trio Cafe (Mediterrean, 222-2196) in downtown Puerto Vallarta. And yes, there is a Hard Rock Cafe (222-2230) and Planet Hollywood (223-2710) in town as well.

To explore Puerto Vallarta **on your own**, we suggest you visit http://www.puertovallarta.net. There are even fun webcams at http://www.puertovallarta.net/interactive/webcam/index.php and http://www.oiccam.com/webcams/index.html?vallarta.

Embarking on Shore Excursions in Puerto Vallarta

Disney offered the following shore excursions at press time:

■ Tropical Rainforest by Horseback [PV02]

Become a "charro" (cowboy)! Travel 45 minutes to a working ranch and saddle up a horse suited to your size and ability. You'll ride on horseback through orchards and jungles to a 60-foot waterfall, where you can swim and rest with a complimentary beverage. After a half hour, you'll ride back and enjoy a lunch with free soft drinks. Guests must be in good physical condition and weigh no more than 250 lbs. Closed-toe shoes and long pants are recommended. Riding helmets will be provided. Typical meeting time is 9:15 am.

Sports
Very active
Ages 10 & up
$95
6.25 hours

■ Paradise Beach Adventure [PV03]

Visit the Paradise Village Beach Resort in Nuevo Vallarta for relaxing, swimming, playing beach volleyball, and exploring underwater caves, Mayan-style pyramids, and a small zoo. A complimentary buffet lunch, three beverages (including beer), lounge chair, umbrella, and the use of an ocean kayak is included. The resort offers a swimming pool with two water slides. Requires a 20-minute ride to and from the resort (included). Typical meeting times are 7:40 am and 12:40 pm. (On Your Own: http://www.paradisevillage.com)

Beach
Leisurely
All ages
$59/$30 (3-9)
5 hours

■ Puerto Vallarta City Tour [PV04]

Enjoy a walking tour of Puerto Vallarta. After a 20-minute scenic ride, your tour begins in the center of town and you'll visit the Malecón (seawall), historic buildings, and Our Lady of Guadalupe cathedral. You'll then take a 30-minute ride to an eatery for complimentary drinks and snacks—local crafts are on display here as well. After the tour, you can choose to stay downtown to shop or explore (if you do stay, you'll need to find your own way back to the dock). Typical meeting times are 8:40 am and 12:50 pm.

Tour
Active
All ages
$35/$25 (3-9)
4.5 hours

■ Sierra Madre Hiking [PV05]

Break out the hiking shoes! This 3.5-mile hike takes you through fields, riverbeds, rainforests, and rocky terrain up to a scenic point high above the city of Puerto Vallarta. Refreshments will be provided halfway through the hike. After you hike back down through a rainforest, you'll finish at an eatery where you'll enjoy complimentary drinks and snacks. Requires a 50-minute ride to and from the trailhead (included). Typical meeting times are 8:40 am and 12:50 pm. You'll want to be in good shape and be wearing good shoes for this excursion.

Sports
Very active
Ages 12 & up
$39
5 hours

■ Historic Towns and Tequila Making [PV07]

Want to see the more traditional side of Mexico? This van tour takes you to the village of Mezcales to visit a tequila refinery that still makes its liquor by hand. Cruisers 21 and over can sample tequila and try their hand at agave-mashing. Then it's over to Porvenir to sample tortillas. From there you go to San Juan to see the village's church and plaza. You'll also visit El Valle before driving to a restaurant for a complimentary lunch. Your last stop will be a woodcarving studio before the 40-minute ride back to the ship. Typical meeting time is 9:20 am.

Tour
Leisurely
All ages
$50/$29 (3-9)
5.5 hours

See page 172 for a key to the shore excursion description charts and their icons.

Embarking on Shore Excursions
in Puerto Vallarta *(continued)*

☐ Canopy Adventure [PV08] ☼ 🛍

You can make-believe you're Tarzan on this unique excursion. A 5-minute boat ride and 50-minute bus ride get you to a rainforest with a series of 90-foot high platforms and zip lines. After safety instructions and equipment are received, you'll zip from platform to platform along the cables to marvel at the rainforest wonders below (don't worry—you're always secured with two safety ropes). There are 14 observation platforms, 11 horizontal traverses, a "Tarzan" swing, two hanging bridges, and a vertical descent (rappel). Afterwards you'll receive complimentary snacks. This is for guests at least 48 in./122 cm. tall and under 250 pounds who are physically fit; you must wear closed-toe shoes and shorts/pants. If you bring a bag, it should be a backpack. Typical meeting times are 7:45 am, 8:15 am, 9:45 am, 10:15 am, 12:45 pm, and 1:15 pm. (On Your Own: Vallarta Adventures, http://www.vallarta-adventures.com, 866-256-2739)

Sports
Very active
Ages 10 & up
$95
4.5-5 hours

☐ Marietas Islands Snorkel and Kayak Tour [PV09] ☼ 🛍 🖸

Enjoy a 90-minute catamaran ride through Banderas Bay to the Marietas Islands, a national wildlife preserve. At the reserve you'll embark on a guided bird-watching trip (by boat), after which it is time to explore by kayak and snorkel. All necessary equipment and instruction is provided. After the adventure, a complimentary lunch is served on a secluded beach, where you can relax, swim, and take a guided nature walk. It then takes an hour and 45 minutes to return to the dock. Typical meeting time is 8:15 am.

Sports
Very active
Ages 5 & up
$75/$40
(5-9)
7-7.5 hours

☐ Scuba Dive Marietas Islands for Certified Divers Only [PV10] ☼ 🛍 🖸

Take the same 90-minute catamaran ride described above to the Marietas Islands for some of the best Mexican diving. All equipment (including wet suit) is provided for this two-tank dive. The first dive is 40 minutes down to 60 feet, and the second dive is 30 minutes down to 50 feet. Complimentary beverages are available and lunch is served after the second dive. Afterwards, relax on a secluded beach before your journey back. Must show certification and have logged a dive in the last year. Typical meeting time is 8:15 am.

Sports
Very active
Ages 12 & up
$115
7-7.5 hours

☐ Dolphin Encounter [PV10] ☼ 🛍

This is your chance for a hands-on encounter with a dolphin! You'll take a 25-minute ride to Nuevo Vallarta Marina where you'll learn more about dolphins. Then you'll stand in waist-deep water in a 14,500-square-foot enclosure to meet Pacific bottlenose dolphins. Your 15-minute encounter will include a dolphin kiss! Guests must be at least 53 in./135 cm. tall and must not wear sunscreen or jewelry or take cameras into the pools. Includes lunch and sparkling soda. Typical meeting times are 9:00 am, 11:00 am, noon, and 3:00 pm.

Sports
Active
Ages 3 & up
$125/$105 (3-9)
2.5 hours

☐ Dolphin Encounter for Kids [PV12] ☼ 🛍

This is the same excursion as described above but geared towards kids ages 4-9 who are accompanied by a parent (parents are required to purchase the Dolphin Observer excursion—see next page). Kids will be in knee-deep water and will have a chance to feed, pet, hug, and dance with the dolphins. Kids must not wear sunscreen or jewelry or take cameras into the pools. Includes lunch and sparkling soda. Typical meeting times are 9:00 am and 11:00 am.

Sports
Active
Ages 4-9
$105
3-3.5 hours

See page 172 for a key to the shore excursion description charts and their icons.

Embarking on Shore Excursions
in Puerto Vallarta *(continued)*

Dolphin Swim Experience [PV13]

This is the same excursion as described on the previous page except you actually enter 15-foot-deep water with the dolphins for 30 minutes. You can then swim and play with the dolphins and even get a tow on a dolphin's fin or a belly ride. Do not wear sunscreen or jewelry or take cameras into the pools. You should be comfortable swimming in water where you cannot touch the bottom for an extended period of time (lifejackets will be provided, however). Includes lunch and sparkling soda. Typical meeting times are 9:00 am, 11:00 am, noon, and 3:00 pm.

Sports
Active
Ages 5 & up
$175/ $155 (5–9)
3–3.5 hours

Dolphin Trainer For a Day [PV23]

New! This is a unique opportunity to learn the basics of training dolphins and sea lions. Training starts at the state-of-the-art Dolphin Adventure Center located in Nuevo Vallarta. Upon arrival you will change into a trainer's uniform and follow the dolphin training team as they perform their daily activities. You will visit the food preparation facility and life support systems. Here you will see what dolphins and sea lions like to eat and will learn the basic skill needed to care for dolphins. After meeting with the on-site vet for some dolphin anatomy lessons, you will get into the water for a 40-minute, one-of-a-kind dolphin swim. In this swim, you will get one-on-one experience with dolphins as they swim and "dance" around you. Includes an authentic Mexican lunch.

Sports
Active
Ages 12 & up
$285
6.5 hours

Sea Lion Encounter [PV26]

New! Located at the Dolphin Adventure Center in Nuevo Vallarta is a special sea lion encounter experience you won't soon forget. You first meet with a marine mammal trainer who goes over the basic anatomy and physiology of sea lions. Then with the assistance of the trainer, you are taken to a shallow pool, where you have 15 minutes to pet and touch sea lions. During this time you will see some of the special techniques that the trainers use in their day-to-day activities with the sea lions. After your time with the sea lions, you will be served a complimentary lunch consisting of Mexican dishes, sandwiches, and burgers.

Sports
Active
Ages 5 & up
$89/$79 (5–9)
2.5 hours

Dolphin Observer [PV14]

If you want to accompany your friends or family on one of the Dolphin Encounters or Dolphin Swims previously mentioned but don't want to get in the water, or just want to watch, this is the one for you. You can ride with them to and from the marina and watch them interact in the water with the dolphins. Includes lunch and sparkling soda. (On Your Own: Dolphin Adventure, http://www.dolphin-adventure.com, *866-256-2739)*

Tour
Leisurely
All ages
$35 (3+)
3–3.5 hours

Las Caletas Hideaway [PV15]

Visit the retreat of the late film director John Huston ("Prizzi's Honor" and many other films) at the tip of the bay of Puerto Vallarta. The beautiful hideaway is only accessible by a 60-minute boat ride. Once you're there, you'll have more than four hours to relax, swim, kayak, snorkel, walk, tour Huston's former home, and learn how to make paella and tortillas. A complimentary lunch buffet with beverages is included. Massages and souvenirs are also available for purchase. Life jackets are provided and required. Typical meeting time is 8:30 am.

Beach/Tour
Leisurely
All ages up
$89/$49 (3–9)
7–7.5 hours

See page 172 for a key to the shore excursion description charts and their icons.

Embarking on Shore Excursions
in Puerto Vallarta (continued)

Banderas Bay Luxury Sailing Adventure [PV16]

Learn the basics of sailing on a private charter, monohull, single-mast sailboat. Your sail will take you north for two hours while you relax on the cushioned deck and enjoy complimentary beverages and fresh fruit. You'll arrive at a secluded beach where you can relax, swim, or snorkel for two hours. After a complimentary lunch served onboard, you'll sail back to the ship. Everyone has the chance to help sail the craft. Typical meeting time is 9:55 am. Note that you must download and submit the private vehicle request on Disney's web site.

Sports
Active
Ages 5 & up
Price based on boat
6 hours

Sierra Madre Off-Road Expedition [PV017]

Get off the beaten path and explore the Mexican outback. After a 20-minute ride, you'll board Mercedes Benz all-terrain, open-air vehicles for a 45-minute journey over bumpy terrain and through streams to a small Mexican village. Here you'll have a 30-minute walking tour and complimentary snacks and beverages. Then it's back in the vehicles for a 60-minute ride to the heart of the Sierra for a 30-minute nature walk through the jungle. After this, you'll ride to a secluded beach for a BBQ lunch buffet with your tour guides. Typical meeting time is 9:00 am. (On Your Own: Vallarta Adventures, http://www.vallarta-adventures.com, 866-256-2739)

Tour
Active
Ages 8 & up
$85/$75 (8-9)
6.5 hours

Pirate Boat Sail and Snorkel Adventure [PV19]

Here be pirates! Board the pirate ship "Marigalante" for a rousing good time. Your wacky pirate Captain Crispin and his friendly crew will treat you to breakfast, dancing, pirate contests, and surprises during the two-hour cruise to Majahuitas Beach. On dry land, you'll have two hours to swim, snorkel, and relax (snorkel equipment is provided). Volleyball, beach games, and a sand sculpture contest are held at the beach, too. Back onboard you'll enjoy a BBQ lunch, a pirate show, and a fiesta during the two-hour cruise back to the dock. Typical meeting time is 8:00 am. (On Your Own: Marigalante Pirate Ship, http://www.marigalante.com.mx, 322-223-0309)

Sports
Active
All ages
$75/$60 (3-9)
5.5 hours

Yelapa & Majahuitas [PV28]

New! Snorkeling and sightseeing is in store for you with this excursion. First, you are taken on a 75-minute catamaran cruise where you get views of the coast of Banderas Bay. You will see Las Caletas, a large rock formation that comes out over the bay and shoots high into the sky. After the catamaran voyage, you will drop anchor in the secluded cove of Majahuitas. Here you will get to snorkel and kayak in crystal-clear water where stunning reef formations and tropical fish are abundant. Afterward, you will visit the sea side village of Yelapa for a guided, jungle hike to the magnificent Cola de Caballo waterfalls. You will have about 2.5 hours in Yelapa before returning to the catamaran for lunch during the journey back to the ship.

Tour/Sports
Active
Ages 5 & up
$69/$39 (5-9)
7 hours

Sea Safari [PV27]

New! Enjoy a 45-minute powerboat ride along the Mexican coastline to South Bay. Once here, you will venture on a guided hike through the jungle to the 100-foot-high waterfalls in Tecomata. After this, travel by sea to the small seaside village of Pizota, where you can swim, snorkel, and kayak. If you don't want to get in the water, there is a hiking trail that will lead you through a tropical forest. By now you've worked up an appetite, and a picnic lunch is provided for you before the cruise back to the ship.

Tour/ Sports
Active
Ages 8 & up
$95/$75 (8-9)
5 hours

Embarking on Shore Excursions
in Puerto Vallarta *(continued)*

Banderas Bay Snorkeling Treasure Hunt [PV31]

New! Board a 68-foot schooner and sail along the coastline of Puerto Vallarta to reach a large rock formation known as Los Arcos. In one of Mexico's best snorkeling areas, you will swim past expansive coral formations as you look for underwater clues to help you with your treasure hunt. Back on board the schooner, scores will be tabulated and awards will be given to those who found the hidden treasure. On the journey back to the ship, refreshments will be served.

Sports
Moderate
Ages 5 & up
$62/$52
(5-9)
4 hours

Outdoor Adventure [PV24]

New! A short speedboat ride across Banderas Bay will take you to the shores of Boca de Tomatlan. Here, you will board an all-terrain, 4x4 Unimog and travel 2,000 feet above sea level to the heart of the Sierra Madre jungle. Once at your base camp, you will go from canyon side to canyon side via a network of pulleys 250 feet above the ground. Then race along a 1,000-foot zip line through the treetops. At the end of the zip line you will then set out on a secret path through the jungle. You will rappel a waterfall and walk across steep jungle bridges. Once you return to base camp, you will be treated to light refreshments before returning to the ship.

Sports
Active
Ages 12 & up
$110
5.5 hours

Extreme Amphibian Adventure [PV30]

New! A 50-minute drive through the countryside brings you to a private ranch. Here you will meet your guide and learn to operate an amphibious Argo 8x8 wheel all-terrain vehicle. You'll drive past lush vegetation, lagoons, sand dunes, and rolling hills and through washed-out riverbeds. After the two-hour trek, you return to the ranch where you will be provided with light snacks and bottled water. Look for the animals that live at the ranch, such as pot-bellied pigs, ostriches, and ferrets.

Sports
Active
Ages 10 & up
$89
4 hours

Mexican Cooking Experience [PV32]

New! Take a 50-minute motorcoach to a private ranch in the Sierra Madre. At the ranch, you'll be led to the on-site kitchen, where you'll meet your chef instructor for the day. You will learn how to make some of Mexico's best-loved dishes, such as salsas, guacamole, and stuffed peppers ... and then you get to try them all! After lunch, you can wander the ranch and see the farm animals or take pictures of the panoramic views. Then sit back and relax on the journey back to the ship.

Tour
Leisurely
Ages 8 & up
$39/$29 (8-9)
5-5.5 hours

Evening Horseback, Country Barbecue, and Show [PV06]

(Only available for the eastbound repositioning cruise.) New! Going north from the ship, you will travel by motorcoach to Rancho Capomo in the foothills of the Sierra Madre. Once at the ranch, you will meet your guide, who will go over safety details before introducing you to your own horse. You will then ride through a rainforest with towering trees and rocky hillsides. As sunset approaches, you will arrive back at the ranch where candlelit dinner tables await. Enjoy a barbeque dinner consisting of grilled chicken, beef strips, ribs, and more. During dinner, you'll see a show that should please the whole family, featuring dancing horses, lasso tricks, and Mexican folkloric dances. Roast marshmallows over a fire before returning to the ship.

Sports
Active
Ages 12 & up
$75
6 hours

See page 172 for a key to the shore excursion description charts and their icons.

Embarking on Shore Excursions in Puerto Vallarta *(continued)*

■ Sunset Sail [PV20]

(Only available for the eastbound repositioning cruise.) New! Just before sunset, board a 50-foot sailboat and sail to the middle of Banderas Bay. Once there, you can sip cocktails and listen to relaxing music as the sun seems to melt into the ocean. Once it is dark, observe a fireworks show from one of the local villages. After the fireworks, enjoy a delicious dinner and relax on the boat. Sit back and look at the stars as you make the 30-minute trip back to the ship.

Tour
Leisurely
Ages 12 & up
$69
3 hours

■ Rhythms of the Night [PV25]

(Only available for the eastbound repositioning cruise.) New! A catamaran will take you on a one-hour cruise across Banderas Bay to the home that once belonged to film director John Huston. Once at Las Caletas, musicians and dancers will greet you dressed in traditional Aztec clothing. You'll then be led to candlelit dinner tables to enjoy a buffet consisting of steak, chicken, seafood, and desserts. After dinner, make your way to an outdoor amphitheater and be entertained by those who greeted you. The show highlights Mexico's ancient past through song and dance. After the 40-minute show, you will return to the catamaran for the trip back to the ship.

Tour/Show
Leisurely
Ages 10 & up
$75
5 hours

■ Private Cars & Vans [PV00]

New! See Puerto Vallarta at your own pace in the comfort of a private car or van. This excursion lets you reserve a vehicle before you ever leave home! Your car or van includes an English-speaking driver/guide, who will take you on a tour of the sights that interest you. Your driver will meet you in Puerto Vallarta and the tour lasts either 4 or 8 hours. Download and submit a Private Vehicle Request Form through the Disney web site for pricing and availability.

Tour
Leisurely
All ages
4–8 hours
Price varies

■ Teens Cruise [PV01]

New! Board a 60-foot yacht and journey to the middle of Banderas Bay. During your teens-only cruise, you will be entertained by a variety of games and activities. Dance competitions and banana-eating contests keep the fun moving along. While you're partying, the yacht makes its way past several towns along the coast of Puerto Vallarta. Snacks and soft drinks will be provided before returning to the ship.

Tour
Leisurely
Ages 13–17
$45
3.5 hours

See page 172 for a key to the shore excursion description charts and their icons.

Puerto Vallarta On Your Own

For those who want to get a head start on their excursion plans, or just want to do it on their own, here is some information on tour operators in Puerto Vallarta. Please note that we have not used these operators, nor is any mention here an endorsement of their services. For a huge variety of excursions, check out **Vallarta Adventures**, which seems to offer a version of almost every Disney excursion available and then some. You can get loads of information on their excursions at http://www.vallarta-adventures.com, or call toll-free at 866-256-2739. If the canopy tours through the jungle intrigue you, you can book this on your own through **Canopy Tours de Los Veranos**, about which we've heard very good things. For more information, visit http://www.canopytours-vallarta.com, or call 322-223-6060.

Mazatlán
(Mexican Riviera Itineraries)

Don your wide-brimmed sombrero, grab a margarita (or lemonade), and get ready to enjoy the best coastal beach town just south of the Tropic of Cancer. Mazatlán is unashamedly touristy but generally **more laid-back** than other resort towns. And thanks to its history and geography, Mazatlán offers far too many choices for just one day in port.

© Corel

Horseback riding on the beach in Mazatlán

AMBIENCE

Mazatlán's nickname is **"Pearl of the Pacific,"** which has far more to do with its gracious hospitality than actual pearls. The city is sheltered in a hilly harbor on the shores of the Pacific Ocean. Its 13 miles of wide beaches share the spotlight with the best seafood in the country, thanks to a thriving fishing industry. Old Mazatlán downtown has recently been restored to its colonial glory.

HISTORY & CULTURE

Long before the Spanish conquerors arrived, Totorames Indians lived here for centuries—artifacts dating as far back as 10,000 years ago have been found here. In 1531, Nuno de Guzman arrived and the area was named Mazatlán, which means **"land of the deer"** in the ancient Nahuatl language. Few deer are seen here today, of course. After the Spanish departed with all the gold from the mines, Mazatlán was mostly used as a hiding place by French and English pirates. The pirates were chased out by 1800, thanks to a small presidio with watchtowers in the harbor. The settlement itself was actually pioneered by German immigrants who developed the port for agricultural imports. With a functioning port, trade activity began in earnest, bringing with it disease from other foreigners—Mazatlán survived both yellow fever and cholera plagues. Modern Mazatlán was born in the '60s, when tourists discovered its beautiful white sandy beaches and the resort hotels popped up.

FACTS

Size: 6 mi. (9.5 km.) long x 5 mi. (8 km.) wide	
Climate: Subtropical	**Temperatures:** 66°F (19°C) to 92°F (33°C)
Population: 700,000	**Busy Season:** January–March, July–August
Language: Spanish, English	**Money:** Mex. Peso (11 Pesos = $1 U.S.)
Time Zone: Mountain (DST observed)	**Transportation:** Walking, taxis
Phones: Dial 011- from U.S.; dial 060 for emergencies; dial 080 for police	

Introduction   Reservations   Staterooms   Dining   Activities   Ports of Call   Magic   Index

Making the Most of Mazatlán

GETTING THERE

The Disney Magic docks in **Mazatlán's commercial cargo port** south of downtown. No tendering should be necessary. You can expect to go ashore around 7:30 am. A "complimentary and compulsory" shuttle takes you to a more tourist-friendly port area, offering shops and bars. Other than this, there's not much around. Taxis are plentiful and reasonably priced—look for the green and white (or red and white) vehicles known as "eco-taxis." Taxi fare is about $10 to $12 for a trip to the Golden Zone. Or you can get a Pulmonia ride (an open-air taxi that looks a bit like a golf cart) for roughly the same price. Buses are also available for about $7/family. There's an English-speaking Visitor Information Center available upon arrival for transportation questions, too. All aboard time is 5:00 pm.

GETTING AROUND

Mazatlán has **four prime tourist areas**. Old Mazatlán, the city center (Centro), is near the southern end of a peninsula. Its colonial charm is quaint and it's a good spot for some casual exploratory walking. **Zona Dorada** (the Golden Zone) is a 10-mile stretch of sandy beaches—it's the tourist heart of the city, populated with shops, restaurants, and hotels. **Isla de la Piedra** (Stone Island) is east of the Mazatlán peninsula and a short boat ride away—you're most likely to visit it as part of an excursion. And finally, **Isla de Venados** (Deer Island) is a natural reserve protecting the native flora and fauna—again, you're most likely to visit this island as part of an excursion.

STAYING SAFE

El Centro in Old Mazatlán and the Golden Zone are **generally safe** for tourists who take common sense precautions. Avoid the local tap water—opt for bottled water instead. While the water has improved much over the years, it's best not to take the chance here. Few beaches have lifeguards, so be careful and don't swim when you see red flags. We strongly suggest that you rent diving equipment only from outfits that require you to have a certification card—others may not be sufficiently safety-conscious. Like most Mexican destinations, there is no shortage of peddlers. Usually a simple "no" does the trick, but if not, it's best to ignore them outright. Mazatlan is a very large city, with a population approaching a quarter of a million. Use your normal "big city smarts" when going about town. Oh, and if you and tequila don't go well together, let us forewarn you that virtually every mixed drink is made with tequila.

Touring Mazatlán

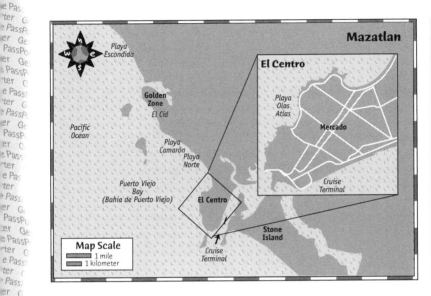

While Disney (and others) offers a guided **walking tour** of Old Mazatlán (El Centro), you can do it on your own as well. Take a taxi to the Continuity of Life dolphin monument ("La Continuidad de la Vida") on Paseo Claussen. From here you can walk south along the coastline to El Clavadista (the cliff divers). After leaving El Clavadista, head south along Olas Atlas to see the La Mujer Mazatleca (the women of Mazatlán) and the El Venaditro (little deer) monuments—if you spot the El Shrimp Bucket Restaurant (at the corner of Olas Atlas and Angel Flores), you'll find it's an excellent spot for breakfast. Take a left on Constitucion and walk five blocks to the tree-filled Plazuela Machado Square, the historic center of Mazatlán. Take a break at Cafe Pacifico, which has tables outside and inside. Just to the south of the square is the Trealto Angela Peralta theater, originally built in 1874 and recently restored (you can tour the building for $1). Now walk north four blocks along Benito Juarez past Revolucion Park to Mazatlán's main cathedral (Catedral de Inmaculada Concepcion), an airy, 19th-century Moorish structure (and, yes, you can go inside). Two more blocks take you to the Central Market (Mercado), a full square block of stalls offering everything from fabrics to jewelry to t-shirts. From here you can get a taxi back to the pier. (By the way, you can see some excellent interactive maps of the downtown area at http://www.maps-of-mexico.com (click on Mazatlán to zoom in the downtown area maps are near the bottom).

Playing in Mazatlán

ACTIVITIES

Mazatlán has seemingly **endless beaches** stretching from El Centro north for more than 13 miles. You'll find wide expanses filled with umbrellas to secluded, romantic coves. Playa Olas Atlas (which means "big waves"), near Old Mazatlán, is a popular beach and is excellent for surfing. Playa Sabalo, located midpoint along the Golden Zone, is the best beach for sunbathing and swimming—parasailing and other watersports are also available here, with a calm surf and plenty of nearby services. For a beach with a more Mexican feel, Playa Norte to the north is favored by sun-worshippers and fishermen—it's got plenty of "palapas" (thatched, open-air restaurants) with excellent seafood.

Scuba diving is best near the offshore islands, paticularly Deer Island. This isn't the ideal port for diving however—visibility tends to be only 10 ft. (thanks to the waves) and water temperature is a chilly 65°F/18°C. If you're determined to try it, El Cid Aqua Sports Center (669-913-333, ext. 341) offers rentals and trips.

Now, what about **cliff diving**? You can't dive yourself, but you can watch daring locals taking the plunge. You'll need to take a taxi to Playa Olas Atlas (in Old Mazatlán) to see the diving shows performed sporadically throughout the day. Divers jump off a 45-foot cliff (Glorieta del Clavadista) into relatively shallow tidal pools. After the dive show, donations are collected from the spectators.

Fishing is big here—Mazatlán has some of the richest game-fishing waters anywhere! You can get a fishing charter through Star Fleet (800-633-3085), the largest fishing fleet in town. Bass fishing is also available at Lake Comedero and El Salto—book a trip through Aviles Brothers (800-633-3085).

If you're interested in **golfing**, El Cid Resort (800-525-1925) is the place to go. Its 18-hole course is designed by Larry Hughes and measures 6,712 yards. More info at http://www.elcid.com.

Shopping is a mixture of open-air markets and typical port shops. The Golden Zone offers the greatest variety of shopping. The best purchases here are Taxco silver jewelry, onyx, and ceramics. If you're looking for real bargains, the Mercado in Old Mazatlán (see previous page) offers some real deals if you're able to bargain. Bargaining, by the way, is accepted and encouraged in Mazatlán.

Embarking on Shore Excursions in Mazatlán

☐ Mazatlan Beach Escape [MZ02]

Take a 20-minute scenic ride to the Los Sabalos Resort for a morning on the Mazatlán waterfront. The resort is situated at the start of the "Golden Zone" strip of beaches and hotels. You'll be provided with towels and a place to change into your swimsuit. A Mexican lunch buffet is included. You can choose from two departure times back to the ship. Typical meeting time is 9:00 am.

Beach	
Leisurely	
All ages	
$49/$39 (3-9)	
4-7 hours	

☐ Sierra Madre Tour [MZ03]

Tour the Sierra Madre mountain communities, including an adobe brickyard, a tile factory, a baker, a 223-year-old church, a pottery farm, and a visit to Copala. You'll have the opportunity to explore several historic sites. Lunch and beverages are included. Kids have the opportunity to make a clay memento to take home. Typical meeting time is 8:45 am.

Tour	
Leisurely	
All ages	
$74/$49 (3-9)	
7 hours	

☐ Hacienda Las Moras & Horseback Riding [MZ04]

Experience an hour-long horseback ride through the Mexican countryside. Afterwards, you can swim at a pool or just relax with complimentary snacks and beverages. Guests should wear long pants and closed-toe shoes, be in good physical condition, between 10 and 65 years old, and weigh no more than 220 lbs. Riding helmets are provided. Wear closed-toe shoes and long pants. Typical meeting times are 7:30 am and 12:30 pm.

Sports	
Very active	
Ages 10-65	
$75	
5 hours	

☐ Mexican Family Ranch Party [MZ05]

A family-friendly fiesta in the country can be had at the Los Moras Ranch. After a 45-minute drive, you'll arrive at the 2,000-acre ranch for swimming, relaxing, strolling in the gardens, and enjoying Mexican art and architecture. Includes lunch, too. The finale is the breaking of a piñata! You can get more information on the ranch at http://www.lasmoras.com. Typical meeting time is 9:15 am.

Tour	
Leisurely	
All ages	
$77/$49 (3-9)	
5 hours	

☐ Old Mazatlán Walking Tour [MZ06]

Hit the highlights of historic Mazatlán with this 3.5-hour walking tour. You'll see the Continuity of Life monument, the famous cliff divers, Ice Box Hill, an old bakery, a restored opera house, Machado Square, and a 19th-century church. You'll have time to do some shopping before returning. Wear comfortable walking shoes. Includes beverages. Typical meeting time is 7:45 am.

Tour	
Active	
All ages	
$31/$19 (3-9)	
4.5 hours	

☐ Tequila, Saddles, and Huaraches [MZ09]

An hour's ride gets you to the village of La Vinata to visit a tequila distillery where you can see how tequila is made and even enjoy a sample if you're 21+. Then it's off to La Noria to visit shops where items such as saddles and huaraches (sandals) are made. After a complimentary lunch at a cafe, you'll take a 50-minute ride back to Mazatlán. Typical meeting time is 9:15 am.

Tour	
Leisurely	
All ages	
$62/$42 (3-9)	
6.5-7 hours	

See page 172 for a key to the shore excursion description charts and their icons.

Embarking on Shore Excursions
in Mazatlán *(continued)*

Shrimp Fest [MZ14]

New! Shrimp, shrimp, and more shrimp is what you will experience with this excursion. Journey to the private residence of Villa de la Cruz above the historic center of Mazatlán, where you will enjoy one of Mexico's finest exports. These mouth-watering crustaceans are plentiful and prepared in a number of different ways. In addition to the shrimp, the all-you-can-eat buffet will have taquitos, rice, beans, guacamole, chips, custard, and alcoholic and non-alcoholic beverages. Travel time to and from the villa is a mere 10 minutes.

Tour
Leisurely
Ages 10 & up
$78
4 hours

Best of Mazatlan [MZ17]

New! Get a feel for what Mazatlán offers with this fun "sampler" excursion. Board an air-conditioned motorcoach and journey to Cerro del Vigia, which offers majestic views of steep cliffs and rolling countryside. Down the road you'll discover a 19th-century lighthouse known as El Faro. Standing 515 feet above sea level, El Faro offers lovely panoramas of neighboring harbors and islands. At the next stop, you get to watch the world-famous cliff divers as they jump into the shallow waters of Olas Atlas. As you finish watching the divers, you will be transported to a beach resort for a complimentary lunch and further entertainment. Lunch consists of an authentic Mexican buffet with beverages. During lunch you'll be entertained by a group of professionally trained dancers performing traditional Mexican dances. After lunch, enjoy 1½ hours of free time at the beach resort, swimming or walking along the coast.

Tour
Leisurely
Ages 3 & up
$89/$59 (3-9)
7 hours

Cross-Country Biking [MZ18]

New! Experience Mazatlán from a vantage point that only a mountain bike tour can offer. A 35-minute van ride will transport you to the starting point, where you will meet your guide and get your mountain bike. From here, you will ride along a bike path that will offer breathtaking views of the Pacific Ocean, steep rock bluffs, and barren plains. After your bike ride, return to the starting point where you can enjoy complimentary bottled water, soda, and fresh fruit.

Sports
Active
Ages 12 & up
$45
3.5 hours

Estrella del Mar Golf Package [MZ19]

New! Play 18 holes on a par 72, 7,045-yard course at Estrella del Mar Golf Course. Included is a shared golf cart, unlimited range balls, and greens fees, plus you can rent clubs if you don't bring your own. Requires a 35-minute taxi or van ride. Also included is a boxed lunch. Drinks are not included but are available for purchase. Golf attire with golf/sport shoes is required.

Sports
Moderate
Ages 10 & up
$170
6.5 hours

Hidden Mazatlán Off-Road Buggy Adventure [MZ20]

New! Nothing shows off the interior of Mexico more than a tour in 4x4 off-road dune buggies. Take a 40-minute motorcoach ride to a local ranch, where you will meet your guide and learn the safety and handling of your dune buggy. Then take off and see sights of Mexico that are otherwise hidden from normal views. You will drive over rocky hilltops and through washed-out riverbeds. See desert flora and unique desert animals. During a beach break, take pictures of breathtaking ocean views. After a two-hour tour, you will arrive back at the ranch, where you will enjoy complimentary snacks and soft drinks.

Sports
Active
Ages 21 & up
$90
5 hours

See page 172 for a key to the shore excursion description charts and their icons.

Embarking on Shore Excursions
in Mazatlán *(continued)*

Mazatlán Highlights, Folkloric Show, & Mexican Buffet [MZ21]

New! Making your way north in an air-conditioned motorcoach, you will travel up and down hills, past steep cliffs, and along the waterfront. Take pictures of a 19th-century lighthouse, El Faro, as you stop at Cerro del Vigia. Here you will see incredible views of the harbor and surrounding areas. Next, you will travel to an upscale beach club for entertainment and lunch, featuring an authentic Mexican buffet with chicken, enchiladas, taquitos, rice, beans, and more. After lunch, enjoy historical dancers in costume performing dances from ancient Mexico. Along with the dancers, there will be singers, comedic performers, and magicians. After the show, return to the ship and marvel at the scenery of Mazatlán.

Tour
Leisurely
All ages
$80/$55 (3-9)
4.5-5 hours

Salsa & Salsa [MZ23]

New! Take 30-minute motorcoach ride to a local beach resort. On your way to the resort, learn about Mazatlán from an onboard tour guide. Once at the resort, meet your instructor who will teach you how to make a variety of authentic Mexican salsas and the Mazatlán version of the margarita. After the demonstrations, enjoy the fruits of your labor. For the second part of the tour, you will be taught how to dance the Salsa from an experienced Salsa dance instructor. After dancing, spend the rest of your time at the resort however you wish. From relaxing in a cozy beach chair, to swimming in the ocean, it is up to you.

Tour
Leisurely
Ages 5 & up
$80/$55 (5-9)
5.5 hours

City Highlights & Mexican Mardi Gras Fiesta [MZ16]

New! Are age-old cathedrals and death-defying cliff divers your thing? Ride in an air-conditioned motorcoach through the magnificent beauty of Mazatlán. During the 15-minute journey, your travel guide will brief you on the fascinating history of the renowned city and bay. Get a chance to view the late 19th-century El Faro lighthouse and snap a picture of the offshore islands during your stop at Cerro del Vigia. Afterwards you will make your way to the center of the city and tour the historic Cathedral of Immaculate Conception, built in 1875. Next you follow the rocky cliffs to view the world-famous divers as they plunge into the shallow waters of Olas Altas. Then you'll be whisked away on a 30-minute drive to the Aztec theater in Mazatlán's Golden Zone to see a traditional Mexican fiesta dance show featuring specially trained adult and child performers. Relax on the 15-minute drive back to the ship. Beverage (bottled water or sparkling soda) is included.

Tour
Leisurely
Ages 3 & up
$35/$25 (3-9)
3-3.5 hours

Hike to the Lighthouse [MZ22]

New! Hike to the top of the famous El Faro lighthouse, perched atop Mazatlán's highest hill. The excursion begins with a 10-minute bus ride to El Creston hill. From there, you will hike 3,642 feet to the top of the lighthouse. You'll be rewarded with gorgeous views at 515 feet above sea level. Enjoy a complimentary drink (bottled water or sparkling soda) before descending along a shorter path. After your descent, you may choose to spend time in the historic downtown district (but if you do, you'll have to find your own transportation back to the ship). Note that you must climb and descend 330 steps to reach the top of the lighthouse. Wear appropriate footwear—no flip-flops or slippery sandals.

Sports
Active
Ages 12 & up
$35
3.5 hours

Introduction · Reservations · Staterooms · Dining · Activities · Ports of Call · Magic · Index

Embarking on Shore Excursions
in Mazatlán *(continued)*

◼ El Rosario Countryside Experience [MZ15] ☀ 🔒 ▣

	Tour
	Active
	All ages
	$82/$55 (3-9)
	7.5 hours

Travel through time on this day-long walking tour of El Rosario town and discover the age-old art of handicraft production at El Tablon Viejo. The excursion begins with an hour-long drive through the Mexican countryside, where you can view the striking landscape of sprawling seaside views, gentle sloping hills, and verdant forest flora along the way. You'll stop and visit a traditional family store and discover the art of making handicrafts from wood and calabash. After this stop, continue on a 20-minute drive to El Rosario, which was once a successful gold- and silver-mining town. You can travel above old mining trails on a guided walking tour. Explore City Hall, the Main Square, and an age-old Spanish Cemetery. Visit the Mining Museum and bask in the history both above and below ground. Sample Sinaloa's favorite vanilla-flavored soda, Toni-Col, during a tour of the Toni-Col factory. After viewing the sights during a 100-minute walking tour, enjoy your complimentary lunch in a relaxed setting at the local Bella Vista restaurant. Children are invited to a piñata party before embarking on the 75-minute drive back to the ship.

See page 172 for a key to the shore excursion description charts and their icons.

Mazatlan On Your Own

For those who want to get a head start on their excursion plans, or just want to do it on their own, here is some information on tour operators in Mazatlán. Please note that we have not used these operators, nor is any mention here an endorsement of their services. A cruiser favorite here is **Randi's Happy Horses** for fun and gentle horseback rides through a plantation and along an undeveloped beach—get more information at http://www.randishappyhorses.com, or call 669-985-2740. Another popular option is **Frank's Mazatlán Tours** with tour guide Frank Thiel-Arenta—he offers both city and country tours. Visit http://www.mazatlan-frank.com/FrankEng.html, or call 669-669-2189 or 669-117 0604. Consider also the **Mazatlán Aquarium**, about a block and a half from Señor Frogs restaurant (between downtown and the Golden Zone). The aquarium has both fresh and saltwater fish, sea lions, and birds. Admission is is $6/adult and $3/kids.

© Rob Lee

A gorgeous Mazatlán sunset

Cabo San Lucas
(Mexican Riviera and Repositioning Itineraries)

Perched on the southern tip of the **Baja California** peninsula, Cabo (Cape) San Lucas and its sister-town, San José de Cabo is a pleasure destination, pure and simple. Pleasant bars, pleasant beaches, pleasant shopping, and some of the best sport fishing you'll find anywhere. These towns were barely on the map until wealthy sportsmen started flying in after World War II.

Lands End in Cabo San Lucas

This is a **Lifestyles of the Rich and Famous** destination, and the restaurants, hotels, and shops cater to this upscale market. You won't find many bargain-rate tourists driving in here—it's more than 1000 miles from anywhere else, over a highway that's short on fuel, water, and other services. The town is compact, although resort development stretches along the 20 miles of coast between Cabo San Lucas and neighboring San José de Cabo (together, these towns are known as Los Cabos). Picturesque beaches are scattered along the rocky coastline, and the sea beckons fishermen, scuba divers, and surfers alike.

Dry and mountainous, Baja was always **sparsely populated**. It's thought that the indigenous people may have migrated here across the Pacific—there's no evidence that Mexico's major civilizations ever put down roots here. Spanish missionaries didn't get to Baja's deserts, mountains, and rocky coast until the late 1600s. Most missionaries moved on, leaving little behind of either historical or archeological interest in Cabo San Lucas. On the other hand, San José de Cabo has a historic Spanish mission, tales of visits by buccaneers, and an attractive downtown district. After World War II, high-end fishing resorts were soon hooking wealthy fishermen. Mexico completed the Transpeninsular Highway in the early '70s, and realizing Cabo's popularity, started making major investments in the '80s.

Size: 14 mi. (23 km.) long x 11 mi. (18 km.) wide	
Climate: Tropical	**Temperatures**: 81°F (27°C) to 87°F (31°C)
Population: 68,000	**Busy Season**: November to April
Language: Spanish, English	**Money**: Mexican Peso (11 Pesos = $1 U.S.)
Time Zone: Atlantic (no DST)	**Transportation**: Walking, taxis, scooters
Phones: Dial 33-977 or 119 for emergencies	

AMBIENCE

HISTORY & CULTURE

FACTS

Introduction
Reservations
Staterooms
Dining
Activities
Ports of Call
Magic
Index

Making the Most
of Cabo San Lucas

GETTING THERE

Although there are rumors of a full-fledged cruise ship pier under development, for now, expect to be **tendered** into the small inner harbor of Cabo San Lucas. From the small ferry terminal, the town is easily explored on foot, with the town square, restaurants, and shopping just a few blocks distant. A waterfront boardwalk makes for a pleasant stroll, and if your interest is game fishing, you'll find charter boats close by the pier. San José de Cabo is 20 miles to the east, along Highway 1. Beaches along this route are marked, if you want to stop and explore. But if you stray outside of Cabo San Lucas, hurry back! For Mexican Riviera itineraries, "all ashore" time is about 9:00 am, and "all aboard" is about 5:30 pm—just over eight hours in port. The west-bound repositioning cruise has a little more time, arriving at 8:00 and departing at 7:30 pm. The east-bound cruise has even less time in port, arriving at 9:00 am and departing at 4:30 pm.

GETTING AROUND

Car rentals are available in downtown Cabo San Lucas from most major agencies, including Alamo, Avis, Budget, Dollar, Hertz, and National (reserve in advance), but you should only rent if you have an out-of-town destination in mind. Taxis are plentiful, but are only really necessary to get to the beaches. Everything else is **within walking distance**. As nearly all points of interest are visited by shore excursions, they remain, as always, your safest bet—you don't want to miss your ship's departure! Due south of the inner harbor is Lands End (see photo on previous page), the southernmost point of Baja, where the Sea of Cortez meets the Pacific Ocean (you'll get a great view of this as you tender into shore). The entire area has been set aside as a natural preserve. Scuba diving is popular, as are sightseeing cruises. Los Arcos is an oft-photographed natural stone arch at Lands End, and next door is beautiful and isolated Lover's Beach, which can only be reached by sea (water taxis operate from the inner harbor and Playa El Médano across the bay).

SAFETY

Cabo is **safer than most tourist ports**, so no special warnings apply—just use standard cautions and procedures. And just one word for you, just one... sunblock!

Charter fishing boats

© Corel

Touring Cabo San Lucas

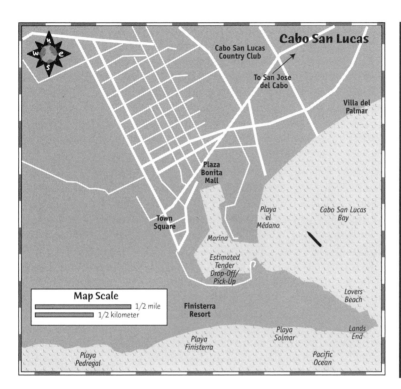

CABO SAN LUCAS MAP

For **swimming and recreation**, Playa El Médano is the place, just east of the inner harbor's entry. You'll find every sort of water sport rental and beach amenity on this broad beach with modest surf and numerous resort hotels. While it's just across the bay from the pier, a short cab ride is probably the best way to get there. Previously mentioned, Lover's Beach is a short boat ride away. It's reputed to be one of the most picturesque beaches anywhere, but swimming is dangerous. Attractive Solmar Beach is also a short cab ride from the pier and guarded by resort hotels, but it, too, is not suitable for swimming. Most other area beaches are also too dangerous for swimming, although several along the road to San Jose de Cabo attract scuba divers, snorkeling, or surfers (see next page). Of those, Playa Chileno, with its offshore reef, offers the best swimming opportunities. None of the beaches have safety patrols, so you're on your own. If you want to book your own excursions, consider Cabo San Lucas Tours at http://www.cabosanlucastours.net or 866-348-6286.

RECREATION

Introduction

Reservations

Staterooms

Dining

Activities

Ports of Call

Magic

Index

Playing in Cabo San Lucas

Scuba diving, snorkeling, and surfing are all popular activities at beaches scattered across more than 20 miles of rugged coastline. Prime surfing beaches are just west of San Jose de Cabo. A good rundown is at http://www.wavehunters.com/cabo/cabo_surf.asp. There's fine scuba and snorkel action at Lands End, so you don't have to stray very far. But if you must venture out, Playa Palmilla (17 mi./ 27 km. east of town) and Playa Chileno (9 mi.,/14 km. east of town) both offer top-notch diving, snorkeling, and general beach facilities. Both have dive shops. Playa Chileno has the added advantage of being a no-motorized-watersports area. Golf is another attractive pastime here, although you'll need an awfully early tee time if you want to get back to the ship in time—play it safe and book that shore excursion!

Los Cabos are especially famous for **blue marlin fishing**, but that legendary game fish will be out of season when the Magic is in port. There's always something biting, though. The fishing pier is right next to the ferry terminal if you want to snag a charter boat.

While plentiful and pleasant, the **shopping** in Cabo San Lucas is not particularly exciting. The jewelry and craft boutiques of San Jose de Cabo, apparently, are another matter. The quality is said to be high and the prices fair.

Surprise, surprise, here's another Mexican port with a Carlos 'n' Charlie's! If you're looking for an **eatery with deeper local roots**, El Squid Roe Bar & Grill seems to have a good reputation. Cabo Wabo Cantina has the added allure of being owned by rock and roll's Sammy Hagar (Van Halen)—definitely a party spot! You'll find these and many more a short walk away in the harbor area. You'll also not lack for lunch choices if you head for Playa El Médano or San Jose de Cabo.

For something a bit out of the ordinary, the **Vitrofusion Y Arte** glass works is located on the outskirts of Cabo San Lucas (take a cab). You can watch the artisans produce functional mouth-blown glassware and art glass (hand-blown doesn't seem to be the right term), and naturally, there's a retail shop on premises, too. You'll also find Vitrofusion goods on sale at some downtown shops.

Embarking on Shore Excursions in Cabo San Lucas

Cabo Beach Break [CLO1]

Hang out at the Beach Club Resort, a 15-minute ride from the ship. You get two complimentary beverages plus chips, salsa, and guacamole. You can also rent sailboats, banana boats, boogie boards, and get parasailing rides. After 2.5 hours at the beach, you can either get a ride back to the ship or walk back on your own, one mile to the pier. Typcial meeting times are 8:05 am and 9:05 am.

Beach
Leisurely
All ages
$38/$24 (3-9)
4-4.5 hours

Cabo del Sol Golf Outing [CLO2]

Play the Desert Course at Cabo del Sol, about 30 minutes from the ship. The par-72, 7,097-yard course was designed by Tom Weiskopf. A cart and bottled water are provided; you can rent clubs if you didn't bring your own. Typcial meeting times are 7:45 am and 8:45 am. About 6.5-7 hours.

Sports
Active
Ages 10 & up
$249

Scuba Diving Odyssey [CLO3]

Certified scuba divers can explore the Sea of Cortez and San Lucas Bay. This one-tank dive goes to depths of 25-100 ft. Complimentary beverages served after the dive. All necessary equipment provided. Divers must have completed a dive in the last year and present certification. Typical meeting times are 9:25 am and 12:30 pm (westbound) or 10:25 am and 1:30 pm (eastbound).

Sports
Very active
Ages 12 & up
$110
2.5-3 hours

Cabo San Lucas Sportfishing Excursion [CLO4]

Board a 28-foot cabin cruiser for a 30-minute cruise to a prime fishing site. Guests will have a chance to fight and reel in fish from the fishing chair. A boxed lunch and beverage are included in the price. Note that catch-and-release of all billfish is mandatory. Mexican fishing license is included in price, but a tip of $5-$10 is not included. Typical meeting times are 7:45 am and 8:45 am.

Sports
Active
Ages 12 & up
$189
5.5-6 hours

Pacific Side Horseback Riding [CLO5]

Ride to the Villa del Palmar Hotel to get matched up with a horse. Then it's off to explore the shoreline of the Sea of Cortez for an hour. After the sedate ride you'll have 45 minutes to relax on the beach. Afterward, you can get a ride back to the pier or get dropped off downtown. Bottled water included. Maximum rider weight is 240 lbs. and riders must be between the ages of 12 and 65.

Sports
Active
Ages 12-65
$79
3-3.5 hours

Harbor Cruise and Scenic Drive [CLO6]

Begin with a 40-minute catamaran trip to the tip of the Baja peninsula to see Lands End and Los Arcos (the arches). Along the way, you'll hear a narration by Cousteau and enjoy a complimentary beverage. Then it's time for a 20-minute drive to Giorgio's clifftop site with its amazing view. Get a ride back to the pier or be dropped off downtown. Typical meeting times are 8:45 am and 9:45 am.

Tour
Leisurely
All ages
$39/$28 (3-9)
3-3.5 hours

Chileno Bay Snorkeling Adventure [CLO7]

Board the "Tropicat," a 65-foot catamaran—it even has a water slide! You'll cruise by many points of interest, including Lover's Beach, the arch at Lands End, and the sea lion colony on the 45-minute trip. You'll then drop anchor at Chileno Bay for snorkeling; equipment is provided. You'll also receive complimentary snacks and drinks on the way back. Typical meeting times are 7:40 am and 8:40 am.

Sports
Active
Ages 5 & up
$69/$38 (5-9)
4-4.5 hours

See page 172 for a key to the shore excursion description charts and their icons.

Embarking on Shore Excursions in Cabo San Lucas *(continued)*

☐ Los Arcos Sea Kayak and Snorkel [CL09]

A 5-minute water taxi ride brings you to your kayak launch site, where you'll receive instructions, gear, and bottled water before boarding your 2-person kayak. Then it's time to paddle into Cabo San Lucas Bay, past Los Arcos to Lover's Beach. You'll have 45 minutes to snorkel at the beach before paddling back. Max. weight is 250 lbs. Typical meeting times are 9:20 am and 10:20 am.	**Sports**
	Very active
	Ages 10 & up
	$49
	3 hours

☐ Coastal Highlights Tour [CL10]

Enjoy a scenic bus tour to various Cabo San Lucas highlights, including a glassblowing shop, the town of San Jose del Cabo, and the clifftop restaurant of Cabo Bello (plus a complimentary beer or soda). Afterward, return to the pier, or visit downtown Cabo San Lucas and then take the 20 min. stroll back to the ship. Typical meeting times are 7:55 am, 8:30 am, 8:55 am, and 9:30 am.	**Tour**
	Leisurely
	All ages
	$45/$29 (3-9)
	4-4.5 hours

☐ Santa Maria Sail & Snorkel Experience [CL11]

Sail aboard a catamaran to Santa Maria Cove, passing by Lover's Beach, the sea lion colony, and Lands End along the way. At the cove, you'll get your snorkeling equipment to explore the reefs (or just swim) for an hour. Life vests are provided and required. Back onboard, you'll enjoy beverages and snacks during the return. Typical meeting times are 9:20 am and 10:00 am.	**Sports**
	Active
	Ages 5 & up
	$65/$36 (5-9)
	4-4.5 hours

☐ Cabo Resort Pool Getaway [CL13]

Take a 10-minute ride to Finisterra Resort to lounge by the resort's pool, play games on the beach, and enjoy a buffet lunch with complimentary beverages and buffet-style lunch. Kids can also paint ceramic figurines, which they can take home. Ocean swimming is not permitted due to strong currents. Typical meeting times are 9:35 am and 10:35 am.	**Beach**
	Leisurely
	All ages
	$59/$49 (3-9)
	4.5-5 hours

☐ Lands End Coastal Cruise [CL14]

Enjoy a 45-minute cruise on a catamaran around the Baja peninsula to see Lands End, Los Arcos, sea lions, and rock formations. Includes a narration by Cousteau. A complimentary beverage (bottled water, beer, or soda) is provided. Typical meeting times are 12:15 pm and 1:15 pm. About 1-1.5 hours.	**Tour**
	Leisurely
	All ages
	$31/$19 (3-9)

☐ Baja 1000 Test Track [CL33]

New! You begin by hopping on a motorcoach for the 15-mile ride from the city center to a private race course. Here you will get to race in an actual off-road racecar like the Baja racers. Your instructor and a team of trainers will go over safety and handling details before they turn you loose. The off-road buggy will have you going over rough and tumble terrain. You get four laps around the track, for a total of 10 miles. After your ride, enjoy an ice-cold beverage before your ride back to town.	**Sports**
	Active
	Ages 25 & up
	$325
	3 hours

☐ Exclusive Private Villa [CL26]

New! Enjoy Cabo from the privacy of your own manor overlooking the Sea of Cortez and the Pacific Ocean. An air-conditioned van ride will take you to the elegant hilltop abode of Casa Miramar. Includes a private chef (and lunch). Max 12 guests. Download and submit form on Disney's site.	**Special**
	Leisurely
	All Ages
	Price varies

Embarking on Shore Excursions in Cabo San Lucas

Talofa Tall Ship [CL29]

New! View the coastline of Mexico from the deck of a tall ship with traditional rigging. You'll sail aboard "Talofa," which was built in the last century. Learn what life was like on one of these ships as you get to help sail the vessel. If you do choose to help sail, you will be required to sign a liability waiver (no sailing experience is necessary). Enjoy a provided lunch and cool beverages (including "grog").

Sports
Active
All ages
$92/$62 (3-9)
3.5 hours

Chileno Power Snorkel [CL27]

New! Snorkel with the speed of a fish using an underwater, power scooter. Take a 75-minute catamaran ride to Chileno Bay, where you'll be met by your guide who will instruct you on how to operate the power scooter safely. You will be able to effortlessly view stunning coral formations and beautiful tropical fish. On your way back to the ship, enjoy complimentary snacks and beverages.

Sports
Active
Ages 12 & up
$78
4.5 hours

Dolphin Kids [CL22]

New! Kids will be talking about this adventure for a long time after the cruise. You and your child will set out on a short 5-minute walk to the Cabo Dolphin Center, where your child will meet with dolphin trainers. The trainers will teach the basics about life in the wild and how the trainers care for the dolphins. After the information session, your child will get a 20-minute, one-on-one session with a Pacific Bottlenose dolphin under the direct supervision of a dolphin trainer. Note that this a not a "swim with the dolphins" experience. A bottle of water is provided and food is available for purchase.

Sports
Active
Ages 4-9
$105
1.5 hours

Dolphin Swim [CL23]

New! Take a short 5-minute walk to the Cabo Dolphin Center for a one-of-a-kind dolphin experience. The Cabo Dolphin center is a state-of-the-art facility designed for educational and interactive programs. At the center, you will meet your guide, who will educate you on dolphin anatomy and physiology, along with the daily activities of the dolphin trainers. After the instruction period, get into the water with Pacific Bottlenose dolphins where you can swim, touch, and interact with them. After your 30-minute swim, enjoy a complimentary bottle of water (food is available for purchase) before you walk back to the ship.

Sports
Active
Ages 5 & up
$175/$155 (5-9)
4 hours

Teen Surfin' Safari [CL28]

New! Designed exclusively for teens, this excursion combines surfing and sun for an unforgettable day. A private van will take you on a 45-minute drive to a prime beach on the Pacific Ocean. After a brief meeting with your instructor, you will be assigned a surfboard and gear for the afternoon. You will then go with your instructor into the water for an hour-long training session. After this, you will be turned loose to catch some waves and splash with your friends. Afterward, enjoy a complimentary beverage before heading back to the ship. Maximum surfboard weight is 220 lbs. Wet suits and life vests are provided.

Sports
Very active
Ages 13-17
$89
5 hours

See page 172 for a key to the shore excursion description charts and their icons.

Embarking on Shore Excursions in Cabo San Lucas *(continued)*

4X4 Rhino Mini Jeep Adventure [CL17]

New! Take a ride on a scenic drive through the Mexican countryside to a private ranch. Here you will meet your guide, who will go over operating and safety protocols before handing you the keys to a two-person Rhino 4x4 all-terrain vehicle. Then you're off, being led through rocky terrain and washed-out riverbeds. Look for towering cactus that stand over 20 feet tall! After your 90-minute drive, head back to the ranch, where beverages will be served.

Sports
Active
Ages 10 & up
$95
4 hours

ATV Beach & Desert Expedition [CL18]

New! A 40-minute van ride will take you to a private ranch along the coast of the Pacific Ocean. Once there you will meet your guide, who will show you how to operate your ATV. The guide will then lead you out of the ranch as you travel the rocky terrain in your ATV. Along the hilltops and riverbeds, there will be frequent stops for photo opportunities. Before returning to the ranch, you will ride along the coast of the Pacific Ocean. Upon your return, enjoy a complimentary beverage before the ride back to the ship.

Sports
Active
Ages 18 & up
$95
4 hours

Canyon Canopy Adventure [CL21]

New! An air-conditioned van will take you through countryside surrounding Cabo and bring you to Boca de la Sierra, a protected site in the High Sierras. Here you will meet with your guide and then travel across the canyons by a network of pulley systems. You will speed across a zip line and fly through the treetops. You will also get to do a bit of rock climbing and then rappel 90 feet down the canyon wall. Finally, climb onto another zip line and sail over 800 feet back to the base camp. In camp, enjoy a bottle of water and fresh fruit and granola. Max. weight is 250 lbs. Min. height is 48 in./122 cm.

Sports
Very active
Ages 10 & up
$95
5.5 hours

Beach Buggy & Swim [CL32]

New! See Cabo San Lucas by both land and sea in this unique excursion. Board a dune buggy and follow your guide as you pass through desert landscapes and small rural villages. After 90 minutes of driving, you arrive at the ocean. Here, you can swim, soak up the sun, or explore one of the many coves along the coast. Then enjoy a light snack and beverages before returning to the ship.

Sports
Active
Ages 10 & up
$86
3.5–4 hours

Cabo My Way [CL00]

New! Do you want to visit Cabo, but none of the other excursions pique your interest? Then this one is for you. You can arrange to have a private van cater to you and your interests. You could visit one of the many beaches or take in a round of golf, all on your own timetable. If you would like to go on a driving tour, an experienced guide can be provided as well. Tours typically are four hours in duration, but you can reserve additional hours if needed. Max. guests is 6 or 12. You will need to download and submit a Private Vehicle Request form through the Disney Cruise Line web site for pricing and availability.

Tour
Leisurely
All ages
4 hours

See page 172 for a key to the shore excursion description charts and their icons.

Acapulco
(Repositioning Itineraries)

Acapulco is the **Monte Carlo** of the Mexican Riviera. It's known for its fabled playground of the rich and famous, with a miles-long arc of prime downtown beachfront, one of the Pacific's great natural harbors, dramatic encircling mountains, and daring cliff divers plunging into a narrow gap in the rocks like matadors in the bull ring.

The famous cliff diving of Acapulco

The **broad arc of Acapulco bay** provides the focus for tourist activities. Nearly every address seems to be on Avenida Costera Miguel Alemán ("Costera"), the waterfront boulevard that hugs the beach, and whenever your eyes lift from the blue waters, the encircling peaks of the Sierra Madre mountains provide a dramatic backdrop. As with many ports, the colorful old city is within walking distance of the piers, while the glamorous high-rise hotels and nightclubs are farther down the coast.

You've docked in one of the West Coast's **oldest and most historic Spanish ports**. During Spanish colonial days, Acapulco had a royal monopoly on trade across the Pacific to the Far East. Can you say, "Buccaneer magnet?" Acapulco's fortress repelled attacks of all sorts, until the end of Spanish rule left the port a has-been in the transoceanic trade. By the time it was rediscovered by the tourist trade in the 1930s, Acapulco had become a sleepy fishing town, ripe for a much more peaceful kind of invasion. The city is the model for nearly every other Mexican beachfront resort, and while she eventually lost her crown to younger glamour queens, Acapulco's still got plenty of class. Today, only one-fifth of Acapulco's visitors are international travelers; the bulk of Acapulco's tourism comes from Mexico City's middle class.

Size: 4 mi. (6.5 km.) x 5 mi. (8 km.)	
Climate: Tropical	**Temperatures**: 87°F (30°C) to 90°F (32°C)
Population: 620,000	**Busy Season**: November to April
Language: Spanish	**Money**: Mexican Peso (11 Pesos = $1 U.S.)
Time Zone: Central (DST observed)	**Transportation**: Walking, taxis, buses
Phones: Dial 011-52-744 from U.S; dial 060 for emergencies; 485-0650 for police	

Making the Most of Acapulco

GETTING THERE

Acapulco's cruise terminal is located on the **west end of Acapulco** Bay, close to the old downtown area (El Centro), with its Zócalo (town square), Municipal Market (Mercado), historic Fort (Fuerte) San Diego, and the waterfront Malecón promenade and dock area, home to fishing charters and other pleasure boats. The famous cliff divers of La Quebrada (see photos on previous page) are a short cab ride away. Cruise pier amenities include a tourist information booth with free maps, an Internet café, and a variety of shops. On the westbound itinerary, "all ashore" time is Monday at 12:00 pm, with "all aboard" at 9:30 pm. On the eastbound itinerary, "all ashore" time will be 6:30 am Friday, with "all aboard" at 1:00 pm (yes, that's just 6 1/2 hours in port).

GETTING AROUND

Here's another port where car rentals are not advisable. While there are some out-of-town beach destinations beckoning the adventuresome, **walking is best** if you're headed for nearby El Centro, and taxis or the plentiful public buses are a better bet than driving in this parking-starved city. Authorized tour guides/drivers can be found under an awning outside the terminal—be sure to refer to the posted price list. The waterfront boulevard Costera Miguel Alemán goes right past the pier and to all points around the bay, so buses and taxis are easy to find. If you have a sense of adventure, buses may be your most economical and efficient alternative. Buses marked "Base" head toward the naval base on the east end of the bay, while "Caleta" buses head west toward the westernmost beaches and La Roqueta Island. "Hornos" buses follow the entirety of Costera Miguel Alemán. An open air tourist "trolley" may be in service. If it is, you can get all-day, flat-rate service to many popular tourist destinations.

STAYING SAFE

This is a **large city with a growing population**. This alone should be enough to put you on your guard. All the usual warnings apply—don't bring valuables ashore (and especially to the beach). Hold purses and bags securely. Be careful of hustlers with high-pressure pitches, and don't "fly" solo to the various public markets—there's safety in numbers. Agree on a fare before you hop in a taxicab. Don't stroll around with shopping bags from upscale shops—disguise your purchases and head right back to the ship. Water? Tourist restaurants use purified water, but otherwise, depend on brand-name bottled water, just to be sure. If you get lost, catch a cab and ask for "La Terminal de Cruceros" to get back to the ship.

Touring Acapulco

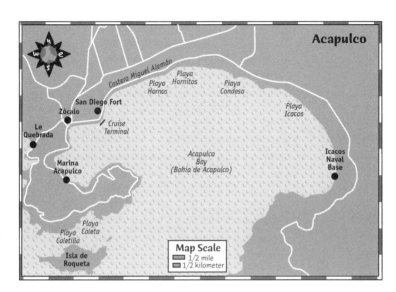

Like many ports of call, **Acapulco has grown** far beyond the bounds of its historic port area, with most of the modern resort hotels quite a distance from the cruise ships. El Centro offers several sights and points of interest. Fort San Diego overlooks the cruise pier and houses a history museum. The fort is closed on Mondays, unless opened by special arrangement for a shore excursion. Nearby is a museum of ceremonial masks. Just a few more blocks inland, the Zócalo is surrounded by shops, restaurants, and a striking cathedral. Several blocks from there is the Municipal Market, which mostly serves the locals with produce and other necessities. At the far southwest end of El Centro are Playa Caleta, Playa Caletilla, and Isla de Roqueta. If you're looking for glitz and glamour, you'll have to head to the "golden" (Costera) and "diamond" (Puerto Marqués) resort areas, clockwise around the bay from the pier via the ever-present Costera Miguel Alemán. The Costera district is at the top of the map, encompassing Playa Hornos, Playa Hornitos, Playa Condesa, and Playa Icacos. You'll also find plenty of restaurants and nightclubs, resort hotels, upscale shopping, and the CiCi water park, the destination for dolphin-related excursions and water slide addicts. Acapulco Diamante includes the hillsides of southeast Acapulco Bay plus Puerto Marqués, a small bay just beyond the southeast end of Acapulco Bay. Head here for the fanciest shops, discos, and restaurants, and ogle the villas of the rich and famous.

Playing in Acapulco

Nearly all of Acapulco Bay is lined with **beaches** offering gentle surf, numerous watersport rentals, and many snack shacks and restaurants. Convenient Costera Miguel Alemán will get you to all the in-town beaches, and there may be a ferry service to Playa Caleta and Playa Caletilla that leaves from the Malecón, close to the cruise pier. While the city is working to clean up the waters of the bay, they may not be as clean as you'd hope. Closest to the pier (but not within walking distance) are Playa Hornos to the northeast in the Costera district, and Playa Caleta and Playa Caletilla, on the peninsula directly to the southwest of the pier. Cozy Playa Caleta and Playa Caletilla form the old-time beach resort area, and are now more popular with local families than visitors. There's a run-down aquarium and water park there that may best be avoided. Glass bottom boats also depart from there to nearby Isla de Roqueta, which is a popular shore excursion destination. East of Playa Hornos in the Costera district is Playa Hornitos, followed by Playa Condesa in the heart of the action, and Playa Icacos, a bit quieter and more remote. Two out-of-town beaches (Revolcadero and Pie de la Cuesta) are more peaceful but have rough surf and a strong undertow. Revolcadero sports some surfing action.

Acapulco Bay and its many beaches

The city has tried to divert **craft and souvenir vendors** into several public markets. The quality of goods is said to be spotty, but if you have a good eye and sharp bargaining instincts (counterbid with 30% of the quoted price, and work your way towards the middle) you may do all right. El Parazal Market is near the Zócalo, as is the Municipal Market. The La Diana Market is in the Costera, along with several shopping malls and countless name-brand boutiques. The cruise terminal hosts a variety of shops, and if you find what you want, you can take your purchases right back to the ship.

Playing in Acapulco

Acapulco has always been known for **freshly caught seafood**, especially red snapper (huachinango). You'll find it at inexpensive beach snack bars and street vendors and at the finest restaurants. While we're not in a position to make specific recommendations, if you want to go "native," find a spot near the Zócalo or at the beach—prices are fair, and quality is supposed to be quite good. For a bit of drama with your meal, La Perla, the Mirador Hotel's sit-down restaurant, overlooks the cliff divers of La Quebrada. It's not about the food, and there's a $13 cover charge to dine or $31 (including two drinks) to sit at the bar. Around the bay in the Costera you'll find Señor Frog's and Carlos 'n' Charlies, popular chain restaurants found in most Mexican tourist ports.

Sport-fishing excursion boats can be hired along the Malecón, by the cruise pier. The CiCi water park in the Costera district has all the water slides and swimming pool action a child could want, plus dolphin shows (its swim-with-the-dolphin activities are usually fully booked by official shore excursions). Scuba is not big around here, but there are several operators, including Fish-R-Us (also offers fishing charters and pleasure cruises) at 877-3-FISH-R-US, and Acapulco Scuba Center at 744-480-1962. Acapulco does have a bull ring, but it'll be closed when the Magic is in port.

Cliff divers (clavadistas) are the classic Acapulco sight. Daring locals dive 130 feet into a narrow, rocky ocean inlet. They live on the $3 fees collected directly from spectators or funneled to them by tour operators and other businesses. While most shore excursions take you to the Hotel Mirador's restaurant in order to squeeze your wallet, there are also outdoor public viewing areas where only the $3 fee is collected. Looking at the map, you may be tempted to walk there, but it's easy to get lost along the way. A cab ride should be around $9. The divers put on one show at 1:00 pm, and hourly shows in the evening starting at 7:30 pm. As evening falls, the divers carry flaming torches, making the show more dramatic. We loved it! Alas, cruisers on the eastbound cruise may not have time to see them.

Taxco is a legendary name among **silver jewelry** aficionados. If you're tempted to make a pilgrimage to this town 170 miles (275 km) north of Acapulco, plan carefully—the Magic will sail without you if you're late! You can also find high-quality silver in Acapulco, but take great care. All that glitters is not silver (or gold). Sterling silver should be stamped 0.925.

ACTIVITIES

Introduction

Reservations

Staterooms

Dining

Activities

Ports of Call

Magic

Index

Embarking on Shore Excursions in Acapulco

Acapulco Highlights, Shopping, and Cliff Divers [AC04]

Hit the major sites of Acapulco with this bus tour. Begin with a stroll to the fascinating Fort San Diego to explore its museum of Acapulco history. Then board an air-conditioned motorcoach for a 20-minute ride to La Quebrada and the famous cliff divers show. Next stop is the Hotel Los Flamingos atop a cliff overlooking Acapulco Bay, where you'll enjoy a complimentary snack and beverage. From here, journey to Acapulco's Zócalo (main square) to explore the pretty plaza, visit a cathedral, peek into the "Forgotten Office," and do some shopping. We took this excursion on our repositioning cruise in 2005 and really enjoyed it—we felt it offered an excellent overview of Acapulco.

Tour
Leisurely
All ages
$59/$42 (3–9)
5–5.5 hours

Acapulco By Horseback [AC05]

Take a 60-minute bus ride to a horse ranch, where you'll be matched with a horse. After putting on your riding helmets (provided) and listening to a short orientation, you're off on a sedate one-hour horseback ride through the Mexican countryside. You'll pass a coconut farm, streams, orchards, and a small village on your way to a sandy beach. After your ride, you'll enjoy a complimentary box lunch and bottled water before returning to the ship. Guests must be in good physical condition, between 12 and 65 years old, and weigh no more than 240 pounds/109 kg. Riders should wear closed-toe shoes and long pants for the horseback ride.

Sports
Active
Ages 12–65
$85
4–4.5 hours

Cultural Walking & Shopping Tour [AC07]

Take a 15-minute walk a few blocks from the ship to Fort San Diego. From there it's another 10-minute walk to a mask shop, then another 15-minute walk to the Zócalo, the traditional town square of Acapulco. You can stay and shop for an hour and walk back with the others, or return at your leisure (it's a 20-minute walk back to the ship). Wear comfortable walking shoes for this excursion. A light snack and soft drink is provided.

Tour
Active
All ages
$31/$20 (3–9)
4 hours

Golf at Mayan Palace [AC08]

Enjoy 18 holes at a par-72, 6,507-yard championship course set between the Pacific Ocean and the Sierra Madre mountains. The course is covered with Bermuda-type grass and has many dunes. A shared cart, range balls, and greens fees are included, as is the one-hour trip to and from the course. Clubs may be rented for about $40. Golf attire (long pants/golf shorts, polo shirt, and golf/sport shoes) is required. (On Your Own: Maya Resorts, http://www.acapulco.com/en/golfsports/mayangolf, 866-765-0608)

Sports
Active
Ages 10 & up
$169
7.5–8 hours

La Roqueta Island Getaway [AC09]

Enjoy a 30-minute cruise south to La Roqueta Island and its gorgeous panoramic views of Acapulco and the Pacific Ocean. Here you can swim, snorkel, and relax on the pristine beach. Included in the excursion is a Mexican buffet lunch (fajitas, rice, beans, fruit, guacamole, tortillas, salsa, chips, and two beverages) and a Mexican folk dancing performance. Must be at least 10 to snorkel.

Beach
Leisurely
Ages 8 & up
$56/$49 (8–9)
4.5 hours

See page 172 for a key to the shore excursion description charts and their icons.

Embarking on Shore Excursions
in Acapulco (continued)

■ Shotover Jet Adventure [AC11]

A thrilling cruise through the Mexican jungle. You'll begin with a 45-minute ride to the Puerto Marquez Lagoon to board a bright red, 12-passenger jet boat which skims the water at 45 mph/70 kmph in just 4 in./10 cm. of water. You'll pass through the mangroves, making thrilling 360° spins and hairpin turns. A soft drink is included. (On Your Own: Shotover Jet Acapulco, http://www.shotoverjet.com.mx/contenido_acapulco.htm, 744-484-1154)	**Sports**
	Active
	Ages 10 & up
	$85
	3-3.5 hours

■ Dolphin Swim Adventure at CiCi Water Park [AC15]

Again, the same excursion as described above, but this time you actually get to swim with the dolphins for 30 minutes. Includes a 10-minute training session before your swim. A beverage is included, but there probably won't be time to play much at the water park. We don't recommend doing this on your own as the dolphin swim fills up with cruisers on official excursions. If you want to observe a family member or friend, book the Dolphin Observer excursion.	**Sports**
	Active
	Ages 5 & up
	$189/$169
	(5-9)
	3.5 hours

■ Dolphin Observer at CiCi Water Park [AC19]

If you want to accompany your friends or family on one of the Acapulco Dolphin Encounters at CiCi Water Park previously mentioned but don't want to get in the water, or just want to watch, this is the one for you. You can ride with them to and from the marina and watch them interact in the water with the dolphins. Food and beverages are available for purchase.	**Tour**
	Leisurely
	All ages
	$20 (3 & up)
	2.5 hours

■ Mini Jeep Rhino Adventure [AC20]

New! Driving an hour outside of Acapulco, you will arrive at your base camp, where your two-person Yamaha Rhino all-terrain vehicle is waiting. You will then follow your guide through palm nurseries, over bumpy roads, and along dirt racetracks. Pass through a local fishing village as you make your way to the first stop at Tres Palos lagoon for photos. Next, zip through "New Acapulco" and then on to one of the area's beaches for sand dune driving. Wind down after driving with a swim in the ocean and a picnic lunch.	**Sports**
	Active
	Ages 10 & up
	$98
	4 hours

■ Acapulco Beach Break [AC21]

Take a 15-minute ride to the El Morro Beach on Acapulco Bay, learning the interesting history of the region along the way. Lounge chairs, boogie boards, volleyball, football, and a trampoline are all available for your use during your three to four hours on the beach. Also included is bottled water, a soft drink, or a beer. While you're there, try the local tropical drink known as Coco Loco, made with dark rum, light rum, vodka, creme de bananas, pineapple juice, coconut cream, and sugar syrup—it's supposed to be pretty good.	**Beach**
	Leisurely
	All ages
	$52/$42 (3-9)
	3.5-4 hours

■ Acapulco City Tour With Cliff Divers [AC22]

New! Start out with a 30-minute bus tour of Acapulco's popular beaches, ultimately arriving at the cliff of La Quebrada, home of the famous cliff divers. You'll watch the diving show at the Hotel El Mirador while enjoying a snack and beverage (soda, rum punch, Piña Colada, or beer). After the show, a Mexican folkloric show is presented. You'll have a half-hour to shop before your two-hour city tour, during which you'll learn about Acapulco's history as you journey through the Golden Zone and get amazing views of Acapulco Bay.	**Tour**
	Leisurely
	All ages
	$45/$35 (3-9)
	4.5-5 hours

Introduction
Reservations
Staterooms
Dining
Activities
Ports of Call
Magic
Index

Embarking on Shore Excursions
in Acapulco *(continued)*

Shopping, Flavors, & Traditions [AC23]

	Tour
New! Take a 30-minute journey in an air-conditioned bus to the heart of the city, where you'll visit a restaurant named El Jaguar. Here you will learn the basics of authentic Mexican cuisine during a food preparation event in which you can participate. After the presentation, indulge in some of the dishes that were prepared as well as some additional dishes. You'll also see dancers performing traditional dances of Acapulco. Afterward, go to the open-air market, el Parasal, for souvenir hunting and photo opportunities of the Mexican coastline.	Leisurely
	All ages
	$85/$72 (3-9)
	3.5 hours

ATV Adventure [AC24]

	Sports
New! Take a 45-minute motorcoach ride through the Mexican countryside and arrive at a local ranch. Once here, you will meet your guide, who will go over safety and handling issues. You will then ride your ATV through palm nurseries, over rolling hills, and along the streets of a Mexican village. Eventually, you will arrive at Bonfil Beach, where you will drive along the coast and up and down sand dunes. After your ATV adventures at the beach, return to the ranch for a picnic-style lunch and beverage. Helmets and goggles are provided.	Active
	Ages 18 & up
	$94
	4 hours

Ancient Petroglyphs of Palma Sola [AC06]

	Tour
New! Viewing a more authentic side of Acapulco is possible only a short distance from town. A 30-minute drive to El Veladaro National Park, which is home to early stone carvings of people and animals. These carvings, believed to be made as early as 600 A.D., offer a unique view into early Mexican civilization. After your two-hour visit at the park, stop at a local handicraft market, where you can shop for local handmade goods such as pottery, jewelry, and baskets. After the market, you'll stop at a seaside restaurant, where a snack and beverage will be provided as part of the excursion price.	Active
	Ages 10 & up
	$52
	4.5 hours

See page 172 for a key to the shore excursion description charts and their icons.

Acapulco On Your Own

For those who want to get a head start on their excursion plans, or just want to do it on their own, here is some information on tour operators in Acapulco. Please note that we have not used these operators, nor is any mention here an endorsement of their services. **Acuario Tours** offers city tours, history tours, and birds and botanical tours. For more information, visit http://www.acapulco.com/en/tours/acuario, or call 744-485-6100. Beyond this, we were unable to find good excursion operators. If you want to do it on your own, we suggest you either stick to spots you can walk to or take a taxi, or use one of Disney's excursions.

© MediaMarx, Inc.

Dave at Fort San Diego in Acapulco

Panama Canal
(Repositioning Itineraries)

Welcome to one of the great, **man-made wonders** of the world. While Disney Cruise passengers won't be debarking in Panama, the roughly eight hours spent traversing this fabled passage may be more eventful and fascinating than any other port along this grand voyage, with the possible exception of Los Angeles.

Disney Magic transversing the Panama Canal

To a large extent, the tale of Panama is the **tale of the canal**, and you'll be witnessing it first-hand as the Magic passes through its massive locks and cruises across man-made lakes and through a towering, man-made gorge. You'll follow in the footsteps of Spanish explorers, American railroaders, French canal-builders, and the most "bully" of American Presidents. You can only begin to imagine what the canal has meant to world growth and commerce as you contemplate the ships that had to sail 'round the Horn of South America in the era before the canal. And you can watch it all from the comfort of your verandah or from the height of deck 10.

The **notion for a canal** (and a route very close to today's actual path) goes back to the early days of Spanish rule. The explorer Vasco Nuñez de Balboa was the first to cross Panama (and "discover" the Pacific) in 1513. By 1534, King Carlos V of Spain commissioned a survey to plan a canal, which concluded that current technology wasn't up to the task. Gold from Peru and other Pacific Coast Spanish holdings crossed the isthmus by mule train instead. In the wake of the California Gold Rush of 1849, U.S. interests built a railroad across the narrow isthmus, so for the first time, transcontinental cargoes could bypass the long route around South America. However, passing goods from ship to rail and back to ship again wasn't the easiest or cheapest way to get things done.

Continued on next page

Size: 50 miles/80 km. long	
Transit Time: 8 hours (with waiting time prior to entry, 24 hours)	
Gain in Altitude: 85 feet/26 meters	
Narrowest Channel: 630 feet/192 meters (in Gaillard Cut)	
Climate: Tropical	**Temperatures:** 79°F (26°C) to 84°F (34°C)
Time Zone: Eastern (DST not observed)	

Sidebar tabs: Introduction · Reservations · Staterooms · Dining · Activities · Ports of Call · Magic · Index

AMBIENCE · HISTORY · FACTS

HISTORY (continued)

Introduction
Reservations
Staterooms
Dining
Activities
Ports of Call
Magic
Index

Discovering the History of the Panama Canal

The **notion of a canal across Panama** was studied by the U.S. in the 1870s, but it was the French who moved it forward, fresh from their triumphal success building the Suez Canal and flush with the machinery and optimism of the Industrial Revolution. The same Ferdinand de Lesseps who led the construction of Suez leapt to the challenge of Panama, and Alexandre Gustave Eiffel (yes, the fellow responsible for the structural supports for the Statue of Liberty and the tower that bears his name) was among the French engineers involved. Alas, de Lesseps was overconfident and under-equipped—he originally aimed to build a sea-level canal, similar to the one he built in Egypt, with no locks at all, just a deep trench all the way across the isthmus. French investors poured huge sums into the 20-year project, but Panama's landslide-prone hillsides consumed all the money, while accidents and tropical diseases consumed the lives of more than 20,000 construction workers who had been recruited by the French from throughout the Caribbean basin. Confident from its military success in the Spanish American War and now a global power, the United States was more than eager to see the project finished for its military and commercial benefits. President Theodore Roosevelt led the charge. The government of Colombia, which then controlled the isthmus, wasn't well-inclined to let the U.S. follow in France's footsteps. So the U.S. lent its support to the local Panamanian independence movement and received the 50-mile-long, 10-mile-wide Panama Canal Zone as a thank you from the new nation. The U.S. paid the French $40 million to take ownership of the project, and placed the U.S. military in charge of construction. Learning from French mistakes, the Army engineers brought massive, innovative machinery to the task and chose to build a canal with locks and man-made lakes, rather than try to dig all the way down to sea level. At about the same time, Army surgeon Walter Reed (then stationed in Cuba), learned that mosquitoes were responsible for both Yellow Fever and Malaria. The canal project was among the first times this knowledge was applied, through a Herculean effort at controlling the insects' habitat and propagation. Without the improved health conditions, the canal may never have been finished. Although it's hard to believe, this huge government project actually came in under budget and six months ahead of schedule, opening with little fanfare (thanks to the start of World War I) on August 15, 1914, ten years after the U.S. started construction. Proving to be a masterwork of design and construction, the Panama Canal continued to operate under U.S. ownership until December 31, 1999, when the U.S. ceded the canal and the Canal Zone to the government of Panama.

Enjoying the Sights of the Panama Canal

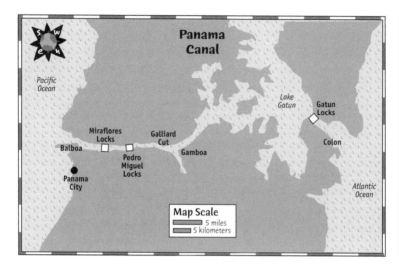

Whether your eyes are fixed on verdant hillsides or the mechanical marvels of the canal's locks, you'll be **viewing it all from the comfort of the ship**. The lower decks offer the most intimate view of your passage through the locks. Outside staterooms on decks 1 and 2, and public areas on deck 3, have an ultra-close-up view of the walls of the locks, until the ship rises above them. You can even catch some of the action from the windows in Parrot Cay during breakfast or lunch. Diversions on deck 3 forward, and the big portholes in Route 66, are also comfy viewing spots. Otherwise, we highly recommend heading to the promenade on deck 4. For those preferring a bird's-eye view, deck 10 has its advantages, and lunch on the deck behind Topsider's Buffet (deck 9 aft) is particularly scenic. Cruisers do crowd deck 10 forward, so consider abandoning that deck for a lower deck to see the action at the locks. In 2005, the Panama Canal Authority provided a tour guide on the Disney Magic as it passed through the canal, giving us all expert commentary over the ship's public address system.

Geographical Facts—Though we may casually imagine that the canal runs east/west between the Caribbean and Pacific, thanks to a little kink of geography, it actually runs from the Caribbean on the north to the Pacific on the south! The flood-prone Chagres River provides much of the water for the canal. A large dam and reservoir controls the river's flow into Gatun Lake, and from there, the river's waters flow into both the Caribbean and Pacific.

Knowing the Most
About the Panama Canal

TIPS AND TRIVIA

When constructed, **Gatun Lake** was the largest man-made lake in the world, its dam the largest earthen dam on Earth, and the canal's locks were the largest structures ever built of concrete. More than 900,000 vessels have passed through the canal since it opened. More than 5% of the world's trade goods pass through every year.

No water pumps are required to fill and drain the lock chambers (66 million "gallons per flush"/250 million liters). Electrically controlled valves are opened and closed, and gravity does the rest in about eight minutes. Each chamber's water requirements are met by 18-foot/5.5-m. diameter water tunnels. • Up to eight custom-built electric locomotives help guide ships through each lock. • Electricity to operate the canal's locks and locomotives is generated by dams along the canal. • The Panama Canal is a two-lane "highway," with a pair of side-by-side lock chambers at every elevation. • The largest of the steel lock gates are 65 feet/19.8 m. wide, 82 feet/25 m. tall, and 7 feet/2.13 m. thick and weigh more than 662 tons/600 metric tons. • Each lock chamber is 1,000 feet/305 m. long and 110 feet/35 m. wide—the Disney Magic is just 36 feet /11 m. shorter, and 6 feet/1.8 m. narrower than the locks.

What do we save by going through the Panama Canal instead of the **old route around the "horn" (southern tip) of South America**? More than 9,000 nautical miles/16,668 km., greater than the distance from Los Angeles to Hong Kong! Port Canaveral to Los Angeles 'round the Horn is approx. 14,500 mi./26,850 km. To look at it another way, the earth's circumference at the equator is 21,600 nautical miles/40,000 km. At the Magic's cruising speed of 21.5 knots (and ignoring stops at such fabled ports-of-call as Caracas, Rio de Janeiro, Montevideo, Santiago, and Lima), that would be at least 20 more days at sea. Not that another 20 days on the Magic would be such a tragedy, but we'd also have to cope with some of the worst oceangoing weather on Earth. And since it'd be the depths of winter down at Cape Horn... no, we wouldn't want to go there!

The Magic's beam (width) and length are at the canal's (current) maximum size. That makes the Magic a **"Panamax" vessel**. Did you know there's an entire class of "Post-Panamax" cruise ships, including the Queen Mary II and Royal Caribbean's Voyager of the Seas, that can't fit through the canal at all? Disney's new ships will be "Post-Panamax," but by 2014 the canal will expand to handle them.

Passing Through the Panama Canal

POINTS OF INTEREST

Introduction

Reservations

Staterooms

Dining

Activities

Ports of Call

Magic

Index

In the absence of shore excursions, here's a step-by-step description of the **canal's major points of interest**, in Caribbean-to-Pacific order. Just work your way up from the bottom if you're on the August, Port Canaveral-bound sailing.

Colon—The second-largest city in Panama guards the canal's Caribbean entrance. Canal-bound ships pass the long Cristobal breakwater and one of the most extensive port facilities in the Caribbean.

Gatun Locks—Three successive lock chambers take ships from the Caribbean Sea to the canal's maximum altitude of 85 feet/26 m. All together, the lock complex is about a mile long, and each lock lifts the ship between 27 and 30 feet.

Gatun Lake—This was the world's largest man-made lake when it was built, at 163 square miles/422 km. sq. All the water necessary to operate the canal is impounded here and in an auxiliary lake and dam farther up the Chagres River. Various engineering improvements recently increased the lake's depth by one foot, resulting in a substantial increase in the maximum cargo that can be carried through the canal.

Gaillard Cut (Culebra Cut)—This 8.75-mile/14-km. man-made passage cuts through the ridge of hills that marks the Continental Divide. The cut runs from Gamboa on the Chagres River on the north to the town of Pedro Miguel on the south. To cross the Continental Divide, a gap was punched through the lowest point (333.5 feet/102.26 m.) on the ridge connecting Gold Hill (587 feet/179 m.) on the east and Contractors Hill on the west. Landslides were a constant problem during construction and are still a concern today. Contractors Hill, named in honor of the companies that worked on the project, was originally 377 feet/115 m. tall, but it has been cut down to reduce the risk of landslides. Originally named for the nearby village of Culebra, the passage was renamed in honor of the engineer who led the American construction of this section of the canal. The channel has been widened several times during the canal's history, most recently in 2002. Two Panamax-sized ships can now pass in the night (or any other time). With more than a third of all ships passing through the canal Panamaxed-out, easy two-way traffic is critical to the efficient use of the canal.

Passing Through
the Panama Canal

Pedro Miguel Locks—One lock chamber moves ships in a single, 31-foot step between the canal's maximum elevation in the Gaillard Cut and Gatun Lake and the intermediate level of Miraflores Lake.

Miraflores Lake—This mile-long man-made lake is 45 feet above sea level and exists to connect the Pedro Miguel and Miraflores locks.

Miraflores Locks—Two lock chambers move ships in 27-foot steps between Miraflores Lake and the Pacific Ocean. The lower chamber of the two has the tallest gates on the canal, necessary to accommodate the Pacific's tidal variations. This is also the site of the canal's visitor center (not that we'll be landing to pay it a visit).

Balboa and Panama City—You're through the locks and headed to the Pacific! Dramatic Centennial Bridge crosses the channel, connecting Balboa to the west with Panama City to the east. Other sights include the Amador Causeway, a 3.25-mile-long breakwater and recreational development built with rock from the construction of the Gaillard Cut, and the canal's Administration Building on a hill overlooking the canal.

You can get a **preview** of your Panama Canal crossing at the official Panama Canal web site at http://www.pancanal.com. Not only does the web site offer helpful descriptions of the various points of interest you'll pass, but there are live webcams, too!

Wondering how we can get through the locks without bumping the sides when the Disney Magic is a mere 6 feet narrower than the locks themselves? While the Magic runs under its own propulsion, four to eight small **railroad engines called "mules"** run on tracks on either side of the locks to keep the ship centered with attached cables. The mules can also help with towing and braking.

© MediaMarx, Inc.

A "mule" alongside the Disney Magic

While we can't say for sure **how much it costs** the Disney Magic to pass through the Panama Canal, we can say that ships of similar size have had to pay from $150,000 to $200,000 for passage! And you thought the tolls on the New Jersey Turnpike were high!

Cartagena
(Eastbound Repositioning Itinerary)

Whether the name Cartagena conjures images of "Romancing the Stone" with Michael Douglas and Kathleen Turner, marauding pirates chasing Spanish gold, or less romantic images of drug cartel-related crime, Cartagena's popular image does not match the port city's reality. Upscale beach resorts, a glittering, high-rise skyline, and a beautifully preserved **old city** that has earned UNESCO World Heritage Site status will be more than enough to fill your eight hours ashore.

© Lobo

Castillo San Felipe de Barajas

AMBIENCE

This is a **vibrant**, **cosmopolitan city** with deep colonial roots and an optimistic future, as well as Colombia's number one tourist destination. Cartagena has a large harbor protected by barrier islands; a well-preserved Spanish Colonial old city; ancient fortresses; glamorous, densely packed beachfront high-rises; and glitzy shopping districts, yet pristine beaches and nature areas are a short drive (or sail) away.

HISTORY & CULTURE

When the Spanish Conquistadors plundered Peru and Colombia of its gold, it was hoarded and then loaded onto galleons in Cartagena. This appealing fact was not lost on pirates like Francis Drake, and even military forces from France and England. For years the marauders came and fortifications rose up around the thriving port. Certainly, Walt Disney's **Pirates of the Caribbean** could have been inspired by Cartagena. Alas, the locals don't forgive or forget the actions of the British and French, or the American politicians who managed to wrest Panama from Colombia so the canal could be built without local opposition. Warfare has dominated recent Colombian history, although Cartagena was affected less than many other areas. The current government of President Alvaro Uribe is credited with doing much to reduce violence and build the local economy, leading to Cartagena's return to the ranks of popular tourist destinations.

FACTS

Size: 235 sq. mi./609 sq. km.	
Climate: Tropical	**Temperatures**: 87°F (30°C) to 90°F (32°C)
Population: 895,000	**Busy Season**: November to March
Language: Spanish	**Money**: Colombian Peso (1,935 Pesos = $1 U.S.)
Time Zone: Eastern (DST observed)	**Transportation**: Walking, taxis, buses
Phones: Dial 112 for police, 132 for Red Cross, 113 for tourist info	

Introduction
Reservations
Staterooms
Dining
Activities
Ports of Call
Magic
Index

Making the Most of Cartagena

GETTING THERE

Your ship docks in the busy port's **Manga district**, in a modern container ship facility and close to an upscale neighborhood of luxury high-rise residences and yacht basins. You're a short drive from the old, walled city that will be visited by most excursions. All ashore is at 9:30 am, all aboard at 5:30 pm.

We generally recommend you **book a Disney shore excursion**, which takes care of all your transportation needs. If you want to venture out on your own, a **taxi tour** is popular. Know that taxis are not metered, but operate on a zone system. The minimum fare is around $2; a one-hour drive may cost $8. A taxi to the old city should cost about $5 one way. You will see several taxi drivers at the pier, but if you walk past them and out to the port gates, you'll find more taxis at better rates. Car rentals? Forget about it!

© Lobo

Cartagena bus

STAYING SAFE

All of Colombia is on the U.S. State Department's watch list, but violent crime isn't the problem movies and TV might lead you to believe. **Fleecing tourists**, on the other hand, appears to be high art. Colombian "emeralds," "Cuban" cigars, "Pre-Colombian" art and gold, money changing, picked pockets, swiped handbags, drug purchase shakedowns … you name it, there seems to be a scam built around it. Naturally, the upscale, higher-priced shops are far more reputable, and you undoubtedly pay for the peace of mind. Look for "recommended" shops in your Shopping in Paradise guide. While limited to advertisers, at least the publisher's shopping guarantee offers some recourse. Note that you need an export permit for Pre-Colombian goods of any sort, but reputable dealers should explain that. Fakes, of course, don't require a permit—just make sure you paid a low, low price. Definitely carry only small bills of U.S. currency—getting change will be either expensive or mark you as a juicy target. Despite that, Cartagena is a very popular vacation destination. Fortunately, since you'll be on your way out of town before dark, will most likely be taking a guided excursion, won't talk to or make eye contact with hustlers or beggars, and won't be going off the beaten track (right?), you should be able to avoid major trouble.

Touring Cartagena

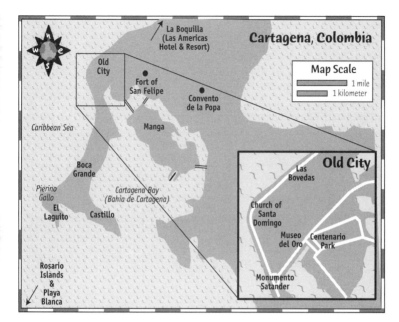

Cartagena, Colombia

Map Scale
1 mile
1 kilometer

Old City

Popular spots visited by official shore excursions include the old city, with four neighborhoods packed within massive city walls; El Centro, with the greatest concentration of historic sites—its Plaza de Bolívar alone can keep you busy for hours, surrounded as it is by the Palace of the Inquisition, the Gold Museum, the Cathedral (Basilica Menor), and La Gobierno, seat of the State of Bolivar. The well-known Clock Tower and the Church and Monastery of San Pedro Claver are also here. Other districts are San Diego, La Matuna, and the oldest, Getsemani, with its large Parque del Centenario. La Popa Hill rises about 500 feet/150 meters above the city in a wooded setting, just a mile from El Centro and beachfront areas. Views from the hilltop Convent la Popa are quite dramatic. Between the walled city and la Popa looms massive Castillo San Felipe de Barajas (see photo on page 281), the largest Spanish fortress in the New World.

For **more information**, visit http://www.cartagenainfo.net, http://www.cartagenacaribe.com/en and http://gosouthamerica. about.com/od/cartagena/Cartagena_Colombia.htm—these are all useful sites for additional information on the city.

CARTAGENA MAP

HIGHLIGHTS

Introduction

Reservations

Staterooms

Dining

Activities

Ports of Call

Magic

Index

Playing in Cartagena

ACTIVITIES

The **beaches** of Bocagrande are well known and convenient, but not necessarily the best of the best. You'll have to visit on your own—perhaps a two-mile taxi ride from the ship. In-town beach excursions take you to La Boquilla, just beyond the airport to the northeast of El Centro. Both these beach areas are dominated by the adjoining hotels, with more elbow room to be had at La Boquilla. A trip to out-of-town Playa Blanca or Islas de Rosario promise far more attractive surroundings, but greatly reduce the time you'll have to tour in-town sights. La Boquilla (Las Americas Hotel), Playa Blanca, and Islas de Rosario are all offered as shore excursions by Disney Cruise Line. Playa Blanca is perhaps the area's finest beach, on Baru Island about 20 miles southwest of the city, often reached by a water taxi leaving from the edge of the old city (opposite the modern convention center). Islas de Rosario is a group of lightly developed islands about 20 miles southwest of El Centro, just offshore from larger Baru Island. The islands host a number of resorts and vacation homes.

Two areas are big on the one-day-visitor's **shopping map**: Las Bóvedas, an arcade of handcraft shops and galleries built into the north corner of the old city's walls in the San Diego district, and the Pierino Gallo shopping mall in Laguito at the far south end of Bocagrande—both are common tour group stops. Leather goods, jewelry, crafts, and antique shops are scattered about the old city for those with time to browse, and a budget-busting combination of high-end leather, fashion, and jewelry shops (emeralds and silver and gold, oh my!) lines Avenida San Martín in Bocagrande and the Pierino Gallo mall.

Popular tourist **destinations** include Manga, a large island in the harbor that is home to upscale residential development, historic forts, yacht clubs, and a modern container port (and the Magic's moorings). Bocagrande (also, Boca Grande) is a long, beachfront peninsula directly to the southwest of El Centro, known for its hotels, shopping, dining, and waterfront promenade. Tierra Bomba is a large, mostly undeveloped island in the mouth of Bahía de Cartagena (Cartagena Bay), south of Bocagrande. The Fort of San José de Bocachica is situated on a small island just offshore of Tierra Bomba. Cienaga de la Virgen, a destination for eco-excursions, is a large lagoon just behind a strip of barrier-beach hotels, about a half-mile from the airport in the northwest corner of the city.

Embarking on Shore Excursions in Cartagena

Best of Cartagena [CT01]

Travel to the center of Cartagena by motorcoach and marvel at the lush vegetation and hillsides that surround you. The first stop will be at Convento de la Popa, a 400-year-old monastery used as a meeting place by local Indians and runaway slaves. After 25 minutes, you'll travel to the largest Spanish fort built in the New World. Fort of San Felipe de Barajas was built in the 17th century with towering walls and sprawling grounds. Next explore the dungeons of Las Bovedas—originally built for storage, they are now occupied by vendors selling handcrafts and jewelry. You'll also visit San Pedro Claver Church and the Navy Museum of the Caribbean. Finish the excursion by traveling to Pierino Gallo mall for some sightseeing and shopping before traveling back to the ship.

Tour
Leisurely
All ages
$42/$29 (3-9)
4.5-5 hours

City Drive, Shopping, and La Popa [CT02]

Learn about the historical and cultural values of Cartagena as you travel by motorcoach to the city center. After the guided tour, stop at Convento de la Popa and marvel at the 400-year-old architecture and well-kept grounds. Next, walk to the dungeons of Las Bovedas filled with vendors selling handmade goods and crafts. Board the motorcoach again and view many colonial buildings and the new modern neighborhood of Bocagrande. Finally, stop at the Pierino Gallo shopping center for some shopping featuring gold, emeralds, and handcrafts, then enjoy the trip back to the ship.

Tour
Leisurely
All ages
$49/$24 (3-9)
3.5 hours

Deluxe Cartagena & Fortress With Folklore Show [CT03]

A short 20-minute drive will take you to the historic Convento de la Popa monastery. This 400-year-old structure was built on La Popa hill and acted as sanctuary for both local Indians and slaves. Next board the motorcoach and an experienced guide will point out different points of interest. You'll also visit the largest fort built by Spain in the New World, Fort of San Felipe de Barajas, the dungeons of Las Bovedas, and the Navy Museum of the Caribbean. You'll then be treated to a Colombian folklore show with traditional dances and songs. Finally, travel to Pierino Gallo shopping mall for shopping before returning to the ship.

Tour
Leisurely
All ages
$49/$32 (3-9)
4.5-5 hours

Historic Cartagena Old City Walking Tour [CT04]

Start out by taking a 20-minute motorcoach ride to the center of Cartagena for a walking tour of the city's historic centers. See Plaza de Bolivar, a tree-lined square with statues representing Colombia's past. See Palaciao de la Inquisicion, housing torture chambers and jails used during the Spanish Inquisition. Visit Museo de Oro, or the Gold Museum, displaying over 600 pre-Colombian gold treasures. Visit the Church of Santo Domingo, Plaza de la Aduana, Plaza de la Proclamation, Plaza de la San Pedro Claver, and the dungeons of Las Bovedas, too.

Tour
Active
All ages
$39/$24 (3-9)
4.5 hours

Mangroves Eco Tour [CT05]

Board an air-conditioned motorcoach for a scenic, 30-minute trip to Las Americas Hotel and Resort. Upon your arrival at the resort, you'll climb into a canoe and glide among the swamps and mangroves of the Cienaga de la Virgen. Your guide will point out flora and fauna during your one-hour trip. After the cruise, relax and enjoy a complimentary beverage before boarding the motorcoach for the return trip. Note that guests do not paddle the canoe. Max. canoe weight is 250 lbs. per person.

Tour
Active
Ages 5 & up
$59/$49 (5-9)
2.5-3 hours

Introduction

Reservations

Staterooms

Dining

Activities

Ports of Call

Magic

Index

Embarking on Shore Excursions
in Cartagena *(continued)*

☐ Tour of the Rosario Islands [CT06]

Take a speedboat ride past the beauty of the Colombian coast to the Rosario Islands to enjoy all that the Islands have to offer. Designated a National Natural Park, the Rosario Islands are made up of 27 islands boasting activities ranging from sightseeing to snorkeling. If you wish to snorkel, a small boat can take you to a nearby reef that is teeming with tropical fish and stunning coral formations. If snorkeling is not your thing, beaches are plentiful for swimming or relaxing in a cozy beach chair. Lunch and beverages are included.

Tour
Leisurely
Ages 5 & up
$110/$89 (5-9)
5.5-6 hours

☐ Spanish History & Fort of San Jose de Bocachica [CT08]

Set off on a 15-minute walk through the port and board a boat that will take you to Fort of San Jose de Bocachica. Sit back and enjoy a 45-minute guided tour along the coast of Cartagena while the guide points out historic points of interest. Once at the fort, take a guided tour to see the barracks and walk over the moat that was once inhabited by sharks that served as a deterrent for bad behavior. After a one-hour visit, you will return to port, viewing quaint fishing villages, mangroves, and the largest Spanish fort in the New World along the way.

Tour
Leisurely
Ages 5 & up
$52/$45 (5-9)
3-3.5 hours

☐ Cartagena Beach & Boating Tour [CT09]

After a short 15-minute walk, you'll board a boat and relax with a 45-minute narrated cruise as you travel past tropical islands and small fishing villages. After a 10-minute stop at the 18th century Fort of San Jose de Bocachica, you will journey to Baru Island and one of Cartegena's finest beaches, Playa Blanca. This beach offers a beautiful sandy coast and crystal clear water. Enjoy a guided tour of the jungle and walk along the coastline, or just relax in beach chairs and enjoy complimentary beverages.

Tour
Leisurely
Ages 5 & up
$78/$62 (5-9)
4 hours

☐ Los Americas Pool and Beach Getaway [CT10]

Take a motorcoach through neighborhoods of elaborate mansions and old world architecture as you make your way to Las Americas Hotel and Resort. Once at the resort, enjoy a beverage and explore the grounds. Take a dip in the Atlantic Ocean or relax in a beach chair. If the ocean is not for you, swim in one of the resort's three pools or play a round of miniature golf. Then enjoy a mouth-watering buffet lunch consisting of grilled chicken, steak, fish, salad, dessert, and more. After lunch, rest a while before returning to the ship.

Tour
Leisurely
All ages
$89/$69 (3-9)
5-5.5 hours

☐ Mangroves, Show, and Lunch [CT11]

As you travel by motorcoach to Las Americas Hotel and Resort, view the tropical landscapes that surround Cartagena. Once at the resort, board a canoe and follow your guide through the mangroves of Cienaga de la Virgen. View the canopies of trees, and as you glide through them smell the sweet scent of the flowers. Returning to the resort, you'll enjoy a buffet lunch and then take a quick dip in one of the resort's three pools. Your adventure concludes with a show featuring the folklore of Colombia's past before returning to the ship.

Tour
Active
Ages 5 & up
$110/$85 (5-9)
5-5.5 hours

See page 172 for a key to the shore excursion description charts and their icons.

Aruba
(Repositioning Itineraries)

© I2UIY/NH7DX

Aruba beach

Baked by the tropical sun and just 17 miles from the coast of Venezuela, Aruba is noteworthy for soft, white sand beaches, reliably sunny, warm weather year-round, and its nice, warm welcome to tourists. Aruba is the quintessential "**desert island**."

AMBIENCE

The island's long southwest coast is blessed by gentle surf and **broad, sandy beaches**, and this is where most of the resorts and population reside. The rugged northeast shore is exposed to rough seas and is sparsely populated, home to a National Park that occupies 18% of the island's area. Downtown Oranjestad (named for the Netherland's House of Orange, not the citrus fruit) boasts colorful Dutch-Antillean buildings, whose masonry outlines borrow heavily from Dutch and Spanish Colonial influences, while sporting the color sense of the islands. The island is mostly flat, with the tallest hills topping off at barely 500 feet above the nearby sea.

HISTORY & CULTURE

It may be soothing to learn that Arubans consider aloe to be one of the islands first sources of wealth (produced for the past 100 years). "Soothing" may also be the word for the island's history. **No pirates or warfare**, for the most part, mar its history. Near-painless exchanges of control between Spain, the Netherlands, England, and back to the Netherlands, a brief gold rush in the 1800s; an easy transition from Dutch colonial rule after World War II; and eventual separation from the rest of the Netherland Antilles leave Aruba as an autonomous part of the Kingdom of the Netherlands. The climate is too dry for most agriculture (although cactus does quite nicely), but it supplies a nice, safe location for oil refineries just 17 miles from the South American mainland. Most of the population still descends from the native Arawaks, a group that was nearly wiped out elsewhere.

FACTS

Size: 21 miles/33 km. long by 6 miles/9 km. wide (75 sq. mi./193 sq. km.)	
Climate: Dry Arid (Desert)	**Temperatures**: 85°F (29°C) to 89°F (32°C)
Population: 100,000	**Busy Season**: November to March
Language: Dutch, Papiamento	**Money**: Aruba Guilder (Florin) (1.79 AWG = $1 U.S.)
Time Zone: Atlantic (DST not observed)	**Transportation**: Walking, taxis, buses
Phones: Dial 112 for police, 132 for Red Cross, 113 for tourist info	

Making the Most of Aruba

GETTING THERE

Your ship docks at one of five cruise ship berths in the heart of Aruba's capital city, **Oranjestad**. Three separate terminal buildings serve the various berths, each providing tourist services and some shopping. Taxis await your fare right on the pier. Shopping and nearby sights are a short walk from the piers. All ashore at 7:30 am (westbound itinerary) or 7:00 am (eastbound itinerary). All aboard is 9:30 pm (westbound) or 11:30 pm (eastbound).

GETTING AROUND

Car rentals are plentiful (the agencies are by the airport, a few miles southeast from the pier), roads are in generally good repair, and Arubans drive U.S.-style, on the right-hand side of the road. Jeeps are popular and useful for driving the dirt roads of the north end of the island. However, unless you're off in search of adventure, we don't see a practical reason to rent—most beaches are within a few miles of town, so taxis will usually be more economical. Taxi fares are government regulated, with fixed fares to various destinations around the island (no meters). As nearly all points of interest are likely to be visited by shore excursions, they remain, as always, your safest bet.

SHOPPING

Befitting a port that can (and does) host five cruise ships at one time, there are plenty of **pleasant shopping opportunities** within comfortable walking distance of the pier. This isn't quite duty-free shopping, though you can still do well if you know your prices and values. Handcrafts and artworks are sold from small stalls on and near the pier. Royal Plaza Mall is the closest major shopping "op," immediately across L.G. Smith Blvd. from the pier. Next to that is Seaport Village Mall, and a bit beyond that, on a landfill jutting into the harbor, is Seaport Market. If you head inland another block to Haven Str./Zoutman Str., and Main Street beyond that, you'll find even more shops there and around the town's colorful central square.

STAYING SAFE

With one of the **highest living standards** in the Caribbean, crimes against tourists are fairly low. Regular precautions are, of course, in order. Specifically, we recommend you keep any money you may have won at a casino under wraps (as Kenny says, "you never count your money when you're sittin' at the table"). Don't leave valuables in your beach bag—when possible, leave them back on the ship, locked in your safe. If you rent a car and plan to get a Jeep, bring a backpack so you can keep all your belongings with you when you get out (Jeeps have no hiding places and are prime targets).

Touring Aruba

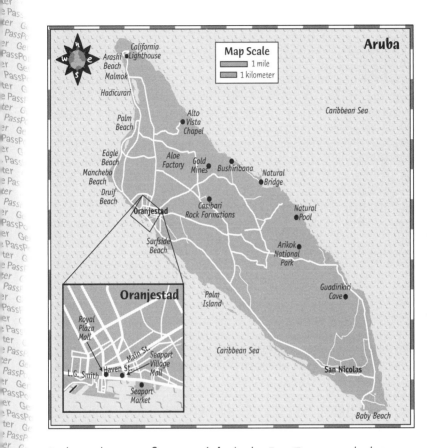

Aruba

Map Scale
- 1 mile
- 1 kilometer

California Lighthouse
Arashi Beach
Malmok
Hadicurari

Caribbean Sea

Palm Beach

Alto Vista Chapel

Eagle Beach
Manchebo Beach
Druif Beach

Aloe Factory
Gold Mines
Bushiribana
Natural Bridge

Oranjestad

Casibari Rock Formations

Natural Pool

Surfside Beach

Arikok National Park

Palm Island

Guadirikiri Cave

Caribbean Sea

San Nicolas

Baby Beach

Oranjestad

Royal Plaza Mall
L.G. Smith
Haven St.
Main St.
Seaport Village Mall
Seaport Market

ARUBA MAP

Introduction
Reservations
Staterooms
Dining
Activities
Ports of Call
Magic
Index

HIGHLIGHTS

Perhaps the **most famous sight** is the Fort Zoutman clock tower, about three blocks southwest of the pier between L.G. Smith Blvd. and Zoutman Str. Until recently it housed the island's principal museum, which may or may not be back in operation in a new location by the time the Magic visits. There is also the Numismatic Museum, just a block from the pier on West Street, with 30,000 coins on display. Probably the most rewarding pursuit is wandering the colorful streets near the pier. Fish, produce, and craft vendors can be found on the waterfront. Haven and Zoutman Streets run a block inland from the waterfront, with Wilhemina Str. branching off at the central square. From the square, Kazeme Str. leads you two blocks to Betico Croes (Main St.), which is about as far inland as a tourist needs to go. The façade of the old City Hall, used for weddings, is a popular sight here.

Playing in Aruba

ACTIVITIES

The nearest **beaches** are not quite walking distance, but very easily reached by taxi or even local bus via L.G. Smith Blvd., which parallels the waterfront. Druif Beach is to the northwest of the pier, Surfside is to the southeast, close to the end of the airport runway. Both are supported by resort facilities. West of Druif Beach is a near-continuous stretch of sand and beach resorts that wrap around the southwest and west shores. While nude sunbathing is illegal (and an affront to local sensibilities), topless sunbathing is hardly unknown at Manchebo Beach (which is also the largest beach on the island). Continuing north up the coast, Eagle and Palm beaches are in the heart of hotel country, offering a wide range of watersport options and amenities. At the north end of the strip, Malmok and Arashi beaches offer good swimming and snorkeling, but few amenities. Off to the extreme southeast beyond the oil refinery, Baby Beach is a popular, reef-protected lagoon with gentle surf but few facilities.

At latest count there are 11 **casinos** in Aruba, most of them associated with the resort hotels that line the beaches to the northwest of Oranjested. These include the Holiday Inn SunSpree, Hyatt Regency, Radisson, La Cabana, and Manchebo resorts. These all have beach and recreational offerings that should keep the whole family happy. Closest to the pier is the Crystal Casino in the Renaissance Aruba hotel, about a block southeast on L.G. Smith Blvd.

Scuba, snorkel, and wind surfing are all popular activities, and thanks to the mostly wild northeast shore, off-road vehicle tours abound. Arashi and Malmok beaches, at the far north of the western beach strip, are popular snorkel destinations, and a bit south of that, Hadicurari is known for windsurfing. Also near Arashi Beach, Tierra del Sol is an 18-hole Robert Trent Jones II golf course—make reservations and find information at http://www.tierradelsol.com/golf.

Out-of-town Sights: Arikok National Park to the northeast offers hiking opportunities amidst cactus and low scrub. One of the island's better-known sights, Natural Bridge (a seaside coral arch), collapsed in 2005. Bashiribana is a stone ruin—a smelting operation leftover from gold mining days. Alto Vista Chapel is a quaint, stone and stucco church on the rugged northern seacoast. California Lighthouse is a tall, photogenic lighthouse on the northwest point of the island near Malmok Beach. Palm Beach hosts Butterfly Farm, one of several such exhibits in the Caribbean.

Embarking on Shore Excursions
in Aruba

☐ Sailing and Snorkeling [AR09] ☀ 🛍 📷

A 45-minute catamaran ride will take you to Boca Cathalina, where you will get up close and personal with schools of tropical fish and coral formations. Next travel to a shipwreck (a German freighter that was sunk in 1940). Enjoy complimentary beverages on the trip back to port. Allow 3.5 hours.	**Sports**
	Active
	Ages 5 & up
	$35/$25 (5-9)

☐ Sailaway Beach & Snorkel [AR02] ☀ 🛍 📷

Journey by motorboat to Arashi Beach to swim and snorkel. View tropical fish and look at unique coral reefs. From here, you will get to snorkel the site of the Antilla shipwreck. After snorkeling, enjoy complimentary lunch and beverages on the beach at Pelican Pier in Palm Beach. Allow 5.5 hours.	**Sports**
	Active
	All ages
	$69/$49 (3-9)

☐ Kayak Adventure [AR07] ☀ 🛍 📷

An open-air bus will take you to Manguel Halto Beach, where you will get to swim and snorkel. Then meet your guide, get your kayak, and start your adventure as you paddle through the Barvadera Channel to view Aruba's Barrier Reef and Spanish Lagoon. Includes a light snack and beverage. Allow 4 hours.	**Sports**
	Very active
	Ages 10 & up
	$75

☐ Scuba Dive [AR08] ☀ 🛍 📷

Get the chance to explore two WWII shipwrecks with a two-tank scuba dive. You'll visit the Antilla (sunk in 1940 by Germany) and the Pedernalis (an oil tanker sunk by a German U-boat). Certified divers only. All scuba gear is provided, as is bottled water. Allow 4 hours.	**Sports**
	Very active
	Ages 12 & up
	$99

☐ Seatrek & De Palm Island [AR10] ☀ 🛍 📷

Cruise by ferry to Palm Island. Here, you will meet your guide, who will take you on a guided-helmet dive. The helmet provides continuous oxygen and is one of the easiest ways to dive. Dive approximately 20 feet to view coral formations and tropical fish. Afterward, enjoy lunch and the beach. Allow 4.5 hours.	**Sports**
	Active
	All ages
	$125

☐ De Palm Island Beach Getaway [AR14] ☀ 🛍 📷

Travel by ferry to Palm Island. At the island enjoy Blue Parrotfish Water Park with more than 70 water attractions. Try one of the hammocks on the beach, which are perfect for napping. Take in a game of beach volleyball or try snorkeling for an underwater adventure. Lunch included. Allow 4.5 hours.	**Sports**
	Active
	All ages
	$72/$36 (3-9)

☐ Natural Pool Jeep Adventure [AR11] ☀ 🛍 📷

You'll meet your guide and board a 4x4 Land Rover for an off-road tour of California Lighthouse, the Natural Bridge, and the Natural Pool. The most memorable point of the trip will be a dip in the Natural Pool, an ocean-filled volcanic stone formation. Beverages included. Allow 5 hours.	**Sports**
	Active
	Ages 6 & up
	$85/$45 (6-9)

☐ Half Day Jeep & Beach [AR12] ☀ 🛍 📷

Just a short distance from the ship, you'll meet your guide and board a 4x4 vehicle. Then travel off-road to the California Lighthouse, the Natural Bridge, and the Alto Vista Chapel. Next, visit a local beach for relaxation or swimming in the ocean after your dusty drive. Beverages included. Allow 4.5 hours.	**Sports**
	Active
	Ages 10 & up
	$59

See page 172 for a key to the shore excursion description charts and their icons.

Introduction
Reservations
Staterooms
Dining
Activities
Ports of Call
Magic
Index

Embarking on Shore Excursions
in Aruba (continued)

Baby Beach Jeep Adventure [AR15]

Meet your guide at the pier and get keys to your off-road vehicle. Set out through the country and make stops at the Natural Bridge, the Baby Natural Bridge, Arikok National Park, and Guadirikiri Cave. End up at the secluded Baby Beach where you can swim, snorkel, or hike. Beverages included. Allow 5 hours.	Sports
	Active
	Ages 10 & up
	$72

ATV Adventure [AR16]

A short 15-minute drive will bring you to base camp where you will meet your guide and get an all-terrain vehicle. You will visit the Balashi Gold Mines, the Arikok National Park, and the Natural Bridge. You'll also see the Bushiribana Gold Mill Ruins before returning to base camp for beverages. Allow 4 hours.	Sports
	Active
	Ages 18 & up
	$110

Aruba Safari Off-Road Adventure [AR17]

Meet your guide right at the pier and go over vehicle operation before going off-road. Drive/ride to the California Lighthouse, the Natural Bridges, Bushiribana Gold Mine, and Alto Vista Chapel. Board a ferry to Palm Island for a barbecue lunch and swimming at the Blue Parrotfish Water Park. Allow 7 hours.	Sports
	Active
	Ages 10 & up
	$99

Seaworld Explorer [AR01]

At Pelican Pier, board a transfer boat that will take you to the Seaworld Explorer. This semi-submarine boasts large glass windows that give the feeling of diving without getting wet. Up close, you will see the freighter Antilla sunk in 1940. Learn the ship's history during the 40-minute dive. Allow 2-2.5 hours.	Tour
	Leisurely
	All ages
	$45/$36 (3-9)

Submarine Expedition [AR04]

Take a 15-minute ferry ride to the submersible vessel, Atlantis. With large windows and comfortable seating, Atlantis explores the sunken ship Mi Dush I. Take pictures of the many fish that call this area home. You'll also visit a newly sunken ship. After the 45-minute dive, you'll return to port. Allow 2 hours.	Tour
	Leisurely
	Ages 4 & up
	$99/$57 (4-9)

Sea & See Island Tour [AR05]

A short ferry trip brings you to the semi-submersible vessel, Seaworld Explorer. Through the underwater viewing area, you'll see the sunken ship Antilla. After a 40-minute dive, enjoy a scenic drive to the California Lighthouse, the Natural Bridge, and Casibari Rock Formations. Allow 4.5 hours.	Tour
	Leisurely
	All ages
	$62/$42 (3-9)

Natural Wonders of Aruba [AR06]

Take a 15-minute bus ride to the Butterfly Farm for a guided tour. Then it's off to the Aloe Balm Facility for another guided tour. You'll then journey to the collapsed Natural Bridge on the coast, followed by a 25-minute tour through Oranjestad. Includes a complimentary beverage. Alow 3-3.5 hours.	Tour
	Leisurely
	All ages
	$45/$35 (3-9)

The Best of Aruba Island Tour [AR13]

Begin with a tour of Oranjestad on an air-conditioned bus, followed by a visit to the Casibari Rock formations. Then it's off to the collapsed Natural Bridge and Baby Bridge. You also visit the Aruba Aloe Factory and afterward relax at a local beach. Includes snack and beverage. Allow 4-4.5 hours.	Tour
	Leisurely
	All ages
	$42/$25 (3-9)

See page 172 for a key to the shore excursion description charts and their icons.

Castaway Cay
(All Caribbean and Repositioning Itineraries)

Castaway Cay is Disney's private island, exclusively for the use of Disney Cruise Line guests and crew. It's clean, safe, and well-themed, and lunch is complimentary on the island. We recommend you get up early on your Castaway Cay day—you don't want to miss a minute of the fun! This port is usually the last stop on most cruise itineraries.

© MediaMarx, Inc.

Megan and Natalie on Castaway Cay

AMBIENCE

Castaway Cay (pronounced "Castaway Key") is a **tropical retreat** with white sandy beaches, swaying palm trees, and aquamarine water. What makes it so magical is its theming—it's not unlike visiting one of Disney's excellent water parks, such as Typhoon Lagoon. The island even has its own legend—they say three explorers set sail with their families to the scattered islands of the Bahamas in search of fame and fortune. Their adventures brought them to this island, where they found sunken treasures, the secret of youth, and the skeletal remains of a giant whale. The explorers and their families remained on the beautiful island for years as castaways—you can still see the original structures and artifacts left behind.

HISTORY

Disney may call this out-island Castaway Cay, but in its previous incarnation it was **Gorda Cay**. The island is a part of the Abaco Bahamas island archipelago. Its history is murky. It may have first been inhabited by Lucayan Indians, "discovered" by the Spanish, later used as a harbor for pirates, and was long used by the Abaconians for farming pumpkins and sweet potatoes. In the '70s and '80s, the island was a base for drug operations. Disney leased the island and, over the next 18 months, spent $25 million to fix up 55 acres (only about 5% of the island). 50,000 truckloads of sand were dredged to make the beautiful beaches. Its extensive facilities are the best in the cruise industry. For more history, visit: http://web.outsideonline.com/magazine/0199/9901blackbeard.html

FACTS

Size: 2 mi. (3.2 km.) x 1.25 mi. (2 km.)	Distance: 260 nautical miles from home port
Climate: Subtropical	Temperatures: 66°F (19°C) to 88°F (31°C)
Language: English	Money: U.S. Dollar/stateroom charge
Time Zone: Eastern (DST observed)	Transportation: Walking, bicycles

Introduction Reservations Staterooms Dining Activities Ports of Call Magic Index

Making the Most of Castaway Cay

GETTING THERE

Thanks to a deep channel Disney dredged when it acquired the island, **your ship pulls right up to the dock** on Castaway Cay. Typical all-ashore time is 8:30 or 9:30 am, and you have until about 5:00 pm (7–8 hours) to play on this delightful island. When you alight from the ship, proceed down the dock (picking up towels on your way) to the island—it's about a 3-minute walk to the tram. Be aware that when the seas are rough, the ship may be unable to dock at Castaway Cay, and therefore, you'll be unable to visit. This is most likely to happen in January and February, but it can occur at any time. Note: We hear that the pier will be expanded and the slip will be deepened in preparation for Disney's new ships, but we're not sure when this will begin.

GETTING AROUND

Castaway Cay is the **easiest port to get around**, thanks to the well-marked paths and convenient trams. As you walk down the dock to the island, you'll pass the Castaway Cay post office on your right and Marge's Barges sea charters dock on your left, after which you'll reach a tram stop—hop aboard the next tram, or simply take the 10-minute walk to the family beach. Once you're at the family beach, you can continue down the path past buildings that house the restrooms, shops, and services. At the far end of the main path is the teen beach. The adults-only beach is accessible by another tram (or a long, hot, 25-minute walk down the airstrip) near the end of the main path. All locations are marked on the map on the next page, as well as on the color map Disney provides with your *Personal Navigator*.

DINING

Unlike the other ports, the Disney Cruise Line provides lunch on Castaway Cay. For complete details on Castaway Cay dining, see page 126 (we've repeated some of the same information here for your reference). Everyone can eat at **Cookie's BBQ** across from the family beach. Cookie's typically serves from 11:30 am to 2:00 pm, and offers the best selection with burgers, BBQ ribs, chicken sandwiches, corn on the cob, fruit, frozen yogurt, and cookies. Food is served buffet-style. Plenty of covered seating is nearby. Basic beverages (including sodas) are also provided, or you can buy an alcoholic beverage across the way at the Conched Out Bar. Adults can eat at the **Castaway Cay Air Bar-B-Q** located at Serenity Bay, the adults-only beach, from about 11:00 am to 1:30 pm. Offerings include burgers, salmon, potato salad, fresh fruit, and fat-free frozen yogurt. Alcoholic beverages can be purchased at the bar nearby. If you choose not to visit Castaway Cay, a buffet is served in Parrot Cay, usually from 8:00 am to 1:30 pm.

Exploring Castaway Cay

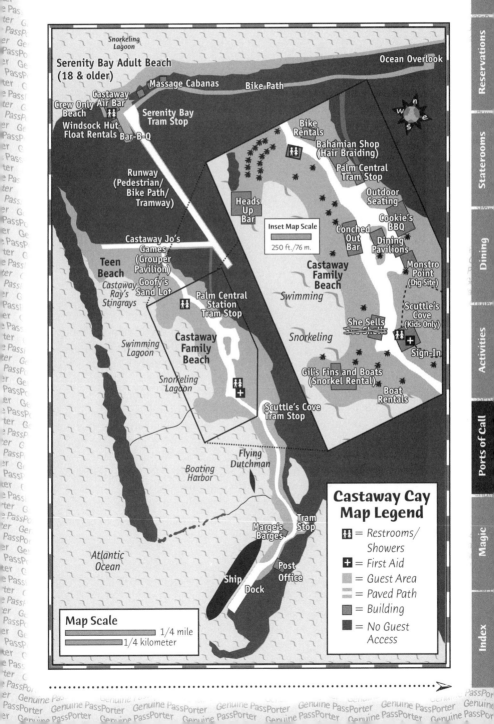

Serenity Bay Adult Beach (18 & older)
Snorkeling Lagoon
Ocean Overlook
Massage Cabanas
Bike Path
Castaway Air Bar
Crew Only Beach
Windsock Hut Float Rentals
Bar-B-Q
Serenity Bay Tram Stop
Bike Rentals
Bahamian Shop (Hair Braiding)
Palm Central Tram Stop
Runway (Pedestrian/Bike Path/Tramway)
Heads Up Bar
Inset Map Scale 250 ft./76 m.
Outdoor Seating
Cookie's BBQ
Conched Out Bar
Dining Pavilions
Castaway Jo's Games (Grouper Pavilion)
Teen Beach
Castaway Ray's Stingrays
Goofy's Sand Lot
Palm Central Station Tram Stop
Castaway Family Beach
Swimming
Castaway Family Beach
Swimming
Snorkeling
She Sells
Monstro Point (Dig Site)
Scuttle's Cove (Kids Only)
Sign-In
Swimming Lagoon
Snorkeling Lagoon
Gil's Fins and Boats (Snorkel Rental)
Boat Rentals
Scuttle's Cove Tram Stop
Flying Dutchman
Boating Harbor
Atlantic Ocean
Marge's Barges
Tram Stop
Post Office
Ship Dock

Map Scale
1/4 mile
1/4 kilometer

Castaway Cay Map Legend
👫 = Restrooms/Showers
✚ = First Aid
= Guest Area
= Paved Path
= Building
= No Guest Access

Side tabs: Introduction · Reservations · Staterooms · Dining · Activities · Ports of Call · Magic · Index

ACTIVITIES

Playing in Castaway Cay

Some **activities** on Castaway Cay require advance booking (see details on page 300). You can reserve floats, bikes, and snorkel equipment rentals in advance, though these are usually available on a walk-up basis. Strollers and beach wheelchairs are free for use on a first-come, first-served basis—while beach wheelchairs are designed to roll on the sand, they are still very hard to push.

The **beautiful beaches** are a big draw at Castaway Cay. The family beach is the largest and busiest—arrive early to get a good beach chair. Float rentals are available near Gil's Fins snorkel rentals and at the bike rental shack. The adults-only beach—Serenity Bay—is a wonderful place to spend a little grown-up time. The beach there is a little more barren than the family beach. Bring some water

© MediaMarx, Inc.

shoes as the bottom is coarser and may be uncomfortable. Walk farther down the beach for the most privacy. The teen beach—which is exclusively for teens— offers teen activities like volleyball and dancing.

The kids' water play area

Stingray encounters, a popular shore excursion on many islands, have finally arrived at Castaway Cay. We think Disney's version of stingray encounters is one of the best, so if you can't decide which port to see stingrays in, choose Castaway Cay! See page 301 for details.

Would you like to see a bit more of the island? You can **rent bicycles** near the family beach—prices are $6/hour for all ages. It takes about one hour to cycle down the airstrip and along the paved trail that borders the Serenity Bay beach and back again. Child seats can be requested. Water is provided along the bike trail, too.

Kids have their own supervised playground at **Scuttle's Cove**. If you've registered your kids for Oceaneer Club or Lab, you can check them in here while you go play at Serenity Bay. Counselors guide kids in structured activities, but they do not take them swimming. Beside Scuttle's Cove is Monstro Point, which has a huge whale "skeleton" to dig up! Programming ends at 3:30 pm. Note that kids can check out sand toys at Scuttle's Cove—first come, first served.

Playing in Castaway Cay

ACTIVITIES

Introduction

Reservations

Staterooms

Dining

Activities

Ports of Call

Magic

Index

Snorkeling is a very popular activity on Castaway Cay, which is an excellent spot for beginners to try out the sport. You can rent equipment at Gil's Fins near the family beach—prices are $25/adult and $10/kid (includes masks, fins, and vest). You can reserve your snorkel rental in advance (see page 300), though this is not necessary. The snorkeling lagoon is extensive—there's plenty of fish and sunken treasure to discover, as well as a submarine from Walt Disney World's "20,000 Leagues Under the Sea." Look for the map that shows the snorkeling course before you get in. Put sunscreen on your back—the water intensifies the sun's rays and you can get badly sunburned. Consider clipping a water bottle to your vest to rinse out your mouth—the saltwater can be bothersome. Note that there is an unofficial snorkeling lagoon at Serenity Bay (it's straight out from the first massage cabana)—rent your equipment at Gil's and tote it over. You can use your own snorkel gear in the lagoons, too. (Disney requires that all snorkelers wear a flotation device—you may need to pay a small fee of $6 for its use.) Some families like to bring their own (better) equipment, or simply purchase cheap snorkel sets for kids and then leave them behind.

Boat rentals are primarily available at the boat beach (Relay Bay). Rent paddle boats ($8 for two-seater, $10 for four-seater), Aqua Trikes ($15),

© MediaMarx, Inc.

sea kayaks ($8 for one-seater, $10 for two-seater), small Aqua Fins sailboats ($15), and Sun Kat sailboats ($20)—all prices are for a half-hour. No advance reservations are necessary for rentals other than Banana Boats.

Watercraft on Castaway Cay

Family games are available at Group Pavilion (sometimes also known as Castaway Jo's), a shaded patio with shuffleboard, billiards, foosball, Ping-Pong, basketball/football toss, horseshoes, a giant checkerboard, and a sandbox with toys. This area is often overlooked, yet can really be a lot of fun, especially when you or a family member need some time out of the sun.

ACTIVITIES

Introduction
Reservations
Staterooms
Dining
Activities
Ports of Call
Magic
Index

Playing in Castaway Cay

Goofy's Sandlot is the **sport beach** on Castaway Cay—it's right next to Castaway Jo's. You can play volleyball and tetherball here. Watch for an organized volleyball game in the late morning. The sport beach is often very quiet and uncrowded, making it an ideal spot for families to hang together. And its proximity to the teen beach (right next door), Castaway Jo's, and the Heads Up Bar make it very convenient, too. This is also a good spot to find a hammock if they are all occupied on other beaches.

Adults can reserve a popular **cabana massage** near Serenity Bay. If you do just one spa treatment, this is the one we recommend. Cabana massages are $139/person—reserve in advance online to avoid disappointment. If you are sensitive to the sun, book a massage for later in the day—the oils make your skin more likely to sunburn. You can bring your sunscreen and ask to have it applied at the end of the massage.

© MediaMarx, Inc.

A massage cabana on Castaway Cay

Shopping is limited to three small shops. She Sells ~~Sea Shells~~ is a Disney-themed shop with unique Castaway Cay logo items. Visit this shop early, as the crowds are huge later in the day and some items and sizes get gobbled up quickly. Two Bahamian-run retail shops near the end of the family beach sell crafts, shirts, and trinkets—this is also where you can get hair braiding for $1/braid or $2/cornrow—expect to pay about $30 for the whole head (which takes about 3 hours). There is sometimes a merchandise cart at Serenity Bay, too. The shops on the ship are closed while the ship is docked at Castaway Cay.

Your can meet your favorite **Disney characters** on Castaway Cay. Check the back of the Disney-provided Castaway Cay map for times. Photo opportunities are available all over the island. Look for ship's photographers near the ship and at the family beach.

Playing in Castaway Cay

While it's not possible to **hike** around the island, you can take a leisurely stroll down the bike path near the adult beach. Water is provided along the trail, and there's a two-story scenic ocean overlook at the end of the hike. If you're looking to see parts of the island that are normally off-limits, we recommend the delightful Walking and Kayak Adventure excursion described on page 302.

If offered on your cruise, the **Pirate Scavenger Hunt** is a fun, free activity—watch your *Personal Navigator* for a "Pirate Scavenger Maps" distribution session the day before your scheduled day in Castaway Cay. At this session, you'll pickup that all-important packet of items that you need for the hunt! (Tip: If you can't make it to this session, ask a friend or tablemate who can attend to pick up a hunt packet for you.) Once you dock at Castaway Cay, you're free to begin your scavenger hunt—it will take you over a wide range and call on your keen observation skills. This is really an adult or family activity, as some of the clues require good reading or logic skills. Record your results in your hunt packet as you go along. If you're following a clue and you're not sure if you've found the right answer, look for a small round plaque—these mark the general location of the answers and are handy for confirming your guesses. Once you've completed your hunt, the answer tells you where to go to claim your treasure. This last step seems to stump a lot of people because not everyone knows the names of the various spots around the island. (Tip: Use our Castaway Cay map!) There's no reward for being the fastest to solve the scavenger hunt, and the reward isn't anything valuable, but it is a lot of fun and we really enjoyed it!

Speaking of pirates, the **Flying Dutchman ghost ship** from Pirates of the Caribbean: Dead Man's Chest is docked at Castaway Cay (at press time). While we can't say for sure how long the 175-foot-long ship will be "in port," it is a sight to behold! You won't be able to board the ship (it's a movie set, after all), but you can get a closer look at it by renting a waverunner or taking the Banana Boat excursion. Also be on the lookout for Captain Jack Sparrow wandering the island!

Let's not overlook one of our favorite activities on Castaway Cay—**relaxing**! You can do it practically anywhere, but we really like lounging about in hammocks on the family beach or adults-only beach. We've had the best luck finding empty hammocks behind Gil's Fins (the snorkel rental shack). If you find a hammock, please enjoy it, but don't try to save it by leaving your things on it.

ACTIVITIES

Introduction
Reservations
Staterooms
Dining
Activities
Ports of Call
Magic
Index

Advance Rentals & Excursions on Castaway Cay

These rentals are nonrefundable unless your cruise skips Castaway Cay.

Snorkel Equipment [CO1] ☀ 🄾

Explore Disney's 12-acre snorkeling lagoon—price includes all-day rental of mask, fins, and vest (light flotation). Beginners can take the Discover Trail; experienced snorkelers may like the longer Explorer Trail. Both trails have lots to see. Pick up your snorkel equipment at Gil's Fins. Note that children under 13 must be with an adult. (On Your Own: Bring your own equipment and use the lagoon!)

| Sports |
| Active |
| Ages 5 & up |
| $25/adult |
| $10/kids 5-9 |

Float/Tube Rentals [CO3] ☀ 🄾

Enjoy the water with a lounge float or tube. (On Your Own: Purchase inflatable floats from a dollar store at home and bring along on your cruise.) Ages 5 & up.

| Beach |
| $6/each |

Bicycle Rental [CO4]   Rating: 8 ☀ 🛍 🄾

Dozens of bikes are available for rent. Training wheels, child seats, and helmets are available. The biking paths are on flat terrain, and there's plenty of drinking water along the way. Look for the ocean outlook at the end of the bike path! Cruiser reviews are positive: The bikes are "comfortable" and the "trail is beautiful." At the end of the trail is a "very peaceful," "secluded beach."

| Sports |
| Active |
| All ages |
| $6/hour |

Castaway Cay Getaway Package [CO5]   Rating: 7 ☀ 🛍 🄾

This package includes a float rental, snorkel equipment rental, and a bike rental for one hour, for a savings of $5-6. Very popular—book early. Cruiser reviews are positive: Cruisers enjoyed having the rentals "secured" and felt it is "good deal," though many noted they weren't able to use all three rentals. Note: The **Extreme Getaway Package** ($54/$39) adds a Castaway Ray's session (see next page for details) to everything else mentioned here, saving $3-$6/person.

| Sports |
| Active |
| Ages 5 & up |
| $32/adult |
| $16/child |

Banana Boat Ride [CO6]   Rating: 8 ☀

Ride a big, yellow, inflatable water "sled" around Relay Bay and out around the ship. The banana boat holds 10 people and is pulled by a Jet Ski. You must be able to swim, as you could fall off. Departure times are every 30 minutes beginning at 8:30 am (Wonder) or 10:30 am (Magic). When we rode it, half the passengers fell off when we hit a big wave. Cruiser reviews are positive: This "very bouncy," "fun" ride is "exhilarating" and "very fast." Many cruisers did get "bounced off" in the water, but "enjoyed it." Most cruisers agree that this is "great fun." We are in the minority as we didn't like this—it was much too rough and we couldn't enjoy the scenery with all the saltwater spray in our eyes. Tip: Wear swim goggles.

| Sports |
| Very active |
| Ages 8 & up |
| $15/person |
| 15-20 minutes |

Parasailing [CO8]   Rating: 9 ☀ 🄾

If you've never tried parasailing, this is a great experience for beginners. You can go solo or tandem, and you'll take off from the boat and land in it when you're done. Expect to be airborne for 5-8 minutes, with 600 feet of rope between you and the boat. Guests must be 90-375 lbs. (40-170 kg.) to parasail. Tandem parasailing is possible if you're both under the maximum weight combined. Be sure to take a disposable camera for some amazing photos while in the air! Cruiser reviews are very positive: "No experience is necessary" to enjoy this "amazing flight" over the water. The "views" are "stunning." It's a "real adrenaline rush" and a "genuine highlight" of the cruise. "Book early" as "spots fill up quickly." Cruisers say "go for it!"

| Sports |
| Active |
| Ages 8 & up |
| $75/person |
| 45 minutes |

Embarking on Shore Excursions on Castaway Cay

Castaway Cay Bottom Fishing [CO2]   Rating: 9

Up to six guests can enjoy a ride around the Abaco Islands for bottom fishing (catch and release). Tackle, bait, and beverages (soda and water) are provided. Guests 12 and under must wear life jackets. Typical meeting times are 9:00 am, 9:30 am, and 1:00 pm. Very popular—book early! Cruiser reviews are very positive: The "friendly" captain takes you out to a "beautiful setting" to fish. There are "lots of fish," and "plenty to catch." Cruisers do note that there is no "head" (restroom) on the boat. All cruisers had a "great time" and considered it a "highlight" of their cruise. This excursion may be suspended without notice depending on the season and other conditions.

Fishing
Active
Ages 6 & up
$117/person
3–3.5 hours

Castaway Ray's Stingray Adventure [C13]   Rating: 9

This adventure begins when you check in at the Castaway Ray's Stingray Hut near the Teen Beach (see Castway Cay map on page 295). After receiving your snorkel equipment (mask, snorkel, and flotation vest), guests gather under a shelter for a fascinating and educational orientation on the stingrays. This program was developed in partnership with The Living Seas at Epcot, and cast members from Epcot are often the ones to give you your orientation. Among other things, you will learn that the barbs have been trimmed from the stingrays that live in the lagoon, so you and your family are safe from stings. After your briefing, you wade into the shallow water with the stingrays. A guide accompanies you and encourages the stingrays to come closer so you can view them up close and touch them. You may even have the chance to feed them! Special U-shaped ramps (see photo below) were created and the stingrays were trained to swim up them, giving you an unparalleled look. After this,

Sports
Active
Ages 5 & up
$35/adult
$29/ages 5–9
1 hour

Dave meets a stingray at Ray's

there's free time to don your snorkel equipment and swim among the stingrays for an underwater look. Note that children under 16 must be accompanied by an adult. A portion of the proceeds from this excursion go to Disney's Wildlife Conservation Fund. Typical meeting times are every hour from 9:00 am to 3:00 pm. Cruiser reviews are very positive: The experience was "enjoyable" as well as "educational." The "innovative" stingray ramps gave cruisers "a better look at the rays" than on other stingray excursions. The stingrays "don't bite" and their "barbs have been removed." Cruisers "did not feel threatened" but the "snorkeling was poor" due to the stirred-up sand. Overall, most cruisers say they want to "do it again" on their next cruise.

Glass-Bottom Boat Scenic Voyage [C11]   Rating: 2

Board a 46-foot trawler with a glass bottom for an hour-long ecotour of the barrier reefs surrounding Castaway Cay. Typical meeting times are 9:45 am, 11:15 am, 12:45 pm, and 2:15 pm. Cruiser reviews are uniform: The "rocky," "overcrowded boat" is filled with people "pushing and shoving" to see out the "cloudy" glass bottom. "Very limited fish" are visible. There are "very few seats," meaning most have to stand the entire time. Overall, cruisers say "don't bother."

Tour
Leisurely
All ages
$35/$25 (0–9)
1 hour

See page 172 for a key to description charts and their icons.

Embarking on Shore Excursions on Castaway Cay

Personal Watercraft Eco Tour (Single and Double) [C12] Rating: 9

Explore Castaway Cay on a personal watercraft (also known as a "WaveRunner" or "Jet-Ski") with a knowledgeable tour guide accompanying you. Note that you must be 18 years or older to drive the personal watercraft (guests ages 16 and 17 may drive with written authorization from parents). Max. weight is 375 lb./170 kg. Typical meeting times are 9:45 am, 10:30 am, 11:15 am, 12:00 pm, 1:00 pm, 1:45 pm, and 2:45 pm. Cruiser reviews are very positive: Guests love "riding the WaveRunners" at a "brisk pace" while getting "gorgeous views" of Castaway Cay and the Abacos. Cruisers recommend you "bring watershoes" and a "waterproof camera" as there are "good photo-ops on the tour." Those who've done this excursion remind us that "just hanging on to the WaveRunner for a long time as you navigate through the waves can leave you a bit tired and even a little sore." Parents also point out that kids who ride double with you "just hang on to your waist—there are no buckles or restraints" to keep them from falling into the water. Most cruisers found this an "excellent excursion" and "highly recommend it" to others.

Sports
Active
Ages 16 & up
$95 single
$160 double
1 hour

Seahorse Catamaran Snorkel Adventure [C09] Rating: 4

If the snorkeling lagoon doesn't satisfy your itch to snorkel, this excursion puts you aboard a 63-foot catamaran to sail to a prime snorkeling area. Snorkel gear and instruction provided. Typical meeting times are 9:15 am and 1:15 pm. Cruiser reviews are mixed: The "excellent" catamaran trip was "delightful" for most. The snorkeling proves trickier, however—some enjoyed an "abundance of sea life," while others battled with "wind and currents." Cruisers felt the "open water can be choppy" and this is "not good for those prone to motion sickness or snorkeling beginners."

Sports
Active
Ages 5 & up
$52/$36 (5-9)
2-2.5 hours

Walking and Kayak Nature Adventure [C10] Rating: 7

Explore areas of Castaway Cay normally off-limits to guests! Start with a 40-min. nature hike to reach your kayak launch site, then enjoy an hour-long kayak trip through mangroves. Afterward, swim at a deserted beach, then take a 20-min. walk back. Typical meeting times are 9:00 am, 9:15 am, and 12:45 pm. We did this ourselves and really enjoyed it—we recommend it to anyone who wants to be active and explore the ecosystem. Wear appropriate footwear. We think it's best for those who've visited the island before. Cruiser reviews are mixed—most think the kayaking is "awesome" but others felt the overall "pace was too slow." Kids were "bored" with the nature aspects and "didn't do much paddling." Cruisers report seeing "lots of wildlife." Other guests recomend you "bring/wear bug repellant" although "bugs aren't too bothersome."

Sports
Very active
Ages 10 & up
$64
2.5-3 hours

The Wild Side (for Teens Only) [C07] Rating: 9

Retrace the adventures of the first teens on the island—Molly and Seth. There's plenty of action, and you'll get to do some snorkeling, biking, and sea kayaking. Typical meeting time is very early for teens—around 9:00 am. Teen cruiser reviews are overwhelmingly positive: First, "wait until you see who else is going" before you book—this tour "is best when you go with people you know" (but don't wait too long—it can book up). On Castaway Cay, you "do the bike ride first," "kayak for about 20 minutes," then bike back to go "snorkeling." After lunch at Cookies, you "hook up with other teens at the teen beach." Many think this was the "highlight" of their cruise; those who disagree had issues with "other teens," not the excursion.

Sports
Very active
Ages 13-17
$35/teen
4 hours

Port Activity Worksheet

Electronic, interactive worksheet available— see page 350

Use this worksheet to keep track of the activities and shore excursions you want to do most on your cruise. List your activities in order of preference— when booking shore excursions with Disney, you'll be more likely to get an excursion if you list a second and third choice along with the first. When you're ready to book your shore excursions through Disney, reserve online or call 877-566-0968 no later than 2 days in advance of your sail date (see page 171). Note that you cannot make excursion reservations until Disney has received the final payment for your cruise. Check off any excursions you've booked with a notation in the "Reserved?" column. Once you know your excursions are confirmed, circle them and cross off the others.

My sail date: _____ less 60 days = _____ (*first reservation date*)

Activity/Excursion	Location	Time	Cost	Reserved?	Notes
Port: _____ Date:					
1.					
2.					
3.					
Port: _____ Date:					
1.					
2.					
3.					
Port: _____ Date:					
1.					
2.					
3.					
Port: _____ Date:					
1.					
2.					
3.					
Port: _____ Date:					
1.					
2.					
3.					

Notes:

Introduction

Reservations

Staterooms

Dining

Activities

Ports of Call

Magic

Index

Cavorting in Port

We predict that some of your favorite cruise memories will be made at your ports of call! Below are tips to help you get the most out of your jaunts, as well as port memories to get you in the mood.

- You can mail a **postcard home from the Castaway Cay post office** and get your stamp canceled with a cool Castaway Cay postmark (see page 16). Be sure to bring some cash to purchase your stamps as you can't use your shipboard charge here. Small bills and change are best, as it can be difficult for the staff to break large bills.

- Pack a disposable **underwater camera**! You'll love it when you swim and snorkel, and you won't worry about it getting wet or stolen.

- The **Caribbean sun** is brutal. Be sure to wear sunscreen on your visits to the shore—you are likely to be in the sun more often than the shade. Sunglasses also come in handy against the glare of the bright sun off sidewalks and water. And don't forget hats with wide brims to protect your face and neck and shield your eyes. You'll find a soft fabric, crushable hat with a chin strap to keep it on your head is invaluable on shore, especially on active excursions.

- "It's not unusual for passengers to **stay onboard** when docked at Nassau. We had a short 3-night cruise, so we decided to stay onboard while everyone else wandered off the ship. We had a relaxing day eating, swimming, and wandering around the ship. We made it our own day at sea since we had such a short cruise. Later in the day we went off the ship for 2–3 hours. That was plenty of time to have a short visit." – contributed by Diana Barthelemy

Magical Memory

- "My three-year-old son Alexander is very much into pirates and treasure chests these days. So I decided to improvise a little 'treasure hunt' on Castaway Cay for him. I began by purchasing a plastic treasure hunt—filled with 'booty'–from Mickey's Mates onboard ($20). Then on the morning of our day at Castaway Cay, I marked a big, bold 'X' on the Disney-provided map of Castaway Cay and presented it to Alexander as a treasure map. He noticed the 'X' immediately and was quite excited. He got out his 'telescope' and a nice big shovel for digging up treasure. On Castaway Cay, we walked to the end of the family beach and Alexander's dad distracted him while I buried the treasure chest and marked an 'X' in the sand over it. Then Alexander came running over, having spotted the 'X.' He began digging for that treasure chest excitedly, happy beyond belief. He was so proud of himself! He proudly showed his treasure chest to Donald Duck before re-boarding the ship. This little treasure hunt is one of my most magical memories ever!"

...as told by Jennifer Marx

Making Magic and Wonder

Is your mind still filled with nagging little questions? This chapter may just banish the last of those concerns. Among other topics, we'll discuss toddler care, special occasions, seasickness, meeting Disney characters, clearing U.S. Customs, how much to tip, and what happens when you arrive back in Port Canaveral. These are some of the little (and not so little) things that can make the difference between an ordinary vacation and a trip filled with magic and wonder.

Is your tot too small for the regular children's programs? We tour Flounder's Reef, the ship's childcare center. Children of all ages can get the lowdown on meeting Disney characters. Learn how to preserve fond memories with your own photographs and glossies from the ship's photographers. Do you have money left after shopping in port? We describe all the stores and shopping opportunities on board, too.

While modern cruises aren't the fancy dress extravaganzas they used to be, every cruise includes opportunities to dress up. In fact, the seven-night sailings include officially designated formal and semi-formal nights (one of each). Here's where we button-down all the details on appropriate attire, tuxedo rentals, and other dress-up options. Do you want a real excuse to dress up? We describe special and celebrity cruises, and deliver tips for creating your own special celebrations on board, whether you're tying the knot or want to give a loved one an extra-special send-off.

Next, there's the business of staying healthy and avoiding that curse of the deep, *mal de mer* (seasickness). Plus, a few tips on keeping up-to-date with your business back home.

It's also time to set your feet back on shore after your cruise. Nobody likes this part, but now is the perfect time to explore the mysteries of "customary gratuities" (tipping), the rules and regulations of U.S. Customs, and the rituals of debarkation. We've had a great time cruising with you! Alas, that it had to end so soon. Bon voyage!

Cruising With Kids

Disney cruises and kids go together like peanut butter and jelly! We've had the pleasure of cruising with kids many times, with our son Alexander (at 4 mo., 11 mo., 1, $1^1/_2$, 2, and 3), our daughter Allie (at 9 and 12), our nieces Megan (at 3, 5, and 8) and Natalie (at 2, 4, and 7), our nieces Kayleigh (at 13 and 16), Melanie (at 11 and 14), and Nina (at 10 and 13), and Dave's second cousins Bradley (2) and Andrea (1). So we've been "around the deck," so to speak. Here are our tips for happy cruising with kids, along with tips from Jennifer's sister Kim Larner, mother of Megan and Natalie.

Introduce kids to Disney cruising before you go. Order the free video/DVD, have a family showing, and encourage your child(ren) to watch it on their own. It builds excitement and also breeds familiarity, which is important to kids. If you have a child with an interest in pirates and treasures, draw a treasure map showing your journey from your home to the ship and review the map in the weeks and days leading up to your cruise (see page 84).

Your stateroom choice depends on your budget, but spring for an **outside stateroom** if possible. The natural light helps kids stay on their regular sleep cycles. Kim says, "The split-bathroom units were very convenient and the large porthole made the room feel very open." These are all big pluses when cruising with kids.

Kids absolutely love **swimming**, and the pools onboard are lots of fun. They also tend to be very crowded, however, and "you'll need to keep an eagle eye on your kids in the pools," according to Kim. She also suggests you make time to go swimming in the ocean at Castaway Cay—"the kids loved the warm water and found crabs and starfish." Keep in mind that diaper-age kids can only use the designated splash areas (see page 154).

The **Oceaneer Club and Lab** tend to be big hits with most kids, though there can be downfalls. Allie tells us she was disappointed when she was put in the age 8 to 9 group and her cousin Nina was in the 10 to 12 group. And while Megan fell in love with the Oceaneer Club at age 3, she had a "potty accident" due to the exciting and unfamiliar environment, and wasn't allowed back in to the Club for a while. Certainly let the kids know about the Oceaneer Club and Lab before you go, but don't build it up too much in the event there are disappointments. Kim also suggests you "put your kid(s) in the Club/Lab for at least one of your meals to allow you the chance to really enjoy the dinner."

© MediaMarx, Inc.

Natalie, Megan, and Alexander coloring their dinner menu in Parrot Cay

Speaking of meals, **early seating** tends to work much better than late seating for kids, especially young kids. Kim says, "the kids enjoyed the start and end of the meal, but were impatient during the middle." We suggest you bring an activity or two with you to dinner to keep the kids entertained after they've grown tired of coloring their menus, such as sticker books or doodle pads. Older kids like Allie also get impatient—consider letting older kids go to the Oceaneer Club, Oceaneer Lab, or the teens club if it's appropriate.

The **stage shows** are popular with kids, though very young kids may find it hard to sit through one of these hour-long shows. We suggest you arrive early enough to either sit close (the proximity tends to better engage the child in the show), sit on an aisle (so you can make a convenient escape), or bring along whatever you need to help your child sleep through the show (bottles/sippy cups, pacifiers, and/or blankie). On-stage characters can present difficulties, too. Kim says that "both Megan and Natalie wanted to go up to the stage and give the characters a hug, and Natalie cried for some time about not being able to do it."

Alexander asleep at the end of a show

Of all the **cruise activities**, it's most common for kids to love swimming and Castaway Cay the best. You may want to take at least two swimsuits so you always have a dry one. We also recommend some water shoes and a bathrobe, for comfortable trips to and from the pool (the air conditioning inside the ship can be quite chilly when you've got nothing on but a wet swimsuit).

The Disney Cruise photographers can capture some **amazing shots of your children** in the pool, in the Club/Lab, and on Castaway Cay—be sure to check Shutters gallery (see page 310) for images of your kids. A Disney cruise is also a great opportunity to get professional photographs of your family or just your kids. To have the best selection of backdrops and characters, and to minimize waits for young kids, plan to arrive in the Lobby Atrium (deck 3 or 4) at least an hour before your dinner begins.

Give serious thought to giving your child a "night out" in Flounder's Reef Nursery or at Oceaneer Club or Lab, thereby giving you at least one **adults-only evening**. The facilities are excellent (much better than other, non-Disney ships on which we've cruised) and the crew members that staff them are very good with kids. Having time alone is as good for your kid(s) as for you.

That said, we also suggest you **savor the time** you'll have to spend with your children on this cruise. You'll have the opportunity for special moments and new discoveries together. Be sure to plan time together every day, whether it's to do a scheduled activity or just

hang together as a family. We've found our cruise time with Alexander provided some of our most treasured moments, including the night we passed through the Panama Canal and he took his very first independent steps, and the day on Castaway Cay when we devised a treasure hunt for him with a real treasure chest buried in the sand under a big "X" (see page 304).

Overall, we've observed that a Disney cruise is **better than a Walt Disney World vacation** when you're with young kids. There's less walking, less overstimulation, less exhaustion, and just as much magic. On every Disney vacation we've gone on with young kids (under 5), the kids (and their parents) were much happier on the ship than at the parks. Kim says, "The cruise was the best part of our vacation."

Sara Varney and her son Ryan

Childcare

Yes, parents, this is your vacation, too! While family time spent together is golden, Disney makes sure there's plenty of time and space for adults-only relaxation and fun. So what do the kids do while the grownups play? They're having a party of their own, in some of the **best childcare** programs you'll find on land or sea.

Kids at least three years of age and potty-trained can enjoy supervised play at the Oceaneer Club or Lab—see pages 148–150 for all the details. If your child is between twelve weeks old and three years old, or not yet toilet-trained, you can use the **Flounder's Reef Nursery**. Flounder's is the ships' full-service childcare center located on deck 5 aft, beside the Buena Vista Theatre. The nursery is equipped with a playroom filled with age-appropriate toys, Disney movies, baby bouncers, and rocking chairs, as well as a separate sleeping room with cribs for infants and mats for toddlers. A smaller third room holds changing tables.

Reservations are required for Flounder's, and you can make them in advance online (see page 139). If you don't reserve in advance, do it very soon after boarding, because it's a popular place. Only a limited number of spaces (about 20) are available, as Disney strives to maintain a child/counselor ratio of 4:1 (infants) and 6:1 (toddlers). You can make reservations in Flounder's on embarkation day, typically from 12:30 pm to 3:15 pm and again from 4:30 pm to 5:30 pm, or by phoning from your stateroom (if no one answers, leave a message with your name, child's name, stateroom, and date and time requested). Once your session is confirmed, you will receive a voice mail on your stateroom phone. Disney initially limits you to ten total reserved hours in order to accommodate more guests. After the initial reservation period, services are offered on a space-available basis. If you are planning to dine at Palo, coordinating the two reservations can be tricky. Get your Palo reservation first, then do your Flounder's Reef Nursery reservation.

Unlike the Oceaneer Club and Lab, which are included in your fare, Flounder's Reef Nursery charges **$6/hour** for the first child and $5/hour for each additional sibling. There is a two-hour minimum. Reservations must be cancelled four hours prior to your reserved time, or you will be charged a cancellation fee equal to 50% of your scheduled time. Flounder's is open daily, typically from 9:00 am to 1:00 or 2:00 pm and again from 5:30 pm to midnight, though times may vary for at-sea days and some port days may offer extended hours to accommodate guests going on shore excursions. You will be issued a pager when your child is signed into the nursery—be sure to return this pager at the end of your child's session or you will incur a $150 fee. Please also be aware that the nursery is unable to accept children who show symptoms of fever, vomiting, diarrhea, or unexplained skin rash, or any child who has other contagious diseases or illnesses. Flounder's Reef Nursery is also unable to administer any medication. If your child has any special needs at all, be sure to mention them so they can accommodate your child.

The Flounder's Reef Nursery crew members are friendly and attentive

When you **check in** your young cruisers to the nursery, bring diapers/pull-ups, wipes, an extra set of clothing/pajamas, and anything else that may be needed, such as premade bottles, sippy cups, baby food in jars, pacifiers, and security items (such as a blanket). The nursery does not provide meals and the official policy states that no outside food is permitted due to allergies. For this reason, we always fed Alexander before bringing him to the nursery. In practice, however, if you have packaged baby food in your diaper bag, the nursery crew _may_ feed it to your baby. We always kept baby/toddler food in our diaper bag as a rule, and we were surprised to learn that the crew had fed it to him when we picked him up at the end of a session (as we assumed they would not). And while the rules state that no meals are provided, on our most recent visit (and probably our last due to Alexander's age), the crew informed us that they gave Alexander some saltine crackers and apple juice during his session. We're sure experiences with food vary from ship to ship and cruise to cruise, but you should be aware of the range of possibilities. Our advice is to assume "no food" and then ask the crew upon your arrival.

If you are **nursing your infant**, you can return to Flounder's Reef in mid-session to nurse—when Jennifer visited with baby Alexander, the crew moved a rocking chair into the

back room for privacy. A reader recently wrote that she encountered resistance from the crew to this on her cruise—the crew did not allow her to enter the nursery itself due to separation anxiety issues with other children in their care. If you encounter such resistance, ask to speak to their superior crew member immediately. When our reader wrote Disney regarding the situation after her cruise, Disney apologized for the miscommunication and stated, "Nursing mothers are allowed to breast feed in the back room."

The back of Flounder's Reef Nursery

Age-appropriate toys are provided.

If you have a **three-year-old who is not yet potty trained** (and therefore unable to be left at Oceaneer Club), you may use Flounder's Reef. The price and other rules are the same as those for kids under 3. Some three-year-olds are okay with this, while others are not (the room is really geared for younger children). If you're considering a Flounder's Reef session with a three-year-old, be sure to visit with your child during their open hours on embarkation day to see if your child finds the room interesting.

Helpful Tips for Parents:

✔ If you are dropping your child off in the evening, put him/her in **pajamas**—it will make the transition back to your stateroom (and to bed) that much easier.

✔ For a **Palo dinner**, reserve at least three hours in Flounder's Reef with the starting time about 15 minutes before your Palo reservation.

✔ Keep in mind that your **pager** won't work off the ship.

✔ Parents **traveling with infants** can request a high chair in the dining room and a pack & play crib for their stateroom.

Photographs

Say cheese! Whether you're taking your own photos or letting a ship's photographer snap the shot, a Disney cruise is the perfect photo op!

Bring your own camera and plenty of film and batteries. Should you forget this essential bit of cruising equipment, you can buy Pentax and Olympus cameras ($200+), Kodak single-use cameras, film, and batteries onboard. We use a digital camera, which allows us to take as many photos as we like and not bother with film—we recommend it! Camcorders are also very popular—if you bring yours, be aware that the high humidity can be a problem for your camcorder. To keep moisture out of your camcorder, keep it in the shade whenever possible and allow at least 30 minutes to adjust to different environments (such as when you go from your air-conditioned stateroom to a steamy port or even out on your verandah).

Onboard photo processing is offered in **Shutters Photo Gallery** (deck 4 aft). Drop off your film before 11:00 am and it'll be ready the same day by 5:00 pm—otherwise your photos are ready the next day. For every roll of film you develop at Shutters, you get a free photo of the ship and a trading pin (as of press time). Developing costs are about $5 for 12 4x6 prints or $10 for 24 (double prints are 35 cents). Shutters processes regular 35mm film and Advantix film, as well as prints from underwater, single-use, and digital cameras. Tip: You can have your digital photos downloaded to a CD for $14.95.

Ship's photographers are everywhere. In fact, the moment you board the ship, you'll be asked to pose for a portrait. Your embarkation photo will be available in Shutters between 5:00 pm and 11:00 pm that same evening. Candid and posed photos may be snapped throughout the cruise—just swing by Shutters to see the photos. Photos taken during the day are typically available in the evening, while photos taken after 5:00 pm or so are displayed the following day. Note that older photos are no longer removed from the displays to make room for new ones. If you aren't sure which photos you want to buy, collect all your photos and stack them behind one another on the display to keep them together. Also, be sure to save your receipts, as you may get quantity discounts. And consider waiting until the end of the cruise to purchase photo packages. If you need photo reprints after your cruise, negatives may be archived for up to ten weeks after your cruise—call 800-772-3470 ext. 11.

© MediaMarx, Inc.

Dave poses for a portrait in the atrium

The **professional photos** at Shutters come in two sizes: 6 x 8 prints are $10 each (10 for $85, 15 for $120, 20 for $150, or 30 for $220); 8 x 10 prints are $20 each (5 for $85, 8 for $130, 10 for $150, or 15 for $220). Formal portraits and some other shots only come in 8 x 10. Purchased photos are placed in flexible cardboard folders, or you can buy padded folders or frames. Photos are copyrighted and you can be fined up to $500 for unauthorized duplication—go to http://www.image.com/html/guest-postcruiseCopyrightReleaseForm.cfm to download a copyright release waiver. Tip: Shutters can turn your family portrait into greeting cards with lots of "character!" These greeting cards are now available year round.

Shutters is **open** all day on at-sea days, and from about 5:00 pm to 11:00 pm on port days. Note that Shutters is also open debarkation morning from 6:45 am to 8:30 am. We recommend you avoid the last night and morning, as they are incredibly busy.

Shopping Onboard

Both ships sport a 5,500-square-foot shopping area—combine that with extra shopping opportunities aboard and great shopping in port (see chapter 6), and you'll find it easy to shop 'til you drop anchor. As you might imagine, prices are a bit on the high side, but the quality is excellent.

Due to U.S. Customs regulations, the onboard shops **cannot be open while in port**. Check your *Personal Navigator* for shop operating hours, and keep in mind that the last night of your cruise is your last opportunity to shop. And before you splurge on that big-ticket item, see page 322 for details on customs allowances.

Mickey's Mates (deck 4 midship) is the Disney character and logo shop, filled with stuffed animals, souvenirs, logowear, trading pins, postcards, etc.

Treasure Ketch (deck 4 midship) is right across the hall from Mickey's Mates and offers more upscale and practical merchandise, such as resort wear, jewelry (including loose gemstones and "gold by the inch"), collectibles, toiletries, film, batteries, books, and magazines. Tax-free gifts are also available here, such as watches and sunglasses. Collectors, check your *Personal Navigator* for Captain's signings—he'll sign posters, hats, T-shirts, pins, and ship models for free.

The shopping area onboard the ship

Preludes Snacks (deck 4 forward) is a small bar that sells packaged snacks such as candy bars, chips, and popcorn. Typically open from 6:00 pm to 10:00 pm.

Up Beat/Radar Trap (deck 3 forward) offers duty-free liquor (50+ brands), fragrances (60+ brands), cigars (25+ brands), and cigarettes, as well as snacks, candy bars, cameras, film, and batteries. Note that duty-free orders are delivered to your stateroom on the last night of your cruise—yes, that means you cannot consume that liquor you bought here while you're onboard. The shop is typically open evenings until midnight.

Shutters (deck 4 aft) sells compact cameras, frames, and photos. See previous page.

Live Auction at Sea (deck 4 forward) features fine art and collectible Disney Cruise Line items auctioned to the highest bidder. See page 165 for all the details.

Pin Trading Station (deck 3 or 4 midship) opens nightly on the port side of the Atrium Lobby, typically from 7:30 pm to 8:30 pm. This is a great place for limited edition pins.

A poolside merchandise cart may be parked near the **Mickey Pool** on certain days.

Let's not forget the **onboard gift brochure** you receive with your cruise documentation before you embark—any items ordered from this brochure will be waiting for you in your stateroom when you board.

Check the **"On-Board Shopping" supplement** distributed with your *Personal Navigator* for daily specials, featured items, operating hours, and a list of where to find what onboard.

Shops are **busiest** from 7:00 pm to 10:00 pm, so you may want to go earlier or later.

Introduction
Reservations
Staterooms
Dining
Activities
Ports of Call
Magic
Index

Formal and Semi-Formal Occasions

What is it about a cruise that brings out our Fred Astaire and Ginger Rogers? It may be passé ashore, but a formal night at sea is still magical!

On the **3- and 4-night** Wonder cruises, there are no official formal nights. Instead, your semi-formal nights are determined by your dining rotation. On your Triton's night, you can wear semi-formal attire, such as a jacket for men and a dress or pantsuit for women, but it isn't required. Wear semi-formal attire for Palo. The other nights are casual or tropical.

On the **7-night** Disney Magic cruises, you have one formal night—day 2 on Eastern Caribbean itineraries and day 3 on Western Caribbean itineraries—and one semi-formal night on day 6 of both itineraries. (Longer cruises have 1–2 more formal and semi-formal occasions.) Formal night is "black tie optional." Many men wear tuxedos or suits and women typically wear evening gowns, but semi-formalwear is fine, too. During the formal and semi-formal nights, the crew sets up backdrops and takes formal portraits (see page 310). In addition, you are asked to wear semi-formal attire when you eat dinner in Lumière's.

Men's Formalwear: Fortunately, you don't have to rent a tuxedo and haul it across the country and back. Cruise Line Formalwear supplies men's formalwear on the Disney Cruise Line, and cruise-long rentals range from $85 to $120 (this price includes everything but

the shoes), plus accessories ($5 to $20). Order at least two weeks before you cruise with the order form in your cruise documents, online at http://www.cruiselineformal.com or on the phone at 800-551-5091. You can also view the tuxedos and accessories on their web site. When you order a tuxedo from them, it'll arrive in your stateroom on your first day aboard (try it on right away to see if it needs any alterations). When the cruise ends, just leave it in your room. Note that Cruise Line Formal does keep extra inventory onboard for exchanges and last-minute rentals. Another option is to buy a tuxedo (try a local tux rental shop or http://www.ebay.com). Perhaps you'd like a Disney-themed vest and tie set to go with your own tux? If so, check on the Internet at http://www.tuxedosdirect.com.

© MediaMarx, Inc.

Jennifer and Dave decked out at Palo

Women's Formalwear: If you don't happen to have an evening gown or old bridesmaid's gown hanging in your closet, you can make do with a nice dress on both semi-formal and formal evenings. A "basic black dress" is a popular choice. Feel free to wear your dress more than once on your cruise—accessorize to change the look. Consider adding a wrap for chilly dining rooms. Formal evenings see most women in long evening gowns—try shopping the department stores (such as J.C.Penney's) for good deals. You could also try Chadwick's (http://www.chadwicks.com) and Victoria's Secret (http://www.victoriassecret.com).

Kids' Formalwear: Dressing the boys in slacks and a button-down shirt is just fine. If your boy really wants to dress up like Dad in a tux, special order rentals are available through Cruise Line Formalwear. You can also look for a good deal at http://www.ebay.com or at http://www.tux4boys.com. The girls look great in sun dresses, and this is the perfect opportunity to wear Disney princess dresses (available beforehand at the Disney Store and onboard in Mickey's Mates). You'll find gorgeous formalwear for both boys and girls at http://www.woodensoldier.com. Of course, that's if they even dine with you. Some kids prefer the company of their peers and have dinner at the Club/Lab.

Special/Celebrity Cruises

Looking for something a bit special on your next cruise? Disney plans many special cruises each year—some are once-in-a-lifetime events, while others just feature celebrity guests. Here are some past and upcoming events to give you an idea of what to expect:

Inaugural Cruises—The first sailing of a new ship, or the first sailing of a ship on a new itinerary is a big deal. On the up side, you get the thrill of being "the first" to sail, and you may get a few extra treats—on the Western Caribbean Inaugural Cruise in May 2002, we were treated to a Mexican mariachi band before embarking, given special "fans" to wave as we set sail, and presented with complimentary champagne glasses. On the down side, an inaugural cruise often doesn't have all the glitches worked out yet (though we didn't notice anything wrong on our inaugural cruise). Unless you count the itineraries to new ports in 2009, we probably won't see another inaugural cruise until the new ships arrive.

Celebrity Cruises—Many cruises have at least a minor celebrity or notable speaker, while others feature bigger names. For example, Roger Ebert and Richard Roeper usually do an annual Film Festival at Sea in the autumn on the Disney Wonder. A special package typically includes a sail-away cocktail reception with the famous film critics, screenings of four of their favorite films, open discussion sessions, and a book signing. Most celebrity guests have some connection with Disney, and include actors, artisans, and authors–recent guests have included Ernie Sabella (voice of "Pumbaa" in Disney's The Lion King—see photo below), Leslie Iwerks (granddaughter of Ub Iwerks), Raven, and former presidents George H.W. Bush and Jimmy Carter. Disney rarely announces their celebrities or speakers ahead of time, but you can call 888-DCL-2500 to inquire.

Holiday Cruises—If your cruise coincides with a major holiday, you can bet Disney has something special planned. Halloween cruises have costume contests, Thanksgiving cruises offer traditional dinners, December cruises feature magical holiday decorations and special holiday events, and so on. New Year's Eve cruises are very, very popular—book early if you're interested in one. Note also that religious holidays (Ash Wednesday, Easter, Passover, Hanukkah, Christmas, etc.) have clergy onboard for observances.

Fan Cruises—Disney fans love to cruise together, and usually one group or another is organizing a group cruise. We're doing a 4-night Disney Wonder cruise as part of MouseFest 2008 on December 7-11, 2008—check http://www.mousefest.org for all the details (see page 315, too). In 2009, PassPorter celebrates its 10th anniversary with a 7-night Disney Magic "Decade of Dreams" cruise to Tortola, St. John, and Castaway Cay, and you're invited—see page 347 for details!

Other Cruises—Keep an ear out for more special cruises, such as pin trading cruises, Disney Vacation Club cruises, and movie premieres. Cruises that feature two stops at Castaway Cay are rare but popular!

© MediaMarx, Inc., used with permission of Ernie Sabella

Ernie Sabella and Dave
at Castaway Cay

Introduction · Reservations · Staterooms · Dining · Activities · Ports of Call · Magic · Index

Celebrating Special Occasions

We firmly believe there's always something to celebrate ... even if it's just the fact that you're going on a cruise! And, of course, there are always birthdays, anniversaries, and holidays to remember. If you are celebrating a special occasion while you're onboard, be sure to let your travel agent or Disney reservation agent know when you book your cruise, or at least three weeks before you sail.

Bon Voyage Celebrations—Why not throw a party before you depart for your cruise? Invite your friends and family and make 'em jealous! Or if you happen to know someone going on a cruise, surprise them with a send-off party or a gift in their stateroom (see sidebar below). And don't forget about a celebratory drink when you board! Note: Only passengers are allowed on board or in the terminal, so parties with non-cruisers must take place before your arrival at the cruise terminal.

Birthdays—Let Disney know about your celebration in advance, and you'll be serenaded by your serving team and receive a small cake. You may also get a birthday pin!

Honeymoons—The Disney Cruise Line is popular with honeymooning couples, and Disney offers some "romance" packages for the celebration (see page 46). Be sure to let Disney know about your honeymoon even if you aren't on a package.

Anniversaries—We celebrated Dave's parents' 50th wedding anniversary aboard the Wonder in 2001—it was magical! Again, tell Disney about your celebration ahead of time and you may get a surprise.

Holidays—Disney does the holidays in grand style, particularly on Christmas and New Year's Eve—look for Santa Goofy, a three-deck-tall tree, holiday feasts, a New Year's Eve party, and a New Year's Day tailgate party.

Door decorations for Dave's "Who Wants to Be a Millionaire —Play It!" winning cruise

Tip: **Decorate your stateroom** and/or stateroom door in honor of your celebration! You can order basic stateroom decorations from Disney (see sidebar below) and they'll put them up before you arrive. Or bring your own decorations from home. Another fun idea is to buy (or make) magnets with which to decorate your metal stateroom door (see photo)—please note that only magnets are allowed on the doors (no tape or glue).

Stateroom Gifts

Disney Cruise Line offers a variety of gifts that you can order ahead of time and have waiting for you in your stateroom (or that of a friend or family member). Check the brochure that comes with your cruise documents, visit http://www.disneycruise.com and search on "gifts," or call 800-601-8455. If you're looking for something extra special, the Cape Canaveral-based company, The Perfect Gift, delivers delightful cruise baskets at good prices to your stateroom—you can even custom design your gift baskets. Call 800-950-4559 or visit http://www.theperfectgift.cc for more information.

Reunions and Group Cruises

A Disney cruise is ideal for a reunion or group event. Unlike a gathering on land, say at Walt Disney World, the Disney cruise allows groups to stay within close proximity of one another, offers a number of built-in activities and meals, and offers fun reunion packages. We've planned a number of reunions and group cruises over the years—here are our tips for a successful gathering:

Pick the best dates. Consult with the members of your group to find the dates that work best for their schedules and wallets. While spring and summer breaks may be best for groups with kids, those are also the priciest and may prevent some from joining you. Whenever possible, go for the less-expensive seasons, such as January, February, May, or early December.

If you're cruising as a family or small group, it may be possible to select staterooms in **close proximity** to one another, which facilitates communications and meetings. But if you cannot, don't fret—the ship isn't that big of a place. You may also be able to get rooms in closer proximity around final payment time (75 days before), when other cruisers cancel.

Keep in **close communication** with your group both before and during your cruise. Simple notes or newsletters, via e-mail or on paper, can be very helpful for educating and notifying them of events. Once onboard, you can leave voice mail and notes on stateroom doors.

When you book your cruise, let Disney know that you're traveling as a group and ask them to **link the reservations together** so you can dine in close proximity to one another. The dining room tables usually hold up to eight guests—on one of our family reunion cruises, we had a family of 16, and we were seated at two tables of eight, end to end. We've found that having this time together at dinner is very important to the success of a group cruise. Keep in mind, however, that everyone in your party needs to be on the same dinner seating—discuss early vs. late seating with your group before making a unilateral decision.

If your group wants to **dine at Palo**, make your reservations online as early as possible! Large groups are hard to accommodate and space goes quickly. Several small tables may be a better idea. Note: If your group's reservations are linked in Disney's system and you book a Palo table large enough to accommodate your group, be aware that other members of your group may not be able to make their own, separate Palo reservations.

Don't expect or try to do everything together. The beauty of a Disney cruise is that you don't have to hang together all the time to enjoy your group. You'll inevitably do some activities together during the day, bump into one another during free moments, and then enjoy quality time together at dinner.

MouseFest Cruise

Interested in joining other Disney Internet fans on a fun cruise? Each year in early December, we host a 4-night cruise—this year it is December 7-11, 2008. We plan all sorts of special activities and enjoy the company of like-minded individuals. And there are fabulous deals available through various travel agents. If you're interested in joining us, visit http://www.mousefest.org for information and an RSVP form. Everyone is invited! (For information on our 10th anniversary cruise, see page 347.)

Introduction

Reservations

Staterooms

Dining

Activities

Ports of Call

Magic

Index

Weddings and Vow Renewals

Ah, what is more romantic (or simple) than getting married or renewing your vows aboard a cruise ship? Disney Cruise Line makes it very easy to do both, and when compared to a land-based wedding, the prices are a good value, too!

First, if you're interested in either a wedding or vow renewal ceremony onboard a Disney ship, be aware that this isn't something you can arrange on your own. You'll need Disney's assistance, and you'll need to purchase their wedding or vow renewal package. To get started, visit http://www.disneycruise.com, click "Reservations," then choose either the "Weddings at Sea" package or the "Vow Renewal" package. This is where you'll find prices and package details. You can also call 321-939-4610 for information.

When you're **ready to book**, call a professional Disney wedding consultant at 321-939-4610 or contact your travel agent. You can book a wedding or vow renewal up to 12 months in advance, though it is not necessary to book it so early—you can plan a cruise wedding or vow renewal in as little as a month or two (based on availability).

Ceremony locations vary. Most wedding ceremonies are held outdoors at the Head's Up Bar at the far end of the family beach on Castaway Cay—the lagoon and ship provide a beautiful backdrop. You can also get married in either Sessions (Magic) or Cadillac Lounge (Wonder) on deck 3 forward. The lounges and Palo are also the typical spots for Vow Renewal ceremonies. Other locations may be possible under certain circumstances—inquire with your Disney wedding consultant.

Wedding ceremonies are **officiated** by an administrator of the Bahamas. Vow renewal ceremonies are usually performed by the Captain or a high-ranking officer.

Those getting married should note that you'll have a **private, legal ceremony** in the cruise terminal before your ship leaves Port Canaveral. This means you're technically married for your entire voyage, even though your public ceremony happens later in the cruise.

We are working on a **Disney Weddings e-book** with author Carrie Hayward. The e-book will cover weddings at Walt Disney World and on the Disney Cruise. We plan to have the e-book available in 2008. For details and to check its status, visit http://www.passporter.com/weddings.asp.

© Disney

A Castaway Cay wedding

Preventing Seasickness

Seasickness—just the thought of it can make some of us a little queasy. And if you actually have it ... no, let's not think about it. Let's think about how fortunate we are to be sailing on a large, modern cruise ship on some of the calmest waters in the world. Two huge stabilizer fins take the bite out of the worst wave action, and modern medicine has provided more than one helpful remedy. If you're looking for that ounce of prevention, read on!

✔ **Purely Natural**—Go topside, take deep breaths, get some fresh air, and look at the horizon. The worst thing you can do is stay in your stateroom. Seasickness is caused by the confusion between what your inner ear senses and what your eyes see. If you can look at something steady, it helps your brain synchronize these. Eventually your brain will get used to the motion and you get your "sea legs," but that can take a day or two. Drink lots of water and have some mild food, such as saltine crackers—avoid fatty and salty foods, and eat lightly.

✔ **Herbs**—Ginger is reported to help reduce seasickness. It comes in pill and cookie form— even ginger ale can help. It's best to begin taking this in advance of feeling sick.

✔ **Bonine, or "Dramamine Less Drowsy Formula"**—These are brand names of Meclizine, which has far fewer side effects than its older cousin Dramamine (which we don't recommend). Try it at home before your cruise to check for side effects, then take it a few hours before departure for maximum effectiveness. Note: For kids ages 6 to 12, look for the new "Bonine for Kids," or use regular Dramamine. Tip: The onboard medical facility (discussed on the next page) provides free chewable Meclizine tablets (25 mg.) from a dispenser next to its door on deck 1 forward. Guest Services (on deck 3 midship) may also have some Meclizine if you can't make it down to deck 1.

✔ **Sea-Bands**—These are elastic wrist bands that operate by applying pressure to the Nei Kuan acupressure point on each wrist by means of a plastic stud, thereby preventing seasickness. Some people swear by them; some say that they don't work. Either way, they are inexpensive (unless you buy them on the ship) and have no medical side effects. They don't yet come in designer colors to match your formal evening gown, however.

✔ **Scopolamine Transdermal Patch**—Available by prescription only. It is the most effective preventative with the least drowsiness, but it also comes with the most side effects, such as dry mouth and dizziness. For more information about scopolamine, speak to your doctor and visit http://www.transdermscop.com.

✔ **Ship Location**—A low deck, midship stateroom is generally considered to be the location on a ship where you'll feel the least movement. If you know you're prone to seasickness, consider requesting a stateroom on decks 1-2, midship. But once you're onboard and you find yourself feeling seasick, the best thing to do is get out of your stateroom, go to deck 4 midship, and lie down in one of the padded deck chairs—then use the tips noted in "Purely Natural" above.

✔ **Choose Excursions Wisely**—Those prone to motion sickness may want to avoid shore excursions that rely heavily on smaller boats such as ferries and sailboats. Read the excursion descriptions in chapter 6 carefully for mentions of motion sickness or rough seas. If you don't want to miss out on anything, begin taking your preferred seasickness remedy well in advance of the excursion.

Introduction

Reservations

Staterooms

Dining

Activities

Ports of Call

Magic

Index

Staying Healthy

Staying healthy is easy with some preparation and knowledge. Folks who are already healthy may only have to worry about getting seasick (see the previous page) or picking up a virus. Here's what you can do to prevent illness:

Getting a virus is less likely than seasickness, but still possible—any time you get people together for more than two or three days at a time, you're going to have some percentage become ill. Cruise ships are significantly less vulnerable than schools, hotels, nursing homes, and restaurants, contrary to the media attention the Norwalk-like virus received in November/December 2002—cruise ships account for 10% of the outbreaks, while restaurants, nursing homes, and schools account for more than 70%. The Centers for Disease Control (CDC) report that normally 1-2% of a cruise population gets sick on a regular basis; during the Norwalk-like virus epidemics, this number may only rise to 2-4%. Nonetheless, Disney takes many precautions to avoid illness on its ships, including thoroughly disinfecting surfaces that are touched, encouraging hand-washing, providing hand wipes in particular situations, and refusing passage to visibly ill passengers to reduce the risk of transmitting a virus to others.

To avoid catching a bug, get a full night's sleep before you embark, eat well, drink lots of water, and wash your hands thoroughly and frequently. Hand-washing cannot be emphasized enough. Wash your hands for at least 15 seconds after using the bathroom, after changing a diaper, and before handling, preparing, or consuming food. Regular soap and water does the trick—there's no need for antibacterial soaps (in fact, the Centers for Disease Control suggest that antibacterial soaps may contribute to the problem and suggest you do not use them). Alcohol-based hand sanitizer can be used as a supplement in between times hands are washed, but it should not replace soap and water and isn't effective after using the bathroom, after changing diapers, or before handling food. There's no need to bring your own Lysol either—all surfaces are disinfected before you board as well as while you're underway (besides, Lysol does nothing to stop the Norwalk-like virus). Tip: To make sure both you and your kids wash your hands for long enough, try singing or humming the "Happy Birthday" song slowly while washing your hands—when the song ends, your hands are clean.

If you get sick, be aware that reporting illness to the cruise staff is taken seriously—the cruise line is required to report any onboard cases of gastrointestinal illness to the CDC. You may be required to visit the medical facility onboard (see below), and if you're found to have a gastrointestinal illness, you may be restricted to your stateroom to avoid passing the illness to others. And if you're sick when you check in at the terminal, you may need to visit a medical professional before boarding—you may even be refused passage.

Viruses aside, there's one medical problem that far too many cruisers contract during their cruise—**sunburn**. Bring that sunscreen (SPF of 30 or higher) and use it. And wear hats and cover-ups whenever possible. Don't take your chances with a sunburn.

As much as we don't like to think about it, accidents happen and guests get sick. Knowing that this is unavoidable, Disney has put a well-equipped **medical facility** aboard—it's equipped with modern medical equipment such as cardiac life support equipment, ventilators, and an X-ray machine. Two doctors and three registered nurses are on staff. The care, we hear, is excellent and the fees are reasonable. Any medical care you receive is billed to your stateroom account and you bill your insurance company separately.

Doing Business Onboard

We know, we know ... "work" is a four-letter word on a cruise. If you can avoid your work entirely on the cruise, we heartily recommend it! Alas, we know better than anyone that sometimes your business doesn't take a vacation just because you do. If you need to keep up with work while you're cruising, here are our tried-and-true tips:

Phone Calls—You have four options when making phone calls: use Disney's ship-to-shore phone system (the phone in your stateroom) for $6.95/minute, use your cellular phone in your stateroom (see page 107), use your cell phone when in port or sailing past islands with cell roaming service, or use a pay phone in port (most cruise terminals have pay phones available). Your stateroom phone system is detailed on page 103. If you opt to bring a cell phone, call your wireless provider to inquire about international roaming.

Laptop Computers—We always bring along our laptop, and now that we can connect to the Internet with it via wireless access onboard (both in public areas and in our stateroom), doing business is much easier. Typically, we use the laptop to download photos from the digital camera, but on one cruise we did some printing (with a portable printer hooked up to our laptop) and faxing through Guest Services. Be sure to bring all necessary cables!

Internet Access—We've devoted two full pages to Internet Access, on pages 158–159. If you're relying on Internet access to keep up with work, keep in mind that the Internet Cafe is the least busy earlier in the day and late at night. Note also that the Internet Cafe may not open on debarkation morning, though recently it has stayed open. We noticed no pattern to the occasional and short downtime experienced with wireless access onboard.

Faxes—You can send and receive faxes from the Guest Services desk (deck 3 midship). Cost is the same as ship-to-shore phone calls—$6.95/minute. We faxed several sheets during a 4-night cruise and found that each page takes about one minute to fax, though fax transmission time does depend on the density of the page.

Copies—The Guest Services desk is also the place to have copies made.

Meeting Space—Both Disney ships have public spaces that may be rented at certain times. You can also get audio-visual equipment. Call Disney for details.

Tip: If your work is portable, take it outside to one of the patio tables behind Topsider's/Beach Blanket Buffet (deck 9 aft) or enjoy the solitude of the small area on deck 7 aft.

Joining the Ship's Crew

Ever thought of working on a Disney ship? If you are at least 21 years old, there are job opportunities. From what we understand, it takes a huge time commitment (you typically sign a six-month contract and work about 70–80 hours a week) and it's difficult to be away from home for the long stretches required. On the flip side, Disney does offer several perks, such as crew-only areas (including a beach on Castaway Cay and an onboard pool), free theme park admission, and so on. If you'd like to learn more, call the job line at 407-566-SHIP or visit http://www.dcljobs.com.

Disney Characters

One of the benefits of a Disney cruise is the opportunity to meet your favorite Disney characters—you won't find them on any other cruise in the world. Typically, the Disney celebrities joining you on your cruise include Mickey, Minnie, Goofy, Pluto, Donald, Chip, Dale, and Stitch (often in tropical attire) as well as appearances from special "face" characters like Cinderella, Snow White, and Alice. Here's where to meet your Disney friends onboard:

Character Appearances—The Lobby Atrium (both decks 3 and 4) is a popular gathering place for Disney friends, typically in the evenings for photo opportunities. If you forget your camera, there are often ship's photographers to snap a shot. You'll also find characters in the terminal before you board, at deck parties, the kids' clubs, and near the Mickey Pool. For schedules, check your *Personal Navigator*, the character appearance display in the Lobby Atrium (or outside Shutters), or call 7-PALS on your stateroom phone.

Character Autographs: Bring a notebook or autograph book to the character meets— you can buy them in Mickey's Mates or just make one at home before you board (see photo on right). Take a photo of the Disney character autographing the book and you can later attach a copy of the picture to each autographed page—this makes a great keepsake!

A homemade autograph book

© MediaMarx, Inc.

Character Breakfasts—Guests on the seven-night and longer cruises get the opportunity to mingle with Mickey, Minnie, Goofy, Pluto, Chip and Dale at a character breakfast in Parrot Cay. For more details, see page 120.

Tea With Wendy—This is a special character event on the seven-night (and longer) cruises. Check your *Personal Navigator* for the day and time to pick up tickets (at no extra charge) and arrive early—this is a popular event and tickets go quickly. The half-hour "tea" is held in Studio Sea (deck 4 midship) on certain afternoons. As you might have guessed, the tea is hosted by Wendy Darling (from Disney's Peter Pan), who demonstrates the proper way to serve tea, and tells a story. Chocolate chip cookies and iced tea are served. The event is attended predominantly by young girls, but everyone is welcome—young or old, male or female. After tea, guests may greet Wendy personally and get a photograph with her. Tip: Crew members select two boys from the audience to play John and Michael, Wendy's brothers.

Character Parties—In addition to the Disney character appearances at the deck parties, there is another special character party for which to check your Personal Navigator. 'Til We Meet Again is a farewell party in the Lobby Atrium held on your last evening (usually at 10:00 or 10:15 pm)—most of the characters come out to bid everyone a special goodbye.

Tipping and Feedback

Tipping is your way of thanking the crew for their fine service. Here are Disney's recommended gratuities for each guest, regardless of age:

Crew Member/Service	Per Night	3-Night	4-Night	7-Night
Dining Room Server	~$3.75	$11.00	$14.75	$25.75
Dining Room Asst. Server	~$2.75	$8.00	$10.75	$18.75
Dining Room Head Server	~$1.00	$2.75	$3.75	$6.50
Stateroom Host/Hostess	~$3.60	$10.75	$14.50	$25.25
Palo Server	Your discretion (on top of the $15/person service charge)			
Bartender/Lounge Server	If no tip was automatically added, 10% to 15%			
Room Service	Your discretion (usually $1 to $2/person)			
Kids' Counselors	Not necessary, but do reward good service			
Shore Excursion Tour Guide	$1 to $2/person			
Baggage Porters (at terminal)	$1 to $2/bag			

Need help calculating your tips? See page 350 for details on how to get an interactive worksheet that does the calculations for you!

Disney's tipping guidelines are **not etched in stone**. Exceptional service deserves an exceptional tip, and substandard service should earn a lesser reward. But don't save all your compliments for the tip envelope—people thrive on appreciation.

On your last day, **tip envelopes** are left in your stateroom so you may give gratuities to the first four crew members noted in the chart above. Fill them with cash, or charge the tips to your stateroom account at Guest Services and they will give you receipts to put in the envelopes (avoid Guest Services on the last evening—it's very busy). Tip: You can now prepay your gratuities up to three days before you leave home at the Disney Cruise Line web site! If you prepay, gratuity vouchers will be left with your tip envelopes. Give the filled envelopes to each crew member—servers typically receive theirs at the last dinner.

Tipping is a form of feedback for services received, but you can give **additional feedback** on your experience. Neither we nor Disney Cruise Line would be where we are today without your feedback. For instance, did you know that those obstructed-view category 7 staterooms we mentioned on page 95 were reclassified (and lowered in price) based on cruiser feedback? And even with PassPorter, our depth of detail is a direct reader request.

The night before you disembark, a **questionnaire** is placed in your stateroom. Fill it out and deposit it in the collection boxes at breakfast or on the gangway. If you had problems, there is a small section to describe what happened—if you need to communicate more, read on.

To send **detailed comments** (complaints or compliments) to Disney once you return home, write a letter and mail it to: DCL Guest Communications, P.O. Box 10238, Lake Buena Vista, FL 32830. You can also send e-mail to dcl.guest.communications@disneycruise.com or visit http://disney.go.com/mail/disneycruiseline. Disney is typically very responsive to guest feedback, and you should hear back from them within six weeks.

Contacting us at **PassPorter Travel Press** is even easier. E-mail feedback@passporter.com or send a letter to P.O. Box 3880, Ann Arbor, MI 48106. We also recommend you visit http://www.passporter.com/register.asp to register your copy, which is another perfect opportunity to tell us what you think. When you register, we'll send back coupons good for discounts on future PassPorters and accessories!

Introduction
Reservations
Staterooms
Dining
Activities
Ports of Call
Magic
Index

Customs Allowances

Ah, U.S. Customs. While we dreaded customs on our first cruise, we quickly found that the rules aren't hard to understand, and the process is smooth if you pay attention. If you feel unsure about customs and debarkation in general, attend the debarkation talk on the afternoon of the day before disembarkation (or catch it on TV in your stateroom later that evening).

You are required to declare everything that you purchased or were given as a gift on the ship, in your ports of call, and on Castaway Cay. Fill out the **U.S. Customs Declaration Form** left in your stateroom on your last night (extra forms are available at Guest Services) Fill it in and sign and date the form—you will hand it to customs during debarkation.

Each guest is allowed a **total duty-free allowance** of $800 (3- and 4-night cruises, 7-night Western Caribbean, repositioning, and Mexican Riviera cruises) or $1,200 (7-night Eastern Caribbean cruises). Liquor and tobacco have special limits. One liter of liquor per person over 21 years of age is exempt from duties (Eastern Caribbean cruisers are allowed four more liters from the Virgin Islands). One carton of cigarettes and 100 cigars (other than Cuban cigars, which are not allowed at all) are exempt (Eastern Caribbean cruisers can add four more cartons of cigarettes if purchased in St. Thomas). If you exceed the customs allowances, you must report to the Customs Inspector before you debark the ship—check

© MediaMarx, Inc.

the debarkation sheet left in your stateroom. If you exceed your customs allowances, you will need to have cash on hand to pay your duties—no checks, traveler's checks, or credit cards are accepted.

Read more about the **U.S. Customs Laws** online at http://www.cbp.gov/xp/cgov/travel (click "Know Before You Go!"). Keep in mind that anything that you don't declare is considered smuggled—don't forget any items you won onboard. The duties on declared items are low, but the penalties for smuggled items are high. And don't try to carry off items that aren't allowed, such as fresh fruit or flowers—you can face a stiff fine. You'd be surprised how many try to "smuggle" a banana unwittingly (see photo).

Fruit taken off the ship

Immigration and International Guests

As we mentioned earlier in the guidebook, international guests yield their passports before boarding the ship. U.S. Immigration requires that all non-U.S. guests (and anyone who joined the ship enroute) present themselves at every U.S. port of entry. International guests on all Caribbean itineraries must go through immigration in Port Canaveral. On the 7-night Eastern Caribbean cruise, immigration inspection may also be held at St. Thomas for all passengers (U.S. and non-U.S.). In both cases, you will be directed to reclaim your passport—the details will be on a note placed in your stateroom the evening before. Alas, immigration happens pretty early in the morning—typically at 5:30 am to 6:00 am. Be sure to bring all members of your party and your passport receipt. All guests must clear immigration before any guests can debark in St. Thomas or Port Canaveral. Note: We've heard from a reader that Disney may be trying out new immigration procedures for international guests which do not involve waking at the crack of dawn!

Debarkation

Yes, your cruise is really over. Wouldn't it be nice if you could just stay onboard and sail forever? Even when it's time to go, nobody gets you to the exit more smoothly than Disney. This is the company that made crowd control a science. There's no waiting in line to depart, nobody calls out your name, and things seem to just flow. Here's the drill:

First, you need to **settle your onboard account**. If you put a credit card on your account at check-in, you're all set. Otherwise, visit Guest Services (deck 3 midship) to check and pay the total with credit card, traveler's checks, or cash. Do this the day before you debark.

On your **last night aboard**, pack your bags, remove old cruise tags, and attach the new tags provided (more tags are at Guest Services if you need them). Don't forget to fill out the tags and make a note of the tag color. When you're ready, place your tagged luggage in the passageway by 11:00 pm-you will not see it again until you're off the ship. Thus, it's crucial that you pack a small day bag to hold your toiletries, nightclothes, and valuables. And don't forget to keep out an outfit (and shoes) to wear the next morning! If you're hoping to get off the ship quickly the next morning, consider keeping your luggage with you and carrying it off the ship yourself—not as convenient, but a bit quicker. This is a good time to fill out the customs forms placed in your stateroom (see previous page). Also, if you have a pager for the kids' clubs, return it to deck 5 midship this evening.

On **debarkation morning**, take your day bags and go to breakfast in the same restaurant in which you dined the previous evening (unless you ate at Palo, in which case you go to the restaurant you would have been in). Guests with early seating eat at 6:45 am, while late seating guests eat at 8:00 am. If you prefer, you can get "early bird" coffee and Danish pastries at 6:00 am to 6:30 am at the Beverage Station (deck 9 aft) or a continental breakfast from 6:30 am to 8:00 am at Topsider's/Beach Blanket Buffet (deck 9 aft). Be aware that guests must vacate their staterooms by 8:00 am. Shutters is open from 7:00 am to 8:30 am, but all other shops are closed. Drop off your questionnaire (see page 321) at breakfast or as you debark. Typically the first guest debarks at 7:45 am and the last guest debarks at 9:45 am.

Now it's time to **say goodbye** to all your "family." After breakfast, go to the gangway (deck 3 midship), stroll off the ship with your day bags, and head off to customs. Keep your photo ID and passport handy. At the customs area, claim your checked baggage in the color-coded area. Photography is not allowed in the customs area—keep your camera down to avoid complications. Pass through customs (usually you just present your customs forms and walk right through) and you're soon in your Disney motorcoach, car, or limousine. Porters are available to help you—don't forget to tip them. If you're flying out of Orlando International Airport, several airlines give you the option of checking your bags on the ship (see "Disney's Onboard Airline Check-In Program" on page 57).

Castaway Club

Once you've got a Disney cruise under your belt, you're an automatic member of Disney's Castaway Club. As a Castaway Club member, you get perks for future cruises, such as a special toll-free number, special check-in area, onboard reception with ship officers, and free gift in your stateroom. If you don't receive any information on the Castaway Club after your cruise, call Disney at 888-DCL-2500 to request it.

Magical and Wonderful Tips

Creating a "magical" and "wonderful" cruise takes a dash of planning, a pinch of knowledge, and a bit of pixie dust! Here are some more tips:

◎ If you feel the Stateroom Celebration decoration package is a bit too spendy and you'd rather have that money for bingo and spa treatments, **bring your own decorations**! My little boy and I usually sail on the Disney Magic right around his birthday, and I like to make a big deal out of his special day. I bring un-inflated mylar birthday balloons (found some Mickey ones at The Dollar Store!), jointed "Happy Birthday" banners, and anything else I can find. I also bring poster putty to put up the decorations without harming the walls. I wait until he is gone to the kids' club, then I "birthday up" the whole stateroom. He loves seeing what I've done, and it makes him feel so special. – *contributed by Disney vacationer Gina Peterson*

◎ Buy a small artist's sketch book (large enough to fit 4x6 photos) to use as a **unique autograph book**. I always have the page open to the next spot for my son to hand the book to the character he is meeting. I have the characters sign on every other page—this way you can put a photo of your child/family on the page opposite of the autograph when you print your photos later. We decorate the front of the book with Disney stickers and the characters are always very impressed with the uniqueness of his album. We also get one of those "chunky" permanent markers for the characters to sign with. The characters always love signing it as the album and marker are large enough for them to handle. When we get home, we print the pictures and mat them on the opposite page of the signature for an instant souvenir. – *contributed by Disney vacationer Susan Zanovitch*

◎ Please **share your memories and tips**. If we publish them, we'll credit you by name and send you a free copy when they're published! Visit http://www.passporter.com/customs/tipsandstories.asp.

Magical Memory

◎ *"Much as we love cruising, there's a lot of stress on that last morning when there's a rush to a standardized breakfast in a dining room crowded with more day bags than two ships' worth of passengers might need. It may just be that it's always at the end of a cruise, but that morning seems the least magical time on board for us. On our last cruise, we dealt with this by grabbing a quick cup of coffee on deck 9 and heading for the gangway at 8:00 am, just as the second seating was starting breakfast. By this time, half the bags are gone from the pickup area, few guests are there, porters are available, and customs is quick. We then head south toward Cocoa Beach for a breakfast at The Omelet Station, a funky little place with great breakfasts and no carry-on bags!"*
...as told by Disney cruiser Bruce Metcalf

Glossary of Terms

While this guide isn't exactly overflowing with salty terms, we thought a brief glossary could be useful, and a bit of fun.

Aft—Towards the rear. The *after* section of the ship. Also *abaft*.

All Aboard— The latest time a passenger may board in a port.

All Ashore—The earliest time a passenger may disembark in a port.

Amidships—The center of the ship, between fore and aft. Also *midship*.

Assistant Server—The crew member who assists your server, typically by looking after drinks, clearing the table, and carrying trays to and from the kitchen. On the Disney Cruise Line, a single assistant server attends your needs throughout your voyage.

Beam—The widest portion of a watercraft.

Berth—Any bed on a ship, but more commonly, the fold-down or fold-out beds in a stateroom.

Boat—A small watercraft, sometimes carried onboard a ship.

Bow—The forwardmost section of the ship, pronounced *bough*.

Bridge—The location from which a ship is steered and speed is controlled.

Bulkhead—A vertical wall or partition.

Captain—Ship's officer responsible for the operation and safety of the vessel. See *Master*.

Cast Member—An employee at Disney's land-based theme parks and resorts.

Castaway Club—Disney's free club for past Disney cruisers.

Catamaran—A very stable, fast watercraft with two parallel, widely spaced hulls joined by a broad deck.

Crew Member—A shipboard employee.

Cruise Director—Officer in charge of all passenger entertainment and recreational activities, including shore excursions. "Is everybody having a good time?"

DCL—Abbreviation for the Disney Cruise Line.

Deck—The covering over a vessel's hull, or any floor on a ship.

Diesel Electric—Propulsion system used by ships of the Disney Cruise Line. Diesel generators provide electricity to operate the ship's propulsion motors and other systems.

Displacement—Weight of the water displaced by a vessel, equivalent to the vessel's weight.

Dock—To come alongside a pier. See also *pier*.

Draft—The depth of the submerged portion of a watercraft.

Fathom—A measure of depth. One fathom is equivalent to 6 feet/1.8288 m.

Fender—A device for padding the side of a watercraft or pier to prevent damage.

Fore—Forward. Toward the front. Also, a golfer's warning call.

Gangway—A location on the side of a vessel where passengers and crew can board and disembark. Also, *a retractable walkway broader than a gangplank, connecting ship to shore.*

Guest Relations—Disney's term for a hotel's front desk operations. On the Disney Cruise Line, equivalent to the Purser's Office. Located on deck 3, adjacent to the Atrium Lobby.

Hawser—Long, thick mooring lines for fastening a ship to a pier.

Head Server—The crew member who supervises dining room servers and assistant servers. A single head server attends your needs throughout your voyage.

Hotel Manager—Ship's officer in charge of all passenger-related operations, including accommodations, housekeeping, food and beverages, and entertainment.

Hull—The main body of a watercraft. From Middle English for *husk*.

Keel—One of the main structural members of a vessel to which frames are fastened.

Key to the World Card—Your personal room key, admission, identification, and charge account. Each member of your party has his/her own Key to the World card.

Introduction

Reservations

Staterooms

Dining

Activities

Ports of Call

Magic

Index

Glossary (continued)

Knot—A measure of speed equal to Nautical Miles Per Hour (6,076 feet/1,852 meters). Also, an undesired tangling of hair.

Latitude—Position north or south of the equator, expressed in degrees.

League—20,000 Leagues = 60,000 miles = 96,560 kilometers

Leeward—Away from, or sheltered from, the wind.

Line—Rope and cord used on a watercraft, or a tall tale told at a bar.

Longitude—Position east or west of Greenwich, England, expressed in degrees.

Mal de Mer—(French) Seasickness. Popular English language euphemism, akin to "green around the gills."

Master—The captain of a ship. *Master Mariner* is a government-issued license for merchant ship captains.

PFD—Personal Floatation Device. Life jacket. Sometimes known as a Mae West, for the pulchritude (physical appeal) added to those who wear it.

Pier—A platform extending from shore for mooring and loading watercraft.

Pitch—The rising and falling of the bow and stern. See *Roll*. Also, black, tar-like substance used for waterproofing wooden vessels.

Port—The left side of the watercraft when facing Forward. Also, harbor. Also, a fortified wine named for the Portuguese port town of Oporto.

Porthole—An opening in the hull of a vessel. A round window.

Porthos—One of Alexandre Dumas' Three Musketeers.

Propeller—A rotary fan-like device connected to the ship's engines. When it turns, the ship moves. When stationary, the ship is at rest.

Purser—The ship's officer responsible for banking, payroll, and passenger records. See Guest Relations.

Roll—Side-to-side, rocking motion of a vessel. In extremes, this can lead to capsizing.

Rudder—A flat, submerged surface at the stern, used to steer a vessel while underway.

Server—The crew member who attends your table in the dining room, takes food and beverage orders, and supervises the assistant server. Similar to a restaurant waiter. On the Disney Cruise Line, the same server attends your needs throughout your voyage.

Ship—A large watercraft, typically oceangoing, too dignified to be called a boat and big enough to carry boats of its own.

Shorex—Cruise industry abbreviation for Shore Excursion.

Stabilizer—Horizontal, mechanized, submerged flaps that can be extended from a vessel to reduce rolling motion.

Staff Captain—A ship's second-in-command, responsible for crew discipline and ship's maintenance. Also known as "Number One."

Starboard—The right-hand side of the vessel when facing Forward.

Stateroom Host/Hostess—The crew member responsible for your stateroom's housekeeping, baggage pickup/delivery, and your housekeeping-related requests. Sometimes known as a Stateroom Attendant or Steward.

Stem—The part of the bow that is farthest forward.

Stern—The rearmost section of the ship. Also, humorless.

Tender—A watercraft used to convey passengers and cargo from a ship to the shore. Also, easily chewed, as in Filet Mignon.

Tonnage—A measure of the size or cargo capacity of a ship. Also, what you may think you will weigh after a long cruise.

Thruster—A propeller positioned to move the ship laterally while docking and at other times when the ship has little or no forward motion.

Waterline—A line painted on the hull of a watercraft to indicate its typical draft when properly loaded.

Whorf—A character on "Star Trek the Next Generation." See *Pier*.

Windward—Travel into the wind.

Index

We feel that a comprehensive index is very important to a successful travel guide. Too many times we've tried to look something up in other books only to find there was no entry at all, forcing us to flip through pages and waste valuable time. When you're on the phone with a reservation agent and looking for that little detail, time is of the essence.

You'll find the PassPorter index is complete and detailed. Whenever we reference more than one page for a given topic, the major topic is in **bold** to help you home in on exactly what you need. For those times you want to find everything there is to be had, we include all the minor references. We have plenty of cross-references, too, just in case you don't look it up under the name we use.

P.S. This isn't the end of the book. The Web Site Index begins on page 333.

Introduction · Reservations · Staterooms · Dining · Activities · Ports of Call · Magic · Index

Introduction
Reservations
Staterooms
Dining
Activities
Ports of Call
Magic
Index

Web Site Index

(continued on next page)

Introduction

Reservations

Staterooms

Dining

Activities

Ports of Call

Magic

Index

Web Site Index *(continued from previous page)*

Introduction

Reservations

Staterooms

Dining

Activities

Ports of Call

Magic

Index

Web Site Index *(continued from previous page)*

Introduction

Reservations

Staterooms

Dining

Activities

Ports of Call

Magic

Index

My Cruise Journal

Introduction

Reservations

Staterooms

Dining

Activities

Ports of Call

Magic

Index

My Cruise Journal

....

....

....

....

....

....

....

....

....

....

....

....

....

....

....

....

....

....

....

....

....

....

....

Introduction
Reservations
Staterooms
Dining
Activities
Ports of Call
Magic
Index

My Cruise Journal

Introduction

Reservations

Staterooms

Dining

Activities

Ports of Call

Magic

Index

My Cruise Journal

....

....

....

....

....

....

....

....

....

....

....

....

....

....

....

....

....

....

....

....

....

Introduction

Reservations

Staterooms

Dining

Activities

Ports of Call

Magic

Index

My Cruise Journal

Introduction

Reservations

Staterooms

Dining

Activities

Ports of Call

Magic

Index

My Cruise Journal

....

....

....

....

....

....

....

....

....

....

....

....

....

....

....

....

....

....

....

....

....

....

....

....

Introduction

Reservations

Staterooms

Dining

Activities

Ports of Call

Magic

Index

My Cruise Journal

Introduction

Reservations

Staterooms

Dining

Activities

Ports of Call

Magic

Index

My Cruise Journal

....

....

....

....

....

....

....

....

....

....

....

....

....

....

....

....

....

....

....

....

....

....

PassPorter Online

A wonderful way to get the most from your PassPorter is to visit our active web site at http://www.passporter.com/dcl. We serve up valuable PassPorter updates, plus useful Disney Cruise information and advice we couldn't jam into our book. You can swap tales (that's t-a-l-e-s, Mickey!) with fellow Disney fans, enter contests, find links to other sites, get plenty of details, and ask us questions. You can also order PassPorters and shop for PassPorter accessories! The latest information on new PassPorters to other destinations is available on our web site as well. To go directly to our latest list of page-by-page PassPorter updates, visit http://www. passporter.com/customs/bookupdates.htm.

Register this guidebook and get more discounts

We are **very** interested to learn how your vacation went and what you think of PassPorter, how it worked (or didn't work) for you, and your opinion on how we could improve it! We encourage you to register your copy of PassPorter with us—in return for your feedback, we'll send you coupons good for discounts on PassPorters and gear when purchased directly from us. Register your copy of PassPorter at http://www.passporter.com/register.asp.

Get weekly updates delivered to your e-mailbox

We publish a free, weekly newsletter filled with feature articles about Disney Cruise Line, Walt Disney World, Disneyland, and travel in general, as well as recent news, reader tips, contests, answers to reader questions, and specials on PassPorter guidebooks and gear. To subscribe, visit http://www.passporter.com/news.htm.

View our cruise photos online before you go

Would you like to see photos from Disney cruises in full color? The PassPorter Photo Archive is a large (and free) collection of photos from Disney cruises, Walt Disney World, Disneyland, and beyond! The archive is fully searchable and each photo carries a description and date. Visit http://www.passporter.com/photos.

Cruise with Jennifer & Dave in 2007 & 2008

We warmly invite you to join us at one of several cruises in 2008 and 2009:

December 7-11, 2008: We'll be onboard the Disney Wonder for the MouseFest 2008 cruise! This is our annual gathering of readers, fellow Disney fans, friends, and family ... and the sixth year we take to the sea! MouseFest is a casual, family-friendly affair for the Disney fan community, during which we and others host informal events—everyone is welcome! To learn more about MouseFest, visit http://www.mousefest.org.

April 25-May 2, 2009: We're celebrating PassPorter's 10th anniversary onboard the Disney Magic for our special "Decade of Dreams" Tour! This is a very special, once-in-a-lifetime cruise and we'd love to cruise with you. See the next page for all the details!

December 6-10, 2009: We'll be back onboard the Disney Wonder for MouseFest 2009 (see details above). We're planning a special PassPorter anniversary meet for this cruise, too.

PassPorter's Decade of Dreams
Our Tenth Anniversary Coast-to-Coast Celebration

2009 marks the realization of a dream ... a decade of dreams! Join PassPorter as we celebrate our dreams and your dreams together with a tenth anniversary coast-to-coast celebration in 2009: **PassPorter's "Decade of Dreams" Tour!**

In 1999, Jennifer and Dave Marx set out to **follow their dreams** by writing and publishing a small Disney guidebook called "PassPorter." Of course, "small" doesn't describe the task they took on, tackling the biggest vacation destination in the United States. Together with the help of a core team and tens of thousands of readers, PassPorter grew and expanded, year by year. Along the way, PassPorter has won awards and hit the bestseller list time and time again. None of this would have happened without the love and support of PassPorter readers. We may have started out small, but together we have built PassPorter into something mighty! In 2009, we will celebrate our achievement together with a year-long celebration from coast to coast! Everyone is invited and all are warmly welcome to join us at all or part of our celebration. We are combining small parties (meets) with grand, multiday trips, including a 7-night Disney Cruise (see below), a 4-night stay at Walt Disney World, and a Disneyland visit that includes park time and an Adventures by Disney expedition.

PassPorter's "Decade of Dreams" Disney Cruise is the 7-Night Eastern Caribbean Cruise to Tortola, St. Thomas, & Castaway Cay, departing on April 25, 2009, and returning on May 2, 2009. This is the Disney Magic's first-ever visit to the port of Tortola, one of Disney's special itineraries, and we'll be onboard to usher her in! If you book with our travel provider (Mouse Fan Travel), you'll be able to join us at exclusive PassPorter "Decade of Dreams" events, meets, and shore excursions, including a special reception with treats, a cruise-long PassPorter Treasure Hunt with daily prizes and a grand prize, customized port guides prepared by Jennifer and Dave, a group photo shoot of all our fellow Dreamers to be published in the 2010 edition of *PassPorter's Disney Cruise Guide*, loads of time to hang out with your fellow PassPorter friends, members, and readers, and a special "Dream Pass" to the PassPorter's Club (see page 350).

For all the details—and our story of how PassPorter came to be—please visit http://www.passporter.com/decade-of-dreams.asp

PassPorter Guidebooks

Deluxe Cruise Edition

Design first-class cruises with this loose-leaf ring-bound edition. Our popular Deluxe Edition features the same great content as this guidebook, plus fourteen of our famous organizer "PassPockets" to plan and record your trip. Special features of the Deluxe Edition include ten interior storage slots in the binder to hold maps, ID cards, and a pen (included). The Deluxe binder makes it easy to add, remove, and rearrange pages ... you can even download, print, and add updates and supplemental pages from our web site or worksheets from the PassPorter's Club (see page 350). Refill pages and pockets are available for purchase. Learn more and order a copy at http://www.passporter.com/wdw/deluxe.htm. The Deluxe Edition is also available through bookstores by special order—just give your favorite bookstore the ISBN code for the 2008 Deluxe Edition (ISBN-13: 978-1-58771-056-8).

PassPorter's Walt Disney World

Our best-selling Walt Disney World guidebook covers everything you need to plan a practically perfect vacation, including fold-out park maps, resort room layout diagrams, KidTips, descriptions, reviews, and ratings for the resorts, parks, attractions, and restaurants, and much more! Learn more and order at http://www.passporter.com/wdw or get a copy at your favorite bookstore. Available in a spiral-bound edition (ISBN-13: 978-1-58771-049-0) and a Deluxe Edition (ISBN-13: 978-1-58771-050-6).

PassPorter's Open Mouse for Disney World & Disney Cruise

Authors Deb Wills and Debra Martin Koma have prepared more than 400 pages of in-depth information for Walt Disney World and Disney Cruise Line vacationers of all abilities, delivering in-depth coverage from a distinctive "special challenges" perspective. This is a perfect supplement to this guidebook. Learn more at http://www.openmouse.com or get a copy at your favorite bookstore (ISBN-13: 978-1-58771-018-6).

PassPorter's Disneyland Resort and S. California Attractions

PassPorter tours the park that started it all! California's Disneyland Park, Disney's California Adventure, and Downtown Disney get PassPorter's expert treatment, and we throw in Universal Studios Hollywood, Knott's Berry Farm, Hollywood and Downtown Los Angeles, San Diego, SeaWorld, the San Diego Zoo and Wild Animal Park, LEGOLAND, and Six Flags Magic Mountain. Learn more and order a copy at http://www.passporter.com/dl, or pick it up at your favorite bookstore (ISBN-13: 978-1-58771-042-1).

PassPorter's Treasure Hunts

Gain a whole new appreciation of Disney's fabulous attention to detail as you search through the ships, parks, and resorts for the little (and big) things that you may never have noticed before. Great for individuals, families, and groups, with hunts for all ages and levels of Disney knowledge. Learn more about this fun book at http://www.passporter.com/hunts or get a copy at a bookstore (ISBN-13: 978-1-58771-026-1).

To order any of our guidebooks, visit http://www.passporterstore.com/store or call toll-free 877-929-3273. PassPorter guidebooks are also available in your local bookstore.

PassPorter E-Books

Looking for more in-depth coverage on specific topics? Look no further than PassPorter E-Books! Our e-books are inexpensive (most just $4.95) and available immediately as a download on your computer (Adobe PDF format). If you prefer your books printed, we have options for that, too! And unlike most e-books, ours are fully formatted just like a regular PassPorter print book. We offer seven e-books at press time, and have plans for many, many more!

PassPorter's Cruise Clues: *First-Class Tips for Disney Cruise Trips*
Get the best tips for the Disney Cruise Line—all categorized and coded—as well as cruise line comparisons, a teen perspective, and ultimate packing lists! This e-book is packed with 250 cruiser-tested tips—all edited by award-winning author Jennifer Marx.

PassPorter's Disney Character Yearbook
Who, What, and Where at Walt Disney World, Disneyland, and the Disney Cruise Line
A 268-page compendium of all the live Disney characters you can find at Walt Disney World, Disneyland, and on the Disney Cruise Line. Also includes tips on finding, meeting, photographing, and getting autographs, plus a customizable autograph book to print!

PassPorter's Disney 500: *Fast Tips for Walt Disney World Trips*
Our most popular e-book has more than 500 time-tested Walt Disney World tips—all categorized and coded! We chose the best of our reader-submitted tips over a six-year period for this e-book and each has been edited by author Jennifer Marx.

PassPorter's Disney Speed Planner: *The Easy Ten-Step Program*
A fast, easy method for planning practically perfect vacations—great for busy people or those who don't have lots of time to plan. Follow this simple, ten-step plan to help you get your vacation planned in short order so you can get on with your life.

PassPorter's Free-Book
A Guide to Free and Low-Cost Activities at Walt Disney World
It's hard to believe anything is free at Walt Disney World, but there are actually a number of things you can get or do for little to no cost. This e-book documents more than 150 free or cheap things to do before you go and after you arrive. It's the most comprehensive collection!

PassPorter's Sidekick for the Walt Disney World Guidebook
This is a customizable companion to our general Walt Disney World guidebook—you can personalize worksheets, journals, luggage tags, and charts, plus click links to all the URLs in the guidebook and get transportation pages for all points within Walt Disney World!

PassPorter's Festivals and Celebrations at Walt Disney World
An 83-page overview of all the wonderful and magical festivals, celebrations, parties, and holidays at Walt Disney World. Includes beautiful color photos and tips!

PassPorter's Walt Disney World for Brit Holidaymakers
Brits, you can get super in-depth information for your Walt Disney World vacation from fellow Brit and PassPorter feature columnist Cheryl Pendry. More than 300 pages long!

Learn more about these and other titles and order e-books at:
http://www.passporterstore.com/store/ebooks.aspx

Introduction
Reservations
Staterooms
Dining
Activities
Ports of Call
Magic
Index

Do you want more help planning your Disney cruise vacation? Join the PassPorter's Club and get all these benefits:

✔ "All-you-can-read" access to EVERY e-book we publish (see current list on the previous page). PassPorter's Club passholders also get early access to these e-books before the general public. New e-books are added on a regular basis, too.

✔ Interactive, customizable "e-worksheets" to help make your trip planning easier, faster, and smoother. These are the electronic, interactive worksheets we've been mentioning throughout this book. The worksheets are in PDF format and can be printed for a truly personalized approach! We have more than 45 worksheets, with more on the way. You can see a sample e-worksheet to the right—this one calculates your cruise gratuities for you!

✔ Access to super-sized "e-photos" in the PassPorter Photo Archives—photos can be zoomed in up to 25 times larger than standard web photos. You can use these e-photos to see detail as if you're actually standing there—or use them for desktop wallpaper, scrapbooking, whatever!

✔ Our best discount on print guidebooks ... 35% off!

There's more features, too! For a full list of features and current e-books, e-worksheets, and e-photos, visit http://www.passporter.com/club. You can also take a peek inside the Club's Gallery at http://www.passporterboards.com/forums/passporters-club-gallery. The Gallery is open to everyone—it contains two FREE interactive e-worksheets to try out!

Price: A PassPorter's Club pass is currently $4.95/month (the cost of just one e-book)!

How to Get Your Pass to the PassPorter's Club

Step 1. Get a free community account. Register simply and quickly at http://www.passporterboards.com/forums/register.php.

Step 2. Log in at http://www.passporterboards.com/forums/login.php using the Member Name and password you created in step 1.

Step 3. Get your pass. Select the type of pass you'd like and follow the directions to activate it immediately. We currently offer monthly and annual passes. (Annual passes save 25% and get extra perks!)

Questions? Assistance? We're here to help! Please send e-mail to club@passporter.com.

You may also find many of your questions answered in our FAQ (Frequently Asked Questions) in the Gallery forum (see link above).

Planning Timeline

Electronic, interactive worksheet available—see page 350

Track the important dates of your cruise vacation with this worksheet.

What To Do	When?			My Date	Done?
Book your cruise	Up to 22 months in advance				
Pay your deposit	Within 7 days of making cruise reservation				
Book travel insurance	Within 7–14 days of deposit				
Arrange transportation	3–6 months in advance				
Order birth certificates and/or passports	3–6 months in advance				
Arrange lodging for pre- or post-cruise	1–6 months in advance				
Arrange ground transportation	1–3 months in advance				
Pay in full	*Categories 1–3*	*Categories 4–12*			
	90 days before	75 days before			
Cancel (full credit)	non-refundable	75 days before			
Cancel (lose deposit)	45+ days	45–74 days			
Cancel (lose 50%)	8–44 days	8–44 days			
Cancel (lose all)	0–7 days	0–7 days			
Book excursions, spa, childcare, and Palo	*Cat. 1–3*	*Castway Club*	*Others*		
	3–105 days	3–90 days	3–75 days		
Receive documents	Within 28 days before your cruise				

Introduction
Reservations
Staterooms
Dining
Activities
Ports of Call
Magic
Index

Cruise at a Glance

Electronic, interactive worksheet available— see page 350

Create an overview of your itinerary in the chart below for easy reference. You can then make copies of it and give one to everyone in your traveling party, as well as to friends and family members who stay behind.

Name(s):	
Departing on:	Time: #:
Arriving at:	
Resort/Hotel:	Cruise Ship:
Date:	Date:
Location/Port:	Location/Port:
Shore Excursion(s):	Shore Excursion(s):
Activity(ies):	Activity(ies):
Meal(s):	Meal(s):
Other:	Other:
Date:	Date:
Location/Port:	Location/Port:
Shore Excursion(s):	Shore Excursion(s):
Activity(ies):	Activity(ies):
Meal(s):	Meal(s):
Other:	Other:
Date:	Date:
Location/Port:	Location/Port:
Shore Excursion(s):	Shore Excursion(s):
Activity(ies):	Activity(ies):
Meal(s):	Meal(s):
Other:	Other:
Date:	Date:
Location/Port:	Location/Port:
Shore Excursion(s):	Shore Excursion(s):
Activity(ies):	Activity(ies):
Meal(s):	Meal(s):
Other:	Other:
Date:	Date:
Location/Port:	Location/Port:
Shore Excursion(s):	Shore Excursion(s):
Activity(ies):	Activity(ies):
Meal(s):	Meal(s):
Other:	Other:
Departing on:	Time: #:
Returning at:	